'Read this remarkable book and the bewildering complexity of Afghan politics and the deadly over-spill of chaos, narcotics and sectarian violence into the surrounding region will become clear.' Patrick Seale, *Sunday Times*

'The first credible account of the rise to power of the Taliban.' Tariq Ali, *New Left Review*

'Rashid has a feel for the characters in this imbroglio, who are as outlandish as any from the old Great Game.' Rupert Edis, *Sunday Telegraph*

'Ahmed Rashid's book describes the stuff that Bond [films] are made of. Warring tribes, clashing empires, fanatics with dreams of world domination, violence and sex . . . If anyone understands the place Rashid does.' Jason Burke, *Observer*

'Rashid tells a complicated story clearly. He places the rise of the Taliban in the context of the Afghan civil war, the energy policies of the Central Asian republics and the interests of American, Saudi and Pakistani intelligence services.' Robin Banerji, *Daily Telegraph*

'This is a riveting, balanced and well-informed book.' *International Herald Tribune*

'In this excellent, highly readable book, Ahmed Rashid succeeds in mixing detailed analysis not only with anecdote but also with a heartfelt sympathy for innocent peoples who for decades have been caught up in games of international rivalry and who appear fated to remain for ever in a Hobbesian state of war.' Roger Howard, *Spectator*

'The author describes the insights he has gained, through personal experience of Afghanistan over the past decade, into the secretive and bizarre Taliban leadership.' Richard Beeston, *New Statesman*

'Rashid has written the most thorough account of the Taliban to date, and has enclosed it within a history of Afghanistan relating back to the Great Game.' Neil Quilliam, *BRISMES Newsletter*

'Thanks to Ahmed Rashid's analysis of the manoeuvrings of companies and governments, oil executives now have an up-to-date bible, and those interested in the new Turkic republics can get a sense of where these mysterious entities may be heading.' Michael Church, *Independent*

TALIBAN

*The Story
of the Afghan
Warlords*

Ahmed Rashid

including a
New Foreword
following the terrorist attacks
of 11 September 2001

Pan Books

For my mother,
what I have seen she taught me to see.
I hope I have honoured it.
And for Angeles.

First published 2000 by I. B. Tauris & Co. Ltd.
as *Taliban: Islam Oil and the New Great Game in Central Asia*

This edition published 2001 with a new foreword by Pan Books
an imprint of Pan Macmillan Ltd
Pan Macmillan, 20 New Wharf Road, London N1 9RR
Basingstoke and Oxford
Associated companies throughout the world
www.panmacmillan.com

ISBN 0 330 49221 7

1 3 5 7 9 8 6 4 2

A CIP catalogue record for this book is available from
the British Library.

Printed and bound in Great Britain by
Mackays of Chatham plc, Chatham, Kent

CONTENTS

NEW FOREWORD
POST-TERRORIST ATTACKS,
SEPTEMBER 2001

Since 1989 the US and the West have ignored Afghanistan's continuing civil war. On 11 September 2001 the world changed forever, as Afghanistan visited the world in a brutal, tragic fashion. The nineteen suicide bombers, who hijacked four planes and then rammed three of them into the twin towers of the World Trade Center in New York and the Pentagon in Washington, belonged to the Al'Qaida organisation led by Osama Bin Laden, which is based in Taliban-ruled Afghanistan. Their targets were the heart of the post-Cold War world, the nerve centre of globalization and the supposed international efforts to make the world a safer, better place.

Within hours of the fiery attacks President George W. Bush said America was at war with international terrorists. "Those who make war on the United States have chosen their own destruction," he said on 15 September after declaring a national state of emergency. He warned that the US response would be "a conflict without battlefields or beach-heads" and that "the conflict will not be short." He pledged to build an international alliance through NATO and other allies to punish Al'Qaida and the Taliban.

The suicide bombers who had trained as pilots in the US and Germany came from a new generation of Islamic militants. They were educated, middle class, with jobs and families and girlfriends. Yet they were filled with an implacable rage and anger which they had quietly nurtured for years that enabled them to think nothing of killing some 7,000 people – many of them ordinary, pious American Muslims. Understanding this rage and the organisation that trained and inspired them is what this book is partly about.

Yet Al'Qaida could not have spent the years of planning and organisation that went into the attacks without a safe sanctuary where everything was available – training, funding, communications and inspiration. The long years of US and Western neglect have allowed the Taliban to turn Afghanistan into just such a sanctuary for extremist groups from more than two dozen countries. Al'Qaida with its 2,500–3,000 fighters in Afghanistan drawn from at least thirteen Arab countries and its global network spread in thirty four countries, is only the tip of a very large iceberg. The Taliban also host Islamic extremist groups from Russia, Pakistan, China, Burma, Iran, Central Asia and several countries of the Far East, who all fight for the Taliban while quietly carrying out their political agendas at home. Afghanistan has become the hub of a worldwide terrorist network, even though none of this is the fault of the misery-stricken Afghan people who are facing drought, famine, civil war and enormous deprivation as a result of the continuing war between the Taliban and the anti-Taliban forces of the United Front (UF).

The harbinger of the 11 September attack was the assassination just two days earlier of the UF leader Ahmad Shah Masud, the most plausible opposition leader to the Taliban. Two young Moroccans with Belgian passports who had travelled through Brussels, London and Islamabad to Kabul posing as journalists had hidden a bomb in a video camera. As they began their interview with Masud in the far north of the country, they blew up Masud and themselves. With shrapnel lodged in his head and body, Masud survived only a few hours. There was little doubt that the assassination was organised by Al'Qaida as a means to further cement its close relationship with the Taliban leadership and to deprive the UF of its most gifted leader, at the precise moment when Al'Qaida was planning an even bigger act of terrorism, which it knew would suck revenge-seeking US forces into Afghanistan. Bin Laden and Taliban leader Mullah Mohammed Omar apparently have no doubts that just as the Afghan Mujaheddin had destroyed the Soviet army after a ten year war, they would now do the same to any US invasion force.

Taliban anger against the West had already escalated at the beginning of the year. On 19 January the UN Security Council (UNSC) passed Resolution 1333, imposing sanctions on the Taliban, which included a complete arms ban, a seizure of Taliban assets outside Afghanistan and the stoppage of all Taliban travel or international flights by the national airline Ariana. The UNSC said Taliban-controlled Afghanistan was the world centre for international terrorism and demanded the extradition of Bin Laden. The Taliban reacted angrily saying they would never expel Bin Laden. What angered the Taliban even more was that there was no ban on arms supplies to the UF who continued to receive military aid from Russia, Iran, India and the Central Asian Republics.

Pakistan, the principal supplier of weapons and fuel to the Taliban was now in an awkward position, but pledged to abide by the UN sanctions. However the 30 April annual report on global terrorism released by the US State Department said Pakistan was continuing to back the Taliban with "fuel, funding, technical assistance and military advisers." At the same time the New York-based Human Rights Watch issued a blistering report saying that Pakistan was breaking the UN sanctions by continuing to provide military supplies and men to the Taliban. With increasing international suspicion that Pakistan was continuing to supply arms to the Taliban, the UNSC passed Resolution 1363 on 31 July, setting up a team of monitors to be placed on Afghanistan's borders to ensure that the UN arms embargo was enforced. The Taliban and Pakistan's Islamic parties which supported them, responded by saying they would kill any UN monitors who were placed on the Pakistan-Afghanistan border.

Moreover in the first nine months of 2001 there were several warning signals that a terrorist attack could be imminent. On 5 February the trial began in a New York courthouse of four Arab accomplices of Bin Laden, who were charged with the bombing of the two US embassies in Africa in 1998. On 29 May the four men were found guilty on 302 charges of terrorism and were convicted to long jail terms. In April an Algerian, Ahmad Ressam, was convicted of bringing explosives from Canada into the US, where he had planned to blow up Los Angeles airport in 2000. Between January and August, Italy, Germany, Spain and Britain arrested twenty Algerians who were allegedly planning several terrorist attacks in Europe. They had close links with Bin Laden and had been trained in Afghanistan. On 23 June US forces in the Arabian Sea went on the highest state of alert, after a terrorism alert was issued. US embassies were shut down in several countries in Africa and the Gulf as Washington warned the Taliban that it would hold them responsible if Bin Laden mounted any attack.

As a result of UN sanctions the Taliban leadership became internationally isolated, but they too went on the offensive determined to defy Western pressure, even as the drought continuing from last year, the civil war and the collapse of agriculture led to an ever worsening humanitarian crisis and a flood of some one million new refugees both inside and outside the country. There was heavy fighting in January as the Taliban and the UF fought for control of the Hazarajat region in central Afghanistan, which is populated by the Hazara ethnic group who are Shia Muslims and therefore loathed by the Sunni Taliban. The Taliban recaptured Yakowlang on 8 January and human rights groups later documented that the Taliban massacred 210 civilians in and around the town. The UF recaptured Bamiyan city on 13 February, but it was quickly recaptured by the Taliban.

On 26 February, as punishment and in a bid to cower the Hazaras, the Taliban leader Mullah Mohammed Omar ordered his troops to destroy two giant 1,800 year old statues of Buddha that dominated the Bamiyan valley. As the Taliban assembled dynamite and tanks in Bamiyan, there was widespread international condemnation with many countries including Japan, Sri Lanka and Egypt sending delegations to plead with the Taliban to halt their destruction of the statues. There were anti-Taliban demonstrations by Buddhists, Afghans and art lovers in many world capitals, but the Taliban refused to relent and on 10 March the statues were destroyed by dynamite and tank fire. The Taliban also destroyed some forty statues in the Kabul Museum and a massive ancient statue of a reclining Buddha in Ghazni. The Taliban accused the world of isolating its regime and ignoring its starving people in favour of the statues, even though they were the least concerned about their peoples' plight.

The destruction of the Buddhas awoke some countries from their slumber regarding the dangers posed by the Taliban. UF leader Ahmad Shah Masud paid his first visit to Europe in April. He addressed the European Parliament in Strasbourg, was received by the European Community in Brussels and the French Foreign Minister in Paris. The UF had been strengthened by the return to the country of General Rashid Dostum, who with the help of Turkey, set up a base in northern Afghanistan to rally Uzbek ethnic fighters against the Taliban and Ismael Khan, the former Governor of western Afghanistan, who set up a new resistance base against the Taliban supported by Iran in Ghor province in western Afghanistan. The UF were thus able to open two new fronts stretching Taliban forces during the summer.

The head of the Taliban Shura or cabinet in Kabul and deputy leader of the movement, Mullah Mohammed Rabbani died of cancer in a Karachi hospital on 16 April. Rabbani was considered a moderate, who had been an advocate of a Taliban dialogue with Masud. His death signalled the end of any serious attempt by moderate Taliban leaders to resist the hardliners in the regime, who were determined to confront the West in order to create what they claimed was the purest Islamic state in the world.

Taliban defiance included the escalation of confrontation with UN and other international humanitarian agencies working in Afghanistan as well as passing new laws, which created grave human rights violations and antagonised many Afghans. On 19 May, the Taliban closed down an Italian hospital in Kabul forcing European doctors to flee after they were accused of consorting with Afghan women. Two days later the Taliban refused to cooperate with a polio immunisation campaign of children by UN agencies. On 22 May the Taliban declared that all Hindus in the country would have to wear yellow badges on their clothes for identification purposes, resulting in more international condemnation, which continued for several weeks before the Taliban backed down saying Hindus would instead carry identity papers. There are an estimated 1,700 Hindus and Sikhs still in Afghanistan. On 31 May the Taliban banned foreign female aid workers from driving cars.

The Taliban's most serious dispute with the aid community was its refusal to allow the UN World Food Program (WFP), which feeds some three million Afghans, to carry out a survey of recipients of subsidised bread at WFP bakeries in Kabul. After months of failed negotiations, the WFP threatened to close down its 157 bakeries in Kabul by 15 June. The Taliban sought help from Arab and Muslim relief agencies, but little aid was forthcoming. The WFP shut down its bakeries on 15 June, prompting the Taliban to agree to a compromise solution two days later. On 13 July the Taliban banned the use of the internet inside the country. A week later the Taliban issued another decree banning the import of thirty items including games, music cassettes and lipstick. The Taliban's confrontation with aid agencies escalated on 5 August when they arrested eight foreigners and sixteen Afghans belonging to 'Shelter Now International', accusing them of trying to promote Christianity – a charge punishable by death. The trial of the eight foreigners, which included four Germans, under Sharia or Islamic law started on September 4 at the Supreme Court in Kabul.

The annual summer offensive of the Taliban began on 1 June when some 25,000 Taliban troops, including some 10,000 non-Afghans (Arabs, Pakistanis and Central Asians) attacked UF front lines outside Kabul, in the Takhar province in the north east of the country and in the Hazarajat. The UF was unable to capture territory, but it held the line against the Taliban and the UF's new battle fronts in the north and the west of the country were effective in stretching Taliban forces. In August in a report to the UNSC, Secretary General Kofi Annan urged a new "comprehensive approach" to try and bring peace to Afghanistan, terming past attempts "fruitless endeavours" and outlining the need for a strategy of incentives and disincentives as well as the need for a reconstruction plan for the country. Annan also mentioned that there were now more foreign Islamic radicals fighting on the side of the Taliban than ever before.

Through this political crisis the suffering of the Afghan people has risen inexorably, with Afghanistan rated as the world's worst humanitarian disaster zone in 2001. Afghans constitute the largest refugee population in the world with 3.6 million refugees outside the country, of which 2.2 million are in Pakistan and 1.2 million in Iran. By September there were more than one million new victims – 800,000 newly displaced Afghans inside the country, 200,000 new refugees in Pakistan and another 100,000 in Iran. The long-running drought forced millions of people off the land and into the cities, where aid agencies were overwhelmed due to their lack of resources and Taliban harassment. In January one hundred Afghans, many of them children, died of severe cold in six refugee camps in Herat where some 80,000 people had gathered. In northern Afghanistan where there were some 200,000 displaced Afghans, people had turned to eating grass, animal fodder and rodents and were selling their daughters for a pittance in order to buy food.

The UN was overwhelmed by the crisis in agriculture. A WFP survey of 24 provinces in April, stated that 50 per cent less land would be culti-vated in 2001 because of the drought and seed shortages, while 70 per cent of the country's livestock had been destroyed due to the acute water shortages and lack of grazing. In June the UN warned of mass star-vation and deaths due to lack of food, unless the international commu-nity responded with greater aid. However the Taliban's harassment of aid agencies made many Western donor countries reluctant to commit aid. WFP said it would need to feed 5.5 million destitute people in the winter of 2001–2002 compared to 3.8 million in 2000. The plight of Afghans became an international issue at the end of August, when Australia refused to give asylum to 438 refugees, mostly Afghan, who were plucked by a Norwegian container ship from a sinking Indonesian boat as they tried to make their way to Australia. Afghans now consti-tute the largest number of illegal migrants to Europe.

The economic crisis was also ironically aggravated by the Taliban's single compliance with international demands – the ban on poppy culti-vation. The poppy flower is converted into opium and heroin which has provided a major source of financing for all the warring Afghan factions. Mullah Omar had banned poppy cultivation in July 2000 and the ban was rigorously enforced. In March 2001, the UN and the US acknowl-edged that the Taliban had prevented any poppy from being cultivated in the growing season and several countries pledged direct aid to thou-sands of farmers, who had lost everything because they had no seed or fertilizer to grow alternative crops. Many of the new refugees were farm labourers who had now lost their livelihood. Nevertheless opium stocks from previous years continued to be smuggled into neighbouring coun-tries such as Tajikistan and Iran for onward journey to Russia and Europe, and between 2000 and 2001 the price of opium rose tenfold.

Before 11 September all the signs were there that Afghanistan had become a major threat to international and regional stability. The drought, the civil war, the mass migrations, drug trafficking, the hard line espoused by Taliban leaders and the increase in terrorist groups operating from the country should have alerted Western powers that a crisis was at hand. The world only realised the significance of Afghani-stan when on that sunny morning in New York people watched aghast as two planes flew into the twin towers of the World Trade Center. Now as the US and its Western allies prepared a devastating military campaign against the Taliban and Al'Qaida, the question was whether there would also be a political and economic strategy to bring about a new government in Afghanistan and deal with the economic crisis that had only helped to fuel extremism and terrorism.

PREFACE
AND
ACKNOWLEDGEMENTS

This book has been 21 years in the writing – about as long as I have covered Afghanistan as a reporter. The war in Afghanistan has taken out a good chunk of my life even though as a Pakistani journalist there was enough going on at home to report on and later there was Central Asia and the collapse of the Soviet Union to cover.

Why Afghanistan? Anyone who has been touched by an Afghan or visited the country in peace or in war, will understand when I say the country and the people are amongst the most extraordinary on earth. The Afghans have also been affected by one of the greatest tragedies of this century – the longest running civil war in this era which has brought untold misery.

Their story and their character involve immense contradictions. Brave, magnificent, honourable, generous, hospitable, gracious, handsome, Afghan men and women can also be devious, mean and bloody-minded.

Over the centuries, trying to understand the Afghans and their country was turned into a fine art and a game of power politics by the Persians, the Mongols, the British, the Soviets and most recently the Pakistanis. But no outsider has ever conquered them or claimed their soul. Only the Afghans could have been capable of keeping two empires – Britain and the Soviet Union – at bay in this century. But in the last 21 years of conflict they have paid an enormous price – over 1.5 million dead and the total destruction of their country.

For me, luck has also played a role in my relationship with Afghanistan. Many times I just happened to be at the right place at the right time. I watched as army tanks blasted their way into the Kabul palace of President Mohammed Daud in 1978, a coup that was to set off Afghanistan's disintegration. A year later I was sipping tea in Kandahar's bazaar when the first Soviet tanks rolled in. As I covered the Soviet Union's war with the Mujaheddin my family urged me to write a book, as so many journalists were doing at the time. I abstained. I had too much to say and did not know where to start.

I was determined to write a book after spending several months in Geneva covering the excruciating UN sponsored negotiations in 1988, which ended with the Geneva Accords and the withdrawal of Soviet troops from Afghanistan. Packed in with 200 journalists I was fortunate enough to be privy to many of the internal stand-offs between diplomats from the UNA, the USA, the Soviet Union, Pakistan, Iran and Afghanistan. That book never got written as my first love, the Afghans, drove straight from Geneva into a bloody, senseless civil war that still continues today.

Instead I went to Central Asia to see the ancestors of the Afghans and became a witness to the collapse of the Soviet Union, which I wrote a book about from the perspective of the newly independent Central Asian states. But Afghanistan always drew me back.

I should have written another book in 1992 when I spent a month dodging bullets in Kabul as the regime of President Najibullah collapsed and the city fell to the Mujaheddin. By then the Afghan saga had taken me to Moscow, Washington, Rome, Jeddah, Paris, London, Ashkhabad, Tashkent and Dushanbe. Ultimately it was the unique nature of the Taliban and the lack of literature about their meteoric rise, which convinced me I had to tell their story as a continuation of the last 21 years of Afghanistan's history and my history.

For years I was the only Pakistani journalist covering Afghanistan seriously, even though the war was next door and Afghanistan sustained Pakistan's foreign policy and kept the military regime of General Zia ul Haq in power. If there was another abiding interest, it was my conviction as early as 1982 that Islamabad's Afghan policy would play a critical role in Pakistan's future national security, domestic politics and create an Islamic fundamentalist backlash at home. Today, as Pakistan teeters on the edge of a political, economic and social abyss while a culture of drugs, weapons, corruption and violence permeates the country, what happens in Afghanistan has become even more important to Pakistan.

Pakistan's policy-makers did not always agree with what I wrote. It was not easy to disagree with Zia. In 1985 I was interrogated for several hours by Zia's intelligence agencies and warned not to write for six months because of my criticism. I continued to write under pseudonyms. My phones were constantly tapped, my movements monitored.

Afghanistan, like the Afghans themselves, is a country of contradictions that are constantly played out for any reporter. Gulbuddin Hikmetyar, the extremist Mujaheddin leader sentenced me to death for being a communist sympathiser – along with George Arney of the BBC – and for a year published my name in his party newspaper, like a wanted ad. Later, in Kabul, a crowd chased and tried to kill me when I arrived moments after a rocket fired by Hikmetyar had killed two small boys in the Microyan housing complex. The Afghans thought I was a Hikmetyar agent checking out the damage.

In 1981 when Najibullah was head of the notorious KHAD, the Afghan communist secret service modelled on the KGB, he personally interrogated me after KHAD officers arrested me for reading a banned copy of *Time* magazine at Kabul's Post Office. After he became president and I had interviewed him several times, he thought I could carry a conciliatory message from him to Prime Minister Benazir Bhutto. I told him she would not listen to me, and she did not.

And many times I have been caught in the contradiction of crossfires, between Afghan communist troops and the Mujaheddin, between rival Mujaheddin warlords and between the Taliban and Ahmad Shah Masud's tank-gunners. I have never been the warrior type and mostly ducked.

My interest in Afghanistan could not have been sustained without the help of many people, above all the Afghans. To the Taliban mullahs, the anti-Taliban commanders, the warlords who went before them, the warriors on the battlefield and the taxi-drivers, intellectuals, aid-workers and farmers – too many to mention and mostly too sensitive to mention – my many thanks.

Apart from the Afghans I have received the greatest help from Pakistani ministers, diplomats, generals, bureaucrats and intelligence officers, who either wanted to take me on or were sincerely sympathetic to my views. Many of them have become firm friends.

Over the years the UN agencies and the non-governmental aid organizations have provided a home for me all over Afghanistan and have given me ideas, information and support. At the UN Office for Co-ordination of Humanitarian Assistance to Afghanistan I owe many thanks to its successive chiefs, Martin Barber, Alfredo Witschi-Cestari and Erick de Mul and to Brigette Neubacher, who has been in the Afghan business almost as long as I have. At the UN High Commission for Refugees I thank Robert Van Leeuwen, Shamsul Bari, Sri Wijaratne, Jacques Muchet, Rupert Colville and Monique Malha. At the World Food Programme the indefatigable Adan Adar understood the Taliban better than any other UN officer.

At the UN Special Mission for Afghanistan many thanks are due to Francis Okelo, James Ngobi, Hiroshi Takahashi, Arnold Schifferdecker and Andrew Tesoriere and at the UN in New York, Benon Sevan and Andrew Gilmour. At the International Committee of the Red Cross, Thomas Gurtner and Oliver Durr, at Acted aid agency Frederick Rousseau

and Marie Pierre Caley and at Save the Children Andrew Wilder and
Sofie Elieussen. The friendship and support of Lakhdar Brahimi, the UN
Secretary General's Special Representative to Afghanistan has been crit-
ical to this work.

For 16 years I have reported on Afghanistan for the *Far Eastern Economic Review* and I owe my editors, especially Nayan Chanda, enormous
thanks for giving me space in the magazine, travel funds and sustaining
an interest in running stories from what has now become an obscure war
on the edge of Asia. The former foreign editor V.G. Kulkarni took a huge
risk when he convinced sceptical bosses that my 1997 story on the oil
and gas pipeline battle in Afghanistan and Central Asia was worthy of a
cover story. From that story was to emerge the now common phrase, 'the
new Great Game'. Foreign editors Andrew Waller and Andrew Sherry
have continued that tradition.

My thanks to the *Daily Telegraph*'s successive foreign editors Nigel
Wade, Patrick Bishop and Stephen Robinson for not totally forgetting
about Afghanistan. And to fellow journalists and friends at the BBC
World Service, Radio France International and Radio Australia for constantly letting me air my views.

In Pakistan, Arif Nizami, editor of the *Nation* has stood by me as
I wrote reams on Afghanistan. He always gave me front page space and
he always took the flak, fielding phone calls from invariably angry
Pakistani government officials. Sherry Rehman, former editor of the
Herald also allowed me to fill her magazine with my photographs and
stories.

This could not have been accomplished without the enormous support
and friendship – not to speak of the website – of Barnett Rubin, who
knows more about Afghanistan than anyone I know. I owe heartfelt
thanks to the Afghanistan brigade of scholars, journalists and human
rights activists who like me cannot leave the story and from whom I
have learnt so much – Olivier Roy, Nancy Hatch Dupree, Ashraf Ghani,
William Maley, Anders Fange, Citha Maass, Eqbal Ahmad, Patti
Gossman, Abbas Faiz, Steve Levine, Tony Davis, Edward Giradet, Sadao
Sakai, Tim McGirk, Bob Nicklesberg, Maleeha Lodhi, Rahimullah
Yousufzai, Leslie Cockburn, Francois Chipaux, Jennifer Griffin and
Gretchen Peters.

I am deeply grateful to Cathy Gannon, the bureau chief of
Associated Press in Islamabad and Kabul, who deserves several Pulitzer
Prizes for her excellent coverage over the years, not to speak of her gener-
osity and modesty. My many thanks to successive Reuters bureau chiefs
in Islamabad, Jane Macartney, Alistair Lyon and Andy Hill. Many thanks
to Sarah Hunt Cooke, my editor at I.B.Tauris who believed in the project
from the start and was patient with deadlines.

This book could not have been written without the patience, love and understanding of my wife Angeles and my two children, who have put up with my wanderings and absences and have shared my feelings for Afghanistan for a long time.

Ahmed Rashid
Lahore

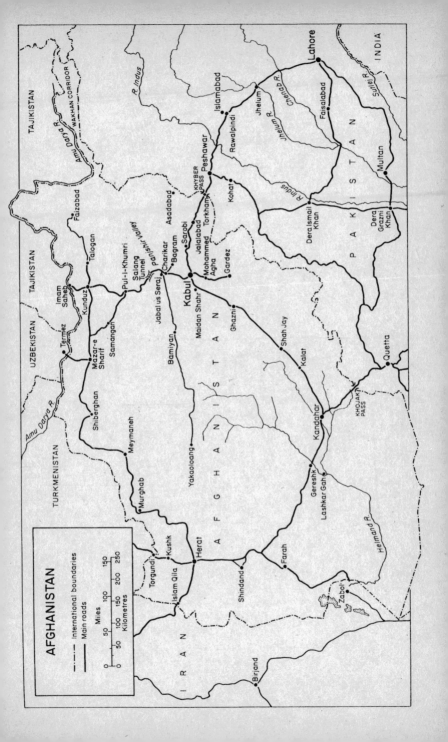

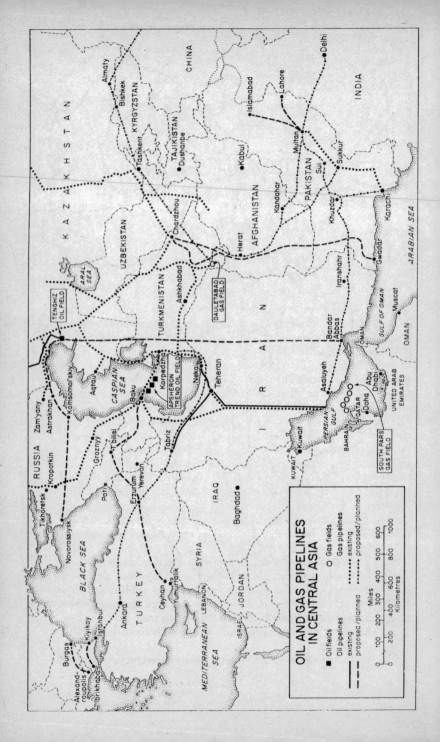

OIL AND GAS PIPELINES
IN CENTRAL ASIA

- Oil fields
- ○ Gas fields
- Oil pipelines
  - ········ existing
  - ––– proposed/planned
- Gas pipelines
  - ········ existing
  - ––– proposed/planned

Miles
0 100 200 300 400 500 600
0 200 400 600 800 1000
Kilometres

INTRODUCTION: AFGHANISTAN'S HOLY WARRIORS

On a warm spring afternoon in the southern city of Kandahar, Afghan shopkeepers were pulling down their shutters in preparation for the weekend. Heavy-set Pashtun tribesmen with long beards and black turbans tied tightly around their heads made their way through the narrow, dusty alleyways to the city's football stadium just beyond the main bazaar. Children, many of them orphaned and in rags, ran up and down the alleys, gesticulating and shouting with excitement at the thought of the spectacle they were about to witness.

It was March 1997 and for two and a half years Kandahar had been the capital of the fierce Taliban Islamic warriors, who had conquered two-thirds of Afghanistan and were now battling to conquer the rest of the country. A handful of Taliban had fought the Soviet Red Army in the 1980s, more had fought the regime of President Najibullah who had hung on to power for four years after Soviet troops withdrew from Afghanistan in 1989, but the vast majority had never fought the communists and were young Koranic students, drawn from hundreds of *madrassas* (Islamic theology schools) that had been set up in Afghan refugee camps in Pakistan.

Since their dramatic and sudden appearance at the end of 1994, the Taliban had brought relative peace and security to Kandahar and neighbouring provinces. Warring tribal groups had been crushed and their leaders hanged, the heavily armed population had been disarmed and the roads were open to facilitate the lucrative smuggling trade between Pakistan, Afghanistan, Iran and Central Asia which had become the mainstay of the economy.

The Taliban, drawn from the majority Pashtun ethnic group which accounts for some 40 per cent of Afghanistan's 20 million people, had also galvanized Pashtun nationalism. The Pashtuns had ruled Afghanistan for 300 years but had recently lost out to the country's other smaller ethnic groups. The Taliban victories revived hopes that once again the Pashtuns would dominate Afghanistan.

But the Taliban had also implemented an extreme interpretation of the Sharia or Islamic law that appalled many Afghans and the Muslim world. The Taliban had closed down all girls' schools and women were rarely permitted to venture out of their homes, even for shopping. The Taliban had banned every conceivable kind of entertainment including music, TV, videos, cards, kite-flying and most sports and games. The Taliban's brand of Islamic fundamentalism was so extreme that it appeared to denigrate Islam's message of peace and tolerance and its capacity to live with other religious and ethnic groups. They were to inspire a new extremist form of fundamentalism across Pakistan and Central Asia, which refused to compromise with traditional Islamic values, social structures or existing state systems.

A few weeks earlier in Kandahar the Taliban had lifted their long-standing ban on football. The United Nations (UN) aid agencies – seizing a rare chance to do something for public entertainment – rushed in to rebuild the stands and seats of the bombed out football stadium. But on this balmy Thursday afternoon – the beginning of the Muslim weekend – no foreign aid-workers had been invited to watch the stadium's inauguration. No football match was scheduled. Instead there was to be a public execution and the victim was to be shot between the goalposts.

I had just got off a UN plane arriving from Pakistan and was told about the execution in hushed tones by depressed and embarrassed foreign aid-workers. 'This is not exactly going to encourage the international community to give more funds for aid projects in Afghanistan. How do we explain the use the Taliban are putting our renovation of the football stadium to?' said one Western aid-worker.

They also looked nervously at my colleague Gretchen Peters, an American journalist. A tall, lanky blonde with a broad face and chiselled features, she was dressed in a one-size-too-small shalwar kameez – the local dress comprising baggy cotton pants, a long shirt that extended to below the knee and a long scarf that covered her head. But that did not hide her height or her striking American looks, which posed a threat to every concept the Taliban held – that women should be neither seen nor heard because they drove men away from the proscribed Islamic path and into wild temptation. Whether it was a fear of women or their abhorrence of femininity, Taliban leaders had frequently refused to give interviews to female journalists.

Ever since the winter of 1994, when the mysterious Taliban first emerged to conquer Kandahar and then swept north to capture Kabul in September 1996, I had been reporting on the Taliban phenomenon, making more than a dozen trips to Taliban strongholds in Kandahar, Herat and Kabul. I was even more interested in trying to get to grips with who they were, what motivated them, who supported them and how they had arrived at this violent, extreme interpretation of Islam.

Now here there was another Taliban surprise, both a nightmare and a gift to any reporter – a horrific event that made me tremble with both fear and anticipation. I had witnessed much death during the years of war, but that did not make it any easier to be a spectator at the execution of a fellow human being. And to view it as an entertainment, shared with thousands of people and as an expression of Islamic justice and Taliban control, was harder still.

At the stadium the Taliban first resisted our entry but then allowed me in if I stood quietly at the touch-line and promised not to talk to anyone. Gretchen Peters slipped in, but she was quickly ousted by a posse of panic-stricken armed Taliban guards who nudged her in the back with their kalashnikov automatic rifles.

By mid-afternoon every seat in the stadium was taken as more than 10,000 men and children packed the stands and overflowed on to the sandy football pitch. Children played games of dare by running on to the pitch before they were pushed back behind the touch-line by angry guards. It seemed as though the whole city's male population had turned up. Women were banned from appearing at any public events.

Suddenly the roar of the crowd subsided as two dozen armed Taliban, wearing plastic flip-flop sandals, black turbans and the male version of the shalwar kameez, came charging onto the pitch. They ran alongside the touch-line pushing the playful children back into the stands with their gun barrels and yelling to the crowd to be silent. As the crowd quickly obeyed, the only sound was the Taliban's flip-flops.

Then, as if on cue, several Datsun two-door pick-ups – the Taliban's favourite mode of transport – drove onto the football pitch. One pick-up sprouted a tinny sounding loudspeaker – the kind seen on thousands of mosques in Pakistan and Afghanistan. An elderly man with a white beard stood up in the vehicle and began to lecture the crowd. Qazi Khalilullah Ferozi, a judge of the Taliban's Supreme Court of Kandahar spoke for over an hour, extolling the crowd on the virtues of the Taliban movement, the benefits of Islamic punishment and a full history of the case.

Abdullah Afghan, a young man in his early 20s had allegedly stolen medicines from Abdul Wali, a farmer who lived in their common village near Kandahar. When Wali resisted, Abdullah had shot him dead. After several weeks of searching for him, Wali's relatives tracked Abdullah down, arrested him and bought him to the Taliban for justice. Abdullah was tried and sentenced to death, first by the Islamic High Court of Kandahar and then on appeal by the Taliban Supreme Court. These were trials without lawyers where the accused is presumed guilty and expected to defend himself.

The Taliban's interpretation of the Sharia or Islamic law demanded the execution of the murderer by the victim's family, but not before a last-minute appeal is made by the judge to the victim's relatives to spare the murderer. If they granted mercy the victim's family would receive blood money or monetary compensation. But how much of this interpretation of Islamic law by the Taliban is owed to the Sharia and how much is owed to the Pashtun tribal code of behaviour or Pashtunwali, is what is disputed by many Muslim theologians, both inside Afghanistan and beyond.

By now some 20 male relatives of the victim had appeared on the pitch and the Qazi turned to them. Raising his arms to the sky, he appealed to them to spare the life of Abdullah in exchange for blood money. 'You will go to Mecca ten times if you spare this man. Our leaders have promised to pay a huge sum to you from the Baitul Mal [Islamic fund] if you forgive him,' he told the relatives. As the relatives all shook their heads in refusal, the Taliban guards pointed their guns at the crowd and warned that they would shoot anyone who moved. There was silence in the stands.

Abdullah, who had been seated throughout the proceedings in another pick-up guarded by armed Taliban, was now let out. Wearing a bright yellow skullcap and new clothes, his feet shackled with heavy manacles, his arms chained behind his back, he was told to walk to the goalposts at one end of the stadium. His legs visibly shook with fear as he shuffled across the pitch, his chains clanking and glinting in the sunlight. When he reached the goalposts, he was made to kneel on the ground with his face turned away from the crowd. A guard whispered to him that he could say his last prayer.

A guard handed a kalashnikov to a relative of the murdered victim. The relative swiftly stepped up to Abdullah, cocked the automatic and from a few feet away shot him three times in the back. As Abdullah fell on to his back the executioner moved alongside his twitching body and at point-blank range pumped three more bullets into his chest. Within seconds his body was thrown into the back of a pick-up and driven away. The crowd quickly and silently dispersed. As we drove back into town, thin slivers of smoke arose from the bazaar as tea stalls and kebab stands lit up for their evening trade.

A mixture of fear, acceptance, total exhaustion and devastation after years of war and more than 1.5 million dead have forced many Afghans to accept the Taliban ways of justice. The next day in a village near Kabul, a woman was stoned to death by a baying crowd after being sentenced for trying to flee Afghanistan with a man who was not her blood relative. Amputations of either one hand or one foot or both are common Taliban punishments for anyone caught stealing. When they captured Kabul in September 1996, to be initially welcomed as liberators, many Kabulis and the world turned away in disgust after the Taliban tortured and then publicly hanged former President Najibullah, the ex-communist strongman who for four years had been living in a UN compound under UN protection.

Since the end of the Cold War no other political movement in the Islamic world has attracted as much attention as the Taliban in Afghanistan. For some Afghans the Taliban created hopes that a movement led by simple Islamic students with an agenda of bringing peace to the country might succeed in finally disposing of the warlord factions which had devastated people's lives since the communist regime in Kabul had been overthrown in April 1992. Others feared that the Taliban movement would quickly degenerate into one more warlord faction, determined to thrust despotic rule upon the hapless Afghan people.

The Pashtun Taliban have also brought the question of inter-ethnic relations in a multi-ethnic state to the forefront, as well as other issues including the role of Islam versus clan, tribal and feudal structures and the question of modernization and economic development in a conservative Islamic society. Understanding the Taliban phenomenon is made even more difficult because of the excessive secrecy that surrounds their political structures, their leadership and the decision-making process within the movement. The Taliban do not issue press releases, policy statements or hold regular press conferences. With their ban on photography and television, nobody knows what their leaders even look like. The one-eyed Taliban leader Mullah Mohammed Omar remains an enigmatic mystery. After the Khmer Rouge in Cambodia, the Taliban are the most secretive political movement in the world today.

Yet the Taliban have inadvertently set a new agenda for Islamic radicalism in the entire region, sending shock waves through Afghanistan's neighbours. Not surprisingly, Iran, Turkey, India, Russia and four of the five Central Asian Republics – Uzbekistan, Kazakhstan, Kyrgyzstan and Tajikistan – have backed the anti-Taliban Northern Alliance with arms and money to try and halt the Taliban's advance. In contrast Pakistan and Saudi Arabia have backed the Taliban. In the post-Cold War era, this has created unprecedented polarization across the region. The Taliban victories in northern Afghanistan in the summer of 1998 and their control of over 90 per cent of the country, set in motion an even fiercer regional conflict as Iran threatened to invade Afghanistan and accused Pakistan of supporting the Taliban.

At the heart of this regional stand-off is the battle for the vast oil and gas riches of landlocked Central Asia – the last untapped reserves of energy in the world today. Equally important has been the intense competition between the regional states and Western oil companies as to who would build the lucrative pipelines which are needed to transport the energy to markets in Europe and Asia. This rivalry has in effect become a new Great Game – a throwback to the nineteenth century Great Game between Russia and Britain over control and domination in Central Asia and Afghanistan.

Since late 1995, Washington had strongly backed the US company Unocal to build a gas pipeline from Turkmenistan to Pakistan across Taliban-controlled Afghanistan. But there was another, unexpected player in this new Great Game. The day after the execution I arrived at the mansion of Mullah Mohammed Hassan, the Governor of Kandahar, to interview him. As I walked up the drive past the heavily armed Taliban guards, I froze. Coming out of the Governor's office was a handsome, silver-haired business executive dressed in an impeccable blue blazer with gold buttons, a yellow silk tie and Italian loafers. With him were two other businessmen, both as impeccably dressed and carrying bulging briefcases. They looked as though they had just concluded a deal on Wall Street, rather than holding negotiations with a band of Islamic guerrillas in the dusty lanes of Kandahar.

The executive was Carlos Bulgheroni, Chairman of Bridas Corporation, an Argentinean oil company which since 1994 had been secretly negotiating with the Taliban and the Northern Alliance to build the same gas pipeline across Afghanistan. Bridas were in bitter competition with Unocal and in a court case filed in California, they had even accused Unocal of stealing the idea from them.

For a year I had been trying to discover what interests an Argentinean company, unknown in this part of the world, had in investing in such a high-risk place as Afghanistan. But both Bridas and Unocal had kept a discreet silence. The last thing Bulgheroni wanted was to be seen by a journalist coming out of a Taliban leader's office. He excused himself and said his company plane was waiting to fly him to the Northern Alliance's capital in Mazar-e-Sharif.

As the battle for pipelines from Central Asia intensified, the Islamic world and the West were also concerned whether the Taliban represented the new future of Islamic fundamentalism – aggressive, expansionist and uncompromising in its purist demands to turn Afghan society back to an imagined model of seventh-century Arabia at the time of the Prophet Mohammed. The West also feared the repercussions from the ever-expanding drugs trade from Afghanistan and the Taliban's harbouring of international terrorists such as the Saudi extremist Osama Bin Laden, whose group Al'Qaida carried out the devastating bombings of US embassies in Kenya and Tanzania in August 1998.

Moreover, experts wondered whether the Taliban's back-to-basics Islamic ideals fulfilled the dire predictions of some American intellectuals that in the post-Cold War era, a new militant Islamic world would oppose the West and create another version of the Cold War in a new clash of civilisations.[1]

For Afghanistan to be at the centre of such conflict is nothing new. Today's Taliban are only the latest in a long line of conquerors, warlords, preachers, saints and philosophers who have swept through the Afghan corridor destroying older civilizations and religions and introducing new ones. The kings of the ancient world believed the Afghanistan region was the very centre of the world and this view has persisted to modern times. The famous Indian poet Mohammed Iqbal described Afghanistan as 'the heart of Asia', while Lord Curzon, the early twentieth-century British Viceroy of India called Afghanistan 'the cockpit of Asia'.[2]

For few countries in the world is it more true that geography determines history, politics and the nature of a people. Afghanistan's geo-strategic location on the crossroads between Iran, the Arabian Sea and India and between Central Asia and South Asia has given its territory and mountain passes a significance since the earliest Aryan invasions 6,000 years ago. Afghanistan's rough, rugged, deserted and arid terrain has produced some of the best fighters the world has ever seen, while its stunning scenery of gaunt mountains and lush green valleys with fruit-laden trees have proved to be an inspiration to poets.

Many years ago a wise old Afghan Mujahed once told me the mythical story of how God made Afghanistan. 'When Allah had made the rest of the world, He saw that there was a lot of rubbish left over, bits and pieces and things that did not fit anywhere else. He collected them all together and threw them down on to the earth. That was Afghanistan,' the old man said.

Modern Afghanistan encompasses 245,000 square miles. The country is split by a north-south divide along the massive Hindu Kush mountain range. Although there was much intermingling of races in the twentieth century, a rough division shows that to the south of the Hindu Kush live the majority of Pashtuns and some Persian-speaking ethnic groups, to the north live the Persian and Turkic ethnic groups. The Hindu Kush itself is populated by the Persian-speaking Hazaras and Tajiks. In the far north-east corner, the Pamir mountains, which Marco Polo called 'the roof of the world', abut Tajikistan, China and Pakistan.[3] The inaccessibility of the Pamirs means that there is little communication between the myriad of diverse and exotic ethnic groups who live in its high, snow-bound valleys.

In the southern foothills of the Hindu Kush lies Kabul; the adjoining valleys are the most agriculturally productive region in the country. Western and southern Afghanistan marks the eastern end of the Iranian plateau – flat, bare and arid with few towns and a sparse population. Much of this region is just called 'registan' or desert by local Afghans. The exception is the oasis town of Herat, which has been a centre of civilization for more than 3,000 years.

North of the Hindu Kush the bare Central Asian steppe begins its long sweep, which stretches thousands of miles north into Siberia. With its extremes of climate and terrain the north's Turkic peoples are some of the toughest in the world and make the fiercest of fighters. In eastern Afghanistan lie smaller mountain ranges including the Suleman range which straddle the border with Pakistan and are populated on both sides by the Pashtun tribes. Passes through these mountains such as the famous Khyber Pass have for centuries given conquerors access to the fertile Indian plains.

Only 10–12 per cent of Afghanistan's terrain is cultivable and most farms, some hanging from mountain slopes, demand extraordinary amounts of labour to keep them productive. Until the 1970s nomadism – the grazing of goats and the fat-tailed Afghan sheep – was a major source of livelihood and the Kochi nomads travelled thousands of miles every year in Pakistan, Iran and Afghanistan in search of good pasture. Although the war against the Soviets destroyed Kochi culture and livelihood in the 1980s, animal herding is still vital in sustaining impoverished farmers. Yesterday's Afghan nomads are today's traders and truck-drivers, who are a crucial support base and revenue generator for the Taliban by running trucks along the smuggling routes across Afghanistan.

Roads and routes have been at the centre of Afghanistan since the dawn of history. The landlocked territory was the crossroads of Asia and the meeting place and battleground for two great waves of civilization, the more urbane Persian empires to the west and the Turkic nomadic empires to the north in Central Asia. As a result Afghanistan is immensely rich in archaeological remains.

For these two ancient civilizations, which ebbed in greatness and conquest according to the momentum of history, control over Afghanistan was vital for their survival. At other times Afghanistan served as a buffer keeping these two empires apart, while at other times it served as a corridor through which their armies marched north to south or west to east when they desired to invade India. This was a land where the first ancient religions of Zoroastrianism, Manichaeanism and Buddhism flourished. Balkh, the ruins of which are still visible a few miles from Mazar-e-Sharif, is according to UNESCO one of the oldest cities in the world and it was a thriving centre of Buddhist, Persian and Turkic arts and architecture.

It was through Afghanistan that pilgrims and traders working the ancient Silk Route carried Buddhism to China and Japan. Conquerors swept through the region like shooting stars. In 329 BC the Macedonian Greeks under Alexander the Great conquered Afghanistan and Central Asia and went on to invade India. The Greeks left behind a new, vibrant Buddhist-Greek kingdom and civilization in the Hindu Kush mountains – the only known historical fusion between European and Asian cultures.

By 654 AD Arab armies had swept through Afghanistan to arrive at the Oxus river on the border with Central Asia. They brought with them their new religion of Islam, which preached equality and justice and quickly penetrated the entire region. Under the Persian Saminid dynasty which lasted from 874 to 999 AD, Afghanistan was part of a new Persian renaissance in arts and letters. The Ghaznavid dynasty ruled from 977 to 1186 and captured north west India Punjab and parts of eastern Iran.

In 1219 Genghis Khan and his Mongol hordes swept through Afghanistan destroying cities such as Balkh and Herat and piling up mounds of dead bodies. Yet the Mongols contributed too, by leaving behind the modern day Hazaras – who were the result of inter-marriage between the Mongols and local tribes.

In the next century Taimur, or Tamerlane as he is called in the West, a descendent of Genghis Khan, created a vast new empire across Russia and Persia which he ruled from his capital in Samarkand in modern-day Uzbekistan. Taimur captured Herat in 1381 and his son Shah Rukh moved the capital of the Timurid empire to Herat in 1405. The Timurids, a Turkic people brought the Turkic nomadic culture of Central Asia within the orbit of Persian civilization, establishing in Herat one of the most cultured and refined cities in the world. This fusion of Central Asian and Persian culture was a major legacy for the future of Afghanistan. A century later the emperor Babur, a descendent of Taimur, visited Herat and wrote, 'the whole habitable world had not such a town as Herat'.[4]

For the next 300 years the eastern Afghan tribes periodically invaded India, conquering Delhi and creating vast Indo-Afghan empires. The Afghan Lodhi dynasty ruled Delhi from 1451 to 1526. In 1500 Taimur's descendent Babur was driven out of his home in the Ferghana valley in Uzbekistan. He went on to conquer first Kabul in 1504 and then Delhi. He established the Mogul dynasty which was to rule India until the arrival of the British. At the same time Persian power declined in the west and Herat was conquered by the Uzbek Shaybani Khans. By the sixteenth century western Afghanistan again reverted to Persian rule under the Safavid dynasty.

This series of invasions resulted in a complex ethnic, cultural and religious mix that was to make Afghan nation-building extremely difficult. Western Afghanistan was dominated by speakers of Persian or Dari as the Afghan Persian dialect is known. Dari was also spoken by the Hazaras in central Afghanistan, who were converted to Shiism by the Persians, thereby becoming the largest Shia group in an otherwise Sunni territory. In the west the Tajiks, the repositors of Persia's ancient culture also spoke Dari. In northern Afghanistan the Uzbeks, Turcomans, Kyrgyz and others spoke the Turkic languages of Central Asia. And in the south and east the Pashtun tribes spoke their own tongue Pashto, a mixture of Indo-Persian languages.

It was the southern Pashtuns who were to form the modern state of Afghanistan at the historical conjuncture when the Persian Safavid dynasty in the west, the Moguls in India and the Uzbek Janid dynasty were all in a period of decline in the eighteenth century. The Pashtun tribes were divided into two major sections, the Ghilzai and Abdali who later called themselves Durrani, which frequently competed against each other.

The Pashtuns trace their genealogy to Qais, a companion of the Prophet Mohammed. As such they consider themselves a Semitic race although anthropologists consider them to be Indo-Europeans, who have assimilated numerous ethnic groups over the course of history. The Durranis claim descent from Qais's eldest son Sarbanar while the Ghilzais claim descent from his second son. Qais's third son is said to be the ancestor of other diverse Pashtun tribes such as the Kakars in Kandahar and the Safis around Peshawar. In the sixth century Chinese and Indian sources speak of the Afghans/Pashtuns living east of Ghazni. These tribes began a westward migration to Kandahar, Kabul and Herat from the fifteenth century. By the next century the Ghilzais and Durranis were already fighting each other over land disputes around Kandahar. Today the Ghilzai homeland lies south of the Kabul river between the Safed Koh and Suleman range on the east to Hazarajat in the west and down to Kandahar in the south.[5]

In 1709, Mir Wais, the chief of the Hotaki tribe of Ghilzai Pashtuns in Kandahar rebelled against the Safavid Shah. This was partly a result of the Shah's attempts to convert the fervently Sunni Pashtuns into Shias – a historical animosity that was to re-emerge with the Taliban's hostility towards Iran and Afghan Shias three centuries later.

A few years later Mir Wais's son defeated the Safavids and conquered Iran. But the Afghans were driven out of Iran in 1729. As Ghilzai power ebbed, their traditional rivals in Kandahar, the Abdalis, formed a confederation and in 1747 after a nine-day Loya Jirga or meeting of tribal chiefs, they chose Ahmad Shah Abdali as their king. The tribal chiefs wrapped a turban around his head and placed blades of grass in it, signifying loyalty. The Loya Jirga was to become the traditional legal instrument which legitimized new rulers thus avoiding a hereditary monarchy. The rulers themselves could claim that they were elected by the tribes represented in the Jirga. Ahmad Shah changed the name of the Abdali confederation to Durrani, united all the Pashtun tribes and began a series of major conquests, quickly taking control over much of modern day Pakistan.

By 1761 Ahmad Shah Durrani had defeated the Hindu Mahrattas and captured the Delhi throne and Kashmir, thereby creating the first Afghan empire. Considered the father of the Afghan nation, Ahmad Shah Durrani was buried in an ornate mausoleum in his capital Kandahar, where Afghans still come to pray. Many Afghans have conferred a kind of sainthood on him. His son Taimur Shah moved the empire's new capital from Kandahar to Kabul in 1772, making it easier to control the newly conquered territories north of the Hindu Kush mountains and east of the river Indus. By 1780 the Durranis had concluded a treaty with the Amir of Bukhara, the principal Central Asian ruler, which designated the Oxus or Amu Darya river as the border between Central Asia and the new Pashtun state of Afghanistan. It was the first border delineation that marked the northern boundary of the new Afghanistan.

In the next century the Durranis were to lose their territories east of the Indus river while feuds between various Durrani clans dissipated their power. However, one or another Durrani clan was to rule Afghanistan for over 200 years until 1973, when King Zahir Shah was deposed by his cousin Mohammed Daud Khan and Afghanistan was declared a Republic. Meanwhile the bitter rivalry between the Ghilzai and the Durrani Pashtuns was to continue and intensify in the aftermath of the Soviet invasion of Afghanistan and the subsequent emergence of the Taliban.

The weakened and bickering Durrani kings had to hold off two new empires, the British in the east and the Russians to the north. In the nineteenth century, fearful of an ever expanding Russian empire in Central Asia which might covet Afghanistan for a thrust against Britain's Indian empire, the British made three attempts to conquer and hold Afghanistan until they realised that the intractable Afghans could be bought much more easily than fought. The British offered cash subsidies, manipulated the tribal chiefs and managed to turn Afghanistan into a client state. What followed was 'the Great Game' between Russia and Britain, a clandestine war of wits and bribery and occasional military pressure as both powers kept each other at a respectful distance by maintaining Afghanistan as a buffer state between them.

The feuds amongst the ruling Durranis which were fuelled by British intelligence officers ensured that Afghan kings remained weak and dependent on British largesse to make up for their inability to raise revenues. As a consequence the non-Pashtun groups in the north exercised increasing autonomy from central control in Kabul. The Pashtuns were also weakened by the British conquest of north-west India, which for the first time divided the Pashtun tribes between British India and Afghanistan. This partition of the Pashtuns was formalised by the Durand Line, a formal border drawn up by Britain in 1893.

After the second Anglo-Afghan war, the British supported Amir Abdul Rehman's claim to the throne. The 'Iron Amir' (1880–1901), as he was called, received British support to centralize and strengthen the Afghan state. The Amir used British subsidies and arms supplies to create an effective administration and a standing army. He subdued rebellious Pashtun tribes and then moved north to ruthlessly end the autonomy of the Hazaras and Uzbeks. Using methods that were to be closely followed a century later by the Taliban, he carried out a nineteenth-century version of ethnic cleansing, massacring non-Pashtun opponents and transporting Pashtuns to settle farms in the north thereby creating a loyal Pashtun population amongst the other ethnic minorities.

Abdul Rehman crushed over 40 revolts by the non-Pashtuns during his reign and created Afghanistan's first brutal secret police force, a precursor to the communist Khad in the 1980s. Although these moves integrated Afghans of all ethnic groups and solidified the Afghan state as never before, much of the subsequent ethnic tensions in northern Afghanistan and the inter-ethnic massacres after 1997 can be traced back to the Iron Amir's policies. His other legacies, which were to indirectly influence the Taliban, included the isolation of Afghanistan from Western or modernizing influences including education, his emphasis on Islam by enhancing the powers of the Pashtun mullahs and introducing the concept of a divine right to rule rather than the traditional concept of election by the Loya Jirga.

The successors of the Iron Amir in the early part of the twentieth century were by and large modernizers, who established full formal independence from Britain in 1919, established the country's first constitution and set about creating a small urban educated elite. Nevertheless the fact that two Afghan kings were assassinated and that there were periodic tribal revolts demonstrated the difficulties rulers faced in turning a multi-ethnic tribal society into a modern state.

The end of the Durrani dynasty came when King Zahir Shah, who had ruled since 1933 was deposed by his cousin and brother-in-law Sardar Mohammed Daud who sent Zahir Shah into exile in Rome. Afghanistan was declared a Republic and Daud ruled as president. Daud was helped by leftist officers in the army and the small, urban-based Parcham party led by Babrak Karmal, to crush a nascent Islamic fundamentalist movement. The leaders of this movement fled to Peshawar in 1975 and were backed by Pakistan's Prime Minister Zulfiqar Ali Bhutto to continue their opposition to Daud. These leaders, Gulbuddin Hikmetyar, Burhanuddin Rabbani and Ahmad Shah Masud were later to lead the Mujaheddin.

Daud turned to the Soviet Union for aid to try and modernize the state structure. From 1956 to 78 the Soviet Union gave a total of US$1.26 billion in economic aid and US$1.25 billion in military aid to Afghanistan, as the Soviets welded the country into their sphere of influence at the height of the Cold War. During the same period, the US gave Afghanistan US$533 million in total aid, much of it in the 1950s after which Washington lost interest. By the time Daud seized power Afghanistan had become a rentier state with 40 per cent of state revenues coming from abroad. Yet Daud, like his royal predecessors failed to build institutions. Instead, a loose centrally administered bureaucracy was laid over the existing society with little public representation except in the now largely nominated Loya Jirga.[6]

Just five years later in April 1978, Marxist sympathizers in the army, who had been trained in the Soviet Union and some of whom had helped Daud to power in 1973, overthrew him in a bloody military coup. Daud, his family and the Presidential Bodyguard were all massacred. But the communists were bitterly divided into two factions, Khalq (the masses) and Parcham (the flag) and their lack of understanding of Afghanistan's complex tribal society led to widespread rural revolts against them. As mullahs and khans declared jihad or holy war against the infidel communists, the communist ruling elite were themselves trapped in internecine violence. The first Khalqi communist President Nur Mohammed Taraki was murdered, while his successor Hafizullah Amin was killed when Soviet troops invaded Afghanistan in December 1979 and installed the Parcham leader Babrak Karmal, as President.

Within a few short, dramatic months Afghanistan had been catapulted into the centre of the intensified Cold War between the Soviet Union and the USA. The Afghan Mujaheddin were to become the US-backed, anti-Soviet shock troops. But for the Afghans the Soviet invasion was yet another attempt by outsiders to subdue them and replace their time-honoured religion and society with an alien ideology and social system. The jihad took on a new momentum as the USA, China and Arab states poured in money and arms supplies to the Mujaheddin. Out of this conflict, which was to claim 1.5 million Afghan lives and only end when Soviet troops withdrew from Afghanistan in 1989, would emerge a second generation of Mujaheddin who called themselves Taliban (or the students of Islam.)

Part 1

History of the Taliban Movement

~1~

KANDAHAR 1994:
THE ORIGINS
OF THE TALIBAN

The Taliban Governor of Kandahar, Mullah Mohammed Hassan Rehmani, has a disconcerting habit of pushing the table in front of him with his one good leg. By the time any conversation with him is over, the wooden table has been pushed round and round his chair a dozen times. Hassan's nervous twitch is perhaps a psychological need to feel that he still has a leg or perhaps he is just exercizing, keeping his one good leg on the move at all times.

Hassan's second limb is a wooden peg-leg, in the style of Long John Silver, the pirate in Robert Louis Stevenson's *Treasure Island*. It's an old wooden stump. The varnish rubbed off long ago, scratches cover its length and bits of wood have been gouged out – no doubt by the difficulties of negotiating the rocky terrain outside his office. Hassan, one of the oldest Taliban leaders at over 40 and one of the few who actually fought Soviet troops, was a founder member of the Taliban and is considered to be number two in the movement to his old friend Mullah Omar.

Hassan lost his leg in 1989 on the Kandahar front, just before Soviet troops began their withdrawal from Afghanistan. Despite the availability of new artificial limbs now being fitted to the country's millions of amputees by international aid agencies, Hassan says he prefers his peg-leg. He also lost a finger tip, the result of another wound caused by shrapnel. The Taliban leadership can boast to be the most disabled in the world today and visitors do not know how to react, whether to laugh or to cry. Mullah Omar lost his right eye in 1989 when a rocket exploded close by. The Justice Minister Nuruddin Turabi and the former Foreign Minister Mohammed Ghaus are also one-eyed. The Mayor of Kabul,

Abdul Majid, has one leg and two fingers missing. Other leaders, even military commanders, have similar disabilities.

The Taliban's wounds are a constant reminder of 20 years of war, which has killed over 1.5 million people and devastated the country. The Soviet Union poured some US$5 billion a year into Afghanistan to subdue the Mujaheddin or a total of US$45 billion – and they lost. The US committed some four to five billion dollars between 1980 and 1992 in aid to the Mujaheddin. US funds were matched by Saudi Arabia and together with support from other European and Islamic countries, the Mujaheddin received a total of over US$10 billion.[1] Most of this aid was in the form of lethal modern weaponry given to a simple agricultural people who used it with devastating results.

The war wounds of the Taliban leaders also reflect the bloody and brutal style of war that took place in and around Kandahar in the 1980s. The Durrani Pashtuns who inhabit the south and Kandahar received far less aid through the CIA and Western aid pipeline which armed, financed and provided logistics such as medical facilities to the Mujaheddin, as compared to the Ghilzai Pashtuns in the east of the country and around Kabul. The aid was distributed by Pakistan's Interservices Intelligence (ISI), who tended to treat Kandahar as a backwater and the Durranis with suspicion. As a consequence the nearest medical facilities for a wounded Kandahari Mujaheddin was a bone-shaking two-day camel ride to Quetta across the border in Pakistan. Even today first-aid amongst the Taliban is rare, doctors are all too few and surgeons on the front line non-existent. Virtually the only medical practitioners in the country are the hospitals of the International Committee of the Red Cross (ICRC).

By chance I was in Kandahar in December 1979 and watched the first Soviet tanks roll in. Teenage Soviet soldiers had driven for two days from the Soviet Republic of Turkmenistan in Central Asia to Herat and then on to Kandahar along a metalled highway that the Soviets had themselves built in the 1960s. Many of the soldiers were of Central Asian origin. They got out of their tanks, dusted off their uniforms and ambled across to the nearest stall for a cup of sugarless green tea – a staple part of the diet in both Afghanistan and Central Asia. The Afghans in the bazaar just stood and stared. On 27 December Soviet Spetsnatz or Special Forces had stormed the palace of President Hafizullah Amin in Kabul, killed him, occupied Kabul and appointed Babrak Karmal as President.

When the resistance began around Kandahar it was based on the tribal network of the Durranis. In Kandahar the struggle against the Soviets was a tribal jihad led by clan chiefs and *ulema* (senior religious scholars) rather than an ideological jihad led by Islamicists. In Peshawar there were seven Mujaheddin parties which were recognised by Pakistan and received a share of aid from the CIA pipeline. Significantly none of the seven parties were led by Durrani Pashtuns. In Kandahar all seven parties had a following, but the most popular parties in the south were those based on tribal ties such as the Harakat-e-Inquilab Islami (Movement of the Islamic Revolution) led by Maulvi Mohammed Nabi Mohammedi and another Hizb-e-Islami (Party of Islam) led by Maulvi Younis Khalis. Before the war both leaders were well known in the Pashtun belt and ran their own *madrassas* or religious schools.

For commanders in the south party loyalty depended on which Peshawar leader would provide money and arms. Mullah Omar joined Khalis's Hizb-e-Islami while Mullah Hassan joined Harakat. 'I knew Omar extremely well but we were fighting on different fronts and in different groups but sometimes we fought together,' said Hassan.[2] Also popular was the National Islamic Front led by Pir Sayed Ahmad Gailani, who advocated the return of the Durrani ex-King Zahir Shah to lead the Afghan resistance – a move that was strongly opposed by Pakistan and the USA. The ex-King was living in Rome and continued to be a popular figure amongst the Kandaharis, who hoped that his return would reassert the leadership role of the Durrani tribes.

The contradictions within the Pashtun Mujaheddin leadership were to weaken the Pashtuns as the war progressed. The *ulema* valued the historical ideals of early Islamic history and rarely challenged traditional Afghan tribal structures like the Jirga. They were also much more accommodating towards the ethnic minorities. The Islamicists denigrated the tribal structure and pursued a radical political ideology in order to bring about an Islamic revolution in Afghanistan. They were exclusivists which made the minorities suspicious of them.

Thus Harakat had no coherent party structure and was just a loose alliance between commanders and tribal chiefs, many of whom had just a rudimentary *madrassa* education. On the other hand Gulbuddin Hikmetyar's Hizb-e-Islami built a secretive, highly centralized, political organization whose cadres were drawn from educated urban Pashtuns. Prior to the war the Islamicists barely had a base in Afghan society, but with money and arms from the CIA pipeline and support from Pakistan, they built one and wielded tremendous clout. The traditionalists and the Islamicists fought each other mercilessly so that by 1994, the traditional leadership in Kandahar had virtually been eliminated, leaving the field free for the new wave of even more extreme Islamicists – the Taliban.

The battle for Kandahar was also determined by its own particular history. Kandahar is Afghanistan's second largest city with a 1979 pre-war population of about 250,000 and twice that today. The old city has been inhabited since 500 BC, but just 35 miles away lies Mundigak, a Bronze-Age village settled around 3,000 BC, which was once part of the Indus Valley civilization. Kandaharis have always been great traders as the city was located at the intersection of ancient trade routes – eastwards across the Bolan Pass to Sind, the Arabian Sea and India and westwards to Herat and Iran. The city was the main crossing point for trade, arts and crafts between Iran and India and the city's numerous bazaars have been famous for centuries.

The new city has changed little from that laid out in grand proportions in 1761 by Ahmad Shah Durrani, the founder of the Durrani dynasty. The fact that the Durranis from Kandahar were to create the Afghan state and rule it for 300 years gave the Kandaharis a special status amongst the Pashtuns. As a concession to their home base, Kabul's kings absolved the Kandaharis from providing manpower for the army. Ahmad Shah's mausoleum dominates the central bazaar and thousands of Afghans still come here to pray and pay their respects to the founder of the nation.

Next to his tomb is the shrine of the Cloak of the Prophet Mohammed – one of the holiest places of worship in Afghanistan. The Cloak has been shown only on rare occasions such as when King Amanullah tried to rally the tribes in 1929 and when a cholera epidemic hit the city in 1935.[3] But in 1996 in order to legitimise his role as leader and one ordained by God to lead the Afghan people, Mullah Omar took out the cloak and showed it to a large crowd of Taliban who then named him Amir-ul Momineen or Leader of the Faithful.

However, Kandahar's fame across the region rests on its fruit orchards. Kandahar is an oasis town set in the desert and the summer heat is devastating, but around the city are lush, green fields and shady orchards producing grapes, melons, mulberries, figs, peaches and pomegranates which were famous throughout India and Iran. Kandahar's pomegranates decorated Persian manuscripts written one thousand years ago and were served at the table of the British Governor General of India in Delhi during the last century. The city's truck transporters, who were to give major financial support to the Taliban in their drive to conquer the country, began their trade in the last century when they carried Kandahar's fruit as far as Delhi and Calcutta.

The orchards were watered by a complex and well-maintained irrigation system until the war, when both the Soviets and the Mujaheddin so heavily mined the fields that the rural population fled to Pakistan and the orchards were abandoned. Kandahar remains one of the most heavily mined cities in the world. In an otherwise flat landscape, the orchards and water channels provided cover for the Mujaheddin who quickly took control of the countryside, isolating the Soviet garrison in the city. The Soviets retaliated by cutting down thousands of trees and smashing the irrigation system. When the refugees were to return to their devastated orchards after 1990, they were to grow opium poppies for a livelihood, creating a major source of income for the Taliban.

With the Soviet withdrawal in 1989 there followed a long struggle against the regime of President Najibullah until he was overthrown in 1992 and the Mujaheddin captured Kabul. Much of Afghanistan's subsequent civil war was to be determined by the fact that Kabul fell, not to the well-armed and bickering Pashtun parties based in Peshawar, but to the better organized and more united Tajik forces of Burhanuddin Rabbani and his military commander Ahmad Shah Masud and to the Uzbek forces from the north under General Rashid Dostum. It was a devastating psychological blow because for the first time in 300 years the Pashtuns had lost control of the capital. An internal civil war began almost immediately as Hikmetyar attempted to rally the Pashtuns and laid siege to Kabul, shelling it mercilessly.

Afghanistan was in a state of virtual disintegration just before the Taliban emerged at the end of 1994. The country was divided into warlord fiefdoms and all the warlords had fought, switched sides and fought again in a bewildering array of alliances, betrayals and bloodshed. The predominantly Tajik government of President Burhanuddin Rabbani controlled Kabul, its environs and the north-east of the country, while three provinces in the west centring on Herat were controlled by Ismael Khan. In the east on the Pakistan border three Pashtun provinces were under the independent control of a council or Shura (Council) of Mujaheddin commanders based in Jalalabad. A small region to the south and east of Kabul was controlled by Gulbuddin Hikmetyar.

In the north the Uzbek warlord General Rashid Dostum held sway over six provinces and in January 1994 he had abandoned his alliance with the Rabbani government and joined with Hikmetyar to attack Kabul. In central Afghanistan the Hazaras controlled the province of Bamiyan. Southern Afghanistan and Kandahar were divided up amongst dozens of petty ex-Mujaheddin warlords and bandits who plundered the population at will. With the tribal structure and the economy in tatters, no consensus on a Pashtun leadership and Pakistan's unwillingness to provide military aid to the Durranis as they did to Hikmetyar, the Pashtuns in the south were at war with each other.

International aid agencies were fearful of even working in Kandahar as the city itself was divided by warring groups. Their leaders sold off everything to Pakistani traders to make money, stripping down telephone wires and poles, cutting trees, selling off factories, machinery and even road rollers to scrap merchants. The warlords seized homes and farms, threw out their occupants and handed them over to their supporters. The commanders abused the population at will, kidnapping young girls and boys for their sexual pleasure, robbing merchants in the bazaars and fighting and brawling in the streets. Instead of refugees returning from Pakistan, a fresh wave of refugees began to leave Kandahar for Quetta.

For the powerful mafia of truck transporters based in Quetta and Kandahar, it was an intolerable situation for business. In 1993 I travelled the short 130 miles by road from Quetta to Kandahar and we were stopped by at least 20 different groups, who had put chains across the road and demanded a toll for free passage. The transport mafia who were trying to open up routes to smuggle goods between Quetta and Iran and the newly independent state of Turkmenistan, found it impossible to do business.

For those Mujaheddin who had fought the Najibullah regime and had then gone home or to continue their studies at madrassas in Quetta and Kandahar, the situation was particularly galling. 'We all knew each other – Mullahs Omar, Ghaus, Mohammed Rabbani (no relation to President Rabbani) and myself – because we were all originally from Urozgan province and had fought together,' said Mulla Hassan. 'I moved back and forth from Quetta and attended madrassas there, but whenever we got together we would discuss the terrible plight of our people living under these bandits. We were people of the same opinions and we got on with each other very well, so it was easy to come to a decision to do something,' he added.

Mullah Mohammed Ghaus, the one-eyed Foreign Minister of the Taliban said much the same. 'We would sit for a long time to discuss how to change the terrible situation. Before we started we had only vague ideas what to do and we thought we would fail, but we believed we were working with Allah as His pupils. We have got so far because Allah has helped us,' said Ghaus.[4]

Other groups of Mujaheddin in the south were also discussing the same problems. 'Many people were searching for a solution. I was from Kalat in Zabul province (85 miles north of Kandahar) and had joined a madrassa, but the situation was so bad that we were distracted from our studies and with a group of friends we spent all our time discussing what we should do and what needed to be done,' said Mullah Mohammed Abbas, who was to become the Minister of Public Health in Kabul. 'The old Mujaheddin leadership had utterly failed to bring peace. So I went with a group of friends to Herat to attend the Shura called by Ismael Khan, but it failed to come up with a solution and things were getting worse. So we came to Kandahar to talk with Mullah Omar and joined him,' Abbas added.

After much discussion these divergent but deeply concerned groups chalked out an agenda which still remains the Taliban's declared aims – restore peace, disarm the population, enforce Sharia law and defend the integrity and Islamic character of Afghanistan. As most of them were part-time or full-time students at madrassas, the name they chose for themselves was natural. A talib is an Islamic student, one who seeks knowledge compared to the mullah who is one who gives knowledge. By choosing such a name the Taliban (plural of *Talib*) distanced themselves from the party politics of the Mujaheddin and signalled that they were a movement for cleansing society rather than a party trying to grab power.

All those who gathered around Omar were the children of the jihad but deeply disillusioned with the factionalism and criminal activities of the once idealised Mujaheddin leadership. They saw themselves as the cleansers and purifiers of a guerrilla war gone astray, a social system gone wrong and an Islamic way of life that had been compromised by corruption and excess. Many of them had been born in Pakistani refugee camps, educated in Pakistani *madrassas* and had learnt their fighting skills from Mujaheddin parties based in Pakistan. As such the younger Taliban barely knew their own country or history, but from their *madrassas* they learnt about the ideal Islamic society created by the Prophet Mohammed 1,400 years ago and this is what they wanted to emulate.

Some Taliban say Omar was chosen as their leader not for his political or military ability, but for his piety and his unswerving belief in Islam. Others say he was chosen by God. 'We selected Mullah Omar to lead this movement. He was the first amongst equals and we gave him the power to lead us and he has given us the power and authority to deal with people's problems,' said Mullah Hassan. Omar himself gave a simple explanation to Pakistani journalist Rahimullah Yousufzai. 'We took up arms to achieve the aims of the Afghan jihad and save our people from further suffering at the hands of the so-called Mujaheddin. We had complete faith in God Almighty. We never forgot that. He can bless us with victory or plunge us into defeat,' said Omar.[5]

No leader in the world today is surrounded by as much secrecy and mystery as Mullah Mohammed Omar. Aged 39, he has never been photographed or met with Western diplomats and journalists. His first meeting with a UN diplomat was in October 1998, four years after the Taliban emerged, when he met with the UN Special Representative for Afghanistan Lakhdar Brahimi, because the Taliban were faced with a possibly devastating attack by Iran. Omar lives in Kandahar and has visited the capital Kabul twice and only then very briefly. Putting together the bare facts of his life has become a full-time job for most Afghans and foreign diplomats.

Omar was born sometime around 1959 in Nodeh village near Kandahar to a family of poor, landless peasants who were members of the Hotak tribe, the Ghilzai branch of Pashtuns. The Hotaki chief Mir Wais, had captured Isfahan in Iran in 1721 and established the first Ghilzai Afghan empire in Iran only to be quickly replaced by Ahmad Shah Durrani. Omar's tribal and social status was non-existent and notables from Kandahar say they had never heard of his family. During the 1980s jihad his family moved to Tarinkot in Urozgan province – one of the most backward and inaccessible regions of the country where Soviet troops rarely penetrated. His father died while he was a young man and the task of fending for his mother and extended family fell upon him.

Looking for a job, he moved to Singesar village in the Mewand district of Kandahar province, where he became the village mullah and opened a small madrassa. His own studies in madrassas in Kandahar were interrupted twice, first by the Soviet invasion and then by the creation of the Taliban.[6] Omar joined Khalis's Hizb-e-Islami and fought under commander Nek Mohammed against the Najibullah regime between 1989 and 1992. He was wounded four times, once in the right eye which is now permanently blinded.

Despite the success of the Taliban, Singesar is still like any other Pashtun village. Mud-brick homes plastered with more mud and straw are built behind high compound walls – a traditional defensive feature of Pashtun homes. Narrow, dusty alleyways, which turn into mud baths when it rains, connect village homes. Omar's madrassa is still functioning – a small mud hut with a dirt floor and mattresses strewn across it for the boys to sleep on. Omar has three wives, who continue living in the village and are heavily veiled. While his first and third wives are from Urozgan, his teenage second wife Guljana, whom he married in 1995, is from Singesar. He has a total of five children who are studying in his madrassa.[7]

A tall, well-built man with a long, black beard and a black turban, Omar has a dry sense of humour and a sarcastic wit. He remains extremely shy of outsiders, particularly foreigners, but he is accessible to the Taliban. When the movement started he would offer his Friday prayers at the main mosque in Kandahar and mix with the people, but subsequently he has become much more of a recluse, rarely venturing outside Kandahar's administrative mansion where he lives. He now visits his village infrequently and when he does he is always accompanied by dozens of bodyguards in a convoy of deluxe Japanese jeepsters with darkened windows.

Omar speaks very little in Shura meetings, listening to other points of view. His shyness makes him a poor public speaker and despite the mythology that now surrounds him, he has little charismatic appeal. All day he conducts business from a small office in the mansion. At first he used to sit on the cement floor alongside visiting Taliban, but he now sits on a bed while others sit on the floor – a move that emphasises his status as leader. He has several secretaries who take notes from his conversations with commanders, ordinary soldiers, ulema and plaintiffs and there is always the crackle of wireless sets as commanders around the country communicate with him.

Business consists of lengthy debate and discussions which end with the issuing of 'chits' or scraps of paper on which are written instructions allowing commanders to make an attack, ordering a Taliban governor to help out a plaintiff or a message to UN mediators. Formal communications to foreign embassies in Islamabad were frequently dictated by Pakistani advisers.

In the early days of the movement I collected numerous chits written on cigarette boxes or wrapping paper, allowing me to travel from city to city. Now more regular paper pads are used. Beside Omar is a tin trunk from which he dishes out wads of Afghani notes to commanders and plaintiffs in need. As success came, another tin trunk was added – this one containing US dollars. These tin trunks are the treasury of the Taliban movement.

In important meetings, Mullah Wakil Ahmad, Omar's trusted confidant and official spokesman is usually beside him. Wakil, a young *madrassa* student from the Kakar tribe who studied under Omar, started out as his companion, driver, food taster, translator and note-taker. He quickly progressed to higher things such as communicating with visiting foreign diplomats and aid agency officials, travelling to meet Taliban commanders and meeting with Pakistani officials. As Omar's spokesman he is the Taliban's main contact with the foreign press as well as its chastizer, when he feels that journalists have criticized the Taliban too harshly. Wakil acts as Omar's ears and eyes and is also his doorkeeper. No important Afghan can reach Omar without first going through Wakil.

There is now an entire factory of myths and stories to explain how Omar mobilized a small group of Taliban against the rapacious Kandahar warlords. The most credible story, told repeatedly, is that in the spring of 1994 Singesar neighbours came to tell him that a commander had abducted two teenage girls, their heads had been shaved and they had been taken to a military camp and repeatedly raped. Omar enlisted some 30 *Talibs* who had only 16 rifles between them and attacked the base, freeing the girls and hanging the commander from the barrel of a tank. They captured quantities of arms and ammunition. 'We were fighting against Muslims who had gone wrong. How could we remain quiet when we could see crimes being committed against women and the poor?' Omar said later.[8]

A few months later two commanders confronted each other in Kandahar, in a dispute over a young boy whom both men wanted to sodomise. In the fight that followed civilians were killed. Omar's group freed the boy and public appeals started coming in for the Taliban to help out in other local disputes. Omar had emerged as a Robin Hood figure, helping the poor against the rapacious commanders. His prestige grew because he asked for no reward or credit from those he helped, only demanding that they follow him to set up a just Islamic system.

At the same time Omar's emissaries were gauging the mood of other commanders. His colleagues visited Herat to meet with Ismael Khan and in September Mulla Mohammed Rabbani, a founding member of the Taliban, visited Kabul and held talks with President Rabbani. The isolated Kabul government wished to support any new Pashtun force that would oppose Hikmetyar, who was still shelling Kabul, and Rabbani promised to help the Taliban with funds if they opposed Hikmetyar.

However the Taliban's closest links were with Pakistan where many of them had grown up and studied in *madrassas* run by the mercurial Maulana Fazlur Rehman and his Jamiat-e-*Ulema* Islam (JUI), a fundamentalist party which had considerable support amongst the Pashtuns in Baluchistan and the North West Frontier Province (NWFP). More significantly Maulana Rehman was now a political ally of Prime Minister Benazir Bhutto and he had access to the government, the army and the ISI to whom he described this newly emerging force.

Pakistan's Afghan policy was in the doldrums. After the collapse of the Soviet Union in 1991, successive Pakistani governments were desperately keen to open up direct land routes for trade with the Central Asian Republics (CARs). The major hindrance was the continuing civil war in Afghanistan, through which any route passed. Pakistan's policy-makers were thus faced with a strategic dilemma. Either Pakistan could carry on backing Hikmetyar in a bid to bring a Pashtun group to power in Kabul which would be Pakistan-friendly, or it could change direction and urge for a power-sharing agreement between all the Afghan factions at whatever the price for the Pashtuns, so that a stable government could open the roads to Central Asia.

The Pakistani military was convinced that other ethnic groups would not do their bidding and continued to back Hikmetyar. Some 20 per cent of the Pakistan army was made up of Pakistani Pashtuns and the pro-Pashtun and Islamic fundamentalist lobby within the ISI and the military remained determined to achieve a Pashtun victory in Afghanistan. However, by 1994 Hikmetyar had clearly failed, losing ground militarily while his extremism divided the Pashtuns, the majority of whom loathed him. Pakistan was getting tired of backing a loser and was looking around for other potential Pashtun proxies.

When Benazir Bhutto was elected as Prime Minister in 1993, she was keen to open a route to Central Asia. The shortest route was from Peshawar to Kabul, across the Hindu Kush mountains to Mazar-e-Sharif and then to Tirmez and Tashkent in Uzbekistan, but this route was closed due to the fighting around Kabul. A new proposal emerged, backed strongly by the frustrated Pakistani transport and smuggling mafia, the JUI and Pashtun military and political officials. Instead of the northern route the way could be cleared from Quetta to Kandahar, Herat and on to Ashkhabad, the capital of Turkmenistan. There was no fighting in the south, only dozens of commanders who would have to be adequately bribed before they agreed to open the chains.

In September 1994 Pakistani surveyors and ISI officers discreetly travelled the road from Chaman on the Pakistani border to Herat, to survey the road. The Pashtun-born Interior Minister Naseerullah Babar also visited Chaman that month. The Kandahar warlords viewed the plan with mistrust, suspecting the Pakistanis were about to try and intervene militarily to crush them. One commander, Amir Lalai, issued a blunt warning to Babar. 'Pakistan is offering to reconstruct our roads, but I do not think that by fixing our roads peace would automatically follow. As long as neighbouring countries continue to interfere in our internal affairs, we should not expect peace,' said Lalai.[9]

Nevertheless, the Pakistanis began to negotiate with the Kandahar warlords and Ismael Khan in Herat to allow traffic through to Turkmenistan. On 20 October 1994, Babar took a party of six Western ambassadors to Kandahar and Herat, without even informing the Kabul government.[10] The delegation included senior officials from the departments of Railways, Highways, Telephones and Electricity. Babar said he wanted to raise US$300 million from international agencies to rebuild the highway from Quetta to Herat. On 28 October, Bhutto met with Ismael Khan and General Rashid Dostum in Ashkhabad and urged them to agree to open a southern route, where trucks would pay just a couple of tolls on the way and their security would be guaranteed.

However, before that meeting a major event had shaken the Kandahar warlords. On 12 October 1994 some 200 Taliban from Kandahar and Pakistani madrassas arrived at the small Afghan border post of Spin Baldak on the Pakistan–Afghanistan border just opposite Chaman. The grimy grease pit in the middle of the desert was an important trucking and fuelling stop for the transport mafia and was held by Hikmetyar's men. Here Afghan trucks picked up goods from Pakistani trucks, which were not allowed to cross into Afghanistan and fuel was smuggled in from Pakistan to feed the warlords' armies. For the transport mafia, control of the town was critical. They had already donated several hundred thousand Pakistani Rupees to Mullah Omar and promised a monthly stipend to the Taliban, if they would clear the roads of chains and bandits and guarantee the security for truck traffic.[11]

The Taliban force divided into three groups and attacked Hikmetyar's garrison. After a short, sharp battle they fled, losing seven dead and several wounded. The Taliban lost only one man. Pakistan then helped the Taliban by allowing them to capture a large arms dump outside Spin Baldak that had been guarded by Hikmetyar's men. This dump had been moved across the border from Pakistan into Afghanistan in 1990, when the terms of the Geneva Accords obliged Islamabad not to hold weapons for Afghans on Pakistani territory. At the dump the Taliban seized some 18,000 kalashnikovs, dozens of artillery pieces, large quantities of ammunition and many vehicles.[12]

The capture of Spin Baldak worried the Kandahar warlords and they denounced Pakistan for backing the Taliban, but they continued bickering amongst themselves rather than uniting to meet the new threat. Babar was now getting impatient and he ordered a 30 truck test-convoy to travel to Ashkhabad with a load of medicines. 'I told Babar we should wait two months because we had no agreements with the Kandahar commanders, but Babar insisted on pushing the convoy through. The commanders suspected that the convoy was carrying arms for a future Pakistani force,' a Pakistani official based in Kandahar later told me.[13]

On 29 October 1994, the convoy drawn from the army's National Logistics Cell (NLC), which had been set up in the 1980s by the ISI to funnel US arms to the Mujaheddin, left Quetta with 80 Pakistani ex-army drivers. Colonel Imam, the ISI's most prominent field officer operating in the south and Pakistan's Consul General in Herat, was also on board. Along with him were two young Taliban commanders, Mullahs Borjan and Turabi. (Both were later to lead the Taliban's first assault on Kabul where Mullah Borjan was to meet his death.) Twelve miles outside Kandahar, at Takht-e-Pul near the perimeter of Kandahar airport, the convoy was held up by a group of commanders, Amir Lalai, Mansur Achakzai, who controlled the airport, and Ustad Halim. The convoy was ordered to park in a nearby village at the foot of low-lying mountains. When I walked the area a few months later the remains of camp fires and discarded rations were still evident.

The commanders demanded money, a share of the goods and that Pakistan stop supporting the Taliban. As the commanders negotiated with Colonel Imam, Islamabad imposed a news blackout for three days on the convoy hijack. 'We were worried that Mansur would put arms aboard the convoy and then blame Pakistan. So we considered all the military options to rescue the convoy, such as a raid by the Special Services Group (Pakistan army commandos) or a parachute drop. These options were considered too dangerous so we then asked the Taliban to free the convoy,' said a Pakistani official. On 3 November 1994, the Taliban moved in to attack those holding the convoy. The commanders, thinking this was a raid by the Pakistani army, fled. Mansur was chased into the desert by the Taliban, captured and shot dead with ten of his bodyguards. His body was hung from a tank barrel for all to see.

That same evening, the Taliban moved on Kandahar where, after two days of sporadic fighting they routed the commanders' forces. Mullah Naquib, the most prominent commander inside the city who commanded 2,500 men, did not resist. Some of his aides later claimed that Naquib had taken a substantial bribe from the ISI to surrender, with the promise that he would retain his command. The Taliban enlisted his men and retired the Mullah to his village outside Kandahar. The Taliban captured dozens of tanks, armoured cars, military vehicles, weapons and most significantly at the airport six Mig-21 fighters and six transport helicopters – left-overs from the Soviet occupation.

In just a couple of weeks this unknown force had captured the second largest city in Afghanistan with the loss of just a dozen men. In Islamabad no foreign diplomat or analyst doubted that they had received considerable support from Pakistan. The fall of Kandahar was celebrated by the Pakistan government and the JUI. Babar took credit for the Taliban's success, telling journalists privately that the Taliban were 'our boys'. Yet the Taliban demonstrated their independence from Pakistan, indicating that they were nobody's puppet. On 16 November 1994 Mullah Ghaus said that Pakistan should not bypass the Taliban in sending convoys in the future and should not cut deals with individual warlords. He also said the Taliban would not allow goods bound for Afghanistan to be carried by Pakistani trucks – a key demand of the transport mafia.[14]

The Taliban cleared the chains from the roads, set up a one-toll system for trucks entering Afghanistan at Spin Baldak and patrolled the highway from Pakistan. The transport mafia was ecstatic and in December the first Pakistani convoy of 50 trucks carrying raw cotton from Turkmenistan arrived in Quetta, after paying the Taliban 200,000 rupees (US$5,000) in tolls. Meanwhile thousands of young Afghan Pashtuns studying in Baluchistan and the NWFP rushed to Kandahar to join the Taliban. They were soon followed by Pakistani volunteers from JUI *madrassas*, who were inspired by the new Islamic movement in Afghanistan. By December 1994, some 12,000 Afghan and Pakistani students had joined the Taliban in Kandahar.

As international and domestic pressure mounted on Pakistan to explain its position, Bhutto made the first formal denial of any Pakistani backing of the Taliban in February 1995. 'We have no favourites in Afghanistan and we do not interfere in Afghanistan,' she said while visiting Manila.[15] Later she said Pakistan could not stop new recruits from crossing the border to join the Taliban. 'I cannot fight Mr [President Burhanuddin] Rabbani's war for him. If Afghans want to cross the border, I do not stop them. I can stop them from re-entering but most of them have families here,' she said.[16]

The Taliban immediately implemented the strictest interpretation of Sharia law ever seen in the Muslim world. They closed down girls' schools and banned women from working outside the home, smashed TV sets, forbade a whole array of sports and recreational activities and ordered all males to grow long beards. In the next three months the Taliban were to take control of 12 of Afghanistan's 31 provinces, opening the roads to traffic and disarming the population. As the Taliban marched north to Kabul, local warlords either fled or, waving white flags, surrendered to them. Mullah Omar and his army of students were on the march across Afghanistan.

~2~

HERAT 1995:
GOD'S INVINCIBLE
SOLDIERS

In March 1995, on the northern edge of the Dashte-e-Mango – the Desert of Death – plumes of fine white dust rose in the air above the narrow ribbon of the battered highway that connects Kandahar with Herat, 350 miles away. The highway, built by the Russians in the 1950s skirted through the brush and sands of one of the hottest and most waterless deserts in the world. After years of war, the highway was now rutted with tank tracks, bomb craters and broken bridges, slowing down the traffic to just 20 miles an hour.

The Taliban war wagons – Japanese two-door pick-ups with a stripped-down trunk at the back open to the elements – were streaming towards Herat laden with heavily armed young men in their bid to capture the city. In the opposite direction a steady flow of vehicles was bringing back wounded Taliban lying on string beds and strapped into the trunk as well as prisoners captured from the forces of Ismael Khan who held Herat.

In the first three months after capturing Kandahar, the Taliban had broken the stalemate in the Afghan civil war by capturing 12 of Afghanistan's 31 provinces and had arrived at the outskirts of Kabul to the north and Herat in the west. Taliban soldiers were reluctant to talk under the gaze of their commanders in Kandahar so the only way to learn something about them was to hitch lifts along the road and back again. In the confines of the pick-ups where a dozen warriors were jam-packed with crates of ammunition, rockets, grenade launchers and sacks of wheat, they were more than eager to share their life stories.

They said that since the capture of Kandahar some 20,000 Afghans and hundreds of Pakistani *madrassa* students had streamed across the border from refugee camps in Pakistan to join Mullah Omar. Thousands more Afghan Pashtuns had joined them in their march northwards. The majority were incredibly young – between 14 and 24 years old – and many had never fought before although, like all Pashtuns, they knew how to handle a weapon.

Many had spent their lives in refugee camps in Baluchistan and the NWFP provinces of Pakistan, interspersed with stints at imbibing a Koranic education in the dozens of *madrassas* that had sprung up along the border run by Afghan mullahs or Pakistan's Islamic fundamentalist parties. Here they studied the Koran, the sayings of the Prophet Mohammed and the basics of Islamic law as interpreted by their barely literate teachers. Neither teachers nor students had any formal grounding in maths, science, history or geography. Many of these young warriors did not even know the history of their own country or the story of the jihad against the Soviets.

These boys were a world apart from the Mujaheddin whom I had got to know during the 1980s – men who could recount their tribal and clan lineages, remembered their abandoned farms and valleys with nostalgia and recounted legends and stories from Afghan history. These boys were from a generation who had never seen their country at peace – an Afghanistan not at war with invaders and itself. They had no memories of their tribes, their elders, their neighbours nor the complex ethnic mix of peoples that often made up their villages and their homeland. These boys were what the war had thrown up like the sea's surrender on the beach of history.

They had no memories of the past, no plans for the future while the present was everything. They were literally the orphans of the war, the rootless and the restless, the jobless and the economically deprived with little self-knowledge. They admired war because it was the only occupation they could possibly adapt to. Their simple belief in a messianic, puritan Islam which had been drummed into them by simple village mullahs was the only prop they could hold on to and which gave their lives some meaning. Untrained for anything, even the traditional occupations of their forefathers such as farming, herding or the making of handicrafts, they were what Karl Marx would have termed Afghanistan's lumpen proletariat.

Moreover, they had willingly gathered under the all-male brotherhood that the Taliban leaders were set on creating, because they knew of nothing else. Many in fact were orphans who had grown up without women – mothers, sisters or cousins. Others were *madrassa* students or had lived in the strict confines of segregated refugee camp life, where the normal comings and goings of female relatives were curtailed. Even by the norms of conservative Pashtun tribal society, where villages or nomadic camps were close-knit communities and men still mixed with women to whom they were related, these boys had lived rough, tough lives. They had simply never known the company of women.

The mullahs who had taught them stressed that women were a temptation, an unnecessary distraction from being of service to Allah. So when the Taliban entered Kandahar and confined women to their homes by barring them from working, going to school and even from shopping, the majority of these *madrassa* boys saw nothing unusual in such measures. They felt threatened by that half of the human race which they had never known and it was much easier to lock that half away, especially if it was ordained by the mullahs who invoked primitive Islamic injunctions, which had no basis in Islamic law. The subjugation of women became the mission of the true believer and a fundamental marker that differentiated the Taliban from the former Mujaheddin.

This male brotherhood offered these youngsters not just a religious cause to fight for, but a whole way of life to fully embrace and make their existence meaningful. Ironically, the Taliban were a direct throwback to the military religious orders that arose in Christendom during the Crusades to fight Islam – disciplined, motivated and ruthless in attaining their aims.[1] In the first few months the sweeping victories of the Taliban created an entire mythology of invincibility that only God's own soldiers could attain. In those heady early days, every victory only reinforced the perceived truth of their mission, that God was on their side and that their interpretation of Islam was the only interpretation.

Reinforced by their new recruits, the Taliban moved north into Urozgan and Zabul provinces which they captured without a shot being fired. The marauding Pashtun commanders, unwilling to test their own supporters' uncertain loyalty, surrendered by hoisting white flags and handing over their weapons in a mark of submission.

In the south the Taliban moved against the forces of Ghaffar Akhunzadeh, whose clan had controlled Helmand province and its lucrative opium poppy fields for much of the 1980s. Here they met with fierce resistance, but by propping up smaller drug warlords against Akhunzadeh and bribing others, the Taliban captured the province by January 1995. They continued westwards reaching Dilaram on the Kandahar–Herat highway and the border of the three western provinces controlled by Ismael Khan. At the same time they moved north towards Kabul, easily slicing through the Pashtun belt where they met with more mass surrenders rather than resistance.

The chaotic and anarchic Pashtun south, where there was only a mob of petty commanders, had fallen to the Taliban easily, but now they came up against the major warlords and the political and ethnic complexities that gripped the rest of the country. In January 1995 all the opposition groups had joined hands to attack President Rabbani's government in

Kabul. Hikmetyar had allied with the Uzbek warlord General Rashid Dostum in the north and the Hazaras of central Afghanistan who held a portion of Kabul. Pakistan had helped broker the new alliance as Hikmetyar was still Islamabad's clear favourite and at the beginning of the year he had received large quantities of Pakistani-supplied rockets to bombard the capital. But even Islamabad was surprised by the rapid Taliban advance. Although the Bhutto government fully backed the Taliban, the ISI remained sceptical of their abilities, convinced that they would remain a useful but peripheral force in the south.

Hikmetyar was clearly worried by this rival Pashtun force sweeping up from the south and tried to halt the Taliban while at the same time launching massive rocket attacks against Kabul, which killed hundreds of civilians and destroyed large tracts of the city. On 2 February 1995, the Taliban captured Wardak, just 35 miles south of Kabul and Hikmetyar's bases around Kabul came under threat for the first time. The Taliban continued to advance in lightning moves, capturing Maidan Shahr on 10 February 1995, after heavy fighting which left 200 dead, and Mohammed Agha the next day. Hikmetyar was now trapped by government forces to the north and the Taliban to the south; morale among his troops plummeted.

On 14 February 1995 the Taliban captured Hikmetyar's headquarters at Charasyab, creating panic among his troops and forcing them to flee eastwards towards Jalalabad. President Rabbani's troops, under his sword-arm Ahmad Shah Masud, withdrew into Kabul city. The Taliban then opened all the roads, allowing food convoys to reach Kabul after the months of blockade imposed by Hikmetyar. It was a popular step, raising the Taliban's prestige amongst the sceptical citizens of Kabul and fulfilled a key demand of the transport mafia backing the Taliban. Appeals for a cease-fire by the UN Special Representative for Afghanistan, the Tunisean diplomat Mehmoud Mestiri, were ignored as Masud and the Taliban now confronted each other.

Masud had another problem even closer to home. Although Hikmetyar had been forced to flee, Masud still faced the forces of the Shia Hazaras under the Hizb-e-Wahadat party, which held the southern suburbs of the capital. Masud tried to buy time and met twice with the Taliban commanders, Mullahs Rabbani, Borjan and Ghaus at Charasayab. These meetings were the first time that the Taliban were to meet with their greatest rival, who was to persist in punishing them for the next four years. The Taliban demanded Rabbani's resignation as President and Masud's surrender – hardly a negotiating stance that would win them support. The Taliban also began negotiating with the Hazaras.

The Taliban also met with Mestiri, the UN mediator, setting down three conditions for their participation in any UN-sponsored peace process. They demanded that their units form a 'neutral force' in Kabul, that only 'good Muslims' form an interim administration in Kabul and that representation be given to all 30 provinces in the country. The Taliban's insistence that only their forces dominate any new government in Kabul, obliged the Rabbani government and the UN to reject their demands.

Masud decided to deal with his enemies one at a time. On 6 March 1995, he launched a blitzkrieg against the Hazaras, sending tanks into Kabul's southern suburbs, smashing the Hazaras and driving them out of Kabul. In desperation the Hazaras cut a deal with the advancing Taliban, yielding their heavy weapons and positions to them. But in the ensuing handover and mêlée, the Hazara leader Abdul Ali Mazari was killed while in Taliban custody. The Hazaras subsequently claimed that Mazari was pushed out of a helicopter to his death by the Taliban, because he tried to seize a rifle while he was being taken to Kandahar as a prisoner.

The death of Mazari, accidental or intentional, was to forever condemn the Taliban in the eyes of the Afghan Shias and their main patron Iran. The Hazaras were never to forgive the Taliban for Mazari's death and took their revenge two years later, when the Hazaras massacred thousands of Taliban in the north. A bloody ethnic and sectarian divide, between Pashtun and Hazara, Sunni and Shia bubbling just below the surface now came into the open.

In the meantime Masud was not going to allow the Taliban to replace the Hazaras in southern Kabul. On 11 March 1995 he launched another punishing attack, pushing the Taliban out of the city after bloody street fighting that left hundreds of Taliban dead. It was the first major battle that the Taliban had fought and lost. Their weak military structure and poor tactics ensured their defeat at the hands of Masud's more experienced fighters.

The Taliban had won over the unruly Pashtun south because the exhausted, war-weary population saw them as saviours and peacemakers, if not as a potential force to revive Pashtun power which had been humiliated by the Tajiks and Uzbeks. Many surrenders had been facilitated by pure cash, bribing commanders to switch sides – a tactic that the Taliban were to turn into a fine art form in later years and which was sustained by the growth in their income from the drugs trade, the transport business and external aid from Pakistan and Saudi Arabia. In their advance they had also captured massive quantities of small arms, tanks and even helicopters enabling them to deploy more troops. In the areas under their rule, they disarmed the population, enforced law and order, imposed strict Sharia law and opened the roads to traffic which resulted in an immediate drop in food prices. These measures were all extremely welcome to the long-suffering population. The defeat in Kabul came as a major blow to the Taliban's prestige, but not to their determination.

The Taliban then turned their attention to the west in a bid to capture Herat. By late February 1995 after heavy fighting they captured Nimroz and Farah, two of the provinces controlled by Ismael Khan and advanced on the former Soviet airbase at Shindand, south of Herat. The Kabul regime was clearly worried by the Taliban advance and Ismael Khan's failure to hold the line against them. Masud's aircraft from Kabul began a bombardment of the Taliban front lines while he airlifted 2,000 of his battle-hardened Tajik fighters from Kabul to help defend Shindand and Herat. With no airpower, poor logistical support from their bases in Kandahar and a weak command structure, the Taliban began to take heavy casualties as they mounted assaults on government positions around Shindand.

By the end of March 1995, the Taliban had been pushed out of Shindand. They retreated losing most of the territory they had captured earlier, suffering at least 3,000 casualties. Hundreds of wounded were left in the desert to die because the Taliban had no medical facilities at the front and their lack of logistics made it impossible for them to provide water and food to their troops. 'We have never seen such an inhospitable environment. Every day we are bombed, 10 to 15 times. There is no food or water and my friends have died of thirst. We lost communication with our commanders and we don't know where our other troops are. We ran out of ammunition. It was a great misery,' Saleh Mohammed, a wounded Taliban told me, as he was transported back to Kandahar.[2]

The Taliban had now been decisively pushed back on two fronts by the government and their political and military leadership was in disarray. Their image as potential peacemakers was badly dented, for in the eyes of many Afghans they had become nothing more than just another warlord party. President Rabbani had temporarily consolidated his political and military position around Kabul and Herat. By May 1995 government forces directly controlled six provinces around Kabul and the north, while Ismael Khan controlled the three western provinces. The Taliban's initial control over 12 provinces was reduced to eight after their defeats. But Herat continued to remain a tantalizing prize, not just for the Taliban, but for the Pashtun transport and drugs mafias who were desperately keen to open up the roads to Iran and Central Asia through Herat for their business.

Few Mujaheddin commanders had the prestige of Ismael Khan and few had sacrificed more than the people of Herat during the war against the Soviets. Ismael Khan was an officer in the Afghan army when the Russians invaded Afghanistan and he had strong Islamic and nationalist leanings. When the Soviets occupied Herat, they viewed the Persian-speaking Heratis as docile and unwarlike and the most cultured of all Afghans. The last time the Heratis were forced into a fight had been more than a cen-

tury earlier when they had resisted a Persian invasion in 1837. Fearing no
resistance, the Soviets developed the Shindand airbase as their largest
airbase in Afghanistan and allowed the families of their army officers to
settle in Herat.

But on 15 March 1979, the population of the city rose up against the
Soviets in an unprecedented urban revolt. As the population killed Soviet
officers, advisers and their families, Ismael Khan staged a coup in the city
garrison, killing Soviet and communist Afghan officers and distributing
arms to the people. Hundreds of Russians were killed. Moscow, fearing
copycat uprisings in other Afghan cities, sent 300 tanks from Soviet Turkmenistan to crush the revolt and began to bomb one of the oldest cities
in the world indiscriminately. Fifteen years later, large tracts of the city
still looked like a lunar landscape with rubble stretching to the horizon.
More than 20,000 Heratis were killed during the next few days. Ismael
Khan escaped to the countryside with his new guerrilla army and tens of
thousands of civilians fled to Iran. For the next decade Ismael Khan waged
a bitter guerrilla war against the Soviet occupation and set up an effective
administration in the countryside, winning the respect of the population.
This was to prove invaluable to him when he was to re-establish himself
in Herat after the departure of Soviet troops.

Herat was the cradle of Afghanistan's history and civilization. An oasis
town, it was first settled 5,000 years ago. Its 200 square miles of irrigated
farmland in a valley rimmed by mountains, was considered to have the
richest soil in Central Asia. The ancient Greek historian Herodotus
described Herat as the breadbasket of Central Asia. 'The whole habitable
world had not such a town as Herat,' wrote the Emperor Babar in his
memoirs. The British likened its beauty to England's home counties. 'The
space between the hills is one beautiful extent of little fortified villages,
gardens, vineyards and cornfields, and this rich scene is brightened by
many small streams of shining water which cut the plain in all directions,'
the British adventurer and spy Captain Connolly wrote in 1831.[3]

For centuries the city was the crossroads between the competing Turkic
and Persian empires and its population was an early convert to Islam. The
main mosque in the city centre dates back to the seventh century and
was rebuilt by the Ghorid dynasty in 1200. In medieval times it was both
a centre for Christianity, under the Nestorian Church and a major centre
for Sufism – the spiritual and mystical side of Islam. Followers of the
Naqshbandi and Chishtyia Sufi brotherhoods became Prime Ministers and
Ministers. Herat's patron saint is Khawaja Abdullah Ansari who died in
1088, a celebrated Sufi poet and philosopher who still has a large following in Afghanistan. When Genghis Khan conquered Herat in 1222, he
spared only 40 of its 160,000 inhabitants. But less than two centuries later
the city had recovered to reach its pinnacle when Taimur's son Shah

Rukh and his Queen Gowhar Shad moved the capital of the Timurid empire from Samarkand to Herat in 1405.

The Timurids were the first to merge the Turkic nomadic steppe culture with the refinements of the settled Persian lands, importing artisans from Persia, India and Central Asia to build hundreds of magnificent monuments. Shah Rukh and Gowhar Shad turned Herat into a vast construction site building mosques, madrassas, public baths, libraries and palaces. Herat's bazaars produced the finest carpets, jewellery, weapons, armour and tiles. Bihzad, considered the finest Persian miniaturist painter of all time worked at the court. 'In Herat if you stretch out your feet you are sure to kick a poet,' said Ali Sher Nawai, Shah Rukh's Prime Minister, who was also an artist, poet and writer.[4] Nawai, who is buried in Herat and is the national poet of modern day Uzbekistan, is considered the father of literary Turkic for he was the first to write poetry in Turkic rather than Persian. The Persian poet Jami was also at court and is buried in Herat while Shah Rukh's son Ulugh Beg, was an astronomer whose observatory in Samarkand monitored the movement of stars. His calendar and tables of the stars were published at Oxford University in 1665 and are still astonishingly accurate.

In 1417, Gowhar Shad, herself a builder of dozens of mosques, completed the construction of a magnificent complex on the outskirts of the city consisting of a mosque, madrassa and her own tomb. The tomb, with its panelled walls of Persian blue tiles bejewelled with floral decorations and topped by a ribbed blue dome with dazzling white Koranic inscriptions, is still considered one of the finest examples of Islamic architecture anywhere in the world. When Byron saw it in 1937, he described it as 'the most beautiful example in colour in architecture ever devised by man to the glory of God and himself.'[5] When Gowhar Shad died at the age of 80 after constructing some 300 buildings in Afghanistan, Persia and Central Asia, the inscription on her tomb read simply 'The Bilkis of the Time.' Bilkis means the Queen of Sheba.[6] Much of the complex was demolished by the British in 1885 and the Soviets later mined the area to keep out the Mujaheddin.

When the Soviets bombed Herat in 1979, they inflicted more damage on the city than even the Mongols had done. 'Herat is the most destroyed and the most heavily mined city in the world today, yet we get no help from anywhere,' Ismael Khan told me in 1993.[7] Despite the devastation around him, Ismael Khan had disarmed the population and established an effective administration with functioning health care and schools in the three provinces.

Short, shrewd and with an elfin smile that made him look much younger than his 47 years, Ismael Khan had 45,000 children studying in Herat's schools, by 1993 half of them were girls – 75,000 students in all across the three provinces. In 1993 he took me to see the Atun Heirvi school where 1,500 girls studied in two shifts, sitting under the open sky as there were no classrooms, desks, books, paper or ink – their desire to learn only re-emphasising Herat's history of learning. In contrast when the Taliban took over Kandahar, the 45 working schools were closed down and only three remained. When the Taliban were later to capture Herat they were to close down every school in the city and disallow girls from even studying at home.

But by 1995 Ismael Khan faced immense problems. He had disarmed the population and created an unpopular conscript army. To face the Taliban, he needed to rearm the population while his conscript army was riddled with corruption, low morale and lack of resources. Official corruption and high-handedness towards civilians had become rampant in the city and customs officials charged trucks passing through Herat the exorbitant sum of 10,000 Pakistan rupees (US$300) – a sure way to make an enemy of the transport mafia. The Taliban were well informed of the problems he faced. 'Ismael is weak, his soldiers will not fight because they have not been paid and he is widely discredited amongst his people because of the corruption in his administration. He stands alone and has to be propped up by Masud,' Mullah Wakil Ahmad told me.[8]

Ismael Khan also made a serious military miscalculation. Believing the Taliban were on the verge of disintegration due to their defeat, he launched an ill-prepared and badly timed offensive against them. With a large mobile force, he captured Dilaram on 23 August 1995 and parts of Helmand a week later thereby threatening Kandahar. But his forces were overstretched in a hostile environment while the Taliban had spent the summer rebuilding their forces with arms, ammunition and vehicles provided by Pakistan and Saudi Arabia and a new command structure created with the help of ISI advisers. The ISI also helped broker an agreement, never made public, between the Taliban and General Rashid Dostum. Dostum sent his Uzbek technicians to Kandahar to repair Mig fighters and helicopters the Taliban had captured a year earlier in Kandahar, thereby creating the Taliban's first airpower. Meanwhile Dostum's own planes began a bombing campaign of Herat.

To meet Ismael Khan's threat, the Taliban quickly mobilized some 25,000 men, many of them fresh volunteers from Pakistan. Their more experienced fighters were deployed in mobile columns in Datsun pick-ups, which harassed Ismael's supply lines. At the end of August at Girishk the Taliban decisively ambushed the intruders and Ismael Khan sounded a general retreat. Within a few days the Taliban pushed back his forces to Shindand, which he inexplicably abandoned on 3 September 1995 without putting up a fight. Then two days later, with his troops in a blind panic as the Taliban mobile columns swept through and around them,

Ismael Khan abandoned Herat fleeing with his commanders and several hundred men to Iran. The next day a pro-government mob in Kabul, incensed at the loss of Herat, attacked and sacked the Pakistan Embassy, wounding the Pakistani Ambassador as government soldiers looked on. Relations between Kabul and Islamabad sunk to an all-time low as President Rabbani openly accused Pakistan of trying to oust him from power through the Taliban.

The Taliban now controlled the entire west of the country, the sensitive border region with Iran and for the first time ruled an area which was not predominantly Pashtun. The Taliban treated Herat as an occupied city, arresting hundreds of Heratis, closing down all schools and forcibly implementing their social bans and Sharia law, even more fiercely than in Kandahar. The city was garrisoned not by local defectors, but hardcore Pashtun Taliban from Kandahar and the administration was handed over to Durrani Pashtuns, many of whom could not even speak Persian and therefore were incapable of communicating with the local population. Over the next few years not a single local Herati was to be inducted into the administration. For the sophisticated population, who were now ruled by what they considered gross, uneducated Pashtuns who had no idea of the past magnificence or history of the city, the only thing left was to go to Jami's tomb and read his sad epitaph.

> When your face is hidden from me, like the moon hidden on a dark night, I shed stars of tears and yet my night remains dark in spite of all those shining stars.[9]

The fall of Herat was also the beginning of the end for the Rabbani government. Bolstered by their victories, the Taliban launched another attack on Kabul during October and November, hoping to gain ground before the winter snows suspended further fighting. Masud counterattacked in late November and pushed them back, resulting in hundreds of dead. But the Taliban were to persist and were now to try other means of conquering the city, weakening Masud's front lines by bribes rather than tank fire.

~3~

KABUL 1996:
COMMANDER OF THE
FAITHFUL

Travelling by jeep, truck and horseback hundreds of Afghan mullahs began to descend on Kandahar in the cool spring weather of 1996. By 20 March more than 1,200 Pashtun religious leaders from south, west and central Afghanistan had arrived in the city. They were housed and fed in government offices, the old fort and the covered bazaar, which were turned into enormous dormitories by the simple act of throwing hundreds of carpets on the floor so that the mullahs could sleep.

It was the biggest gathering of mullahs and *ulema* that had ever taken place in modern Afghan history. Significantly absent were local military commanders, traditional tribal and clan leaders, political figures from the war against the Soviets and non-Pashtun representatives from northern Afghanistan. Only religious leaders had been summoned by Mullah Omar to debate a future plan of action, but more importantly to legitimize the Taliban leader as the all powerful leader in the country.

The ten-month Taliban siege of Kabul had failed to crack the city and as Taliban casualties mounted, there was growing unrest in their ranks. During the long winter months, moderates in the movement openly talked of the need for negotiations with the Kabul regime. Hardliners wanted to continue the conquest of the entire country. There were also broad divisions within the Pashtuns. The Kandaharis grouped around Omar wanted the war to continue, while those representing Pashtun areas recently conquered by the Taliban wanted peace and an end to the conflict.

Everyone outside the country also realised that the Taliban were at a crossroads. 'The Taliban cannot take Kabul nor can Masud take Kandahar. How will the Taliban evolve if they fail to take Kabul? Even if they do manage to take Kabul how will the rest of Afghanistan accept their type of Islamic system?' the UN mediator Mehmoud Mestiri told me.[1] For more than two weeks the Shura continued with meetings lasting all day and all night. Separate Shuras discussed issues such as the political and military future, how best to impose Sharia law and the future of girls' education in Taliban-held areas. The discussions were all held in extreme secrecy and foreigners were banned from Kandahar for the duration. However Pakistani officials were there to monitor the Shura, including the Pakistani Ambassador to Kabul Qazi Humayun and several ISI officers such as Colonel Imam, Pakistan's Consul General in Herat.

To patch over their differences, the core group of Kandaharis around Mullah Omar nominated him to become the 'Amir-ul Momineen' or 'Commander of the Faithful', an Islamic title that made him the undisputed leader of the jihad and the Emir of Afghanistan. (The Taliban were later to rename the country as the Emirate of Afghanistan). On 4 April 1996, Omar appeared on the roof of a building in the centre of the city, wrapped in the Cloak of the Prophet Mohammed, which had been taken out of its shrine for the first time in 60 years. As Omar wrapped and unwrapped the Cloak around his body and allowed it to flap in the wind, he was rapturously applauded by the assembled throng of mullahs in the courtyard below, as they shouted 'Amir-ul Momineen.'

This oath of allegiance or 'baiat' was a procedure similar to when Caliph Omar was confirmed as leader of the Muslim community in Arabia after the death of the Prophet Mohammed. It was a political masterstroke, for by cloaking himself with the Prophet's mantle, Mullah Omar had assumed the right to lead not just all Afghans, but all Muslims. The meeting ended with a declaration of jihad against the Rabbani regime. The Taliban vowed not to open talks with any of their adversaries and declared that a final decision on allowing women to be educated could only be tackled 'when there was a legitimate government in Afghanistan'. The hard-liners and Mullah Omar had won.[2]

But for many Afghans and Muslims elsewhere it was a serious affront to propriety that a poor village mullah with no scholarly learning, no tribal pedigree or connections to the Prophet's family should presume so much. No Afghan had adopted the title since 1834, when King Dost Mohammed Khan assumed the title before he declared jihad against the Sikh kingdom in Peshawar. But Dost Mohammed was fighting foreigners, while Omar had declared jihad against his own people. Moreover, there was no sanction for such a title in Islam, unless all of the country's *ulema* had bestowed it upon a leader. The Taliban insisted that their meeting constituted the Koranic requirement of 'ahl al-hal o aqd', literally 'the people who can loose and bind' or those empowered to take legitimate decisions on behalf of the Islamic community.

For Omar the title gave him badly needed legitimacy and a new mystique amongst the Pashtuns that no other Mujaheddin leader had acquired during the war. It would allow him to distance himself still further from day-to-day politics, give him an additional excuse not to meet foreign diplomats and allow him to be more inflexible in either broadening the base of the Taliban leadership or in talking to the opposition. Omar could now always retreat behind his title and decline to meet opposition leaders on an equal footing.

But the *ulema* meeting had deliberately not come to any decisions on the much more sensitive questions on how the Taliban planned to rule Afghanistan and what if anything they planned for the country's economic and social development. Such questions were to remain permanently unanswered, even after they captured Kabul. 'We have not gone public yet on our structure because we are not strong enough to decide who will be the Prime Minister or the President,' said Mullah Wakil, the aide to Omar. 'The Sharia does not allow politics or political parties. That is why we give no salaries to officials or soldiers, just food, clothes, shoes and weapons. We want to live a life like the Prophet lived 1,400 years ago and jihad is our right. We want to recreate the time of the Prophet and we are only carrying out what the Afghan people have wanted for the past 14 years,' he added.[3] Another Taliban leader put it even more succinctly. 'We can love our enemies but only after we have defeated them.'

Only a day earlier Taliban emissaries had told Mestiri in Islamabad that they were ready to talk to President Rabbani.[4] 'If the Taliban are ready to talk and President Rabbani is ready to talk, then this is really something,' said Mestiri hopefully. The final result of the *ulema* meeting was a blow that neither Mestiri nor the UN peace effort was to recover from and in May Mestiri resigned from his job.

The *ulema* meeting had also been prompted by the regime's growing political successes at wooing other opposition leaders and President Rabbani's increasing international standing. Kabul's military successes at seeing off Hikmetyar, the Hazaras and the Taliban attack had finally persuaded the regime that this was an opportune moment to try and gain greater political acceptability, by broadening the base of their support. President Rabbani began talks with other warlords, holding out the carrot that he was prepared to set up a new government which could include them. In January and February 1996, Rabbani's emissary Dr Abdur Rehman met separately with Gulbuddin Hikmetyar at Sarobi, with General Rashid Dostum in Mazar-e-Sharif and the Hizb-e-Wahadat leadership in Bamiyan. In February all the opposition groups except for the Taliban agreed to set up a ten-man council to negotiate peace terms with Kabul, even as the Taliban continued to demand the surrender of the regime. A few weeks later the council of the Hizb-e-Islami gave Hikmetyar the power to negotiate a power-sharing agreement with Rabbani.

Pakistan was worried by Rabbani's successes and attempted to woo the same warlords to join the Taliban and form an anti-Kabul alliance. The ISI summoned Hikmetyar, Dostum, the Pashtun leaders of the Jalalabad Shura and some Hizb-e-Wahadat chiefs to Islamabad to persuade them to ally with the Taliban. These warlords met with President Farooq Leghari and army chief General Jehangir Karamat as negotiations continued for a week between 7 and 13 February. Pakistan proposed a political alliance and in private a joint attack on Kabul with the Taliban attacking from the south, Hikmetyar from the east and Dostum from the north.[5] To sweeten the Taliban, Babar offered to spend US$3 million to repair the road across southern Afghanistan from Chaman to Torgundi on the Turkmenistan border. But the Taliban refused to turn up to the meeting, spurning their Pakistani mentors yet again, despite personal appeals by Interior Minister Naseerullah Babar, the JUI chief Fazlur Rehman and the ISI. The Taliban declined to have anything to do with the other warlords whom they condemned as communist infidels.

Islamabad's failure to create a united front against Kabul, emboldened Rabbani further. In early March, along with a 60-man delegation, he set off on an extensive tour of Iran, Turkmenistan, Uzbekistan and Tajikistan to lobby for international support and increased military aid. Iran, Russia and India, who backed the Kabul regime, calculated that the conflict had now entered a crucial stage as another battle for Kabul could increase political instability and influence the spread of Islamic fundamentalism in Central Asia. Iran was incensed by the fall of Herat to a Pashtun force that was vehemently anti-Shia and was backed by its regional rivals Pakistan and Saudi Arabia. Russia considered the Kabul regime as more moderate and pliant than the Taliban, as it worried about the security of the Central Asian Republics. Moscow also wanted an end to the four-year-old civil war in Tajikistan between the neo-communist government and Islamic rebels, which was being fuelled from Afghanistan. India backed Kabul simply because of Pakistani support to the Taliban.

All these countries stepped up military aid to the regime forces. Russia sent technical help to upgrade Bagram airport facilities for the regime while Russian transport planes from Russia, Tajikistan and Ukraine delivered Russian arms, ammunition and fuel to Kabul. Iran developed an air bridge from Meshad in eastern Iran to Bagram, where it flew in arms supplies. Pakistani intelligence reported that on a single day, 13 Iranian flights landed at Bagram with supplies. The CIA suspected that Afghan Shia allies of the Rabbani regime had sold Iran five Stinger anti-aircraft missiles for US$1 million each. (The US provided the Mujaheddin with some 900 Stingers in 1986–87 and after 1992 the CIA had launched a clandestine but unsuccessful buy-back operation to try and retrieve those Stingers not utilised.)[6] Iran had also set up five training camps near Meshad for some 5,000 fighters led by the former Herat Governor Ismael Khan. Iran's aid to the regime was significant because Tehran had to swallow its anger with Masud over the slaughter of the Shia Hazaras in Kabul the previous year. India meanwhile helped refurbish Ariana – the Afghan national airline now based in New Delhi – to provide the regime with a reliable arms carrier. India also provided aircraft parts, new ground radars and money.

In turn, Pakistan and Saudi Arabia stepped up arms supplies to the Taliban. Pakistan provided a new telephone and wireless network for the Taliban, refurbished Kandahar airport and helped out with spare parts and armaments for the Taliban's airforce, while continuing to provide food, fuel and ammunition, including rockets. The Saudis provided fuel, money and hundreds of new pick-ups to the Taliban. Much of this aid was flown into Kandahar airport from the Gulf port city of Dubai.

The extent of outside interference worried the Americans: after a lapse of four years they were once again beginning to take an interest in trying to resolve the Afghan conflict. In early March, Congressman Hank Brown, a member of the Senate Subcommittee on Foreign Relations for South Asia, became the first American elected representative in six years to visit Kabul and other power centres. He hoped to call a meeting of all the Afghan factions in Washington.[7]

The US Assistant Secretary of State for South Asia Robin Raphel arrived in Islamabad to review US policy towards Afghanistan. Starting on 19 April 1996, Raphel visited the three power centres of Kabul, Kandahar and Mazar-e-Sharif and later three Central Asian capitals. 'We do not see ourselves inserting in the middle of Afghan affairs, but we consider ourselves as a friend of Afghanistan which is why I am here to urge the Afghans themselves to get together and talk. We are also concerned that economic opportunities here will be missed, if political stability cannot be restored,' said Raphel in Kabul.[8] Raphel was referring to a proposed gas pipeline to be built by the American oil giant Unocal to carry gas from Turkmenistan across Afghanistan to Pakistan. The US waited to make the pipeline acceptable to all Afghan factions and urged Pakistan to make up with the Rabbani regime and bring the Taliban and the Rabbani regime to the peace table.

The US moved on other fronts. During a UN Security Council debate on Afghanistan on 10 April 1996, the first to be held in six years, it proposed an international arms embargo on Afghanistan. Raphel wanted to use this as a lever to persuade all the involved regional countries to agree to non-interference in Afghanistan, while at the same time lending greater weight to UN efforts to convene a conference of all the Afghan factions.[9]

The Clinton administration was clearly sympathetic to the Taliban, as they were in line with Washington's anti-Iran policy and were important for the success of any southern pipeline from Central Asia that would avoid Iran. The US Congress had authorised a covert US$20 million budget for the CIA to destabilize Iran, and Tehran had accused Washington of funnelling some of these funds to the Taliban – a charge that was always denied by Washington. Bhutto sent several emissaries to Washington to urge the US to intervene more publicly on the side of Pakistan and the Taliban, but despite a common antipathy to Iran, Washington resisted, refusing to take sides in the civil war. Raphel vehemently denied that the US was aiding the Taliban. 'We do not favour one faction over another nor do we give any group or individual support,' she told me.

Moreover the US remained sceptical that the Taliban would conquer Kabul in the near future. Raphel described the Taliban as highly fractionalized, inexperienced, lacking strong leadership and inept at administration while their obstinacy had alienated other factions. 'These weaknesses combined with Masud's growing strength, appear to be shifting the balance against the Taliban somewhat, and will prevent them from achieving their stated goal of taking Kabul. While the Taliban appears to have reached the limit of its expansion, its position in the Pashtun south is solid,' she said.[10]

Washington also courted the other warlords. Several visited Washington, starting with General Dostum who met US officials in Washington on 11 April 1996. Afghan leaders or their representatives from all factions participated in an unprecedented Congressional hearing in Washington held by Senator Hank Brown between 25 and 27 June. However in an American election year and with little enthusiasm for renewed involvement in the quagmire of Afghanistan, Washington's aims could only be limited, even though the arms and drugs trade proliferating inside Afghanistan worried Washington.

US reluctance to support the Taliban was also influenced by Pakistan's failure in creating an anti-Rabbani alliance. This proved even more embarrassing for Islamabad when, in May, 1,000 of Hikmetyar's troops arrived in Kabul to support the government and defend the front line against the Taliban. On 26 June 1996 Hikmetyar himself entered Kabul for the first time in 15 years, to take up the post of Prime Minister offered by the regime, while his party accepted nine other cabinet posts in the government. In retaliation, on the same day, the Taliban launched a massive rocket attack on Kabul in which 61 people were killed and over 100 injured.

Rabbani followed up his political breakthrough with Hikmetyar with a visit to Jalalabad where he attempted to persuade the Jalalabad Shura to join his government. He said he was willing to step down in favour of any Afghan leader and proposed an all-party conference in Jalalabad to elect a new head of state. By August Dostum had also agreed to a truce and he reopened the Salang Highway which connected Kabul with the north of the country for the first time in over a year. Rabbani's agreements had finally got his 'intra-Afghan dialogue' off the ground. 'This alliance can be consolidated by bringing in more opposition figures to create a peace axis and I call on others to join the process so that a formula for an interim government can be found,' Rabbani told me in Kabul.[11] It was a significant achievement, which infuriated the Taliban who realized that they would have to move quickly against Rabbani before he consolidated these alliances.

Camped outside the capital, the Taliban had been rocketing Kabul mercilessly throughout the year. In April 1996 alone, the Taliban fired 866 rockets, killing 180 civilians, injuring 550 and destroying large tracts of the city – a repetition of Hikmetyar's attacks in 1993–95. In July 1996 Taliban rockets fell close to the newly appointed UN mediator for Afghanistan, the German diplomat Norbert Holl who was visiting Kabul. Holl was furious. 'This is no way to treat a peace emissary, by shooting at him. If you receive a guest in your house you don't start spitting at him. It demonstrates a sort of contempt for my mission,' he told the Taliban.[12]

The Taliban's rocket attacks were punctuated by frequent ground assaults against Masud's front lines south and west of the city. At the end of May, I stood on a rain-swept hill with Masud's troops outside Kabul and watched through binoculars as dozens of Taliban in pick-ups tried to punch through Masud's lines along a road in the valley below under the cover of a Taliban artillery barrage. In return Masud's Russian-made D-30 howitzers pounded the hidden Taliban artillery. The thud of shells shook the mountains, deafening the ears and making me sway at the knees. The gunners were stone-deaf due to the constant shelling and the lack of ear protectors.

Behind Masud's lines, lorry-loads of fresh troops and ammunition ground their way up the hill through the mud to replenish supplies. 'The Taliban have enormous supplies of ammunition and they shoot off thousands of shells but their gunners are very inaccurate. However they are making better use of their tanks and pick-ups than a year ago,' said a general from Masud's army. 'Their tactics are still poor, relying more on frontal assaults and there seems to be no effective chain of command,' he added. The Taliban were unable to concentrate enough firepower and manpower on one front to achieve a breakthrough into the city and Masud was constantly breaking up their formations. Although he could hold the line around Kabul, his forces, estimated at just 25,000 men, could not extend it and carry out offensives to push the Taliban further south.

The Taliban's stubbornness in refusing to cut deals with other warlords frustrated the Pakistanis, but finally it appeared to pay off when the Taliban persuaded Pakistan and Saudi Arabia to back another major bid to capture Kabul before the winter. The Saudi Intelligence chief Prince Turki al Faisal visited Islamabad and Kandahar in July 1996 to discuss with the ISI a new plan to take Kabul, and both countries stepped up supplies to the Taliban. Within two months of Turki's visit, the Taliban were on the move – not against Kabul but the eastern city of Jalalabad. Pakistan and Saudi Arabia helped engineer the surrender and eventual flight of the head of the Jalalabad Shura, Haji Abdul Qadeer. He was given a large bribe, reported by some Afghans to be US$10 million in cash, as well as guarantees that his assets and bank accounts in Pakistan would not be frozen.[13]

The Taliban launched their surprise offensive on Jalalabad on 25 August 1996. As the main Taliban force moved up on the city from the south, Pakistan allowed hundreds of armed Taliban supporters from Afghan refugee camps in Pakistan to cross the border and move on Jalalabad from the east. There was panic in Jalalabad and the Shura fell apart. Haji Qadeer fled to Pakistan on 10 September and his replacement Acting Governor Mehmoud was killed along with six bodyguards a day later, while also trying to escape to Pakistan. That same evening a Taliban mobile column of pick-ups led by Mullah Borjan drove into Jalalabad after a brief firefight in which some 70 people were killed.

Within the next few days mobile Taliban columns captured the three eastern provinces of Nangarhar, Laghman and Kunar and on the night of 24 September 1996 they moved on Sarobi, 45 miles from Kabul and the gateway to the capital. Their lightning attack, which came from several directions, took the government's troops by total surprise and they fled back to Kabul. The capital was now wide open from the east for the first time. The Taliban did not pause to regroup, but instead pursued Sarobi's defenders back to Kabul. Other Taliban columns moved on Kabul from the south, while another column drove north from Sarobi to capture Bagram airport cutting off Masud's only air link.

The speed of their offensive stunned the government. Taliban columns swept into Kabul on the evening of 26 September 1996, just a few hours after Masud had ordered a general withdrawal to evacuate the city. Small units stayed behind to delay the Taliban advance and blow up ammunition dumps, while Masud escaped northwards with the bulk of his armour and artillery. Masud took the decision to abandon the city without a fight knowing he could not defend it from attacks coming from all four points of the compass. Nor did he want to lose the support of Kabul's population by fighting for the city and causing more bloodshed. The Taliban victory was complete. 'No Afghan force, either government or opposition, had ever carried out such a swift and complex series of operations over such a wide operation area. This was mobile warfare at its most effective.'[14]

The Taliban's first and bloodiest act was to hang former President Najibullah, then aged 50, who had ruled Afghanistan from 1986 to 1992. Najibullah had been staying in a UN diplomatic compound in central Kabul since 1992, when a UN peace plan to set up an interim government fell apart. Just before the Mujaheddin were to capture Kabul, Najibullah was due to be taken out of Kabul by the UN mediator Benon Sevan, but they were stopped at the last moment. All the warring Afghan factions had respected the diplomatic immunity of the UN compound. Najibullah's wife Fatana and three daughters had lived in exile in New Delhi since 1992.

Blunders by the UN were partly responsible for his death. On the day Sarobi fell, Najibullah had sent a message to the UN headquarters in Islamabad asking Norbet Holl to arrange the evacuation of himself and his three companions – his brother, Shahpur Ahmadzai, his personal secretary and bodyguard. But there were no UN officials in Kabul to take responsibility for Najibullah. Only Masud offered him a lift out of the city. On the afternoon of 26 September 1996, Masud sent one of his senior Generals to ask Najibullah to leave with the retreating government troops, promising him safe passage to the north, but Najibullah refused. A proud and stubborn man, he probably feared that if he fled with the Tajiks, he would be for ever damned in the eyes of his fellow Pashtuns.[15]

There were only three frightened Afghan guards employed by the UN on duty inside the compound and they fled as they heard the guns of the Taliban on the outskirts of the city. Najibullah sent a last wireless message to the UN in Islamabad in the early evening, again asking for help. But by then it was too late. A special Taliban unit of five men designated for the task and believed to be led by Mullah Abdul Razaq, the Governor of Herat and now commander of the forces designated to capture Kabul, came for Najibullah at about 1.00 a.m., even before the Taliban had entered central Kabul. Razaq later admitted that he had ordered Najibullah's murder.[16]

The Taliban walked up to Najibullah's room, beat him and his brother senseless and then bundled them into a pick-up and drove them to the darkened Presidential Palace. There they castrated Najibullah, dragged his body behind a jeep for several rounds of the Palace and then shot him dead. His brother was similarly tortured and then throttled to death. The Taliban hanged the two dead men from a concrete traffic control post just outside the Palace, only a few blocks from the UN compound.

At dawn curious Kabulis came to view the two bloated, beaten bodies as they hung from steel wire nooses around their necks. Unlit cigarettes were stuck between their fingers and Afghani notes stuffed into their pockets – to convey the Taliban message of debauchery and corruption. Najibullah's two other companions had escaped from the compound, but they were later caught trying to flee the city and were also tortured and hanged.

Najibullah's execution was the first symbolic, brutal act by the Taliban in Kabul. It was a premeditated, targeted killing designed to terrorize the population. Mullah Rabbani, the newly appointed head of the Kabul Shura proclaimed that Najibullah was a communist and a murderer and that he had been sentenced to death by the Taliban. That was true, but the mutilation of Najibullah's body was beyond the pale of any Islamic injunction, while the lack of a fair trial and the public display of the bodies revolted many Kabulis. People were further repulsed when the Taliban banned an Islamic funeral for Najibullah, even though funeral prayers were said for him the next day in Quetta and Peshawar where he was remembered by Pakistan's Pashtun nationalists. Eventually the bodies were taken down and handed over to the ICRC, who drove them to Gardez, Najibullah's birthplace in Paktia province where he was buried by his Ahmadzai tribesmen.

There was widespread international condemnation of the murder, particularly from the Muslim world. The Taliban had humiliated the UN and the international community and embarrassed their allies, Pakistan and Saudi Arabia. The UN finally issued a statement. 'The killing of the former President without any legitimate judicial procedure not only constitutes a grave violation of the immunity UN premises enjoy, but also further jeopardizes all the efforts which are being made to secure a peaceful settlement of the Afghan conflict.' The Taliban were not deterred and they issued death sentences on Dostum, Rabbani and Masud.

Within 24 hours of taking Kabul, the Taliban imposed the strictest Islamic system in place anywhere in the world. All women were banned from work, even though one quarter of Kabul's civil service, the entire elementary educational system and much of the health system were run by women. Girls' schools and colleges were closed down affecting more than 70,000 female students and a strict dress code of head-to-toe veils for women was imposed. There were fears that 25,000 families which were headed by war widows and depended on working and UN handouts would starve. Every day brought fresh pronouncements. 'Thieves will have their hands and feet amputated, adulterers will be stoned to death and those taking liquor will be lashed,' said an announcement on Radio Kabul on 28 September 1996.

TV, videos, satellite dishes, music and all games including chess, football and kite-flying were banned. Radio Kabul was renamed Radio Shariat and all music was taken off the air. Taliban soldiers stood on main streets arresting men without beards. Unlike the capture of Herat and other cities, a large international press and TV corps were in Kabul and for the first time they reported extensively on the Taliban's restrictions. The Taliban set up a six-man Shura to rule Kabul, which was dominated by Durrani Pashtuns and did not include a single Kabuli. Headed by Mullah Mohammed Rabbani, the Shura included Mullah Mohammed Ghaus as Foreign Minister, Mullah Amir Khan Muttaqi as Information Minister, Mullah Syed Ghayasuddin Agha, Mullah Fazil Mohammed and Mullah Abdul Razaq.

None of the Shura members had ever lived in a large city, most had never even visited Kabul, but they were now running a vibrant, semi-modern, multi-ethnic city of 1.2 million people in which Pashtuns were only a small minority. As the newly formed Taliban religious police went about their business of enforcing 'Sharia', Kabul was treated as an occupied city. There was little understanding that governing a large city was not the same as ruling a village. It appeared that all that lay in the way of a total victory for the Taliban was Ahmad Shah Masud.

Masud was one of the most brilliant military commanders and charismatic personalities to emerge out of the jihad. Dubbed the 'Lion of Panjshir' after his birthplace in his Tajik homeland of the Panjshir valley north of Kabul, he eluded and then fought to a standstill seven huge Soviet offensives against the Panjshir in the 1980s. Soviet generals termed him unbeatable and a master of guerrilla warfare. His army of some 20,000 men adored him and his reputation was at its peak when he took over Kabul in 1992, foiling Hikmetyar's attempt to do the same, as the communist regime crumbled. But four years in power in Kabul had turned Masud's army into arrogant masters who harassed civilians, stole from shops and confiscated people's homes which is why Kabulis first welcomed the Taliban when they entered Kabul.

Born in 1953 into a military family, Masud studied at the French-run Lycée Istiqlal in Kabul. He became one of the young Islamic opponents of the regime of President Daud and fled to Pakistan in 1975, after he led a failed uprising in the Panjshir. In exile in Peshawar, Masud fell out with his colleague Gulbuddin Hikmetyar and their rivalry for the next 20 years was a determining reason why the Mujheddin never united to form a coalition government. His bitterness against Pakistan for first supporting Hikmetyar and then the Taliban became an obsession. During the jihad Masud argued that the strategic direction of the war should be left to the Afghans to decide rather than the ISI. But Pakistan was supplying all the US-provided weapons, which created an enmity which still lasts today. Islamabad was taken by surprise when in 1992 Kabul fell not from the south to the Pashtuns, but from the north to the Tajiks and Uzbeks.

Peacemaking always eluded Masud. He was a poor politician, incapable of convincing other Pashtun warlords who hated Hikmetyar that a Tajik–Pashtun alliance was the only feasible way to bring peace. Masud may have been a masterful military strategist but he was a failure at building political alliances between different ethnic groups and parties. His major problem was that he was a Tajik. Except for one abortive uprising in 1929, the Tajiks had never ruled in Kabul and were mistrusted by the Pashtuns.

In Kabul he remained aloof and refused to acccept government posts, declining the post of Defence Minister in President Rabbani's government even though he commanded the army. 'There is an old Persian saying. When everyone is looking for a chair to sit on, it is better to sit on the floor,' he told me in May 1996, just a few weeks before the Taliban were to drive him out of Kabul. 'Pakistan is trying to subjugate Afghanistan and turn it into a colony by installing a puppet government. It won't work because the Afghan people have always been independent and free,' he added.

Working 18 hours a day with two military secretaries, who took it in shifts to keep up with him, he would sleep four hours a night and because of fears of assasination never spent two nights in the same location. He slept, ate and fought with his men and invariably in the midst of a major battle he could be found on the frontline. In the next few months he was to face his greatest challenge as the Taliban swept him out of Kabul and appeared to be on the verge of conquering the entire country. He survived, but by 1999, aged 46 years old, he had been fighting virtually non-stop for 25 years.

Masud's forces now retreated up the Salang highway to his base area in the Panjshir. As the Taliban pursued them, Masud's men blew up the mountains, creating landslides to block the entrance to the valley. The Taliban launched an abortive attack on the Panjshir but failed to make headway. They pushed up the Salang highway capturing towns along the way until they were blocked at the Salang tunnel by Dostum's forces, who had advanced south from Mazar-e-Sharif. It was still unclear whose side Dostum would take and his forces refrained from engaging the Taliban.

Mullah Rabbani met with Dostum on 8 October 1996 in a bid to try and neutralize the Uzbeks while the Taliban went after Masud, but the talks broke down. The Taliban refused to allow Dostum autonomy and power in the north. Pakistan also launched a diplomatic shuttle in a bid to break Dostum away from Masud. However, Dostum realised that, despite his differences with Masud, the Taliban posed the real threat to all non-Pashtuns. On 10 October 1996, deposed President Rabbani, Masud, Dostum and the Hazara leader Karim Khalili met in Khin Jan on the highway and formed a 'Supreme Council for the Defence of the Motherland' to counter the Taliban. It was the beginning of a new anti-Taliban alliance that would perpetuate the civil war.

In their rapid advance northwards, the Taliban had spread themselves too thin and Masud took advantage of this, launching a major counter-attack along the highway on 12 October 1996. He captured several towns, killing and capturing hundreds of Taliban soldiers as they fled back to Kabul in panic. On 18 October 1996, Masud's forces recaptured the Bagram airbase and began to shell Kabul airport, even as Dostum's airforce bombed Taliban targets in Kabul. The heavy fighting resulted in thousands of civilian casualties and forced 50,000 people to flee their homes in villages along the Salang highway. As these destitute refugees arrived in Kabul, tens of thousands of Kabulis – mostly Tajiks and Hazaras – were trying to escape in the other direction – eastwards to the Pakistan border to escape Taliban reprisals and mass arrests which had begun in the city.

Faced with rising casualties the Taliban began to suffer from manpower shortages and they started conscripting young men from Kabul into their army, entering mosques and seizing worshippers. Thousands more volunteers arrived from Pakistan where some Pakistani *ulema* closed down their *madrassas* so that students would have no choice but to enlist en masse with the Taliban. Thousands of Pakistani students and Afghans from the refugee camps began to arrive daily in Kandahar and Kabul on buses hired by Pakistan's Islamic parties. Pakistan waived all passport and visa requirements for them.

Bolstered by this fresh support, the Taliban launched an attack in western Afghanistan, moving northwards from Herat into Baghdis province. By the end of October 1996 Ismael Khan and 2,000 of his fighters, who had been in exile in Iran, were flown into Maimana on Dostum's aircraft to defend the front line against the Taliban in Baghdis. Iran had rearmed and re-equipped Ismael Khan's forces in a provocative and deliberate attempt to bolster the new anti-Taliban alliance. As heavy fighting took place in Baghdis during November and December, with considerable use of air power by both sides, another 50,000 displaced people fled to Herat. This added to what was now a catastrophic refugee crisis for UN aid agencies as winter, heavy snows and fighting prevented the delivery of humanitarian aid.

Despite heavy snowfall, the Taliban pushed Masud back from the outskirts of Kabul. By the end of January 1997, they had recaptured nearly all the territory they had lost along the Salang highway, retaking the Bagram airbase and Charikar. Masud retreated into the Panjshir as the Taliban pushed up the highway to confront Dostum.

The fall of Kabul and the intense fighting that followed created serious apprehensions in the entire region. Iran, Russia and four Central Asian Republics warned the Taliban not to move north and publicly declared they would help rearm the anti-Taliban alliance. Meanwhile Pakistan and Saudi Arabia sent diplomatic missions to Kabul to see what help they could offer the Taliban. Appeals from the UN and other international bodies for a cease-fire and mediation failed to receive any hearing from the belligerents. The region was now deeply polarized with Pakistan and Saudi Arabia allied to the Taliban and the other regional states backing the opposition. The Taliban were still not to receive the international recognition they so desperately wanted. 'We don't have a friend in the world. We have conquered three quarters of the country, we have captured the capital and we haven't received even a single message of congratulations,' said a wistful Mullah Mohammed Hassan.[17]

Yet it appeared that Mullah Omar's refusal to compromise with the opposition or the UN, along with his unshakeable faith and his determination to achieve a military victory, had finally paid off. Kabul, the capital of Afghan Pashtun kings since 1772 which had been lost for the past four years to Tajik rulers, was back in the hands of the Pashtuns. The student movement, which so many had predicted would never be able to take the capital had done just that. Despite their enormous losses, the Taliban's prestige had never been higher. The cost of their victory however was the deepening ethnic and sectarian divide that was clearly dividing Afghanistan and polarizing the region.

'War is a tricky game,' said Omar, who remained in Kandahar and declined to even visit Kabul. 'The Taliban took five months to capture one province but then six provinces fell to us in only ten days. Now we are in control of 22 provinces including Kabul. Inshallah [God willing] the whole of Afghanistan will fall into our hands. We feel a military solution has better prospects now after numerous failed attempts to reach a peaceful, negotiated settlement,' he added.[18] Northern Afghanistan now appeared ready for the taking.

~4~

MAZAR-E-SHARIF 1997: MASSACRE IN THE NORTH

Everyone expected a Taliban spring offensive on Mazar-e-Sharif, the last stronghold in northern Afghanistan of the anti-Taliban alliance which was under the control of General Rashid Dostum and his Uzbeks. During the long winter months there was growing panic in Mazar as food and fuel supplies ran out due to the Taliban blockade and the Afghani rate of exchange doubled to US$1 and then tripled as wealthy Mazar citizens fled to Central Asia.

Although most of Afghanistan's population is concentrated in the south and was now under Taliban control, 60 per cent of Afghanistan's agricultural resources and 80 per cent of its former industry, mineral and gas wealth are in the north. During the last century, Kabul's control of the north had become the key to state building and economic development. For the Taliban, determined to conquer the country and keep it united, the autonomy enjoyed by the northern warlords had to be crushed. Yet when the Taliban offensive finally came in May, nobody expected the bloody drama of betrayals, counter-betrayals and inter-ethnic bloodshed which was astounding even by Afghan standards and would send the entire Central Asian region into a tailspin.

Ensconced during the winter in the Qila-e-Jhangi, the Fort of War, on the outskirts of Mazar, Dostum suddenly found himself promoted by neighbouring states and many Afghans as a saviour and the last hope against the Taliban. Mazar, situated in the Central Asian steppe which begins north of the Hindu Kush, is culturally and ethnically as far away from Kandahar as Kandahar is from Karachi. The nineteenth-century fort is a surreal pastiche of a European baronial castle with a moat and defence ditches and a fantasy from the Arabian Nights with its massive, mud-baked ramparts and a blue-domed citadel, which Dostum used as his office. Guarded by tanks and artillery and Dostum's well-turned-out troops, who still wore the uniforms of the communist era, the impressive fort was not the only factor he used to win over visitors such as foreign diplomats who now lined up to see him.

He wielded power ruthlessly. The first time I arrived at the fort to meet Dostum there were bloodstains and pieces of flesh in the muddy courtyard. I innocently asked the guards if a goat had been slaughtered. They told me that an hour earlier Dostum had punished a soldier for stealing. The man had been tied to the tracks of a Russian-made tank, which then drove around the courtyard crushing his body into mincemeat, as the garrison and Dostum watched. The Uzbeks, the roughest and toughest of all the Central Asian nationalities, are noted for their love of marauding and pillaging – a hangover from their origins as part of Genghis Khan's hordes and Dostum was an apt leader. Over six feet tall with bulging biceps, Dostum is a bear of a man with a gruff laugh, which, some Uzbeks swear, has on occasion frightened people to death.

Born into a poor peasant family in 1955 in a village near Shiberghan, he was a farm-hand and a plumber until he joined the Afghan army in 1978. He rose through the ranks to become the commander of the armoured corps that defended the Soviet supply line into Afghanistan from Hairatan port on the Amu Darya river. After the Soviet departure in 1989, Dostum led a ferocious Uzbek militia force called Jowzjan, named after their province of origin, which was used by President Najibullah as the regime's storm-troopers against the Mujaheddin. The Jowzjanis fought all over Afghanistan, often being flown in as a last resort to prevent a government garrison being overrun.

In 1992 Dostum was the first to rebel against his mentor Najibullah, thereby establishing his reputation for treachery and political opportunism. The hard-drinking Dostum then became a 'good Muslim'. Since then he had, at one time or another allied himself with everyone – Masud, Hikmetyar, the Taliban, Masud again – and betrayed everyone with undisguised aplomb. He had also been on every country's payroll receiving funds from Russia, Uzbekistan, Iran, Pakistan and lately Turkey. In 1995 he managed to be on the payroll of both Iran and Pakistan, then at daggers drawn over the Taliban.[1] Although he controlled only six provinces in the north, Dostum had made himself indispensable to neighbouring states. Now Iran, Uzbekistan and Russia who had propped up Dostum as a secular buffer against Pashtun fundamentalism, saw him as the only leader capable of saving the north from the Taliban.[2] If there was one consistent trait, it was his deep opposition to the extremist fundamentalism of the Pashtun factions, even before the advent of the Taliban.

Mazar, once a bustling stop on the ancient Silk Route, had regained its pre-eminence as a key staging post in the now massive smuggling trade between Pakistan, Central Asia and Iran. Dostum had inaugurated his own 'Balkh Airlines' which bought in smuggled goods from Dubai, while the truck traffic to the border with Central Asia, just 70 miles from Mazar, provided him with a steady income in transit taxes and duties. Mazar's bazaars were stocked high with Russian vodka and French perfumes for the hard-drinking, womanizing Uzbek troops. But unlike the other war-lords, Dostum ran an efficient administration with a functioning health and educational system. Some 1,800 girls, the majority dressed in skirts and high heels, attended Balkh University in Mazar, the only operational university in the country.

As a consequence he guaranteed security to tens of thousands of refugees from Kabul, who had fled the capital in several waves since 1992, seeking refuge in Mazar which they saw as the last bastion of peace. Famous Afghan singers and dancers who could no longer perform in Kabul moved to Mazar. It was also a city of pilgrimage. Thousands came every day to pray at the blue-tiled Tomb of Ali, the cousin and son-in-law of the Prophet Mohammed and the fourth Caliph of Islam, whom Shia in particular revere. Ali is believed to be buried in what has become Afghanistan's most magnificent mosque and holiest site. Near Mazar lie the ruins of Balkh, called 'The Mother of all Cities' by invading Arabs in the seventh century. Here, Zoroaster preached nearly 3,000 years ago, Alexander the Great set up camp and the Persian poet Rumi was born. Balkh flourished as a centre of continuous civilization and Zoroastrianism, Buddhism and Islam before it was destroyed by Genghis Khan in 1220 and the focus of culture and trade shifted to Mazar.

Dostum was revered for the simple fact that his city had not been touched in the past 18 years of war. Mazar's citizens had never undergone the devastating shelling and street battles that had destroyed other cities. All that was about to change. Uzbek clan history is a long litany of blood feuds, revenge killings, power struggles, loot and plunder and disputes over women. The favourite Uzbek sport of *buzkushi*, a kind of polo with whip-wielding horsemen trying to grab the carcass of a headless goat, is invariably used to describe Uzbek politics. There are no teams and no rules for the sport, an apt analogy for Dostum's relations with his brother officers.

There was a bitter feud between Dostum and his second-in-command General Malik Pahlawan – Dostum was accused of murdering Malik's brother General Rasul Pahlawan, who had been killed in an ambush along with 15 bodyguards in June 1996. This feud, together with fears that Dostum had already ordered Malik's murder, and helped along by Taliban bribes and promises of power, prompted Malik's betrayal of Dostum on 19 May 1997 when Malik called on the Taliban to help him oust his leader.[3] Joining Malik were three other senior Uzbek generals, his half-brother

Gul Mohammed Pahlawan, Ghafar Pahlawan and Majid Rouzi. Moreover, Dostum had not paid his troops for five months and there was unrest in the ranks.

The Taliban moved north swiftly from Herat and Kabul. As the northern provinces fell one after another to this unlikely alliance of Pashtuns and Uzbeks from Malik's power base in Faryab province, Dostum fled with 135 officers and men, first to Uzbekistan and then to Turkey. On the way to Termez on the Uzbekistan–Afghanistan border, Dostum had to bribe his own soldiers with US dollars to let his convoy pass. For the Taliban it was a God-sent opportunity, but they had learnt little from their conquest of other cities, where they refused to share power, remained politically inflexible and would not relax Sharia law in the light of ethnic sensibilities. If Malik thought that the Taliban would give him the kind of autonomy in the north enjoyed by Dostum since 1992, he was badly mistaken. It was a deal made in hell that unravelled by the hour.

When 2,500 heavily armed Taliban troops rolled into Mazar in their pick-ups under Mullah Abdul Razaq (the man who had ordered Najibullah's murder), they declined to share power with Malik and offered him the insignificant post of Deputy Foreign Minister in the Kabul government. The Taliban, the majority of whom had never been in the north before, arrogantly started disarming the fierce Uzbek and Hazara troops, took over the mosques from where they declared the imposition of Sharia law, shut down schools and the university and drove women off the streets. It was a recipe for disaster in a city where a complex mix of ethnic and religious groups lived and which had remained the most open and liberal in the country.

Pakistani diplomats and ISI officers flew into the city in a bid to help the Taliban renegotiate the terms of the agreement, which was already falling apart. Islamabad then aggravated the situation further by prematurely recognizing the Taliban as the legitimate government of Afghanistan and persuading Saudi Arabia and the United Arab Emirates to follow suit.[4] The Uzbeks had been led to believe that this was a power-sharing agreement and now they realized it was a Taliban takeover. Malik was caught in the middle and his betrayal of Dostum was made worse when he also handed over Ismael Khan to them, who had been fighting against the Taliban in Faryab.[5]

On the afternoon of 28 May 1997, a squabble broke out as a group of Hazaras resisted being disarmed. Then all hell broke loose. First Mazar's Hazaras and then the rest of the population rose in revolt. Untrained in street fighting and not knowing the maze of city alleyways, the Taliban were easy victims as they drove their pick-ups into dead ends, trying to escape the withering fire from houses and roof tops. In 15 hours of intense fighting some 600 Taliban were massacred in the streets and over 1,000 were captured at the airport as they tried to flee. Ten top Taliban political and military leaders were either killed or captured. Those captured included Foreign Minister Mullah Mohammed Ghaus, Mullah Razaq and Central Bank Governor Mullah Ehsanullah. Malik's men promptly started looting the city, including the offices of UN agencies, and forced the UN to abandon the city. Dozens of Pakistani students were also killed.

Malik's troops swiftly retook four northern provinces (Takhar, Faryab, Jowzjan and Sari Pul), which the Taliban had captured only five days earlier and there was heavy fighting for control of three other northern provinces (Balkh, Samangan and Kunduz). With their escape routes closed, thousands of Taliban troops and hundreds of Pakistani students were captured and subsequently shot dead and buried in mass graves. In the south, Masud seized the opportunity to launch his own counter-attack, once again capturing Jabal ul Seraj at the southern entrance of the Salang tunnel. He blew up the entrance of the tunnel, trapping the Taliban who were still in the north and were trying to escape down the road to Kabul.

Masud recaptured more territory around Kabul and several towns in north-eastern Afghanistan that had fallen to the Taliban just a week earlier. Hundreds more Taliban were either killed or captured. Meanwhile the Hazaras, spurred on by the Mazar victory also counter-attacked, breaking the nine-month Taliban siege of their homeland, the Hazarajat. Taliban forces at the entrance to the Bamiyan valley were pushed back and Khalili's forces moved south towards Kabul, forcing thousands of Pashtun villagers to flee to the capital.

It was the worst ever Taliban defeat since they had emerged just 30 months earlier to conquer the country. In ten weeks of fighting between May and July the Taliban suffered over 3,000 casualties, killed or wounded, and some 3,600 men were taken prisoner.[6] More than 7,000 troops and civilians were wounded on both sides according to the ICRC. Even more embarrassing for Islamabad, over 250 Pakistanis had been killed and 550 captured during the May–July period. Morale amongst the Taliban plummeted as they had also lost some of their best and most experienced front-line units.

Mullah Omar gave an urgent call for students in Pakistan to come and help the Taliban. Once again Pakistani *madrassas* were closed down as 5,000 new recruits – both Pakistani and Afghan – arrived to enlist with the Taliban. The situation for the Taliban was deemed so serious that even the reclusive Mullah Omar was forced to leave his sanctuary in Kandahar and visit Kabul for the first time to meet his commanders and raise morale amongst his troops.

The Taliban were also forced to recruit increasing manpower from the Ghilzai Pashtun tribes of eastern Afghanistan and Pakistan. But they demanded a political price which the Taliban were not prepared to pay.

The Ghilzais, who had dominated the anti-Soviet war effort were not prepared to be used as cannon fodder by the Taliban without adequate representation in the Durrani-dominated Taliban Shuras. They would come if they were given a share of power. Ghilzai commanders with the Taliban were extremely critical of Taliban tactics in Mazar. 'There were too many mistakes made in Mazar. The initial agreement between Malik and the Taliban happened in too short a time. They should have discussed the agreement for a longer time and built up a dialogue with each other. They also made many military mistakes,' Jalaluddin Haqqani, the leading eastern Pashtun commander with the Taliban told me in Kabul in July 1997.

Haqqani, who commanded Taliban troops on the Kabul front, was a veteran Pashtun commander from Khost in Paktia province who had joined the Taliban in 1995. He was one of the most celebrated commanders from the anti-Soviet war. Although Haqqani was made a minister in Kabul, he and other non-Kandaharis remained extremely bitter that they were kept out of the decision-making process that took place in Kandahar under Omar, rather than in Kabul.[7] After the Mazar defeat the Taliban gave Haqqani a large sum of money to recruit 3,000 Ghilzai tribesmen. Haqqani arrived with his men on the Kabul front, but being powerless to make military decisions and the fact that they were led by Kandahari officers at the front led to mass desertions. Within two months Haqqani had only 300 of his new recruits left. Even more disturbing was that villages around Kandahar were refusing to send their sons to enlist with the Taliban. For the first time the Taliban had a recruitment problem and a manpower shortage.

For the Central Asian states the bloodshed on their doorstep created a paranoid reaction as they considered the spectre of the war crossing into their territories and the thousands of Afghan refugees fleeing across their porous borders. In an unprecedented move, military security was heightened throughout the region. Some 3,000 Russian troops on the Uzbekistan–Afghanistan border, 25,000 Russian troops on the Tajikistan–Afghanistan border, Russian border guards in Turkmenistan and local army divisions all went on a high state of alert. Uzbekistan and Tajikistan closed their borders with northern Afghanistan. At Termez, Uzbek helicopter gunships flew patrol as troops laid tank traps and fortified the bridge that crosses the Amu Darya river, which divides Afghanistan from Central Asia.

Russia offered to send ten battalions of troops to Kyrgyzstan after an appeal by Kyrgyz President Askar Akayev, even though his country has no border with Afghanistan. Russia and Kazakhstan organized an emergency meeting of the Commonwealth of Independent States (CIS) to discuss the crisis, where Russian Foreign Minister Yevgeny Primakov promised 'very tough and effective actions by Russia', if the Taliban advanced further. Turkmenistan, a self-declared neutral state which bordered western Afghanistan, had developed working relations with the Taliban but the Turkmen were unnerved by the fighting around Mazar. For the first time 9,000 Afghan Turkmen crossed the border into Turkmenistan seeking shelter from the fighting.

Iran said it would continue to support the anti-Taliban alliance and appealed to Russia, India and the Central Asian states to help them also. Iranian Foreign Minister Ali Akbar Velayti urged the UN to intervene. The Taliban were furious with all of their neighbours. 'Iran and Russia are interfering and supporting the opposition. They have given aircraft to the opposition to carry out bombardments. Iran is flying up to 22 flights a day to Mazar carrying arms,' said Mullah Mohammed Abbas, the Taliban Minister of Health.[8]

Iranian and Central Asian diplomats bitterly accused Pakistan of not only supporting the Taliban, but of lying and betraying a solemn commitment made by Prime Minister Nawaz Sharif just a week before the Taliban offensive. At a summit of regional heads of state in Ashkhabad, the capital of Turkmenistan, Sharif had promised to reign in the Taliban and prevent the war spreading to the north. 'Pakistan's credibility in Central Asia is zero right now,' a senior Uzbek diplomat told me.[9]

However, the arrival of the Taliban in the north did have a salutary effect on the four-year-old civil war in Tajikistan as it forced both sides in the conflict to quicken the pace of negotiations out of fear of the Taliban. A peace settlement between the Tajik government and the Islamic opposition, brokered by Russia and the UN was finally reached in Moscow on 27 June 1997. The settlement provided a major boost to Masud as Russia could now re-supply him from bases inside Tajikistan. Masud was given the use of the airport in Kuliab in southern Tajikistan where he received Russian and Iranian supplies which he then flew into the Panjshir valley.

The anti-Taliban alliance now tried to cement their unity by reformulating a new political alliance, which had to take into account Dostum's departure from the scene. On 13 June 1997 they set up the 'United Islamic and National Front for the Salvation of Afghanistan' and declared Mazar as their capital. They reappointed Burhanuddin Rabbani as President and Masud as the new Defence Minister and promised to form a new government which would include tribal and Islamic leaders as well as technocrats. But the pact was doomed to failure as again differences between Malik, Masud and Khalili prevented the Uzbeks, Tajiks and Hazaras from working together.

At the root of the split was the other leaders' suspicions of Malik after his string of betrayals. Malik had been unable to prevent a force of some

2,500 Taliban, who had remained behind in the north, from capturing the city of Kunduz which had an airport. The Taliban reinforced this enclave with daily flights of men and materials from Kabul. While Malik could not or would not drive the Taliban out of the north, Masud was moving closer to Kabul.

In mid-July, Masud broke the military stalemate north of Kabul, by recapturing Charikar and the Bagram airbase, killing hundreds more Taliban troops. By September, Masud's forces were once again positioned only 20 miles from Kabul. Both sides traded artillery and rocket bombardments, which forced nearly 180,000 civilians to flee the lush Shomali valley just north of Kabul and now on the front line. As the Taliban retreated from the Shomali, they poisoned water wells and blew up small irrigation channels and dams in a bid to ensure that the local Tajik population would not return in a hurry. The war was now not just uprooting and killing civilians, but destroying their very means of livelihood and turning Kabul's agricultural belt into a wasteland.

The anti-Taliban alliance had now created a huge 180-degree arc that surrounded Kabul. To the west and north of the city were Masud's forces while to the east and south were Khalili's Hazaras. As speculation mounted that they may launch an attack on Kabul, the Taliban remained confident that the opposition was too divided to attack Kabul. 'We have divided the opposition into two parts by putting our forces into Kunduz. The northern groups are disunited against each other. The other Uzbek generals cannot rely on Malik. He has already betrayed them once and now he is just trying to save himself. No group has enough forces to fight the Taliban on their own, so they have to try and unite but they can never unite,' said Haqqani.[10]

Doubts about Malik's loyalty to the alliance appeared to be justified, when in September the Taliban force in Kunduz took him by surprise. The Taliban broke out of their Kunduz enclave and with the help of Pashtun tribes in the area launched another attack on Mazar. On 7 September 1997 they captured the town of Tashkhorgan, creating panic in Mazar. As the Taliban advanced on Mazar, heavy fighting broke out between Uzbek troops loyal to Malik and others loyal to Dostum. Malik's house was burnt down by Dostum's troops and he fled to his base in Faryab province and then escaped to Turkmenistan from where he went on to Iran.

In a dramatic turnaround, Dostum returned to Mazar from exile in Turkey and rallied his troops to defeat Malik's supporters and push the Taliban out of the Mazar region. Mazar descended into chaos as the Uzbeks again looted parts of the city and the offices of UN aid agencies forcing humanitarian aid-workers to abandon Mazar for the second time in a year. As the Taliban retreated they massacred at least 70 Shia Hazaras in Qazil Abad, a village south of Mazar, and perhaps hundreds more. 'The Taliban swept through this village like storm. They killed about 70 people, some had their throats slit, while others were skinned alive,' said Sohrab Rostam, a survivor of the massacre.[11]

With the Taliban retreating back to Kunduz, Dostum tried to consolidate his position, but Mazar was now virtually taken over by Hazara groups and Dostum was forced to abandon the Uzbek capital and set up his base in Shiberghan. Acute tensions between the Uzbeks and the Hazaras undermined the anti-Taliban alliance and Dostum still had to win over Malik's supporters. He did so by exposing the atrocities committed by Malik. Dostum's troops unearthed 20 mass graves near Shebarghan in the Dash-te-Laili desert in Jowzjan province where more than 2,000 Taliban prisoners of war had been massacred and buried. Dostum accused Malik of the massacres, offered the Taliban help to retrieve the bodies and called in the UN to investigate. He released some 200 Taliban prisoners as a gesture of goodwill.[12]

Subsequent UN investigations revealed that the prisoners had been tortured and starved before dying. 'The manner of their death was horrendous. Prisoners were taken from detention, told they were going to be exchanged and then trucked to wells often used by shepherds, which held about 10 to 15 metres of water. They were thrown into the wells either alive or if they resisted, shot first and then tossed in. Shots were fired and hand grenades were exploded into the well before the top was bulldozed over.' said UN Special Rapporteur Paik Chong-Hyun who inspected the graves.[13]

Later there were eye-witness reports which made it clear that vicious ethnic cleansing had taken place, 'At night when it was quiet and dark, we took about 150 Taliban prisoners, blindfolded them, tied their hands behind their backs and drove them in truck containers out to the desert. We lined them up, ten at a time, in front of holes in the ground and opened fire. It took about six nights,' said General Saleem Sahar, an officer loyal to Malik, who had been arrested by Dostum.[14] The use of containers was particularly horrific and they were to be used increasingly as a method of killing by both sides. 'When we pulled the bodies out of the containers, their skin was burned black from the heat and the lack of oxygen,' said another of Malik's generals, who added that 1,250 Taliban had died a container death.

The catastrophe in the north and the heavy fighting that followed through the summer only further widened the ethnic divide in Afghanistan between the Pashtun Taliban and the non-Pashtuns. The country was now virtually split along north–south lines and also along Pashtun and non-Pashtun lines. All sides had carried out ethnic cleansing and religious persecution. The Taliban had massacred Shia Hazara villagers and forced out Tajik farmers from the Shomali valley. The Uzbeks and Hazaras had massacred hundreds of Taliban prisoners and killed Pashtun villagers in the north and around Kabul. The Shia Hazaras had also forced out Pashtuns on the basis of their Sunni beliefs. More than three-quarters of a million people had been displaced by the recent fighting – in the north around Mazar, on the Herat front and around Kabul – creating a new refugee crisis at a time when UN agencies were trying to persuade refugees still living in Pakistan to return home. Moreover, the divisions inside Afghanistan were manipulated and exacerbated by its neighbours, as all countries stepped up aid to their various Afghan proxies. This only worsened the ethnic and sectarian divide.

. Apart from the suffering civilians, the biggest casualty of the stepped-up fighting was the UN. The UN mediator Norbet Holl failed to persuade the Taliban that the UN was a neutral peace broker or the opposition that the UN would protect the interests of the ethnic minorities. Nor was Holl able to put pressure on regional countries to stop arming the factions. Nobody trusted the UN and everyone ignored it. Holl made a blunt statement blaming outside powers for continued interference and the inflexibility of the belligerents. 'We have a standstill in the negotiating process, we just cannot continue business as usual. I do not see the Afghan leaders as puppets but they need to get ammunition from somewhere,' Holl said.[15] A month later Holl had resigned.

The Taliban leadership, unversed in UN procedures and even the UN Charter, proved to be the greatest obstacle. Mullah Omar refused to meet Holl, creating resentment within the UN team while other Taliban leaders publicly mocked UN efforts at promoting a cease-fire. Taliban resentment against the UN increased after the débâcle in Mazar and more so after the UN Security Council refused to take action against the Mazar massacres or hand over Afghanistan's seat at the UN, which was still occupied by President Rabbani.

The Taliban harboured several unrealistic suspicions about the UN, which no amount of diplomacy could dispel. They were convinced that the UN, in league with Western powers, was conspiring against Islam and their imposition of Sharia law. They also accused the UN of being influenced by regional countries in blocking recognition of their government. The crisis within the UN came at a time when it faced dwindling funds from wealthy donor countries for aid programmes because of 'donor fatigue' over the continuing war. Donations were decreasing further because of the Taliban's discrimination against Afghan women. The future survival of aid operations in Afghanistan depended on the UN agencies convincing the Taliban to moderate their gender policies, which the Taliban refused to do. Several Western non-governmental organisations (NGOs) halted their programmes in Kabul because of the Taliban's refusal to let them continue helping women. In the north the fighting had forced the NGOs to pull out twice and they did not return.

Moreover, Taliban hardliners were doing their utmost to promote a crisis with UN humanitarian aid agencies so that they could kick them out of Taliban-held areas, under the pretext that the agencies were imparting Western secular ideas to the population. At the end of September, heads of three UN agencies in Kandahar were ordered to leave the country after they protested that a female lawyer for the UN High Commissioner for Refugees (UNHCR) was forced to talk to Taliban officials from behind a curtain so her face would not be visible. In November, the UNHCR suspended all its programmes when the Taliban arrested four UNHCR Afghan staff. Save the Children shut down several programmes because the Taliban refused to allow women to participate in mine-awareness classes. It was becoming impossible to provide humanitarian aid to the population anywhere, even though winter was approaching and there were growing food shortages.

The Taliban's treatment of women drew enormous adverse publicity and international criticism when Emma Bonino, the European Commissioner for Humanitarian Affairs and 19 Western journalists and aid workers were arrested and held for three hours by the Taliban religious police in Kabul on 28 September 1997. They had been touring a female hospital ward funded by the European Union (EU), when journalists accompanying Bonino were arrested for taking photographs of women patients – all photography was banned by the Taliban.

'This is an example of how people live here in a state of terror,' Ms Bonino told reporters in Kabul.[16] The Taliban apologized, but Western enthusiasm for funding aid to Afghanistan was dealt another blow. The Taliban then declared that they would segregate Kabul's hospitals and not allow women to be treated together with men – and there was only one women's hospital in the city.

It was now becoming difficult for the Clinton administration to maintain its initial sympathy for the Taliban. Powerful US feminist groups lobbied Washington on behalf of Afghan women. In November Secretary of State Madeleine Albright issued the harshest criticism of the Taliban ever made by the US. 'We are opposed to the Taliban because of their opposition to human rights and their despicable treatment of women and children and great lack of respect for human dignity,' Albright said on a visit to Islamabad on 18 November 1997. Her statement was seen as a significant indicator of the US distancing itself both from the Taliban and Pakistan's support for them. Yet the Taliban appeared least concerned about these international pressures and in fact generated greater anti-Western feeling. The *ulema* in Pakistan and Kandahar told Omar that he should throw all aid agencies out of Afghanistan because they were spies and the enemies of Islam.[17]

In a bid to energise UN mediation, Secretary – General Kofi Annan ordered Lakhdar Brahimi, a former Algerian Foreign Minister to tour the region and present a report to the UN Security Council. After visiting 13 countries including Afghanistan between 14 August and 23 September, Brahimi's conclusions were to mobilize greater international pressure on Afghanistan's neighbours to stop aiding the belligerents. In October Annan had set up a Group of Concerned Countries at the UN. The group nicknamed 'Six plus Two', included six of Afghanistan's neighbours, Russia and the United States.[18] Brahami hoped that this forum would encourage Iran to talk to Pakistan as well as re-engage Washington in a search for peace. Another aim was to implement an arms embargo on Afghanistan and to start talks between the Afghan factions.

Annan followed up these steps in mid-November with a blistering report on Afghanistan to the UN Security Council, in which for the first time he used uncompromisingly tough language accusing regional countries, especially Iran and Pakistan, of fomenting the conflict. He said these states were using the UN as a fig leaf to continue providing aid to the factions.[19] 'Foreign military material and financial support continues unabated, fuelling this conflict and depriving the warring factions of a genuine interest in making peace,' Annan said. 'The continued support by these outside forces, combined with the apathy of others not directly involved, is rendering diplomatic initiatives almost irrelevant.' Neither did Annan spare the warlords. 'The Afghan leaders refuse to rise above their factional interests and start working together for national reconciliation. Too many groups in Afghanistan, warlords, terrorists, drug dealers and others, appear to have too much to gain from war and too much to lose from peace.'[20]

Later in Tehran, Annan addressed the summit meeting of the Organization of the Islamic Conference (OIC) and bluntly criticized their apathy in trying to resolve the conflict. After years of neglect, Afghanistan now appeared to feature on the international diplomatic agenda, but that did little to satisfy the Taliban who were determined to conquer the north and their opponents who were equallly determined to resist them.

~5~

BAMIYAN 1998–99:
THE NEVER-ENDING WAR

In the Hazarajat, the country of the Hazaras in central Afghanistan, the temperature was below freezing. Under the shadows of the towering snow – covered peaks of the Hindu Kush mountains that surround Bamiyan, Hazara children with extended stomachs and rake-thin features played their version of a cops and robbers game they called 'Taliban'. The Hazaras were starving and the game involved ambushing a Taliban convoy of wheat and bringing it home to their hungry families. The children were living on roots, berries and a few potatoes their parents managed to grow in tiny, stony fields, dug out from the sides of the steep valleys. Only 10 per cent of the Hazarajat is cultivable and that year's harvests of wheat and maize had failed.

But the Hazaras were also starving simply for who they were. Since August 1997 in a bid to force them to surrender, the Taliban had closed all the roads from the south, west and east that entered their mountain fastness. There was no relief possible from the north, where the break-down of law and order, the shortage of foodstuffs and the mountain passes closed by winter snow made it impossible for food convoys to travel to Bamiyan, which is situated at a height of 7,500 feet. Three hundred thousand Hazaras in the province of Bamiyan were already hungry, while another 700,000 in the three neighbouring provinces of Ghor, Wardak and Ghazni were also suffering from shortages – one million people in all.

For months the UN and its sister organization the World Food Programme (WFP) had been holding tortuous negotiations with the Taliban to allow relief convoys through, but the Taliban had refused. The UN were even more frustrated with the fact that Pakistan had contracted to provide the Taliban with 600,000 tons of wheat, but had made no humanitarian demand on the Taliban to lift their blockade on Bamiyan. It was the first time in the past 20 years of conflict that one faction had used food as a weapon of war against another and it demonstrated the escalation in the ethnic and sectarian divisions that were consuming Afghanistan.

The Hazaras had always been at the short end of the Pashtun stick, but never to such an extent. These short, stocky people with their distinctive Mongol features were, according to one theory, the descendants of inter-marriage between Genghis Khan's Mongol warriors and the indigenous Tajik and Turkic peoples. In 1222 Genghis Khan's grandson was killed by Bamiyan's defenders and, in revenge, he massacred the population.[1] For one thousand years before that Bamiyan was the centre of Buddhism in India and an important *serai* or resting place for the camel caravans on the ancient Silk Route, which linked the Roman Empire with Central Asia, China and India. Bamiyan remained the protector and capital of Buddhism for the whole of Central Asia and India after the Islamic conquests. A Korean monk, Hui-chao who arrived in the town in 827 AD wrote that the King of Bamyan was still a Buddhist and it was not until the eleventh century that the Ghaznavids established Islam in the valley.

The town is still dominated by two magnificent second-century AD Buddha colossi, carved into a sandstone cliff face. The two statues, one 165 feet high, the other 114 feet high, are weathered and cracked while the faces of both the Buddhas are missing, but their impact is stunning. The figures are carved with the classical features of all sub-continental Buddhas, but the figures are draped in Greek robes for they represented the unique fusion of classical Indian and Central Asian art with Hellenism, introduced by the armies of Alexander the Great. The Buddhas were one of the wonders of the ancient world, visited by pilgrims from China and India.

Thousands of Buddhist monks once lived in the caves and grottos carved into the cliffs alongside the statues. These caves, covered with antique stuccoes, were now home to thousands of Hazara refugees who had fled Kabul. The Taliban threatened to blow up the colossi when they captured Bamiyan, generating high-level protests from Buddhist communities in Japan and Sri Lanka. In the meantime they had bombed the mountain above the Buddhas eight times, creating more cracks in the sandstone niches that held the figures.

The Hazarajat had remained virtually independent until 1893 when it was conquered by the Pashtun King Abdul Rehman, who initiated the first anti-Hazara programme, killing thousands of Hazaras, moving thousands more to Kabul where they lived as indentured serfs and servants, and destroying their mosques. The estimated 3–4 million Hazaras are the largest Shia Muslim group in Afghanistan. The sectarian enmity between the Sunni Pashtuns and the Shia Hazaras went back a long way, but the Taliban had brought a new edge to the conflict for they treated all Shias as *munafaqeen* or hypocrites and beyond the pale of true Islam.

Even more irksome for the Taliban, was that Hazara women were playing a significant political, social and even military role in the region's defence. The 80-member Central Council of the Hazara's Hizb-e-Wahadat party had 12 women members, many of them educated professionals. Women looked after UN aid programmes and Wahadat's efforts to provide basic literacy, health care and family planning. Women often fought in battle alongside their men – some had killed Taliban in Mazar in May. Female professors, who had fled Kabul had set up a university in Bamiyan, probably the poorest in the world where classrooms were constructed with mud and straw and there was no electricity or heating and few books.

'We detest the Taliban, they are against all civilization, Afghan culture and women in particular. They have given Islam and Afghan people a bad name,' Dr Humera Rahi, who taught Persian literature at the university and had emerged as a leading poet of the resistance, told me. Nor did the Taliban appreciate Hazara women's style of dress. Dr Rahi and her colleagues wore skirts and high-heeled boots. The poetry of Humera Rahi seemed to echo the Hazaras' new found confidence after centuries of oppression at the hands of the Pashtuns.

'Victory is yours and God is with you, victorious army of Hazarajat. May your foes' chests be the target of your rifle barrels. You are the winner, the victorious, God is with you. My midnight prayers and my cries at dawn, and the children saying "O Lord, O Lord!", and the tears and sighs of the oppressed are with you.'[2]

Despite the siege and decades of poor treatment and prejudice by the Pashtun rulers of Kabul, the Hazaras were now on a roll. They had been instrumental in defeating the Taliban in Mazar in May and again in October 1997. They had also repulsed repeated Taliban attacks against Bamiyan. The Hazaras had once made up the third and weakest link in the Uzbek–Tajik–Hazara alliance confronting the Taliban, but now with the Uzbeks divided and in disarray and the Tajiks in a position of stalemate around Kabul, the Hazaras sensed that their time had come. 'Our backs are to the Hindu Kush and before us are the Taliban and their supporters Pakistan. We will die but we will never surrender,' Qurban Ali Irfani, the defiant deputy chief of Wahadat told me, as we sat trying to warm ourselves in front of a log fire in a room that overlooked the Buddhas, spectacularly draped in moonlight.

There was a new found confidence and pride in their organization and their fighting prowess. 'We saved the north from the Taliban,' said Ahmed Sher, a 14-year-old Hazara soldier, who had already seen two years of battle and held his kalashnikov like a professional soldier. The Hazaras were not without friends. Iran was flying in military supplies to a newly constructed two-mile-long landing strip outside Bamiyan and Karim Khalili, the leader of Wahadat, spent the winter visiting Tehran, Moscow, New Delhi and Ankara looking for more military aid.

But the Hazaras had also overstretched themselves. There were several factions amongst them, all competing for territory, influence and foreign aid. Separate factions of Hizb-e-Wahadat each controlled a part of Mazar and they fought each other as well as the Uzbeks, turning Mazar into a war zone and the anti-Taliban alliance into a political shambles. Iranian and Russian intelligence officers made several attempts at mediating between Dostum, who was then based in Shiberghan, and the Hazaras, as well as between the Hazara factions, but no side would compromise. In February 1998, as heavy fighting erupted inside Mazar between the Uzbeks and the Hazaras, Masud paid his first visit to Tehran to try and persuade the Iranians to do something to save the anti-Taliban alliance before it was too late. Meanwhile the Taliban sat out the winter, watching their enemies tear each other apart while tightening the siege around Bamiyan and preparing for another attack on Mazar.

Fighting continued through the winter months in the western province of Faryab, where the Taliban carried out another massacre in January – this time of some 600 Uzbek villagers. Western aid-workers who later investigated the incident said civilians were dragged from their homes, lined up and gunned down. International censure against the Taliban's policies escalated as they imposed ever stricter Islamic laws and punishments in Kabul. The public amputation of limbs, lashings, stoning of women and executions became weekly events in Kabul and Kandahar. International Women's Day on 8 February 1998 was dedicated to the plight of Afghan women under Taliban rule. A hearing in the US Senate on the Afghan gender issue attracted widespread publicity, as did condemnation of the Taliban's policies by such luminaries as Hillary Clinton.

The Taliban issued new edicts, stipulating the exact length of beards for males and a list of Muslim names with which newborn children had to be named. The Taliban shut down the few home schools for girls that were operating in Kabul, as the religious police went on a rampage forcing all women off the streets of Kabul and insisting that householders blackened their windows, so women would not be visible from the outside. Women were now forced to spend all their time indoors, where not even sunlight could penetrate. Taliban hardliners were determined to force the UN aid agencies out of Afghanistan and they provoked a number of incidents that tested UN patience to the limit.

On 24 February 1998 all UN staff pulled out of Kandahar and halted aid operations there after senior Taliban leaders beat up UN staff and threatened them. Mullah Mohammed Hassan, the usually mild-mannered, one-legged Governor of Kandahar, threw a table and a chair at the head of one UN official and then tried to throttle him, because he had refused to pave a road in Hassan's village. In March, the Taliban refused to allow Alfredo Witschi-Cestari, the head of UN humanitarian aid operations to visit Kabul for talks. And the UN remained deeply frustrated by the Taliban siege of the Hazarajat. 'In the north there is complete insecurity for our aid operations and in the south we have a hell of a horrible time working with the Taliban. In the north there is no authority and in the south there is a very difficult authority,' Lakhdar Brahimi told me.[3]

Despite these problems Brahimi attempted to set up a meeting between the Taliban and the anti-Taliban alliance. Anxious to avoid meeting the opposition's leaders and thereby give them further legitimacy, the Taliban suggested a meeting of *ulema* from both sides. For several months they squabbled with each other as to who qualified to be an *ulema*. The UN mustered the help of the US. Bill Richardson, President Clinton's foreign policy troubleshooter and the US Ambassador to the UN, visited Afghanistan for a day of parachute diplomacy on 17 April 1998 and persuaded both sides to convene the *ulema* meeting.

Both sides were trying to woo the US and the flamboyant Richardson received a rapturous reception. He was deluged with gifts of carpets, saddlebags and turbans. In Kabul the Taliban allowed the accompanying US TV crews to film their leaders for the first time and, as a courtesy to Richardson, they postponed their regular Friday public spectacle of lashings and amputations in the city's football stadium. But although the Taliban leaders in Kabul promised to ease the siege of Hazarajat and discuss their gender policies with the UN, Mullah Omar rejected the agreement just a few hours after Richardson left.

The *ulema* met in Islamabad under UN auspices at the end of April and after four days of talks each side agreed to nominate 20 *ulema* to a peace commission, which would decide on such issues as a cease-fire, lifting the Taliban siege on the Hazarajat and an exchange of prisoners. However, the Taliban then refused to nominate their delegation and by May another peace process had collapsed – even as the Taliban prepared a fresh offensive.

Part of these preparations involved a fresh escalation with the UN. In June the Taliban stopped all women from attending general hospitals and ordered all female Muslim UN staff travelling to Afghanistan to be chaperoned by a *mehram* or a blood relative – an impossible demand to meet, especially as UN agencies had increased the number of Muslim female aid-workers, precisely so as to satisfy Taliban demands and gain access to Afghan women. The Taliban then insisted that all NGOs working in Kabul move out of their offices and relocate to the destroyed building of the Polytechnic College. Twenty-two out of 30 NGOs voted to pull out of Kabul if the Taliban did not retract their demand, but the Taliban said the issue was non-negotiable.

As the EU suspended all humanitarian aid to areas under Taliban control, Brahimi dropped a bombshell by going public on the UN's frustration. 'This is an organization that hands out edicts to us that prevents us from doing our job,' he said. 'The Taliban must know that not only is there a limit to what you can stand but that there are growing pressures on us – in particular from the donor community to say that there's a limit.'⁴ The Taliban refused to relent and on 20 July 1998 they closed down all NGO offices by force and an exodus of foreign aid-workers from Kabul began. The same day the bodies of two Afghans working for UN aid agencies, Mohammed Habibi of UNHCR and Mohammed Bahsaryar of WFP, who had been kidnapped earlier, were found in Jalalabad. The Taliban offered no explanation for their deaths.

With more than half of Kabul's 1.2 million people benefiting in some way from NGO handouts, women and children were immediate victims when aid was cut off. Food distribution, health care and the city's fragile water distribution network were all seriously affected. As people waved empty kettles and buckets at passing Taliban jeeps, their reply to the population was characteristic of their lack of social concern. 'We Muslims believe God the Almighty will feed everybody one way or another. If the foreign NGOs leave than it is their decision. We have not expelled them,' Planning Minister Qari Din Mohammed insisted.⁵

Meanwhile the Taliban had persuaded Pakistan and Saudi Arabia to back them in another offensive to take the north. The Saudi intelligence chief Prince Turki al Faisal visited Kandahar in mid-June, after which the Saudis provided the Taliban with 400 pick-up trucks and financial aid. Pakistan's ISI had prepared a budget of some 2 billion rupees (US$5 million) for logistical support that was needed by the Taliban. ISI officers visited Kandahar frequently to help the Taliban prepare the attack, as thousands of new Afghan and Pakistani recruits from refugee camps and *madrassas* arrived to enlist with the Taliban. Meanwhile in March, Iran, Russia and Uzbekistan began to pour weapons, ammunition and fuel into the anti-Taliban alliance.⁶ While Iran flew in planeloads of weapons to the Hazaras directly from Meshad to Bamiyan, the Russians and Iranians provided Masud with weapons at an airbase in Kuliab in southern Tajikistan, from where he transported them into Afghanistan.

In July, the Taliban swept northwards from Herat, capturing Maimana on 12 July 1998 after routing Dostum's forces and capturing 100 tanks and vehicles and some 800 Uzbek soldiers – the majority of whom they massacred. On 1 August 1998, the Taliban captured Dostum's headquarters at Shiberghan after several of his commanders accepted Taliban bribes and switched sides. Dostum fled to Uzbekistan and later to Turkey. Demoralized by Dostum's desertion, more Uzbek commanders guarding the western road into Mazar also accepted bribes, thereby exposing the 1,500 strong Hazara force just outside the city to a surprise Taliban attack. It came in the early hours of 8 August 1998, when the Hazara forces suddenly found themselves surrounded. They fought until their ammunition ran out and only 100 survived. By 10.00 a.m., the first Taliban pick-ups entered Mazar, as an unsuspecting public was going about its daily business.[7]

What followed was another brutal massacre, genocidal in its ferocity, as the Taliban took revenge on their losses the previous year. A Taliban commander later said that Mullah Omar had given them permission to kill for two hours, but they had killed for two days. The Taliban went on a killing frenzy, driving their pick-ups up and down the narrow streets of Mazar shooting to the left and right and killing everything that moved – shop owners, cart pullers, women and children shoppers and even goats and donkeys. Contrary to all injunctions of Islam, which demands immediate burial, bodies were left to rot on the streets. 'They were shooting without warning at everybody who happened to be on the street, without discriminating between men, women and children. Soon the streets were covered with dead bodies and blood. No one was allowed to bury the corpses for the first six days. Dogs were eating human flesh and going mad and soon the smell became intolerable,' said a male Tajik who managed to escape the massacre.[8]

As people ran for shelter to their homes, Taliban soldiers barged in and massacred Hazara households wholescale. 'People were shot three times on the spot, one bullet in the head, one in the chest and one in the testicles. Those who survived buried their dead in their gardens. Women were raped,' said the same witness. 'When the Taliban stormed into our house they shot my husband and two brothers dead on the spot. Each was shot three times and then their throats were slit in the *halal* way,' said a 40-year-old Tajik widow.[9]

After the first full day of indiscriminate killing, the Taliban reverted to targeting the Hazaras. Unwilling to repeat their mistake the previous year when they entered Mazar without guides, this time the Taliban had enlisted local Pashtuns, once loyal to Hikmetyar, who knew the city well. Over the next few days, these Pashtun fighters from Balkh guided Taliban search parties to the homes of Hazaras. But the Taliban were out of control and arbitrary killings continued, even of those who were not Hazaras. 'I saw that a young Tajik boy had been killed – the *Talib* was still standing there and the father was crying. "Why have you killed my son? We are Tajiks." The Talib responded, "Why didn't you say so?" And the father said, "Did you ask that I could answer?"'[10]

Thousands of Hazaras were taken to Mazar jail and when it was full, they were dumped in containers which were locked and the prisoners allowed to suffocate. Some containers were taken to the Dasht-e-Laili desert outside Mazar and the inmates massacred there – in direct retaliation for the similar treatment meeted out to the Taliban in 1997. 'They brought three containers from Mazar to Shiberghan. When they opened the door of one truck, only three persons were alive. About 300 were dead. The three were taken to the jail. I could see all this from where I was sitting,' said another witness.[11] As tens of thousands of civilians tried to escape Mazar by foot in long columns over the next few days, the Taliban killed dozens more in aerial bombardments.

The Taliban aimed to cleanse the north of the Shia. Mullah Niazi, the commander who had ordered Najibullah's murder was appointed Governor of Mazar and within hours of taking the city, Taliban mullahs were proclaiming from the city's mosques that the city's Shia had three choices – convert to Sunni Islam, leave for Shia Iran or die. All prayer services conducted by the Shia in mosques were banned. 'Last year you rebelled against us and killed us. From all your homes you shot at us. Now we are here to deal with you. The Hazaras are not Muslims and now we have to kill Hazaras. You either accept to be Muslims or leave Afghanistan. Wherever you go we will catch you. If you go up we will pull you down by your feet; if you hide below, we will pull you up by your hair,' Niazi declared from Mazar's central mosque.[12] As the Roman historian Tacitus said of the Roman conquest of Britain, 'the Roman army created a desolation and called it peace.'

With no independent observers around to do a body count, it was impossible to estimate the numbers killed, but the UN and the ICRC later estimated that between 5,000 and 6,000 people were killed. It subsequently became clear that along the route of the Taliban advance similar massacres of Uzbeks and Tajiks had taken place in Maimana and Shiberghan. My own estimate is that as many as between 6,000 and 8,000 civilians were killed in July and August, including the heavy casualties amongst the anti-Taliban troops. But the Taliban's aim to terrorize the population so that they would not rise against them later, was to remain unfulfilled.

The Taliban were to target one more group in Mazar that was to bring down a storm of international protest and plunge them into near war with Iran. A small Taliban unit led by Mullah Dost Mohammed and including several Pakistani militants of the anti-Shia, Sipah-e-Sahaba party entered the Iranian Consulate in Mazar, herded 11 Iranian diplomats, intelligence officers and a journalist into the basement and then shot them dead. Tehran had earlier contacted the Pakistan government to guarantee the security of their Consulate, because the Iranians knew that ISI officers had driven into Mazar with the Taliban. The Iranians had thought that Dost Mohammed's unit had been sent to protect them and so had welcomed them at first.[13] The Taliban had also captured 45 Iranian truck-drivers who had been ferrying arms to the Hazaras.

At first the Taliban refused to admit the whereabouts of the diplomats but then as international protests and Iranian fury increased, they admitted that the diplomats had been killed, not on official orders but by renegade Taliban. But reliable sources said that Dost Mohammed had spoken to Mullah Omar on his wireless to ask whether the diplomats should be killed and Omar had given the go-ahead. True or not the Iranians certainly believed this. Ironically Dost Mohammed later wound up in jail in Kandahar, because he had brought back two Hazara concubines and his wife in Kandahar complained to Mullah Omar. Some 400 Hazara women were kidnapped and taken as concubines by the Taliban.[14]

It was the Taliban victory, their control over most of Afghanistan and their expectation, fuelled by Pakistani officials that they would now receive international recognition, which partly prompted their guest, the Saudi dissident Osama Bin Laden, to become bolder in his declared jihad against the US and the Saudi Royal family. On 7 August 1998, Bin Laden's sympathizers blew up the US Embassies in Kenya and Tanzania, killing 224 people and wounding 4,500. This prompted the US to launch missile strikes on Bin Laden's training camps in north-eastern Afghanistan on 20 August 1998. Dozens of cruise missiles hit six targets killing over 20 people and wounding 30 more. The US claimed that Bin Laden had been present but escaped the attack. In fact there were few Arab casualties. Most of those killed were Pakistanis and Afghans who were training to fight in India-controlled Kashmir.

The Taliban were outraged and organized demonstrations in Afghan cities to protest against the attacks. UN offices in several towns were attacked by mobs. Mullah Omar emerged to blast Clinton personally. 'If the attack on Afghanistan is Clinton's personal decision, then he has done it to divert the world and the American people's attention from that shameful White House affair that has proved Clinton is a liar and a man devoid of decency and honour,' Omar said, in reference to the Monica Lewinsky affair. Omar insisted that Bin Laden was a guest, not just of the Taliban but of the people of Afghanistan and that the Taliban would never hand him over to the US. 'America itself is the biggest terrorist in the world,' Omar added.[15] As UN officials evacuated Kabul because of growing insecurity, gunmen shot dead an Italian UN military officer and wounded a French diplomat. The two killers, Haq Nawaz and Salim both from Rawalpindi, whom the Taliban apprehended and jailed were both Pakistani Islamic militants from the Harkat ul Ansar group.

Instead of trying to placate their international critics and Iran, the

Taliban launched an offensive from three directions on Bamiyan, which fell on 13 September 1998 after some Hazara commanders surrendered to the Taliban. Karim Khalili and other Wahadat leaders, together with much of the population of the town, took to the hills as the first Taliban troops entered. This time, due to repeated international appeals to respect human rights, Mullah Omar ordered his troops to restrain themselves against Hazara civilians. Nevertheless killings did take place in Bamiyan a few weeks after the Taliban entered. In one village near Bamiyan 50 old men, who were left behind after the younger population escaped, were killed by the Taliban.[16]

In another tragedy on 18 September, just five days after they occupied Bamiyan, Taliban fighters dynamited the head of the small Buddha colossus, blowing its face away. They fired rockets at the Buddha's groin, damaging the luxurious folds of the figure and destroying the intricate frescoes in the niche, where the statue stood. The two Buddhas, Afghanistan's greatest archaeological heritage, had stood for nearly 2,000 years and had withstood the assault of the Mongols. Now the Taliban were destroying them. It was a crime that could not be justified by any appeals to Islam.

For the Iranians the fall of Bamiyan was the last straw. Iran said it had the right of self-defence under international law and the UN Charter to take all necessary action against the Taliban – exactly the same argument used by Washington for its missile strike. A week later Iran's Supreme Leader Ayatollah Ali Khomenei warned of a huge war which could engulf the entire region. He accused Pakistan of using troops and aircraft in the capture of Bamiyan, which was denied by Islamabad. Iran–Pakistan relations sunk to a new low as Tehran flexed its muscles. Seventy thousand Iranian Revolutionary Guards, backed by tanks and aircraft, began the largest military exercises ever along the Iran-Afghanistan border. In October some 200,000 regular Iranian troops began another series of exercises along the border as the Taliban mobilized some 5,000 fighters to prevent an expected Iranian invasion.

As the UN Security Council expressed fears of an all – out Iranian attack, it sent Lakhdar Brahimi back to the region. The military tensions between Iran and the Taliban only subsided when Brahimi met with Mullah Omar in Kandahar on 14 October 1998. It was the first time that Omar had ever met with a UN official or foreign diplomat who was not Pakistani. Omar agreed to release all the Iranian truck drivers, return the dead bodies of the Iranian diplomats and promised to improve relations with the UN.

The Taliban's confrontation with Iran had given Masud the time and space to regroup his forces and the remaining Uzbek and Hazara fighters, who had not surrendered. At the same time, increased arms supplies, including vehicles and helicopters, reached him from Russia and Iran.

Masud launched a series of well co-ordinated, lightning attacks in the north east, capturing a huge swathe of territory back from the Taliban, especially along Afghanistan's sensitive border with Tajikistan and Uzbekistan. There were some 2,000 Taliban casualties during October and November as the demoralized, poorly supplied and cold Taliban garrisons fought briefly and then surrendered to Masud. On 7 December 1998 Masud held a meeting of all field commanders opposed to the Taliban in the Panjshir valley. The collapse of the Hazara and Uzbek leadership had left Masud and his Tajiks supreme and the commanders, who included several prominent Pashtuns, appointed Masud as the military commander of all anti-Taliban forces.

The Taliban offensive, the massacre of Hazaras and the confrontation with Iran, along with the US cruise-missile attack dramatically undermined the fragile balance of power in the region. The Taliban's clean sweep also infuriated Russia, Turkey and the Central Asian states who blamed Pakistan and Saudi Arabia for backing the Taliban. The sharpened war of words increased the regional polarization between the two blocks of states. The foreign and defence ministers of Kazakhstan, Kyrgyzstan, Uzbekistan and Tajikistan and Russian officials met in Tashkent on 25 August 1998 to co-ordinate joint military and political plans to halt the Taliban advance.

The consequences of the regional escalation were enormous: there was the danger of a war between Iran and the Taliban, which could also suck in Pakistan on the side of the Taliban; Western investors and oil companies became wary of further investments in the oil-rich Caspian nations; the danger of Islamic fundamentalism spreading to the already economically impoverished Central Asian states increased and anti-US feeling across the region escalated; Pakistan became more deeply polarized as Islamic parties demanded Islamicization.

The international community remained frustrated with the Taliban's intransigence in refusing to form a broad-based government, change its stance on the gender issue and accept diplomatic norms of behaviour. UN aid agencies were unable to return to Kabul. Washington was now obsessed with Bin Laden's capture and the Taliban's refusal to hand him over. Even close ally Saudi Arabia, which felt insulted by the protection that the Taliban were giving Bin Laden, pulled out its diplomatic representation in Kabul and ceased all official funding for the Taliban, leaving Pakistan as their sole provider.

These international frustrations resulted, on 8 December 1998, in the toughest UN Security Council Resolution on Afghanistan to date. The Resolution threatened unspecified sanctions against the Taliban for harbouring international terrorists, violating human rights, promoting drugs trafficking and refusing to accept a cease-fire. 'Afghanistan-based terrorism has become a plague,' said US envoy Nancy Soderberg.[17] Pakistan was the only country that did not support the resolution, calling it biased and by now Pakistan was as internationally isolated as the Taliban.

Increasing pressure by the UN, the US and other states forced both sides back to the negotiating table in early 1999. Under UN auspices, delegations from the Taliban and the opposition met for talks in Ashkhabad on 11 March 1999. The talks ended on a hopeful note, with both sides agreeing to exchange prisoners and continue negotiating. But by April, Mullah Omar ruled out further talks, accusing Masud of duplicity. In fact both sides had used the lull and the talks to prepare for a renewed spring offensive. On 7 April 1999, Masud met with the Russian Defence Minister Igor Sergeyev in Dushanbe, as Russia announced it would build a new military base in Tajikistan. Clearly part of its role would be to step up military aid to Masud. The Taliban were re-equipping themselves and recruiting more students from Pakistani *madrassas*. Masud and the Hazaras launched a series of attacks in the north east and the Hazarajat. In a dramatic reversal Wahadat troops recapatured Bamiyan on 21 April 1999. The north was once again in flames as fighting spread and UN peace-making efforts were back to zero.

At the beginning of 1998 Kofi Annan had warned, 'In a country of 20 million people, 50,000 armed men are holding the whole population hostage.'[18] By the end of 1998 Annan spoke ominously of 'the prospect of a deeper regionalization of the conflict' where Afghanistan had become 'the stage for a new version of the Great Game'.[19] Rather than bring peace, the Taliban victories and their massacres of the peoples of the north, had only brought Afghanistan even closer to the edge of ethnic fragmentation.

Annan's dire predictions appeared to be borne out by the end of the year when UN mediator Lakhdar Brahimi announced his resignation. He blamed the Taliban for their intransigence, the support given to them by thousands of Pakistani *madrassa* students and continued outside interference. His resignation in October followed two Taliban offensives in July and September, which attempted to push Masud's forces out of the Kabul region and cut off his supply links with Tajikistan in the north.

Both offensives failed but the Taliban conducted a bloody scorched-earth policy north of the capital, which led to some 200,000 people fleeing the area and the devastation of the Shomali valley – one of the most fertile regions in the country. As winter set in tens of thousands of refugees who had taken shelter with Masud's forces in the Panjshir valley and with the Taliban in Kabul faced acute shortages food and shelter.

Brahimi's resignation was followed by a much tougher reaction against the Taliban by the international community. The UN Security Council unanimously imposed limited sanctions on the Taliban on 15 October –

banning commercial aircraft flights to and from Afghanistan and freezing Taliban bank accounts world wide – even as Washington stepped up pressure on the Taliban to hand over Bin Laden.

On February 6, 2000 the Taliban came under renewed international pressure after distraught Afghan civilians hijacked an Afghan Airlines passenger plane on an internal flight from Kabul and flew it to London where they asked for asylum. The hijacking ended peacefully four days later. In early March 2000 the Taliban launched abortive offensives against Masud's forces but were pushed back. The Taliban received a major blow to their prestige when two top NA leaders, who had spent three years in a Taliban jail in Kandahar, managed to escape on March 27 and arrived in Iran. The included Ismail Khan, who had led the Mujheddin resistance against Soviet occupying forces in the 1980's and then fought the Taliban.

In April the Taliban issued several appeals to the international community to help draught victims in three southern provinces and a locust plague in Baghlan province. The draught worsened over the summer affecting the entire country, but the Taliban's refusal to announce a ceasefire discouraged international aid. After three months UN agencies had received only US 8 million dollars out of US 67 million dollars for a draught appeal. As the draught worsened, prices for foodstuffs rose by over 75% between January and July and the Afghani currency lost some 50% of its value between February and July. However that did not stop the Taliban from launching their summer offensive against the NA on July 1. thousands of Taliban troops and dozens of tanks attacking from five directions, tried to blast their way through NA positions just 30 kilometers north of Kabul. However, the Taliban lost some 400 men as they were repelled by Masud's forces.

As fighting subsided around Kabul, the Taliban launched an offensive on July 28 in the north east of the country, in a bid to cut Masud's supply lines with Tajikistan. The Taliban carried out intensive bombing of civilian targets as the Taliban slowly made headway towards Taloqan, the political headquarters of the NA. After a four week siege and heavy fighting Taloqan fell on September 5, after Masud conducted a strategic withdrawal from the city to prevent civilian casualties. Masud withdrew to the borders of Badakhshan, the last province under his control as 150,000 refugees fleeing Taloqan and the Taliban advance pressed up against the border with Tajikistan and asked to be given refuge. The Taliban also captured several towns on the Afghanistan–Tajikistan border, creating a wave of panic in Central Asia.

Throughout 2000 there were growing signs of splits and dissent within the Taliban leadership, while the tribal Pashtuns demonstrated growing resentment against the strictures and corruption of Taliban rule and their lack of consideration for the suffering population. On January 13, the money market in Kabul was robbed by its Taliban guards who stole the equivalent of some US 200,000 dollars. The money maket shut down in protest for several days as the 'Afghani' plummeted against the US dollar. On January 25, 400 tribal leaders from four eastern provinces—Paktiya, Khost, Paktika and Gardez—forced the Taliban to replace local Governors, as they protested the conscription drive by the Taliban and the sharp rise in taxes, which they complained were being sent to Kabul rather than being used for local relief. On January 27, over 2000 people held an unprecedented anti-Taliban rally in Khost. The draught and the Taliban's insistence on continued fighting, increased public criticism of the Taliban's lack of concern for the civilian population. Smugglers and transporters blamed the Taliban for harbouring Bin Laden, which had led to UN sanctions and a cut back in the smuggling trade. In late April the Taliban arrested the head of its air force General Akthar Mansuri and 10 other officials in Kandahar for helping Ismael Khan escape.

There was also increasing hostility to the Taliban's expanding support to Islamic fundamentalist and terrorist movements from neighboring countries, especially in Central Asia. The Taliban were playing host to extremist groups from Central Asia, Iran, Kashmir, China and Pakistan whose militants fight for the Taliban. The Islamic Movement of Uzbekistan (IMU), which in the summer of 1999 and again in 2000 launched abortive offensives against Uzbekistan's regime have bases in northern Afghanistan. More than one third of the 15000 strong Taliban force which captured Taloqan was made up of non-Afghans, which included 3000 Pakistani militants, 1000 fighters from the IMU, several hundred Arabs under Bin Laden as well as Kashmiris, Chechens, Philipinos and Chinese Muslims.

International efforts by the US, Russia and the regional states to coordinate anti-terrorism measures were stepped up. Russia's accusations against the Taliban increased dramatically after Kabul recognised the government of the breakaway Republic of Chechnya and allowed the Chechens to open an embassy in Kabul on January 16, 2000. After the military coup in Islamabad on October 12, 1999 Pakistan stepped up its support to the Taliban providing increased military aid to the Taliban for its summer offensive in 2000. Pakistan remained the only country in the world supporting the Taliban and countries in the region became more hostile to the military regime.

Several attempts by the UN and Organisation of the Islamic Conference (OIC) to bring the warring factions to the negotiating table failed to yield positive results. Francesc Vendrell, a Spanish diplomat was appointed as the new UN Secretary General's Special Representative to Afghanistan on January 18. In March and again in May, the OIC organised indirect talks between the Taliban and the NA in Jeddah with no outcome. Even as they appeared to be winning control of the entire country, the Taliban remained internationally isolated and condemned as a pariah movement by all of Afghanistan's neighbors.

Part 2

Islam and the Taliban

~6~

CHALLENGING ISLAM:
THE NEW-STYLE
FUNDAMENTALISM OF
THE TALIBAN

I slam has always been at the very centre of the lives of ordinary Afghan people. Whether it is saying one's prayers five times a day, fasting in Ramadan or giving *zakat* – an Islamic contribution to the poor – few Muslim peoples in the world observe the rituals and the piety of Islam with such regularity and emotion as the Afghans. Islam has been the bedrock for the unity of Afghanistan's diverse and multi-ethnic peoples while jihad has frequently provided the principle mobilizing factor for Afghan nationalism, during the resistance against the British and the Russians.

Rich or poor, communist, king or Mujaheddin it makes little difference. When I met with the ageing ex-King Zahir Shah in Rome in 1988, he quietly interrupted the interview so he could go into the next room to pray. Communist ministers prayed in their offices. Mujaheddin warriors would break off from fighting to pray. Mullah Omar spends hours on his prayer mat, often doing much of his strategic thinking after his prayers. Ahmad Shah Masud leads breaks from directing a battle to pray and then goes into a deep spiritual silence as booming guns and wireless chatter fill the air.

But no Afghan can insist that the fellow Muslim standing next to him prays also. Traditionally Islam in Afghanistan has been immensely tolerant – to other Muslim sects, other religions and modern lifestyles. Afghan mullahs were never known to push Islam down people's throats and sectarianism was not a political issue until recently. Until 1992 Hindus, Sikhs and Jews played a significant role in the country's economy. Traditionally they controlled the money market in urban centres and when Afghan kings went to war they often borrowed money from them.

After 1992 the brutal civil war destroyed this age-old Afghan tolerance and consensus. The civil war has divided Islamic sects and ethnic groups in a way that before was unimaginable to ordinary Afghans. Masud's massacre of the Hazaras in Kabul in 1995, the Hazaras' massacre of the Taliban in Mazar in 1997 and the Taliban massacres of Hazaras and Uzbeks in 1998 has no precedent in Afghan history and perhaps has irreparably damaged the fabric of the country's national and religious soul. The Taliban's deliberate anti-Shia programme has denigrated Islam and the unity of the country as minority groups tried to flee the country en masse. For the first time in Afghanistan's history the unifying factor of Islam has become a lethal weapon in the hands of extremists, a force for division, fragmentation and enormous blood-letting.

Eighty per cent of Afghans belong to the Sunni Hanafi sect, the most liberal of the four Sunni schools of thought.[1] The minority sects were few and scattered along the fringes of the country. Shia Islam is predominant amongst the Hazaras in the Hazarajat, a handful of Pashtun tribes, a few Tajik clans and some Heratis. The Ismaelis, the followers of the Agha Khan, follow a branch of Shiism. They have always lived in the inaccessible north-east, contiguous to the Ismaeli communities in the Pamir mountains which today constitute eastern Tajikistan and Pakistan's northern areas. The Afghan Ismaeli leader Syed Nadir Shah Hussain, who died in 1971 was made head of the community by the Agha Khan. His sons have led the Ismaeli community since then, playing a prominent role in the anti-Taliban alliance. Hindus and Sikhs who arrived with the British as camp followers in the nineteenth century had mostly left the country by 1998 as had the Bukharan Jews although a few dozen remained.

The Sunni Hanafi creed is essentially non-hierarchial and decentralized, which has made it difficult for twentieth-century rulers to incorporate its religious leaders into strong centralized state systems. But for centuries this admirably suited the loose Afghan confederation. Traditional Islam in Afghanistan believed in minimum government, where state interference was as little and as far away as possible. Everyday decisions were carried out by the tribe and the community. Amongst the Pashtuns, village mullahs, although largely uneducated, ensured that the mosque was the centre of village life. Students or *Talibs* studied at the small *madrassas* that were scattered through the tribal areas. In medieval times Herat was the centre of Afghanistan's *madrassa* system but from the seventeenth century Afghan scholars travelled to Central Asia, Egypt and India to study at more renowned *madrassas* in order to join the ranks of the *ulema*.[2]

Islam was also deeply rooted in Afghanistan because Sharia law governed the legal process until 1925, when King Amanullah first began to introduce a civil legal code and the state took on the role of training *ulema* to become *Qazis*, Islamic judges. In 1946 a Sharia Faculty was set up in Kabul University which became the main centre for integrating the new civil code with the Sharia. This merging of the traditional with the modern was epitomized by Mohammed Musa Shafiq, the last Prime Minister under the monarchy, which was overthrown in 1973. Shafiq studied at a madrassa and at the Sharia Faculty in Kabul and then went on to take another degree from Columbia University in New York. When he was executed by the communists in 1979 his death was widely mourned.[3]

Thus it was not surprising that in 1979 the mullahs did not join the radical Islamic Mujaheddin parties, but the more traditional tribal-based parties such as Harakat Inquilabi-Islami headed by Maulana Mohammed Nabi Mohammedi and Hizb-e-Islami led by Maulvi Younis Khalis. Both men were maulvis who had studied for a time at the Haqqania *madrassa* in Pakistan and then established their own *madrassas* inside Afghanistan. After the Soviet invasion they set up loose organisations which were decentralized, unideological and non-hierarchical, but they rapidly lost out as the CIA–ISI arms pipeline supported the more radical Islamic parties.

Another moderating factor for Islam in Afghanistan was the enormous popularity of Sufism, the trend of mystical Islam, which originated in Central Asia and Persia. Sufi means 'wool' in Arabic and the name comes from the rough woollen coats worn by the early Sufi brethren. The Sufi orders or *Tariqah*, which means 'the way', was a medieval reaction against authority, intellectualism, the law and the mullah and thus immensely appealing for poor, powerless people. The Sufis build their faith on prayer, contemplation, dances, music and sessions of physical shaking or whirling in a permanent quest for truth. These rituals create an inner spiritual space within man that the outsider cannot penetrate. Seven centuries ago the famous Arab traveller Ibn Battuta described Sufism: 'The fundamental aim of the Sufi life was to pierce the veils of human sense which shut man off from the Divine and so to obtain communion and absorption into God.'[4]

The two main Sufi orders in Afghanistan of Naqshbandiyah and Qaderiyah played a major role in uniting the anti-Soviet resistance as they provided a network of associations and alliances outside the Mujaheddin parties and ethnic groups. Leaders of these orders were equally prominent. The Mujaddedi family were leaders of the Naqshbandiyah order and had been king makers in Kabul for centuries. In a brutal act, the communists killed 79 members of the Mujaddedi family in Kabul in January 1979 to eliminate potential rivals. Nevertheless one survivor, Sibghatullah Mujaddedi, set up his own resistance party in Peshawar, the Jabha-i Najat Milli Afghanistan, National Liberation Front of Afghanistan, and became a fierce critic of the radical Islamic parties. He was appointed President of the Afghan interim government in 1989 and then became the first Mujaheddin President of Afghanistan in 1992.

Pir Sayed Ahmad Gailani, the head of the Qaderiyah order and related to ex-King Zahir Shah through marriage, set up the Mahaz-e-Milli, National Islamic Front of Afghanistan, in Peshawar. Both leaders were supporters of Zahir Shah and remained the most moderate of all the Mujaheddin leaders. They were also sidelined by the CIA–ISI nexus and by Hikmetyar and Masud and later by the Taliban. They returned to politics in 1999 by setting up a new Peace and National Unity party that attempted to mediate between the Taliban and their opponents.

Before the Taliban, Islamic extremism had never flourished in Afghanistan. Within the Sunni tradition were the Wahabbis, followers of the strict and austere Wahabbi creed of Saudi Arabia. Begun by Abdul Wahab (1703–1792) as a movement to cleanse the Arab bedouin from the influence of Sufism, the spread of Wahabbism became a major plank in Saudi foreign policy after the oil boom in the 1970s. The Wahabbis first came to Central Asia in 1912, when a native of Medina, Sayed Shari Mohammed set up Wahabbi cells in Tashkent and the Ferghana valley. From here and from British India the creed travelled to Afghanistan where it had miniscule support before the war.

However, as Saudi arms and money flowed to Saudi-trained Wahabbi leaders amongst the Pashtuns, a small following emerged. In the early stages of the war, the Saudis sent an Afghan long settled in Saudi Arabia, Abdul Rasul Sayyaf, to set up a Wahabbi party, the Ittehad-e-Islami, Islamic Unity, in Peshawar. The Wahabbi Afghans who are also called Salafis, became active opponents of both the Sufi and the traditional tribal-based parties but they were unable to spread their message because they were immensely disliked by ordinary Afghans, who considered it a foreign creed. Arab Mujaheddin including Osama Bin Laden, who joined the jihad, won a small Pashtun following, largely due to the lavish funds and weapons at their disposal.

Thanks to the CIA–ISI arms pipeline, the engine of the jihad was the radical Islamic parties. Hikmetyar and Masud had both participated in an unsuccessful uprising against President Mohammed Daud in 1975. These Islamic radicals had then fled to Pakistan where they were patronized by Islamabad as a means to pressurize future Afghan governments. Thus when the Soviets invaded Afghanistan in 1979, Pakistan already had effective Islamic radicals under its control which could lead the jihad. President Zia ul Haq insisted that the bulk of CIA military aid was transferred to these parties, until Masud became independent and fiercely critical of Pakistani control.

These Islamic leaders were drawn from a new class of educated university students – Hikmetyar studied engineering at Kabul University, Masud studied at Kabul's French Lycée – who took their inspiration from the most radical and politicized Islamic party in Pakistan, the Jamaat-e-Islami. The Pakistani Jamaat in turn was inspired by the Ikhwan ul Muslimeen or the Muslim Brotherhood which was set up in Egypt in 1928 with the aim of bringing about an Islamic revolution and creating an Islamic state. The founder of the Ikhwan, Hasan al-Banna (1906–1949) was a major influence on Abul-Ala Maududdi (1903–1978), who founded the Pakistani Jamaat in 1941.

The old Ikhwan movements around the Muslim world wanted an Islamic revolution rather than a nationalist or communist revolution to overthrow colonialism. In opposition to the traditional mullahs these Islamicists refused to compromise with the indigenous neo-colonial elite and wanted radical political change, which would create a true Islamic society as constituted by the Prophet Mohammed in Mecca and Medina as well as deal with the challenges of the modern world. They rejected nationalism, ethnicity, tribal segmentation and feudal class structures in favour of a new Muslim internationalism which would reunite the Muslim world or Ummah.[5] To achieve this, parties like the Pakistani Jamaat and Hikmetyar's Hizb-e-Islami set up highly centralized modern parties organized along communist lines with a cell system, extreme secrecy, political indoctrination and military training.

The greatest weakness of the Ikhwan model of political Islam is its dependence on a single charismatic leader, an Amir, rather than a more democratically constituted organization to lead it. The obsession of radical Islam is not the creation of institutions, but the character and purity of its leader, his virtues and qualifications and whether his personality can emulate the personality of the Prophet Mohammed. Thus these movements pre-suppose the Islamic virtue of individuals, even though such virtue can only be logically acquired if a society is already truly Islamic.[6] Invariably, as was the case with Hikmetyar, this model allowed dictatorship to flourish.

Nevertheless these radical Islamicists, as compared to the Taliban, were relatively modern and forward-looking. They favoured women's education and participation in social life. They developed or tried to develop theories for an Islamic economy, banking system, foreign relations and a more equitable and just social system. However, the radical Islamicist discourse suffered from the same weaknesses and limitations as the Afghan Marxist did: as an all-inclusive ideology, they rejected rather than integrated the vastly different social, religious and ethnic identities that constituted Afghan society. Both the Afghan communists and Islamicists wanted to impose radical change on a traditional social structure by a revolution from the top. They wished to do away with tribalism and ethnicity by fiat, an impossible task, and were unwilling to accept the complex realities on the ground.

The Afghan Islamicists' political failure and their inability to produce reality-based theories of change is a widespread phenomenon in the Muslim world. The French scholar Olivier Roy has dubbed it 'the failure of political Islam'.[7] Muslim societies in the twentieth century have been divided between two contradictory structures. The clan, tribe and ethnic group on one hand and the state and religion on the other. It is the small group versus the larger faith or the tribe versus the *Ummah*, which has been the main focus of loyalty and commitment rather than the state.[8] Afghanistan's Islamicists failed to resolve this dichotomy.

The Taliban had set out as an Islamic reform movement. Throughout Muslim history, Islamic reform movements have transformed both the nature of belief and political and social life, as Muslim nomadic tribes destroyed other Muslim empires, transformed them, and then were themselves urbanized and later destroyed. This political change has always been made possible through the concept of jihad. Western thought, heavily influenced by the medieval Christian Crusades has always portrayed jihad as an Islamic war against unbelievers. But essentially jihad is the inner struggle of a Muslim to become a better human being, improve himself and help his community. Jihad is also a testing ground for obedience to God and implementing His commands on earth. 'Jihad is the inner struggle of moral discipline and commitment to Islam and political action.'[9]

Islam also sanctions rebellion against an unjust ruler, whether Muslim or not and jihad is the mobilizing mechanism to achieve change. Thus the life of the Prophet Mohammed has become the jihadi model of impeccable Muslim behaviour and political change as the Prophet himself rebelled, with deep religious and moral anger, against the corrupt Arab society he was living in. The Taliban were thus acting in the spirit of the Prophet's jihad when they attacked the rapacious warlords around them. Yet jihad does not sanction the killing of fellow Muslims on the basis of ethnicity or sect and it is this, the Taliban interpretation of jihad, which appalls the non-Pashtuns. While the Taliban claim they are fighting a jihad against corrupt, evil Muslims, the ethnic minorities see them as using Islam as a cover to exterminate non-Pashtuns.

The Taliban interpretation of Islam, jihad and social transformation was an anomaly in Afghanistan because the movement's rise echoed none of the leading Islamicist trends that had emerged through the anti-Soviet war. The Taliban were neither radical Islamicists inspired by the Ikhwan, nor mystical Sufis, nor traditionalists. They fitted nowhere in the Islamic spectrum of ideas and movements that had emerged in Afghanistan between 1979 and 1994. It could be said that the degeneration and collapse of legitimacy of all three trends (radical Islamicism, Sufism and traditionalism) into a naked, rapacious power struggle created the ideological vacuum which the Taliban were to fill. The Taliban represented nobody but themselves and they recognized no Islam except their own. But they did have an ideological base – an extreme form of Deobandism, which was being preached by Pakistani Islamic parties in Afghan refugee camps in Pakistan. The Deobandis, a branch of Sunni Hanafi Islam has had a history in Afghanistan, but the Taliban's interpretation of the creed has no parallel anywhere in the Muslim world.

The Deobandis arose in British India, not as a reactionary but a forward-looking movement that would reform and unite Muslim society as it struggled to live within the confines of a colonial state ruled by non-Muslims. Its main ideologues were Mohammed Qasim Nanautawi (1833–77) and Rashid Ahmed Gangohi (1829–1905), who founded the first *madrassa* in Deoband near New Dehli. The Indian Mutiny of 1857 was a watershed for Indian Muslims, who had led the anti-British revolt and had been severely defeated. In the aftermath of the Mutiny several philosophical and religious trends emerged amongst Indian Muslims in a bid to revive their standing. They ranged from the Deobandis to pro-Western reformers who set up colleges such as the Aligarh Muslim University based on the British model which would teach Islam and the liberal arts and sciences, so Muslim youth could catch up with their British rulers and compete with the growing Hindu elite.

All these reformers saw education as the key to creating a new, modern Muslim. The Deobandis aimed to train a new generation of learned Muslims who would revive Islamic values based on intellectual learning, spiritual experience, Sharia law and Tariqah or the path. By teaching their students how to interprate Sharia, they aimed to harmonize the classical Sharia texts with current realities. The Deobandis took a restrictive view of the role of women, opposed all forms of hierarchy in the Muslim community and rejected the Shia – but the Taliban were to take these beliefs to an extreme which the original Deobandis would never have recognized. The Deobandis set up *madrassas* all over India and Afghan students, themselves searching for a better understanding of how Islam could cope with colonialism, arrived to study. By 1879 there were 12 Deobandi *madrassas* across India and Afghan students were plentiful, although they were described as 'rowdy and quick tempered'.[10] By 1967 when Deoband celebrated its first centenary, there were 9,000 Deobandi *madrassas* across South Asia.

In the early twentieth century, the Afghan government sought co-operation with Deoband to expand its own attempt to build modern, state controlled madrassas. *Ulema* from the Deoband *madrassa* visited Kabul in 1933 for King Zahir Shah's coronation and said that Deoband would, 'prepare such *ulema* in the changed circumstances of the period that they may co-operate fully with the aim and purpose of the free governments in the world of Islam and prove sincere workers for the state'.[11] A few Deobandi *madrassas* were established by the Afghan state, but they were not hugely popular even in the Pashtun belt.

Deobandi *madrassas* developed much faster in Pakistan after its creation in 1947. The Deobandis set up the JUI, a purely religious movement to propagate their beliefs and mobilize the community of believers. In 1962 its leader in the North West Frontier Province NWFP, Maulana Ghulam Ghaus Hazarvi turned the JUI into a political party, as a result of which it quickly split into several factions. Maulana Mufti Mehmood, a dynamic leader, took over the Pashtun faction of the JUI in the NWFP and remoulded it in a populist form. Mufti Mehmood's JUI played a leading role in the 1970 elections mobilizing support against military rule. He propagated a 22-point Islamic agenda, which included a progressive social programme and a strong anti-American, anti-imperialist stance. The JUI campaign was marked by a bitter feud with the Jamaat-e-Islami and the rift between the two largest Islamic parties persists to this day.[12]

The history of the JUI in Pakistan is not relevant here, but the Deobandi creed was to become the primary religious and ideological influence on the Taliban. During the 1980s Pakistan's Afghan policy was conducted with the help of the Jamaat-e-Islami and Hikmetyar's Hizb-e-Islami, who were also the main rivals of the JUI inside Pakistan. The ISI's connection with the Jamaat-e-Islami was an important policy instrument in the distribution of aid to the Mujaheddin. The JUI, which was now run by Mufti Mehmood's son, Maulana Fazlur Rehman, was given no political role and the small pro-Deobandi Afghan Mujaheddin groups were largely ignored.

However, the JUI used this period to set up hundreds of *madrassas* along the Pashtun belt in the NWFP and Baluchistan where it offered young Pakistanis and Afghan refugees the chance of a free education, food, shelter and military training. These *madrassas* were to train a new generation of Afghans for the post-Soviet period. Even though the Deobandis received no political support, the military regime of President Zia ul Haq funded *madrassas* of all sectarian persuasions. In 1971 there were only 900 *madrassas* in Pakistan, but by the end of the Zia era in 1988 there were 8,000 *madrassas* and 25,000 unregistered ones, educating over half a million students. As Pakistan's state-run educational system steadily collapsed, these *madrassas* became the only avenue for boys from poor families to receive the semblance of an education.[13]

Most of these *madrassas* were in rural areas and Afghan refugee camps and were run by semi-educated mullahs who were far removed from the original reformist agenda of the Deobandi school. Their interpretation of

Sharia was heavily influenced by Pashtunwali, the tribal code of the Pashtuns, while funds from Saudi Arabia to *madrassas* and parties which were sympathetic to the Wahabbi creed, as the Deobandis were, helped these *madrassas* turn out young militants who were deeply cynical of those who had fought the jihad against the Soviets. After the 1992 capture of Kabul by the Mujaheddin, the ISI continued to ignore the JUI's growing influence over the southern Pashtuns. The JUI was politically isolated at home, remaining in opposition to the first Benazir Bhutto government (1988–90) and the first Nawaz Sharif government (1990–93).

However in the 1993 elections the JUI allied itself with the winning Pakistan People's Party (PPP) led by Benazir Bhutto, thus becoming a part of the ruling coalition.[14] The JUI's access to the corridors of power for the first time allowed it to establish close links with the army, the ISI and the Interior Ministry under retired General Naseerullah Babar. Babar was in search of a new Pashtun group which could revive Pashtun fortunes in Afghanistan and give access to Pakistani trade with Central Asia through southern Afghanistan and the JUI offered him that opportunity. The JUI leader Maulana Fazlur Rehman was made Chairman of the National Assembly's Standing Committee for Foreign Affairs, a position that enabled him to have influence on foreign policy for the first time. He was to use his position to visit Washington and European capitals to lobby for the Taliban and Saudi Arabia and the Gulf states to enlist their financial support.

With no centralized hierarchy nor the ability of any locally renowned or learned mullah to start a *madrassa*, the Deobandi tradition resulted in dozens of breakaway, extremist factions emerging out of the mainstream JUI. The most important breakaway faction of the JUI is led by Maulana Samiul Haq, a religious and political leader who has been a Member of the National Assembly and a Senator and whose *madrassa* became a major training ground for the Taliban leadership. In 1999 at least eight Taliban cabinet ministers in Kabul were graduates of Haq's Dar-ul-Uloom Haqqania and dozens more graduates served as Taliban governors in the provinces, military commanders, judges and bureaucrats.[15] Younis Khalis and Mohammed Nabi Mohammedi, leaders of the traditional Mujaheddin parties, both studied at Haqqania.

Haqqania is in Akhora Khatak, in the NWFP. It is a sprawling collection of buildings on the main Islamabad-Peshawar highway. It has a boarding school for 1,500 students, a high school for 1,000 day students and 12 affiliated smaller *madrassas*. It was started in 1947 by Samiul Haq's father Maulana Abdul Haq who was a student and teacher at Deoband. Haqqania offers an eight-year Master of Arts course in Islamic studies and a PhD after an additional two years of study. Funded by public donations it charges its students nothing.

In February 1999, the *madrassa* had a staggering 15,000 applicants for some 400 new places making it the most popular *madrassa* in northern Pakistan. Samiul Haq, a jovial but pious man with a tremendous sense of humour and a flowing red hennaed beard told me that his *madrassa* has always kept some 400 places for Afghan students. Since 1991 60 students are accepted from Tajikistan, Uzbekistan and Kazakhstan who tend to belong to the Islamic opposition in these countries and enter Pakistan without passports or visas.

Haq is still bitter about how he was ignored by the ISI for so long. 'The ISI always supported Hikmetyar and Qazi Hussain Ahmed [leader of the Jamaat-e-Islami] while we were ignored, even though 80 per cent of the commanders fighting the Russians in the Pashtun areas had studied at Haqqania,' he told me as we sat on a rough carpet in his office surrounded by bearded students holding application forms for the class of '99.[16] 'Hikmetyar had 5 per cent of the popular support but 90 per cent of the military aid from the ISI. We were never recognized but, with the arrival of the Taliban, the support of the people of Afghanistan fell into our lap,' he added with a big laugh.

'Before 1994 I did not know Mullah Omar because he had not studied in Pakistan, but those around him were all Haqqania students and came to see me frequently to discuss what to do. I advised them not to set up a party because the ISI was still trying to play one Mujaheddin party against the other in order to keep them divided. I told them to start a student movement. When the Taliban movement began I told the ISI, "let the students take over Afghanistan," ' Haq said. Samiul Haq has deep respect for Mullah Omar. 'I met Omar for the first time when I went to Kandahar in 1996 and I was proud that he was chosen as Amir-ul Momineen. He has no money, tribe or pedigree but he is revered above all others and so Allah chose him to be their leader. According to Islam the man who can bring peace can be elected the Amir. When the Islamic revolution comes to Pakistan it will not be led by the old defunct leaders like me, but by a similiar unknown man who will arise from the masses.'

Samiul Haq is in constant touch with Omar, helps him deal with international relations and offers advice on important Sharia decisions. He is also the principle organizer for recruiting Pakistani students to fight for the Taliban. After the Taliban defeat in Mazar in 1997 he received a telephone call from Omar asking for help. Haq shut down his *madrassa* and sent his entire student body to fight alongside the Taliban. And after the battle for Mazar in 1988, Haq organized a meeting between Taliban leaders and 12 *madrassas* in the NWFP to organize reinforcements for the Taliban army. All the *madrassas* agreed to shut down for one month and send 8,000 students to Afghanistan. The help the Taliban receive from Pakistan's Deobandi *madrassas* is an important level of support they can rely upon, quite apart from the government and the intelligence agencies.

Another JUI faction runs the Jamiat-ul Uloomi Islamiyyah in Binori town, a surburb of Karachi. It was established by the late Maulvi Mohammed Yousuf Binori and has 8,000 students including hundreds of Afghans. Several Taliban ministers have studied there. It also operates with the help of donations from Muslims in 45 countries. 'The funding we get is a blessing from Allah,' said Mufti Jamil, a teacher. 'We are proud that we teach the Taliban and we always pray for their success as they have managed to implement strict Islamic laws,' he added.[17] Binori sent 600 students to join the Taliban in 1997. In November 1997 students from Binori went on a rampage in Karachi after three of their teachers were assasinated. They fought the police and smashed vehicles, video shops and beat up photographers. It was the first time that Pakistan's largest and most cosmopolitan city had experienced Taliban-style unrest.

Another extreme splinter faction of the JUI is the Sipah-e-Sahaba Pakistan (SSP), the most virulent anti-Shia group in Pakistan which is supported by the Taliban. When the government launched a crackdown against the SSP in 1998 after hundreds of Shia had been massacred by the SSP, their leaders fled to Kabul where they were offered sanctuary. Hundreds of SSP militants have trained at the Khost training camp run by the Taliban and Bin Laden, which the US hit with cruise missiles in 1998 and thousands of SSP members have fought alongside the Taliban.

The JUI were to benefit immensely from their Taliban protégés. For the first time, the JUI developed international prestige and influence as a major patron of Islamic radicalism. Pakistani governments and the ISI could no longer ignore the party, nor could Saudi Arabia and the Arab Gulf states. Camps inside Afghanistan which were used for military training and refuge for non-Afghan Mujaheddin, and which had earlier been run by Hikmetyar, were taken over by the Taliban and handed over to JUI groups such as the SSP. In 1996 the Tailiban handed over Camp Badr near Khost on the Pakistan–Afghanistan border to the Harkat-ul-Ansar led by Fazlur Rehman Khalil. This was another JUI splinter group, known for its extreme militancy which had sent members to fight in Afghanistan, Kashmir, Chechnya and Bosnia.[18] The camp was attacked by US cruise missile two years later.

The links between the Taliban and some of the extreme Pakistani Deobandi groups are solid because of the common ground they share. Several Deobandi leaders from both sides of the border originate from the Durrani Pashtun tribes based around Kandahar and Chaman in Pakistan. The Deobandi tradition is opposed to tribal and feudal structures, from which stems the Taliban's mistrust of the tribal structure and the clan chiefs and whom the Taliban have eliminated from any leadership role. Both are united in their vehement opposition to the Shia sect and Iran.

Now, Pakistani Deobandis want a Taliban-style Islamic revolution in Pakistan.

The Taliban have clearly debased the Deobandi tradition of learning and reform, with their ridigity, accepting no concept of doubt except as sin and considering debate as little more than heresy. But in doing so they have advanced a new, radical and, to the governments of the region extremely threatening, model for any forthcoming Islamic revolution. Hikmetyar and Masud are not opposed to modernism. In contrast, the Taliban are vehemently opposed to modernism and have no desire to understand or adopt modern ideas of progress or economic development.

The Taliban are poorly tutored in Islamic and Afghan history, knowledge of the Sharia and the Koran and the political and theoretical developments in the Muslim world during the twentieth century. While Islamic radicalism in the twentieth century has a long history of scholarly writing and debate, the Taliban have no such historical perspective or tradition. There is no Taliban Islamic manifesto or scholarly analysis of Islamic or Afghan history. Their exposure to the radical Islamic debate around the world is minimal, their sense of their own history is even less. This has created an obscurantism which allows no room for debate even with fellow Muslims.

The Taliban's new model for a purist Islamic revolution has created immense repercussions, in Pakistan and to a more limited extent in the Central Asian Republics. Pakistan, an already fragile state beset by an identity crisis, an economic meltdown, ethnic and sectarian divisions and a rapacious ruling elite that has been unable to provide good governance, now faces the spectre of a new Islamic wave, led not by the older, more mature and accommodating Islamic parties but by neo-Taliban groups.

By 1998, Pakistani Taliban groups were banning TV and videos in towns along the Pashtun belt, imposing Sharia punishments such as stoning and amputation in defiance of the legal system, killing Pakistani Shia and forcing people, particularly women to adapt to the Taliban dress code and way of life. Pakistan's support for the Taliban is thus coming back to haunt the country itself, even as Pakistani leaders appear to be oblivious of the challenge and continue to support the Taliban. In Central Asia, particularly Tajikistan and Uzbekistan, neo-Taliban militants are being hunted by the police in the Ferghana valley, which borders both countries.

The Taliban and their supporters present the Muslim world and the West with a new style of Islamic extremism, which rejects all accommodation with Muslim moderation and the West. The Taliban's refusal to compromise with the UN humanitarian agencies or foreign donor countries or to compromise their principles in exchange for international recognition and their rejection of all Muslim ruling elites as corrupt, has inflamed the debate in the Muslim world and inspired a younger generation of Islamic militants. The Taliban have given Islamic fundamentalism a new face and a new identity for the next millenium – one that refuses to accept any compromise or political system except their own.

~7~

SECRET SOCIETY: THE TALIBAN'S POLITICAL AND MILITARY ORGANIZATION

If there was a single inspiration and hope for peace amongst ordinary Afghans after the Taliban emerged, it was the fact that they governed through a collective political leadership, which was consultative and consensus-building, rather than dominated by one individual. The Taliban Shura in Kandahar claimed it was following the early Islamic model where discussion was followed by a consensus amongst 'the believers' and sensitivity and accessibility to the public were deemed important. The Shura model was also heavily based on the Pashtun tribal *jirga* or council where all clan chiefs took part in deciding upon important issues which the tribe faced. On my early visits to Kandahar, I was impressed with the debates, which sometimes went on all night as commanders, mullahs and ordinary fighters were called in to give their views, before Mullah Omar took a decision.

Many Afghans were also impressed by the fact that initially the Taliban did not demand power for themselves. Instead they insisted they were restoring law and order, only to hand over power to a government which was made up of 'good Muslims'. However, between 1994 and the capture of Kabul in 1996, the Taliban's decision-making process was to change and become highly centralized, secretive, dictatorial and inaccessible.

As Mullah Omar became more powerful and introverted, declining to travel to see and understand the rest of the country and meet the people under his control, the movement's power structure developed all the faults of the Mujaheddin and communist predecessors. Moreover after 1996, the Taliban made known their desire to become the sole rulers of Afghanistan without the participation of other groups. They maintained that the ethnic diversity of the country was sufficiently represented in the Taliban movement itself and they set out to conquer the rest of the country to prove it.

The initial hopes generated by the Taliban were a direct result of the degeneration of the former Mujaheddin leadership. During the jihad, the Mujaheddin leadership based in Peshawar was highly factionalized and personalised. The parties were held together by charismatic leaders and warlords rather than an organisation. As the war progressed these leaders became more and more dependent on Western supplied funds and arms to keep their field commanders and guerrilla fighters loyal. They spent much of their time literally buying support inside Afghanistan, while bickering with each other in Peshawar.

Pakistan only helped fuel this process of disunity. General Zia ul Haq had commanded Pakistani troops in Jordan in 1970 and had helped King Hussein crush the Palestinians. He had seen at first hand the threat that a united guerrilla movement posed to the state where it had been given sanctuary. By maintaining a disunited movement with no single leader, Zia was able to keep the Mujaheddin leaders obligated to Pakistan and Western largesse. But when Islamabad desperately needed a coherent Mujaheddin leadership to present a political alternative to the communist regime in Kabul in 1989 as Soviet troops withdrew, and again in 1992 as the Najibullah regime collapsed, the disunity amongst the Peshawar-based Mujaheddin leaders was too far gone to mend – even with significant bribes. This disunity was to have a profound effect on Afghanistan's future inability to achieve a consensus government.

The second element in the anti-Soviet resistance leadership were the field commanders, who became increasingly frustrated by the disunity and corruption of the Peshawar leaders and the ease with which they were held hostage over funds and weapons supplies. The very nature and hardship of the war demanded that they cooperate with each other, despite the feuding of their party chiefs in Peshawar.

There was a passionate desire for greater structural unity amongst the field commanders. Ismael Khan organized the first meeting of field commanders in Ghor province in July 1987, which was attended by some 1,200 commanders from across Afghanistan. They adopted 20 resolutions of which the most important was the demand that they, rather than the Peshawar leaders, dictate the political movement. 'The right of determining the future destiny of Afghanistan lies with the heirs of the martyrs and with the Muslims of the trenches, who are struggling in bloody fronts and are ready to be martyred. Nobody else is allowed to make decisions determining the fate of the nation.'[1]

Some 300 commanders met again in Paktia province in July 1990 and in Badakhshan in October. However, ethnicity, personal rivalries and the urge to be the first into Kabul broke down their consensus as the Mujaheddin competed to seize the capital in 1992. The battle for Kabul brought the divisions between north and south and Pashtuns and non-Pashtuns into the open. Ahmad Shah Masud's inability to compromise with Pashtun commanders opposed to Hikmetyar, even as Masud seized Kabul in 1992, badly dented his political reputation. He was never to regain the trust of Pashtuns, until after the Taliban had conquered the north in 1998.

A third level of leadership within the resistance were the scholars, intellectuals, businessmen and technocrats who had escaped from Kabul to Peshawar. Many remained independent advocating unity amongst all the resistance forces. But this group of educated Afghans was never given a serious political role by the Peshawar parties nor by Pakistan. As a consequence many left Peshawar for foreign countries, adding to the diaspora of Afghan professionals. They became marginal in influencing political events at home and when they were needed after 1992 to help rebuild the country, they were not available.[2] The Pashtun *ulema* and *madrassa* teachers were scattered throughout the resistance movement, some as party leaders in Peshawar, others as field commanders, but they formed no united, powerful presence within the resistance and even their individual influence had waned considerably by 1992. The *ulema* were ripe to be taken over by a Taliban style movement.

When the Taliban emerged in 1994 only the old, bickering resistance leadership was left and President Burhanuddin Rabbani had failed to unite them. In the Pashtun areas there was a total vacuum of leadership as warlordism gripped the south. The Taliban rightly considered the former Mujaheddin leaders as redundant and corrupt. Although the Taliban revered some leaders from the *ulema* who were their earlier mentors, they gave them no political role in their movement. Nor did the Taliban have any liking for the independent-minded field commanders, whom they blamed for the debacle of the Pashtuns after 1992. Important field commanders who surrendered to the Taliban were never elevated within the Taliban military structure. The Taliban also completely rejected Afghan intellectuals and technocrats, as they considered them the spawn of a Western or Soviet-style educational system which they detested.

The Taliban's emergence thus coincided with a fortunate historical juxtaposition, where the disintegration of the communist power structure was complete, the Mujaheddin leaders were discredited and the traditional tribal leadership had been eliminated. It was relatively easy for the Taliban to sweep away what little of the old Pashtun leadership was left. Thereafter, from within the Pashtuns, the Taliban faced no possible political challenges to their rule. They now had the opportunity to build a more tribal-democratic, grass-roots organisation. Imbued with the legitimizing factor of Islam, it could have responded to the population's needs, but the Taliban proved incapable and unwilling to do this.

At the same time, they refused to evolve a mechanism by which they could include the representatives of the non-Pashtun ethnic groups. Their supreme position in the Pashtun areas could not be duplicated in the north unless they had the flexibility to unite the complex mosaic of the Afghan nation under a new style of collective leadership. Instead, what the Taliban ultimately created was a secret society run mainly by Kandaharis and as mysterious, secretive and dictatorial in its ways as the Khmer Rouge of Cambodia or Saddam Hussein's Iraq.

The Taliban's apex decision-making body was the Supreme Shura which continued to be based in Kandahar, a city which Mullah Omar has left only once (to visit Kabul in 1996) and which he turned into the new power centre for Afghanistan. The Shura was dominated by Omar's original friends and colleagues, mainly Durrani Pashtuns, who came to be called the 'Kandaharis', even though they hailed from the three provinces of Kandahar, Helmand and Urozgan. The original Shura was made up of ten members, (see Appendix 2) but military commanders, tribal elders and *ulema* took part in Shura meetings so that it remained loose and amorphous with as many as 50 people often taking part.

Of the ten original Shura members, six were Durrani Pashtuns and only one, Maulvi Sayed Ghiasuddin, was a Tajik from Badakhshan (he had lived for a long time within the Pashtun belt). This was sufficient as long as the Taliban were advancing in the Pashtun belt but after the capture of Herat and Kabul, the Shura became totally unrepresentative. The Kandahar Shura never broadened its base sufficiently to include Ghilzai Pashtuns or non-Pashtuns. It has remained narrowly based and narrowly focused, unable to represent the interests of the entire nation.

Two other Shuras report to the Kandahar Shura. The first is the cabinet of acting ministers in Kabul or the Kabul Shura. The second is the military council or military Shura. Out of 17 members in the Kabul Shura in 1998, at least eight were Durranis while three are Ghilzais and only two were non-Pashtuns (see Appendix 2). The Kabul Shura deals with the day-to-day problems of the government, the city and the Kabul military front, but important decisions are conveyed to the Kandahar Shura where decisions are actually taken. Even minor decisions taken by the Kabul Shura and its chief Mullah Mohammed Rabbani, such as permission for journalists to travel or new UN aid projcts, have been frequently revoked by the Kandahar Shura. It soon became impossible for the Kabul Shura, which acted as the government of Afghanistan, to take any decision without lengthy consultations with Kandahar, delaying decisions interminably.

In Kabul and Herat and later in Mazar – none of which have a Pashtun majority – the Taliban's representatives such as the governor, mayor, police chiefs and other senior administrators are invariably Kandahari Pashtuns who either do not speak Dari, the lingua franca of these cities or speak it poorly. There is no prominent local citizen in any of these local Shuras. The only flexibility the Taliban have demonstrated is in their appointments of governors to the provinces. Of 11 governors in 1998, only four were known to be Kandaharis.[3] In the past the governors and senior local officials were usually drawn from the local elite, reflecting the local ethnic make-up of the population. The Taliban broke with this tradition and appointed outsiders.

However, the political powers of the Taliban governors have been considerably reduced. The paucity of funds at their disposal, their inability to carry out serious economic development or rehabilitate refugees returning from Pakistan and Iran gave governors even less of a political, economic or social role. Mullah Omar has also kept the governors under control and not allowed them to build up a local power base. He has constantly shifted them around and sent them back to the battle front as commanders.

After the Mazar defeat in 1997 there was growing criticism from Ghilzai Pashtun commanders that they were not being consulted on military and political issues, despite the fact that they now provided the bulk of the military manpower. In Mazar the Taliban lost some 3,000 of their best troops, 3,600 were taken prisoner and ten leaders were killed or captured. Thus the Taliban were forced to draw upon new recruits from the Ghilzai tribes of eastern Afghanistan but the Taliban were not prepared to yield them political power or include them in the Kandahar Shura. Increasingly the Ghilzais were not prepared to accept being used as cannon fodder by the Taliban and resisted recruitment.

The military structure of the Taliban is shrouded in even greater secrecy. The head of the armed forces is Mullah Omar although there is no actual definition of his position or his role. Under Omar there is a chief of general staff and then chiefs of staff for the army and air force. There are at least four army divisions and an armoured division based in Kabul. However, there is no clear military structure with a hierarchy of officers and commanders, while unit commanders are constantly being shifted around. For example, the Taliban's Kunduz expeditionary force, which was the only military group in the north after the 1997 Mazar debacle, saw at least three changes of command in three months, while more than half the troops were withdrawn and flown to the Herat front and replaced by less experienced Pakistani and Afghan fighters. The military Shura is a loose body which plans strategy and can implement tactical decisions, but appears to have no strategic decision-making powers. Military strategy, key appointments and the allocation of funds for offensives are decided upon by Omar.

Apart from the general conscription enforced by the Taliban, individual commanders from specific Pashtun areas are responsible for recruiting men, paying them and looking after their needs in the field. They acquire the resources to do so – money, fuel, food, transport, weapons and ammunition – from the military Shura. There is a constant coming and going as family members change places at the front, allowing soldiers to go home for long spells. The regular Taliban army has never numbered more than 25,000 to 30,000 men although these numbers could be rapidly increased before new offensives. At the same time Pakistani *madrassa* students, who by 1999 made up some 30 per cent of the Taliban's military manpower, also served for short periods before returning home and sending back fresh recruits. Nevertheless this haphazard style of enlistment, which contrasted sharply with Masud's 12,000 to 15,000 regular troops, does not allow for a regular or disciplined army to be created.

As such, the Taliban fighters resemble a *lashkar* or traditional tribal militia force, which has long historical antecedents amongst the Pashtun tribes. A *lashkar* has always been quickly mobilized either on orders of the monarch or to defend a tribal area and fight a local feud. Those who joined a *lashkar* were strictly volunteers who were not paid salaries, but shared in any loot captured from the enemy. However, Taliban troops were forbidden from looting and in the early period they were remarkably disciplined when they occupied new towns, although this broke down after the 1997 Mazar defeat.

The majority of Taliban fighters are not paid salaries and it is up to the commander to pay his men an adequate sum of money when they go on home leave. Those who are paid regular salaries are the professional and trained soldiers drawn from the former communist army. These Pashtun tank drivers, gunners, pilots and mechanics are fighting more as mercenaries, having served in the armies of whoever controls Kabul.

Several members of the military Shura are also acting ministers, creating even greater chaos in the Kabul administration. Thus Mullah Mohammed Abbas, the Health Minister, was the second-in-command of the Taliban expeditionary force trapped in the north after the 1997 Mazar defeat. He was then pulled out and sent to Herat to organize another offensive and finally returned to his job as Minister six months later – leaving UN aid agencies whom he was dealing with in consternation. Mullah Ehsanullah Ehsan, the Governor of the State Bank commanded an elite force of some 1,000 Kandaharis, ensuring his financial job received little attention before he was killed in Mazar in 1997. Mullah Abdul Razaq, the Governor of Herat who was captured in Mazar in 1997 and later freed, has been leading military offensives all over the country since 1994. Almost all the members of the Kandahar and Kabul Shura, except for those with physical disabilities, have acted as military commanders at some time or the other.

In one sense this allows for remarkable flexibility amongst the Taliban hierarchy as they all act both as administrators and generals and this keeps them in touch with their fighters. However, the Taliban administration, especially in Kabul, has suffered enormously. While a minister is away at the front no decisions can be taken in the ministry. The system ensured that no Taliban minister became proficient in his job or created a local power base through patronage. Mullah Omar would send any minister who was becoming too politically powerful back to the front at a moment's notice. But the result of this confusion was a country without a government and a movement without clearly defined leadership roles.

The Taliban's excessive secrecy has been a major deterrent in winning public confidence in the cities, the foreign media, aid agencies and the international community. Even after they captured Kabul, the Taliban declined issuing any agenda on how they intended to set up a representative government or foster economic development. For the Taliban to insist upon international recognition when there was no clearly demarcated government only increased the international community's doubts about their ability to govern. The spokesman of the Kabul Shura, Sher Mohammed Stanakzai, a relatively suave English-speaking Ghilzai Taliban from Logar province who had trained in India as a policeman, was the Taliban conduit for the UN aid agencies and the foreign media. However it quickly became apparent that Stanakzai had no real power and did not even have direct access to Mullah Omar in order to convey messages and receive an answer. As a consequence his job became meaningless as aid agencies never knew if their messages were even reaching Omar.

The Taliban increased the confusion by purging Kabul's bureaucracy, whose lower levels had remained in place since 1992. The Taliban replaced all senior Tajik, Uzbek and Hazara bureaucrats with Pashtuns, whether qualified or not. As a result of this loss of expertise, the ministries by and large ceased to function.

Within the ministries the Taliban's work ethic defied description. No matter how serious the military or political crisis, government offices in Kabul and Kandahar are open for only four hours a day, from 8.00 a.m. to noon. The Taliban then break for prayers and a long afternoon siesta. Later, they have long social gatherings or meetings at night. Ministers desks are empty of files and government offices are empty of the public. Thus while hundreds of Taliban cadres and bureaucrats were involved in a drive to force the male population to grow long beards, nobody was available to answer queries in the ministries. The public ceased to expect anything of the minstries while the lack of local representation in urban administrations made the Taliban appear as an occupying force, rather than administrators trying to win hearts and minds.

The Taliban have to date given no indication as to how and when they would set up a more permanent representative government, whether they would have a constitution or not and how political power would be divided. Every Taliban leader has different views on the subject. 'The Taliban are willing to negotiate with the opposition, but on the one condition that no political parties take part in the discussions. Most of the Taliban have come from political parties and we know the conflict they create. Islam is against all political parties,' a minister told me. 'Eventually when we have peace people can select their own government, but first the opposition has to be disarmed,' said another minister. Others wanted an exclusive Taliban government.[4]

After 1996, power was entirely concentrated in the hands of Mullah Omar while the Kandahar Shura was consulted less and less. Mullah Omar's confidant Wakil made this apparent. 'Decisions are based on the advice of the Amir-ul Momineen. For us consultation is not necessary. We believe that this is in line with the Sharia. We abide by the Amir's view even if he alone takes this view. There will not be a head of state. Instead there will be an Amir-ul Momineen. Mullah Omar will be the highest authority and the government will not be able to implement any decision to which he does not agree. General elections are incompatible with Sharia and therefore we reject them.'[5]

To implement his decisions Mullah Omar relied less on the Kabul government and increasingly upon the Kandahari *ulema* and the religious police in Kabul. Maulvi Said Mohammed Pasanai, the Chief Justice of Kandahar's Islamic Supreme Court, who had taught Omar the basics of Sharia law during the jihad, became a key adviser to Omar. He claimed responsibility for ending lawlessness in the country through Islamic punishments. 'We have judges presiding over 13 High Courts in 13 provinces and everywhere there is peace and security for the people,' he told me in 1997.[6] Pasanai, who is in his 80s, said that he had handed out Islamic punishments for nearly half a century in local villages and guided the Mujaheddin in applying Sharia during the jihad.

The Kandahar Islamic Supreme Court became the most important court in the country because of its proximity to Omar. The Court appointed Islamic judges, *Qazis*, and Assistant Qazis in the provinces and once or twice a year assembled them all in Kandahar to discuss cases and the application of Sharia law. A parallel system exists in Kabul where the Justice Ministry and the Supreme Court of Afghanistan are based. The Kabul Supreme Court handles about 40 cases a week and comprises eight departments which deal with laws related to commerce, business, criminal and public law, but it clearly does not have the same powers as the Kandahar Supreme Court. According to Attorney General Maulvi Jalilullah Maulvizada, 'All the laws are being Islamicized. Those laws repugnant to Islam are being removed. It will take several years for us to go through all the old laws and change or remove them.'

The worsening economic situation and political alienation in Taliban-controlled areas along with the massive military losses they suffered, led to increasing internal divisions. In January 1997, the Taliban faced a revolt from within the Kandahar heartland over forced conscription. At least four Taliban recruiters were killed by villagers who refused to join the army. The Taliban were driven out from several villages around Kandahar after gunfights in which there were casualties on both sides.[7] Village elders said that their young men faced death if they joined the army. 'The Taliban had promised peace, instead they have given us nothing but war,' said one village elder.[8] In June, the Taliban executed 18 army deserters in Kandahar jail.[9] There were similar movements against conscription in Wardak and Paktia provinces. Forced conscription has increased the Taliban's unpopularity and forced them to draw more upon recruits from Pakistani madrassas and Afghan refugees settled there.

Meanwhile the simmering differences between the Shuras in Kandahar and Kabul escalated dramatically in April 1998 after the visit of the US envoy Bill Richardson to Kabul. Mullah Rabbani, the head of the Kabul Shura, agreed to implement Richardson's point agenda, but the next day the agreement was rejected by Mullah Omar from Kandahar. Rabbani went off on one of his periodic long leaves and there were rumours he was under arrest. In October 1998, the Taliban arrested over 60 people in Jalalabad, the largest city in eastern Afghanistan, claiming there was a coup attempt by ex-military officers loyal to General Shahnawaz Tanai, the Pashtun general who in 1990 had deserted Najibullah's army and joined the Mujaheddin. His Pashtun officers had supported the Taliban since 1994 and many served in the Taliban army.[10] In December the Taliban shot a student dead and wounded several others during a disturbance at the medical faculty of Nangarhar University in Jalalabad. Strikes and anti-Taliban protests took place in the city.

The growing discontent in Jalalabad appeared to be instigated by supporters of the more moderate Mullah Rabbani, who had built a political base in the city. Jalalabad's powerful traders who ran the smuggling trade from Pakistan also wanted a more liberal attitude from the Taliban. After the Jalalabad incidents Mullah Rabbani was once again recalled from Kabul to Kandahar and disappeared from view for several months. By 1998, the Kabul Shura was keen to moderate Taliban policies so that UN agencies could return to Afghanistan and greater international aid flow to the cities. Taliban leaders in the Kabul and Jalalabad Shuras were feeling the growing public discontent at rising prices, lack of food and the cut-back in humanitarian aid. However, Mullah Omar and the Kandahar leadership refused to allow an expansion of UN aid activities and eventually forced the UN to quit.

In the winter of 1998–99 there were several acts of looting and robbery by Taliban soldiers, reflecting the growing indiscipline caused by economic hardship. In the worst such incident in Kabul in January 1999, six Taliban soldiers had their right arms and left feet amputated for looting. The authorities then hung the amputated limbs from trees in the city centre where they could be seen by the public until they rotted. Although internal differences increased speculation about serious weakness within the Taliban, which could lead to an intra-Taliban civil war, Mullah Omar's exalted position and increased powers allowed him to keep total control of the movement.

Thus the Taliban, like the Mujaheddin before them, had resorted to one-man rule with no organizational mechanism to accommodate other ethnic groups or points of view. The struggle between moderate and hard-line Taliban went underground with no Taliban leader willing to contradict Omar or oppose him. Such a situation is more than likely to lead to an eventual explosion within the Taliban – an intra-Taliban civil war, which can only once again divide the Pashtuns and bring more suffering to the common people.

~8~

A VANISHED GENDER: WOMEN, CHILDREN AND TALIBAN CULTURE

Nobody ever wants to see the inside of Maulvi Qalamuddin's sparse office in the centre of Kabul. Half the population never will anyway, because the Maulvi does not allow women to even enter the building. A huge Pashtun tribesman with enormous feet and hands, a long thick nose, black eyes and a bushy black beard that touches his desk while he talks, Qalamuddin's physique and name generate fear across the city. As head of the Taliban's religious police, the stream of regulations he issues from this office has dramatically changed the lifestyle of Kabul's once easy-going population and forced Afghan women to disappear entirely from public view.

Maulvi Qalamuddin runs the Amar Bil Maroof Wa Nahi An al-Munkar, or the Department of the Promotion of Virtue and Prevention of Vice. He himself prefers the translation as Department of Religious Observances. In the streets, people just call the department's thousands of young zealots, who walk around with whips, long sticks and kalashnikovs, the religious police and even more derogatory names. The day I visited him for a rare interview in the summer of 1997, he had just issued new regulations which banned women from wearing high heels, making a noise with their shoes while they walked or wearing make-up. 'Stylish dress and decoration of women in hospitals is forbidden. Women are duty-bound to behave with dignity, to walk calmly and refrain from hitting their shoes on the ground, which makes noises,' the edict read. How the zealots could even see women's make-up or their shoes, considering that all women were now garbed in the head to toe *burkha* was mystifying (see Appendix 1).

The new edict formalized previous restrictions on disallowing women from working, but it now also banned them from working for Western humanitarian aid agencies, except in the medical sector. 'Women are not allowed to work in any field except the medical sector. Women working in the medical sector should not sit in the seat next to the driver. No Afghan woman has the right to be transported in the same car as foreigners,' the edict continued. Education for boys is also at a standstill in Kabul because most of the teachers are women, who now cannot work. An entire generation of Afghan children are growing up without any education. Thousands of educated families have fled Kabul for Pakistan simply beause their children can no longer receive an education.

I nervously asked Qalamuddin what justified the Taliban's ban on women from working and going to school. 'We will be blamed by our people if we don't educate women and we will provide education for them eventually, but for now we have serious problems,' he replied. Like so many mullahs and despite his size, he is surprisingly soft-spoken and I strained to catch his words. 'There are security problems. There are no provisions for separate transport, separate school buildings and facilities to educate women for the moment. Women must be completely segregated from men. And within us we have those men who cannot behave properly with women. We lost two million people in the war against the Soviets because we had no Sharia law. We fought for Sharia and now this is the organization that will implement it. I will implement it come what may,' Qalamuddin said emphatically.

When the Taliban first entered Kabul, the religious police beat men and women in public for not having long enough beards or not wearing the *burkha* properly. 'We advise our staff not to beat people on the streets. We only advise people how to behave according to the Sharia. For example, if a person is about to reverse his car into another car, then we just warn you not to reverse now,' Qalamuddin said with a broad grin on his face, obviously pleased with his modern metaphor.

The Department is modelled on a similar government organisation in Saudi Arabia and it has recruited thousands of young men, many of them with only a minimum *madrassa* education from Pakistan. The department is also the Taliban's most effective intelligence agency – a bizarre throwback to KHAD, the enormous intelligence agency run by the communist regime in the 1980s. KHAD, which later changed its name to WAD, employed 15,000 to 30,000 professional spies as well having 100,000 paid informers.[1] Qalamuddin admitted that he has thousands of informers in the army, government ministries, hospitals and Western aid agencies. 'Our staff all have experience in religious issues. And we are an independent organization and we don't take advice from the Justice Ministry or the Supreme Court as to what we should implement. We obey the orders of the Amir Mullah Mohammed Omar.'

Qalamuddin's edicts are broadcast regularly on Radio Shariat (formerly Radio Kabul) and cover every aspect of social behaviour for the population (see Appendix 1). One addresses public attendance at sports events, which the Taliban had initially banned. 'All onlookers, while encouraging the sportsmen, are asked to chant Allah-o-Akbar [God is Great] and refrain from clapping. In case the game coincides with prayer time, the game should be interrupted. Both the players and spectators should offer prayers in congregation,' said the edict. Kite-flying, once a favourite pastime in the spring for Kabulis, is still banned as are all sports for women.

For the Taliban anyone questioning these edicts, which have no validity in the Koran, is tantamount to questioning Islam itself, even though the Prophet Mohammed's first task was to emancipate women. 'The supreme, unmistakable test of Islam was the emancipation of women, first beginning to be proclaimed, then – more slowly – on the way to be achieved,' said Ferdinand Braudel.[2] But the Taliban did not allow even Muslim reporters to question these edicts or to discuss interpretations of the Koran. To foreign aid-workers they simply said, 'You are not Muslim so you have no right to discuss Islam.' The Taliban were right, their interpretation of Islam was right and everything else was wrong and an expression of human weakness and a lack of piety. 'The Constitution is the Sharia so we don't need a constitution. People love Islam and that is why they all support the Taliban and appreciate what we are doing,' said Attorney General Maulvi Jalilullah Maulvizada.[3]

However the plight of Afghan women and Afghan society as a whole began well before the Taliban arrived. Twenty years of continuous warfare has destroyed Afghan civil society, the clan community and family structure which provided an important cushion of relief in an otherwise harsh economic landscape. Afghanistan has one of the lowest rated indices for the human condition in the world. The infant mortality rate is 163 deaths per 1,000 births (18 per cent) the highest in the world which compares to an average of 70/1000 in other developing countries. A quarter of all children die before they reach their fifth birthday, compared to one tenth that number in developing countries.

A staggering 1,700 mothers out of 100,000 die giving birth. Life expectancy for men and women is just 43–44 years old, compared to 61 years for people in other developing countries. Only 29 per cent of the population has access to health and 12 per cent has access to safe water, compared to 80 per cent and 70 per cent respectively in developing states. Children die of simple, preventable diseases like measles and diarrhoea because there are no health facilities and no clean water.[4]

Illiteracy was a major problem before the Taliban appeared, affecting 90 per cent of girls and 60 per cent of boys. There were huge swathes of rural Afghanistan where schools had been destroyed in the war and not a single one remained. Thus the Taliban's gender policies only worsened an ongoing crisis. Within three months of the capture of Kabul, the Taliban closed 63 schools in the city affecting 103,000 girls, 148,000 boys and 11,200 teachers, of whom 7,800 were women.[5] They shut down Kabul University sending home some 10,000 students of which 4,000 were women. By December 1998, UNICEF reported that the country's educational system was in a state of total collapse with nine in ten girls and two in three boys not enrolled in school.[6]

The Afghan people's desperate plight was largely ignored by the outside world. Whereas in the 1980s the war in Afghanistan attracted attention and aid, the moment the Soviets withdrew their troops in 1989, Afghanistan dropped off the radar screen of world attention. The ever dwindling aid from wealthy donor countries, which did not even meet the minimum budgetary requirements of the humanitarian aid effort, became a scandal.

In 1996 the UN had requested US$124 million for its annual humanitarian aid programme to Afghanistan, but by the end of the year, it had only received US$65 million. In 1997 it asked for US$133 million and received only US$56 million or 42 per cent and the following year it asked for US$157 million but received only US$53 million or 34 per cent. By 1999 the UN had drastically scaled down its request to just US$113 million. In the words of scholar Barnett Rubin: 'If the situation in Afghanistan is ugly today, it is not because the people of Afghanistan are ugly. Afghanistan is not only the mirror of the Afghans: it is the mirror of the world. "If you do not like the image in the mirror do not break the mirror, break your face," says an old Persian proverb.'[7]

When Kabul's women looked at themselves in the mirror, even before the Taliban captured the city, they saw only despair. In 1996 I met Bibi Zohra in a tiny bakery in Kabul. She was a widow who led a group of young women who prepared *nan*, the unleavened baked bread every Afghan eats, for widows, orphans and disabled people. Some 400,000 people in Kabul depended on these bakeries funded by the WFP, which included 25,000 familes headed by war widows and 7,000 families headed by disabled men. Zohra's mud shack was pockmarked with shrapnel and bullet holes. It had first been destroyed by rockets fired by Gulbuddin Hikmetyar's forces in 1993, then shelled by the Taliban in 1995.

With six children and her parents to support she had donated part of the tiny plot of land where her house once stood to WFP for a bakery. 'Look at my face, don't you see the tragedy of our lives and our country marked all over it?' she said. 'Day by day the situation is worsening. We have become beggars dependent on the UN to survive. It is not the Afghan way. Women are exhausted, depressed and devastated. We are just waiting for peace, praying for peace every minute of the day.'

The plight of Bibi Zohra's children and other kids was even worse. At a playground set up by Save the Children in the battered, half-destroyed Microyan housing complex, rake-thin Afghan children played grimly on the newly installed swings. It was a playground littered with reminders of the war – discarded artillery shell cases, a destroyed tank with a gaping hole where the turret once was and trees lopped down by rocket fire. 'Women and children face the brunt of the conflict,' Save the Children's Director Sofie Elieussen told me. 'Women have to cope with no food and malnutrition for their children. Women suffer from hysteria, trauma and depression because they don't know when the next rocket attack will come. How can children relate to a mother's discipline or affection when they have seen adults killing each other and mothers are unable to provide for their basic needs? There is so much stress that the children don't even trust each other and parents have stopped communicating with their kids or even trying to explain what is going on,' said Elieussen.

A UNICEF survey of Kabul's children conducted by Dr Leila Gupta found that most children had witnessed extreme violence and did not expect to survive. Two-thirds of the children interviewed had seen somebody killed by a rocket and scattered corpses or body parts. More than 70 per cent had lost a family member and no longer trusted adults. 'They all suffer from flashbacks, nightmares and loneliness. Many said they felt their life was not worth living anymore,' said Dr Gupta. Every norm of family life had been destroyed in the war. When children cease to trust their parents or parents cannot provide security, children have no anchor in the real world.

Children were caught up in the war on a greater scale than in any other civil conflict in the world. All the warlords had used boy soldiers, some as young as 12 years old, and many were orphans with no hope of having a family, an education or a job except soldiering. The Taliban with their linkages to the Pakistani *madrassas* encouraged thousands of children to enlist and fight. Entire units were made up of kids as loaders for artillery batteries, ammunition carriers, guarding installations and as fighters. Significantly a major international effort in 1998 to limit the age of soldiers to 18, rather than the current minimum age of 15 met with resistance by the US, Pakistan, Iran and Afghanistan. A 1999 Amnesty International report said there were over 300,000 children under 18 enlisted as soldiers worldwide.[8] The plight of women and children would get much worse after the Taliban capture of Kabul.

Every Kabuli woman I met during 1995–96 – and reporters could then easily meet and talk to women on the street, in shops and offices – knew their precarious lives would only get worse if the Taliban captured Kabul. One such woman was Nasiba Gul, a striking 27-year-old single woman who aspired to be part of the modern world. A 1990 graduate of Kabul

University, she held down a good job with an NGO. Dressed in a long skirt and high heels, she rarely bothered to cover her face, throwing just a small scarf over her head when she travelled across the city. 'The Taliban just want to trample women into the dust. No woman, not even the poorest or most conservative wants the Taliban to rule Afghanistan,' said Nasiba. 'Islam says women are equal to men and respect should be given to women. But the Taliban's actions are turning people against even Islam,' she added. Nasiba's fears were justified, for when the Taliban captured Kabul, women disappeared from public view. Nasiba was forced to stop working and left for Pakistan.

The Taliban leaders were all from the poorest, most conservative and least literate southern Pashtun provinces of Afghanistan. In Mullah Omar's village women had always gone around fully veiled and no girl had ever gone to school because there were none. Omar and his colleagues transposed their own milieu, their own experience, or lack of it, with women, to the entire country and justified their policies through the Koran. For a time, some aid agencies claimed that this was the Afghan cultural tradition which had to be respected. But in a country so diverse in its ethnicity and levels of development, there was no universal standard of tradition or culture for women's role in society. Nor had any Afghan ruler before the Taliban ever insisted on such dress codes as compulsory beards for men and the *burkha*.

The rest of Afghanistan was not even remotely like the south. Afghan Pashtuns in the east, heavily influenced by Pakistani Pashtuns, were proud to send their girls to school and many continued to do so under the Taliban, by running village schools or sending their families to Pakistan. Here aid agencies such as the Swedish Committee supported some 600 primary schools with 150,000 students of whom 30,000 were girls. When Pashtun tribal elders demanded education for girls, Taliban governors did not and could not object.[9] In Afghan refugee camps in Pakistan tens of thousands of Pashtun girls studied. Outside the Pashtun belt, all other ethnic groups vigorously encouraged female education. Afghanistan's strength was its ethnic diversity and women had as many roles as there were tribes and nationalities.

Afghanistan's cities were even more diverse. Kandahar was always a conservative city but Herat's female elite once spoke French as a second language and copied the fashions of the Shah's court in Tehran. Forty per cent of Kabul's women worked, both under the communist regime and the post-1992 Mujaheddin government. Women with even a smattering of education and a job exchanged their traditional clothes for skirts, high heels and make-up. They went to the movies, played sports and danced and sang at weddings. Common sense alone should have dictated that to win hearts and minds, the Taliban would have to relax their gender policy according to the prevalent realities in the areas they took control of. Instead they viewed Kabul as a den of iniquity, a Sodom and Gomorrah where women had to be beaten into conforming with Taliban standards of behaviour. And they viewed the northerners as impure Muslims who had to be forcibly re-Islamicized.

The Taliban's uncompromising attitude was also shaped by their own internal political dynamic and the nature of their recruiting base. Their recruits – the orphans, the rootless, the lumpen proleteriat from the war and the refugee camps – had been bought up in a totally male society. In the *madrassa* milieu, control over women and their virtual exclusion was a powerful symbol of manhood and a reaffirmation of the students' commitment to jihad. Denying a role for women gave the Taliban a kind of false legitimacy amongst these elements. 'This conflict against women is rooted in the political beliefs and ideologies, not in Islam or the cultural norms. The Taliban are a new generation of Muslim males who are products of a war culture, who have spent much of their adult lives in complete segregation from their own communities. In Afghan society, women have traditionally been used as instruments to regulate social behaviour, and as such are powerful symbols in Afghan culture,' said Simi Wali, the head of an Afghan NGO.[10]

Taliban leaders repeatedly told me that if they gave women greater freedom or a chance to go to school, they would lose the support of their rank and file, who would be disillusioned by a leadership that had compromised principles under pressure. They also claimed their recruits would be weakened and subverted by the possibility of sexual opportunities and thus not fight with the same zeal. So the oppression of women became a benchmark for the Taliban's Islamic radicalism, their aim to 'cleanse' society and to keep the morale of their troops high. The gender issue became the main platform of the Taliban's resistance to UN and Western governments' attempts to make them compromise and moderate their policies. Compromise with the West would signal a defeat that they were wrong all along, defiance would signal victory.

Hardline Taliban turned the argument of the outside world on its head. They insisted that it was up to the West to moderate their position and accommodate the Taliban, rather than that the Taliban recognize universal human rights. 'Let us state what sort of education the UN wants. This is a big infidel policy which gives such obscene freedom to women which would lead to adultery and herald the destruction of Islam. In any Islamic country where adultery becomes common, that country is destroyed and enters the domination of the infidels because their men become like women and women cannot defend themselves. Anybody who talks to us should do so within Islam's framework. The Holy Koran cannot adjust itelf to other people's requirements, people should adjust themselves to the requirements of the Holy Koran,' said Attorney General Maulvi Jalil-ullah Maulvizada.[11] The Taliban could not explain how a deeply rooted religion like Islam could be so undermined at the hands of adulterers.

All tribal Pashtuns also followed Pashtunwali, a social code which gave the tribal *jirga* or council the right to make judgments on cases from a traditional pantheon of laws and punishments, especially when it came to disputes over ownership of land and women and murder. The line between Pashtunwali and Sharia law has always been blurred for the Pash-tuns. Taliban punishments were in fact drawn largely from Pashtunwali rather than the Sharia. But Pashtunwali was practised in varying degrees, to a lesser or greater extent across the Pashtun belt and it certainly did not govern the practices of other ethnic groups. The fact that the Taliban were determined to impose Pashtunwali–Sharia law on these ethnic groups by force only deepened the ethnic divide in the country. Non-Pashtuns saw this is an attempt to impose Kandahari Pashtun laws on the entire country.

There were no political conditions in which the Taliban were prepared to compromise. After every military defeat they tightened their gender policies ferociously, under the assumption that harsher measures against women would sustain morale amongst their defeated soldiers. And every victory led to another tightening because the newly conquered popula-tions had to be shown Taliban power. The policy of 'engagement' with the Taliban to moderate their policies, advocated by the international community, gave no dividends. And their insistence that they would allow women's education after the war was over became more and more meaningless. The capture of Herat in 1995 was the first indicator to Afghans and the outside world that the Taliban would not compromise on the gender issue. Herat, the heart of medieval Islam in the entire region, was a city of mosques and *madrassas*, but it had an ancient, liberal, Islamic tradition. It was the home of Islamic arts and crafts, miniature painting, music, dance, carpet-making and numerous stories about its redoubtable and beautiful women.

Heratis still recount the story of Queen Gowhar Shad, the daughter-in-law of the conquerer Taimur who moved the Timurid capital from Samar-kand to Herat in 1405 after Taimur's death. One day in the company of 200 'ruby-lipped', beautiful ladies-in-waiting, the Queen inspected a mosque and *madrassa* complex she was building on the outskirts of Herat. The *madrassa* students (or *taliban*) had been asked to vacate the premises while the Queen and her entourage visited, but one student had fallen asleep in his room. He was awoken by an exquisitely attractive lady-in-waiting. When she rejoined the Queen, the lady was panting and dishev-elled by the exertions of passionate love-making and thus she was disco-vered. Instead of punishing her or the student, the Queen ordered all her ladies-in-waiting to marry the students in a mass ceremony so as to bless them and ensure they avoided temptation in the future. She gave each student clothes and a salary and ordered that husband and wife should meet once a week as long as the students studied hard. It was the kind of story that epitomized the liberal, human tradition of Islam and *madrassa* education in Herat.

The Taliban had no knowledge of Herat's history or traditions. They arrived to drive Herati women indoors. People were barred from visiting the shrines of Sufi saints of which Herat had an abundance. The Taliban cancelled out years of effort by the Mujaheddin commander Ismael Khan to educate the population, by shutting down all girls' schools. Most boys' schools also closed as their teachers were women. They segregated the few functioning hospitals, shut down bathhouses and banned women from the bazaar. As a result Herati women were the first to rebel against Taliban excesses. On 17 October 1996 more than 100 women protested outside the office of the Governor against the closure of the city's bathhouses. The women were beaten and then arrested by the Taliban religious police, who went from house to house warning men to keep their women indoors.

The international media and the UN largely chose to ignore these events in Herat, but several Western NGOs realized the profound implications for their future activities. After a long internal debate and fruitless negotiations with the Taliban in Herat, UNICEF and Save the Children suspended their educational programmes in Herat because girls were excluded from them.[12] The suspension of these aid programmes did not deter the Taliban, who quickly realized that other UN agencies were not prepared to take a stand against them on the gender issue. Moreover they had succeeded in dividing the aid-giving community. UN policy was in a shambles because the UN agencies had failed to negotiate from a common platform. As each UN agency tried to cut its own deal with the Taliban, the UN compromised its principles, while Taliban restrictions on women only escalated. 'The UN is on a slippery slope. The UN thinks by making small compromises it can satisfy the international community and satisfy the Taliban. In fact it is doing neither,' the head of a European NGO told me.[13]

The world only woke up to the Taliban's gender policies after they captured Kabul in 1996. The UN could not avoid ignoring the issue after the massive international media coverage of the Taliban's hanging of former President Najibullah and the treatment of Kabul's women. Protest statements from world leaders such as UN Secretary General Boutros Boutros-Ghali, the heads of UNICEF, UNESCO, UNHCR and the European Commissioner for Human Rights met with no Taliban response.[14] Beauty, hair and make-up salons were shut down in Kabul, as were women's bathhouses – the only place where hot water was available.

Tailors were ordered not to measure women for clothes, but learned to keep the measurements of their regular customers in their heads. Fashion magazines were destroyed. 'Paint your nails, take a snapshot of a friend, blow a flute, clap to a beat, invite a foreigner over for tea and you have broken a Taliban edict,' wrote an American reporter.[15]

Until Kabul, the UN's disastrous lack of a policy had been ignored but then it became a scandal and the UN came in for scathing criticism from feminist groups. Finally the UN agencies were forced to draw up a common position. A statement spoke of 'maintaining and promoting the inherent equality and dignity of all people' and 'not discriminating between the sexes, races, ethnic groups or religions'.[16] But the same UN document also stated that 'international agencies hold local customs and cultures in high respect'. It was a classic UN compromise, which gave the Taliban the lever to continue stalling, by promising to allow female education after peace came. Nevertheless, by October 1996 the UN was forced to suspend eight income-generating projects for women in Kabul, because women were no longer allowed to work in them.

During the next 18 months, round after round of fruitless negotiations took place between the UN, NGOs, Western governments and the Taliban, by which time it became clear that a hardline lobby of Taliban *ulema* in Kandahar were determined to get rid of the UN entirely. The Taliban tightened the screws ever further. They closed down home schools for girls which had been allowed to continue and then prevented women from attending general hospitals. In May 1997 the religious police beat up five female staff of the US NGO Care International and then demanded that all aid projects receive clearance from not just the relevant ministry, but also from the Ministries of Interior, Public Health, Police and the Department of the Promotion of Virtue and Prevention of Vice. This was followed by a demand that all Muslim female humanitarian workers coming to Afghanistan be accompanied by a male relative. Finally in July 1997 the Taliban insisted that all 35 UN and NGO agencies move out of their offices to one pre-selected compound at the destroyed Polytechnic building. As the European Union suspended further humanitarian aid, the UN and the NGOs left Kabul.

The plight of Afghanistan's women often hid the fact that urban males did not fare much better under the Taliban, especially non-Pashtuns. All Kabul males were given just six weeks to grow a full beard, even though some of the ethnic groups such as the Hazaras have very limited beard growth. Beards could not be trimmed shorter than a man's fist, leading to jokes that Afghanistan's biggest import–export business was male facial hair and that men did not need visas to travel to Afghanistan, they just needed a beard. The religious police stood at street corners with scissors cutting off long hair and often beating culprits. Men had to wear their shalwars or baggy trousers above the ankle and everyone had to say their prayers five times a day.

The Taliban also clamped down on homosexuality. Kandahar's Pashtuns were notorious for their affairs with young boys and the rape of young boys by warlords was one of the key motives for Mullah Omar in mobilizing the Taliban. But homosexuality continued and the punishments were bizarre if not inhuman. Two soldiers caught indulging in homosexuality in Kabul in April 1998 were beaten mercilessly and then tied up and driven around Kabul in the back of a pick-up with their faces blackened by engine oil. Men accused of sodomy faced the previously unheard of 'Islamic' punishment of having a wall toppled over them.

In February 1998 three men sentenced to death for sodomy in Kandahar were taken to the base of a huge mud and brick wall, which was then toppled over them by a tank. They remained buried under the rubble for half an hour, but one managed to survive. 'His eminence the Amir-ul Momineen [Mullah Omar] attended the function to give Sharia punishment to the three buggerers in Kandahar,' wrote Anis, the Taliban newspaper.[17] In March 1998 two men were killed by the same method in Kabul. 'Our religious scholars are not agreed on the right kind of punishment for homosexuality,' said Mullah Mohammed Hassan, epitomizing the kind of debates the Taliban were preoccupied with. 'Some say we should take these sinners to a high roof and throw them down, while others say we should dig a hole beside a wall, bury them, then push the wall down on top of them.'[18]

The Taliban also banned every conceivable form of entertainment, which in a poor, deprived country such as Afghanistan was always in short supply anyway. Afghans were ardent movie-goers but movies, TV, videos, music and dancing were all banned. 'Of course we realize that people need some entertainment but they can go to the parks and see the flowers, and from this they will learn about Islam,' Mullah Mohammed Hassan told me. According to Education Minister Mullah Abdul Hanifi, the Taliban 'oppose music because it creates a strain in the mind and hampers study of Islam'.[19] Singing and dancing were banned at weddings which for centuries had been major social occasions from which hundreds of musicians and dancers made a living. Most of them fled to Pakistan.

Nobody was allowed to hang paintings, portraits or photographs in their homes. One of Afghanistan's foremost artists, Mohammed Mashal, aged 82, who was painting a huge mural showing 500 years of Herat's history was forced to watch as the Taliban whitewashed over it. Simply put, the Taliban did not recognize the very idea of culture. They banned Nawroz, the traditional Afghan New Year's celebrations as anti-Islamic. An ancient spring festival, Nawroz marks the first day of the Persian solar calendar when people visit the graves of their relatives. People were forcibly stopped from doing so. They banned Labour Day on 1 May for being a communist holiday, for a time they also banned Ashura, the Shia Islamic month of mourning and even restricted any show of festivity at Eid, the principle Muslim clelebration of the year.

Most Afghans felt demoralized by the fact that the Islamic world declined to take up the task of condemning the Taliban's extremism. Pakistan, Saudi Arabia and the Arab Gulf states have never issued a single statement on the need for women's education or human rights in Afghanistan. Nor did they ever question the Taliban's interpretation of Sharia. Asian Muslim countries were also silent. Surprisingly, Iran issued the toughest defence of women's rights under Islam. 'Through their fossilized policies the Taliban stop girls from attending school, stop women working out of their homes and all that in the name of Islam. What could be worse than committing violence, narrow-mindedess and limiting women's rights and defaming Islam,' said Ayatollah Ahmad Jannati, as early as 1996.[20] Iranian criticism of Taliban policies escalated dramatically after the deaths of their diplomats in Mazar in 1998.

In Mazar stands the Tomb of Rabia Balkhi, a beautiful, tragic medieval poetess. She was the first woman of her time to write love poetry in Persian and died tragically after her brother slashed her wrists as punishment for sleeping with a slave lover. She wrote her last poem in her own blood as she lay dying. For centuries young Uzbek girls and boys treated her tomb with saint-like devotion and would pray there for success in their love affairs. After the Taliban captured Mazar, they placed her tomb out of bounds. Love, even for a medieval saint, was now out of bounds.

~9~

HIGH ON HEROIN:
DRUGS AND THE
TALIBAN ECONOMY

Just two miles from Kandahar's city centre poppy fields stretch as far as the horizon. In the spring of 1997, farmers were carefully tending the young, green, lettuce-like leaves of the plants which had been planted a few weeks earlier. They meticulously hoed the soil to uproot weeds, sprinkled fertilizer and repaired irrigation ditches destroyed by the Soviet army in the 1980s to provide water to the fields. In a few weeks the leaves would sprout a bright red flower which would bloom until its petals fell away to reveal a hardened capsule.

Four months after sowing the poppy seeds, the capsules would be ready to be lanced with thin, home-made blades for their liquid gold. The farmer would squeeze each capsule with his fingers until a milky-white gooey substance oozed out. By the next day the opium would solidify into a brown gum which would be scraped off with a trowel. This operation would be repeated every few days until the plant stopped yielding any gum. The raw opium would be collected, slapped together in a cake and kept wet in plastic bags until the dealers arrived. The best quality opium, generally obtained from well-irrigated land, has a dark brown colour and sticky texture. It is called *tor*, the substance which lubricates the finances of all the Afghan warlords, but particularly the Taliban.[1]

'We cannot be more grateful to the Taliban,' said Wali Jan, a toothless, elderly farmer as he weeded his fields. 'The Taliban have brought us security so we can grow our poppy in peace. I need the poppy crop to support my 14 family members,' he added. The Taliban objective of re-establishing peace and security in the countryside has proved to be an immense boon to opium farming. On his small plot of land Wali Jan produces 45 kilograms of raw opium every year and earns about

US$1,300 – a small fortune for Afghan farmers. Wali Jan knows that refined heroin fetches 50 times that price in London or New York, but he is more than happy with what he gets. The results of this cash flow are evident everywhere, for there is more reconstruction going on in villages around Kandahar than anywhere else in Afghanistan.

The Taliban have provided an Islamic sanction for farmers like Wali Jan to grow even more opium, even though the Koran forbids Muslims from producing or imbibing intoxicants. Abdul Rashid, the head of the Taliban's anti-drugs control force in Kandahar, spelt out the nature of his unique job. He is authorised to impose a strict ban on the growing of hashish, 'because it is consumed by Afghans and Muslims'. But, Rashid tells me without a hint of sarcasm, 'Opium is permissable because it is consumed by kafirs [unbelievers] in the West and not by Muslims or Afghans.' There are other political imperatives for letting poppy farming flourish. 'We let people cultivate poppies because farmers get good prices. We cannot push the people to grow wheat as there would be an uprising against the Taliban if we forced them to stop poppy cultivation. So we grow opium and get our wheat from Pakistan,' he said.[2]

Governor Mohammed Hassan justifies this unique policy with another twist. 'Drugs are evil and we would like to substitute poppies with another cash crop, but it's not possible at the moment, because we do not have international recognition.' Over the next two years, Mullah Omar was to periodically offer the US and the UN an end to poppy cultivation, if the Taliban were given international recognition – the first time a movement controlling 90 per cent of a country had offered the international community such an option.

The Taliban had quickly realized the need to formalize the drugs economy in order to raise revenue. When they first captured Kandahar they had declared they would eliminate all drugs and US diplomats were encouraged enough by the announcement to make immediate contact with the Taliban. However, within a few months the Taliban realized that they needed the income from poppies and would anger farmers by banning it. They began to collect an Islamic tax called *zakat* on all dealers moving opium. According to the Koran, Muslims should give 2.5 per cent of their disposable income as *zakat* to the poor, but the Taliban had no religious qualms in collecting 20 per cent of the value of a truckload of opium as *zakat*. Alongside this, individual commanders and provincial governors imposed their own taxes to keep their coffers full and their soldiers fed. Some of them became substantial dealers in opium or used their relatives to act as middlemen.

Meanwhile the Taliban crackdown against hashish, a staple part of Afghan truck-drivers diets was extremely effective – demonstrating that any crackdown on opium could be just as strictly implemented. In two warehouses in Kandahar hundreds of sacks of hashish were stored after being confiscated from growers and dealers. Ordinary people said they were too scared to take hashish after the Taliban had forbidden it. For those who continued to do so clandestinely, the Taliban had devised a novel approach to curing hashish addiction. 'When we catch hashish smugglers or addicts we interrogate and beat them mercilessly to find out the truth,' said Abdul Rashid. 'Then we put them in cold water for many hours, two or three times a day. It's a very good cure,' he added.[3] Rashid then strode into the jail and pulled out several terrified prisoner-addicts to talk to me. They had no hesitation in agreeing that the Taliban's shock therapy was effective. 'When I am beaten or in the cold water I forget all about hashish,' said Bakht Mohammed, a shopkeeper and hashish dealer who was serving three months in jail.

Between 1992 and 1995 Afghanistan had produced a steady 2200–2400 metric tonnes of opium every year, rivalling Burma as the world's largest producer of raw opium. In 1996 Afghanistan produced 2,250 metric tonnes. Officials of the United Nations Drugs Control Programme (UNDCP) said that in 1996 Kandahar province alone produced 120 metric tonnes of opium harvested from 3,160 hectares of poppy fields – a staggering increase from 1995, when only 79 metric tonnes was produced from 2,460 hectares. Then, in 1997, as Taliban control extended to Kabul and furthur north, Afghanistan's opium production rose by a staggering 25 per cent to 2,800 metric tonnes. The tens of thousands of Pashtun refugees arriving in Taliban-controlled areas from Pakistan were farming their lands for the easiest and most lucrative cash crop available.

According to the UNDCP, farmers received less than 1 per cent of the total profits generated by the opium trade, another 2.5 per cent remained in Afghanistan and Pakistan in the hands of dealers, while 5 per cent was spent in the countries through which the heroin passed while en route to the West. The rest of the profits were made by the dealers and distributors in Europe and the US. Even with this low rate of return, it is conservatively estimated that some one million Afghan farmers are making over US$100 million dollars a year on account of growing poppies. The Taliban were thus raking in at least US$20 million in taxes and even more on the side.

Ever since 1980, all the Mujaheddin warlords had used drugs money to help fund their military campaigns and line their own pockets. They had bought houses and businesses in Peshawar, new jeeps and kept bank accounts abroad. Publicly they refused to admit that they indulged in drugs trafficking, but always blamed their Mujaheddin rivals for doing so. But none had ever been so brazen, or honest, in declaring their lack of intention to control drugs as the Taliban. By 1997, UNDCP and the US estimated that 96 per cent of Afghan heroin came from areas under Taliban control.

The Taliban had done more than just expand the area available for opium production. Their conquests had also expanded trade and transport routes significantly. Several times a month heavily armed convoys in Toyota landcruisers left Helmand province, where 50 per cent of Afghan opium is grown, for a long, dusty journey. Some convoys travelled south across the deserts of Baluchistan to ports on Pakistan's Makran coast, others entered western Iran, skirted Tehran and travelled on to eastern Turkey. Other convoys went north-west to Herat and Turkmenistan. By 1997 dealers began flying out opium on cargo planes from Kandahar and Jalalabad to Gulf ports such as Abu Dhabi and Sharjah.

Central Asia was the hardest hit by the explosion in Afghan heroin. The Russian mafia, with ties to Afghanistan established during the Soviet occupation, used their networks to move heroin through Central Asia, Russia, the Baltics and into Europe. Tajikistan and Kyrgyzstan developed important opium routes and became significant opiate producers themselves. Whereas previously Afghan opium would be refined in laboratories in Pakistan, a crackdown in Pakistan and the new diversification in routes encouraged dealers to set up their own laboratories inside Afghanistan. Acetic anhydride, a chemical necessary to convert opium into heroin was smuggled into Afghanistan via Central Asia.

The explosion in heroin production began ironically not in Afghanistan but in Pakistan. Pakistan had become a major opium producer during the 1980s producing around 800 metric tonnes a year or 70 per cent of the world's supply of heroin until 1989. An immense narcotics trade had developed under the legitimizing umbrella of the CIA–ISI covert supply line to the Afghan Mujaheddin. 'During the 1980s corruption, covert operations and narcotics became intertwined in a manner which makes it difficult to separate Pakistan's narcotics traffic from more complex questions of regional security and insurgent warfare,' said a landmark 1992 study on the failure of US narcotics policy.[4] As in Vietnam where the CIA chose to ignore the trade in drugs by anti-communist guerrillas whom the CIA was financing, so in Afghanistan the US chose to ignore the growing collusion between the Mujaheddin, Pakistani drugs traffickers and elements in the military.

Instances of this collusion that did come to light in the 1980s were only the tip of the iceberg. In 1983 the ISI Chief, General Akhtar Abdur Rehman had to remove the entire ISI staff in Quetta, because of their involvement with the drugs trade and sale of CIA supplied weapons that were meant for the Mujaheddin.[5] In 1986, Major Zahooruddin Afridi was caught while driving to Karachi from Peshawar with 220 kilograms of high-grade heroin – the largest drugs interception in Pakistan's history.

Two months later an airforce officer Flight Lieutenant Khalilur Rehman was caught on the same route with another 220 kilograms of heroin. He calmly confessed that it was his fifth mission. The US street value of just these two caches was US$600 million dollars, equivalent to the total amount of US aid to Pakistan that year. Both officers were held in Karachi until they mysteriously escaped from jail. 'The Afridi-Rehman cases pointed to a heroin syndicate within the army and the ISI linked to Afghanistan,' wrote Lawrence Lifschultz.[6]

The US Drugs Enforcement Administration (DEA) had 17 full-time officers in Pakistan during the 1980s, who identified 40 major heroin syndicates, including some headed by top government officials. Not a single syndicate was broken up during that decade. There was clearly a conflict of interest between the CIA which wanted no embarrassing disclosures about drug links between the 'heroic' Mujaheddin and Pakistani officials and traffickers and the DEA. Several DEA officials asked to be relocated and at least one resigned, because the CIA refused to allow them to carry out their duties.

During the jihad both the Mujaheddin and officers in the communist army in Kabul seized the opportunity. The logistics of their operations were remarkably simple. The donkey, camel and truck convoys which carried weapons into Afghanistan were coming back empty. Now they carried out raw opium. The CIA–ISI bribes that were paid off to the Pashtun chiefs to allow weapons convoys through their tribal areas, soon involved the same tribal chiefs allowing heroin runs along the same routes back to Pakistan. The National Logistics Cell, an army-run trucking company which transported CIA weapons from Karachi port to Peshawar and Quetta, was frequently used by well-connected dealers to transport heroin back to Karachi for export. The heroin pipeline in the 1980s could not have operated without the knowledge, if not connivance, of officials at the highest level of the army, the government and the CIA. Everyone chose to ignore it for the larger task was to defeat the Soviet Union. Drugs control was on nobody's agenda.

It was not until 1992, when General Asif Nawaz became Pakistan's army chief, that the military began a concerted effort to root out the narcotics mafia that had developed in the Pakistani armed forces. Nevertheless, heroin money had now penetrated Pakistan's economy, politics and society. Western anti-narcotics agencies in Islamabad kept track of drugs lords, who became Members of the National Assembly during the first governments of Prime Minister Benazir Bhutto (1988–90) and Nawaz Sharif (1990–93). Drugs lords funded candidates to high office in both Bhutto's Pakistan People's Party and Sharif's Pakistan Muslim League. Industry and trade became increasingly financed by laundered drugs money and the black economy, which accounted for between 30 and 50 per cent of the total Pakistan economy, was heavily subsidised by drugs money.

It was only after the Soviet withdrawal from Afghanistan that US and Western pressure began to mount on Islamabad to curtail the production of opium in Pakistan. Over the following decade (1989–99) some US$100 million dollars of Western aid to combat narcotics was made available to Pakistan. Poppy cultivation was drastically reduced from a high of 800 tons to 24 tons in 1997 and two tons by 1999. Crop substitution projects in the NWFP proved to be extremely successful. Nevertheless the dealers and the transport mafia never went away and they received a major boost with the arrival of the Taliban and the subsequent increase in Afghan heroin production. Pakistan was no longer a heroin producer, but it became a major transport route for Taliban heroin exports. The same dealers, truck drivers, *madrassa* and government contacts and the arms, fuel and food supply chain that provided the Taliban with its supplies also funnelled drugs – just as the arms pipeline for the Mujaheddin had done in the 1980s.

Pakistan was slipping back into bad habits. In February 1998 the Clinton administration accused Islamabad of doing little to curb production and exports of heroin. The US refused to certify that Pakistan was curbing narcotics production, but gave a waiver on the grounds of US national security interests.[7] But the drugs problem was now no longer confined to Pakistan and Afghanistan. As export routes multiplied in all directions, there was a dramatic increase in drug consumption across the region. By 1998, 58 per cent of opiates was consumed within the region itself and only 42 per cent was actually being exported.[8] Pakistan, which had no heroin addicts in 1979, had 650,000 addicts in 1986, three million by 1992 and an estimated five million by 1999. Heroin addiction and drugs money fuelled law and order problems, unemployment and allowed ethnic and sectarian extremist groups to arm themselves.

In Iran, the government admitted to having 1.2 million addicts in 1998, but senior officials in Tehran told me the figure was nearer three million – even though Iran had one of the toughest anti-narcotics policies in the world, where anyone caught with a few ounces of heroin faced the death penalty automatically.[9] And Iran had tried much harder than Pakistan to keep the drugs menace away. Since the 1980s Iran had lost 2,500 men from its security forces in military operations to stop convoys carrying drugs from Afghanistan. After Iran closed its borders with Afghanistan during the tensions with the Taliban in September 1998, Iranian security forces caught five tons of heroin on the border in a few weeks. The Taliban faced a major financial crisis as the closed border led to a drop in heroin exports and tax revenue.

Heroin addiction was also increasing in Uzbekistan, Tajikistan, Turkmenistan and Kyrgyzstan as they became part of the heroin export chain. In 1998 guards on the Tajikistan–Afghanistan border confiscated one ton of opium and 200 kilograms of heroin. In January 1999, Tajikistan's President Imomali Rakhmanov told an international conference that drugs were being smuggled into his country from Afghanistan at the rate of one ton a day and addiction was increasing. Uzbekistan said there was an 11 per cent increase of drugs from Afghanistan during 1998.

I saw heroin being openly sold outside five-star hotels in Ashkhabad, the capital of Turkmenistan, and inside the hotels flashy Turkmen and Russian mafioso with their even flashier girlfriends, spoke of their trips to the Afghan border 'to do business'. In 1997 two tons of heroin and 38 tons of hashish were seized by the authorities. By 1999, Turkmenistan, with its conciliatory policy with the Taliban had become the principle route of export for Afghan heroin with corrupt Turkmen officials benefiting from the trade.[10] President Askar Akayev of Kyrgyzstan told me in January 1999, that his country was now 'a major route for drugs trafficking and it is responsible for the growth of crime'. Akayev said the war against drugs could not be won until there was peace in Afghanistan and the civil war had become the most destabilizing factor in the region.[11]

The heroin explosion emanating from Afghanistan is now affecting the politics and economics of the entire region. It is crippling societies, distorting the economies of already fragile states and creating a new narco-elite which is at odds with the ever increasing poverty of the population. 'Drugs is determining the politics of this region as never before,' said a Western ambassador in Islamabad. 'We equate it now with other serious threats such as Islamic fundamentalism, terrorism and potential economic collapse in some of these countries,' he added.[12]

This worsening situation prompted attempts by the international community to talk to the Taliban. After six months of secret negotiations UNDCP concluded an agreement with the Taliban in October 1997. The Taliban agreed to eradicate poppy growing if the international community provided funds to help farmers with substitute crops. Pino Arlacchi, the head of UNDCP asked for US$25 million from donors for a ten-year programme to eliminate poppy farming in areas controlled by the Taliban. 'Afghan heroin supplies 80 per cent of Europe's supply of heroin and 50 per cent of the world's supply of heroin. We are talking about eliminating half the heroin of the world,' Arlacchi said enthusiastically.[13] UNDCP said it would introduce new cash crops, improve irrigation, build new factories and pay for law enforcement.

But the agreement was never implemented by the Taliban and after the pull-out of UN agencies from Afghanistan in 1998, it simply fell apart. Six months later Arlacchi was less optimistic when he told me, 'Afghanistan is one of the most difficult and crucial parts of the world but a wider political settlement is needed before drugs production can be be controlled.'[14] The record of wealthy countries supporting UNDCP initiatives was not particularly hopeful either. Between 1993 and 1997 UNDCP had asked for US$16.4 million from international donors for anti-narcotics work in Afghanistan and received only half that amount.

The taxes on opium exports became the mainstay of Taliban income and their war economy. In 1995 UNDCP estimated that Pakistan–Afghanistan drugs exports were earning some 50 billion rupees (US$1.35 billion) a year. By 1998 heroin exports had doubled in value to US$3 billion. Drugs money funded the weapons, ammunition and fuel for the war. It provided food and clothes for the soldiers and paid the salaries, transport and perks that the Taliban leadership allowed its fighters. The only thing that can be said in the Taliban's favour was that unlike in the past, this income did not appear to line the pockets of their leaders, as they continued to live extremely frugal lives. But it made the Afghan and Pakistani traffickers extremely rich.

Alongside the drugs trade, the traditional Afghan smuggling trade from Pakistan and now the Gulf states, expanded under the Taliban and created economic havoc for neighbouring states. The Afghan Transit Trade (ATT), described in detail in Chapter 15, is the largest source of official revenue for the Taliban and generates an estimated US$3 billion annually for the Afghan economy. Customs officials in Kandahar, Kabul and Herat refuse to disclose their daily earnings but with some 300 trucks a day passing through Kandahar on their way to Iran and Central Asia via Herat and another 200 trucks passing through Jalalabad and Kabul to the north, daily earnings are considerable. The illegal trade in consumer goods, food and fuel through Afghanistan is crippling industries, reducing state revenues and creating periodic food shortages in all neigbouring states – affecting their economies in a way that was never the case during the jihad.

Taliban customs revenues from the smuggling trade are channelled through the State Bank of Afghanistan which is trying to set up branches in all provincial capitals. But there is no book-keeping to show what money comes in and where it goes. These 'official' revenues do not account for the war budget which is accumulated and spent directly by Mullah Omar in Kandahar and is derived from drugs income, aid from Pakistan and Saudi Arabia and other donations. 'We have revenues from customs, mining and zakat, but there are some other sources of income for the war effort that do not come through the State Bank of Afghanistan,' admitted Maulvi Arifullah Arif, the Deputy Minister of Finance.[15]

With the war being run directly by Mullah Omar from his tin trunks stuffed full of money, which he keeps under his bed, making a national budget is next to impossible – even if the expertise was available, which it is not. The Finance Ministry has no qualified economist or banker. The Minister and his deputies are mullahs with a *madrassa* education and knowledgeable bureaucrats were purged. The paucity of official funds can be judged by the fact that in 1997 the Finance Ministry had set a budget of the equivalent of US$100,000 for the entire country's administration and development programmes for the Afghan financial year – February 1997–January 1998. In fact this amount just covered salaries for officials.

Some of the mullah traders within the Taliban are trying to encourage industry and foreign investment, but there appears to be no serious support from the Taliban leadership for these efforts. 'We want to develop Afghanistan as a modern state and we have enormous mineral, oil and gas resources which should interest foreign investors,' said Maulvi Ahmed Jan, the Minister of Mines and Industries, who left his carpet business in Saudi Arabia to join the Taliban and run Afghanistan's industries. 'Before we took control of the south there was no factory working in the country. Now we have reopened mines and carpet factories with the help of Pakistani and Afghan traders,' he added. He agreed that few members of the powerful Kandahar Shura were interested in economic issues as they were too involved with the war.[16]

As an investment incentive to foreigners, particularly Pakistani traders, Ahmed Jan was offering free land to anyone who would build a new factory. But with the collapse of the country's infrastructure, any investor would have to build his own roads and provide electricity and housing. Only a few Pakistani and Afghan transport-traders based in Peshawar and Quetta, who are already involved in either smuggling or the lucrative illegal timber trade from Afghanistan, appear to be taking an interest in projects such as mining.

There is no educated or professional class left in the country. In the several waves of refugees that have left the cities since 1992, all the educated, trained professionals, even telephone operators, electricians and mechanics, have gone. Most of the Taliban running the departments of finance, economy and the social sector are mullah traders – businessmen, truck transporters and smugglers for whom the rationale of nation-building is seen only in the perspective of expanding the market for smuggling and the trucking business across the region.

One such is Mullah Abdul Rashid, a fierce-looking Taliban military commander from Helmand, who gained notoriety in April 1997 when he captured a Pakistani military patrol that had entered Afghan territory from Baluchistan province to chase a gang of drug smugglers. Rashid arrested the soldiers and sent them to Kandahar, sparking off a row with Pakistan. He also runs the Taliban-owned marble mines in Helmand. The mine which employs 500 men with picks, has no mining engineers, no equipment, no electricity and no expertise. Rashid's mining techniques are limited to using explosives to blast (and scar) the marble.

The Taliban's appetite for foreign investment had been first wetted by the competition between two oil companies, Bridas of Argentina and the US company Unocal, who were competing for influence with the Taliban in order to build a gas pipeline from Turkmenistan to Pakistan across southern Afghanistan (see Chapters 12 and 13). The pipeline attracted a few swashbuckling, risk-taking businessmen. These included Afghan and Pakistani traders who built regular petrol pumps in Kandahar and along the route to Herat. They also promised to build roads. A USA-based group provided the Taliban with a mobile telephone network between Kabul and Kandahar in 1999. Such activities did little for re-establishing a regular economy. They were solely aimed at improving the Taliban's smuggling business and making life easier for traders and transporters.

Serious foreign investment and even aid to begin reconstruction is certainly not going to happen until there is an end to the war and a government which can ensure minimum stability and public loyalty. In the meantime Afghanistan is like an economic black hole that is sending out waves of insecurity and chaos to a region that is already facing multiple economic crises. Afghanistan's infrastructure lies in ruins. Basic civic amenities available in any underdeveloped country are non-existent. There is no running water, little electricity, telephones, motorable roads or regular energy supplies. There are severe shortages of water, food and housing and other basic necessities. What is available is too expensive for most people to afford.

The laying of millions of mines during the war has created severe resettlement problems in the cities and the countryside, where agriculture and irrigation in the most fertile areas is hampered by mines. Since 1979, 400,000 Afghans have been killed and another 400,000 injured in mine explosions. A staggering 13 per cent of all Afghan families has had a relative killed or crippled in mine accidents and over 300 people are killed or maimed every month. Although some 4,000 deminers working for the UN and other NGOs are trying to demine the country as fast as possible, it could take another decade before even the major cities are demined. In 1998, after six years of extensive work, Kabul still had some 200 square miles out of a total of 500 square miles of the city which had not been demined.[17]

Apart from mines, the daily battle for most Kabulis is to find enough of the grubby Afghani notes to pay for daily foodstuffs. Although the shops are full of smuggled foodstuffs from Iran and Pakistan, people do not have the money to buy them. Salaries for those Afghan surgeons who have not fled Kabul is the equivalent of US$5 a month. They only survive because their salaries are subsidized by the ICRC. Average salaries are around US$1–3 a month. As a result of grinding poverty and no jobs, a large percentage of the urban population is totally dependent on UN agencies for basic survival and subsidized food supplies. Fifty per cent of Kabul's 1.2 million people receive some kind of food aid from Western humanitarian agencies.

This poses a continuing dilemma for the UN as to whether its humanitarian aid is only sustaining the war, because it gives the warlords the excuse to absolve themselves of taking responsibility for the civilian population. The Taliban continuously insisted that they were not responsible for the population and that Allah would provide. However, the suffering of ordinary Afghans would only increase if the UN and NGOs were to cease their relief operations altogether and in particular stop feeding vulnerable groups such as widows and orphans.

In 1998 the economic situation visibly worsened. Northern Afghanistan was hit by three devastating earthquakes, the Taliban siege of the Hazarajat led to widespread starvation in central Afghanistan, floods in Kandahar submerged villages and crops and the urban population was blighted by the pull-out of aid agencies after the US missile strikes in August 1998. There was visible malnutrition on the streets of Kabul during the freezing winter of 1998–99, when few could afford to eat even one meal a day or heat their homes. However, there were signs of hope, if only peace would come. The WFP estimated that cereal production for 1998 would be 3.85 million tons, five per cent more than 1997 and the best year of production since 1978.

This reflected the improved law and order in rural areas under Taliban control, the lack of fighting and the return of refugees to farm their lands. Although there are still 1.2 million Afghan refugees in Pakistan and 1.4 million in Iran, more than 4 million refugees had returned home between 1992 and 1999. However, the Taliban and the UN agencies still had to import 750,000 tons of wheat in 1998 for the cities to make up the food shortfall. Clearly the Taliban did not create the economic devastation in Afghanistan. Rather they inherited it from the civil war which all the factions waged after 1992. But none of the factions, including the Taliban have paid any attention to the needs of the civilian population.

Thus it is not surprising that Western countries are suffering from 'donor fatigue' – the reluctance to come up with more money for humanitarian aid, when the civil war continues unabated and the warlords are so irresponsible. 'The level of suffering experienced by the Afghan people is literally horrendous,' said Alfredo Witschi-Cestari, the UN Co-ordinator for Afghanistan until 1998. 'As the years go by, funds trickle in slower and slower. We raise less than half the money we ask for.'[18] The warlords are not even remotely concerned with planning for the reconstruction of the country. Afghanistan's economic black hole is getting larger and wider, sucking more and more of its own population and the people of the region into it.

~10~

GLOBAL JIHAD:
THE ARAB-AFGHANS
AND OSAMA BIN LADEN

At Torkham – the border post at the head of the Khyber Pass between Afghanistan and Pakistan, a single chain barrier seperates the two countries. On the Pakistani side stand the smartly turned out Frontier Scouts – paramilitaries in their grey shalwar kameezes and turbans. It was April 1989, and the Soviet withdrawal from Afghanistan had just been completed. I was returning to Pakistan by road from Kabul, but the barrier was closed. Exhausted from my journey I lay down on a grass verge on the Afghan side of the border and waited.

Suddenly, along the road behind me, a truck full of Mujaheddin roared up and stopped. But those on board were not Afghans. Light-coloured Arabs, blue-eyed Central Asians and swarthy Chinese-looking faces peered out from roughly wound turbans and ill-fitting shalwar kameezes. They were swathed in ammunition belts and carried kalashnikovs. Except for one Afghan, who was acting as interpreter and guide, not a single one of the 30 foreigners spoke Pushto, Dari or even Urdu. As we waited for the border to open we got talking.

The group was made up of Filipino Moros, Uzbeks from Soviet Central Asia, Arabs from Algeria, Egypt, Saudi Arabia and Kuwait and Uighurs from Xinjiang in China. Their escort was a member of Gulbuddin Hikmetyar's Hizb-e-Islami. Under training at a camp near the border they were going on weekend leave to Peshawar and were looking forward to getting mail from home, changing their clothes and having a good meal. They had come to fight the jihad with the Mujaheddin and to train in weapons, bomb-making and military tactics so they could take the jihad back home.

That evening, Prime Minister Benazir Bhutto had hosted a dinner for journalists in Islamabad. Among the guests was Lieutenant General

Hameed Gul, the head of the ISI and the most fervent Islamic ideologue in the army after Zia's death. General Gul was triumphant about the Soviet withdrawal. I asked him if he was not playing with fire by inviting Muslim radicals from Islamic countries, who were ostensibly allies of Pakistan. Would these radicals not create dissension in their own countries, endangering Pakistan's foreign policy? 'We are fighting a jihad and this is the first Islamic international brigade in the modern era. The communists have their international brigades, the West has NATO, why can't the Muslims unite and form a common front?' the General replied. It was the first and only justification I was ever given for what were already called the Arab-Afghans, even though none were Afghans and many were not Arabs.

Three years earlier in 1986, CIA chief William Casey had stepped up the war against the Soviet Union by taking three significant, but at that time highly secret, measures. He had persuaded the US Congress to provide the Mujaheddin with American-made Stinger anti-aircraft missiles to shoot down Soviet planes and provide US advisers to train the guerrillas. Until then no US-made weapons or personnel had been used directly in the war effort. The CIA, Britain's MI6 and the ISI also agreed on a provocative plan to launch guerrilla attacks into the Soviet Socialist Republics of Tajikistan and Uzbekistan, the soft Muslim underbelly of the Soviet state from where Soviet troops in Afghanistan received their supplies. The task was given to the ISI's favourite Mujaheddin leader Gulbuddin Hikmetyar. In March 1987, small units crossed the Amu Darya river from bases in northern Afghanistan and launched their first rocket attacks against villages in Tajikistan. Casey was delighted with the news and on his next secret trip to Pakistan he crossed the border into Afghanistan with President Zia to review the Mujaheddin groups.[1]

Thirdly, Casey committed CIA support to a long-standing ISI initiative to recruit radical Muslims from around the world to come to Pakistan and fight with the Afghan Mujaheddin. The ISI had encouraged this since 1982 and by now all the other players had their reasons for supporting the idea. President Zia aimed to cement Islamic unity, turn Pakistan into the leader of the Muslim world and foster an Islamic opposition in Central Asia. Washington wanted to demonstrate that the entire Muslim world was fighting the Soviet Union alongside the Afghans and their American benefactors. And the Saudis saw an opportunity both to promote Wahabbism and get rid of its disgruntled radicals. None of the players reckoned on these volunteers having their own agendas, which would eventually turn their hatred against the Soviets on their own regimes and the Americans.

Pakistan already had standing instructions to all its embassies abroad to give visas, with no questions asked, to anyone wanting to come and fight with the Mujaheddin. In the Middle East, the Muslim Brotherhood, the Saudi-based World Muslim League and Palestinian Islamic radicals organized the recruits and put them into contact with the Pakistanis. The ISI and Pakistan's Jamaat-e-Islami set up reception committees to welcome, house and train the arriving militants and then encouraged them to join the Mujaheddin groups, usually the Hizb-e-Islami. The funds for this enterprise came directly from Saudi Intelligence. French scholar Olivier Roy describes it as 'a joint venture between the Saudis, the Muslim Brotherhood and the Jamaat-e-Islami, put together by the ISI'.[2]

Between 1982 and 1992 some 35,000 Muslim radicals from 43 Islamic countries in the Middle East, North and East Africa, Central Asia and the Far East would pass their baptism under fire with the Afghan Mujaheddin. Tens of thousands more foreign Muslim radicals came to study in the hundreds of new *madrassas* that Zia's military government began to fund in Pakistan and along the Afghan border. Eventually more than 100,000 Muslim radicals were to have direct contact with Pakistan and Afghanistan and be influenced by the jihad.

In camps near Peshawar and in Afghanistan, these radicals met each other for the first time and studied, trained and fought together. It was the first opportunity for most of them to learn about Islamic movements in other countries and they forged tactical and ideological links that would serve them well in the future. The camps became virtual universities for future Islamic radicalism. None of the intelligence agencies involved wanted to consider the consequences of bringing together thousands of Islamic radicals from all over the world. 'What was more important in the world view of history? The Taliban or the fall of the Soviet Empire? A few stirred-up Muslims or the liberation of Central Europe and the end of the Cold War?' said Zbigniew Brzezinski, a former US National Security Adviser.[3] American citizens only woke up to the consequences when Afghanistan-trained Islamic militants blew up the World Trade Centre in New York in 1993, killing six people and injuring 1,000.

'The war,' wrote Samuel Huntington, 'left behind an uneasy coalition of Islamist organizations intent on promoting Islam against all non-Muslim forces. It also left a legacy of expert and experienced fighters, training camps and logistical facilities, elaborate trans-Islam networks of personal and organization relationships, a substantial amount of military equipment including 300 to 500 unaccounted-for Stinger missiles, and, most important, a heady sense of power and self-confidence over what had been achieved and a driving desire to move on to other victories.'[4]

Most of these radicals speculated that if the Afghan jihad had defeated one superpower, the Soviet Union, could they not also defeat the other superpower, the US and their own regimes? The logic of this argument was based on the simple premise that the Afghan jihad alone had brought the Soviet state to its knees. The multiple internal reasons which led to the collapse of the Soviet system, of which the jihad was only one, were conveniently ignored. So while the USA saw the collapse of the Soviet state as the failure of the communist system, many Muslims saw it solely as a victory for Islam. For militants this belief was inspiring and deeply evocative of the Muslim sweep across the world in the seventh and eighth centuries. A new Islamic *Ummah*, they argued, could be forged by the sacrifices and blood of a new generation of martyrs and more such victories.

Amongst these thousands of foreign recruits was a young Saudi student Osama Bin Laden, the son of a Yemeni construction magnate Mohammed Bin Laden who was a close friend of the late King Faisal and whose company had become fabulously wealthy on the contracts to renovate and expand the Holy Mosques of Mecca and Medina. The ISI had long wanted Prince Turki Bin Faisal, the head of *Istakhbarat*, the Saudi Intelligence Service, to provide a Royal Prince to lead the Saudi contingent in order to show Muslims the commitment of the Royal Family to the jihad. Only poorer Saudis, students, taxi-drivers and Bedouin tribesmen had so far arrived to fight. But no pampered Saudi Prince was ready to rough it out in the Afghan mountains. Bin Laden, although not a royal, was close enough to the royals and certainly wealthy enough to lead the Saudi contingent. Bin Laden, Prince Turki and General Gul were to become firm friends and allies in a common cause.

The centre for the Arab-Afghans was the offices of the World Muslim League and the Muslim Brotherhood in Peshawar which was run by Abdullah Azam, a Jordanian Palestinian whom Bin Laden had first met at university in Jeddah and revered as his leader. Azam and his two sons were assassinated by a bomb blast in Peshawar in 1989. During the 1980s Azam had forged close links with Hikmetyar and Abdul Rasul Sayyaf, the Afghan Islamic scholar, whom the Saudis had sent to Peshawar to promote Wahabbism. Saudi funds flowed to Azam and the Makhtab al Khidmat or Services Centre which he created in 1984 to service the new recruits and receive donations from Islamic charities. Donations from Saudi Intelligence, the Saudi Red Crescent, the World Muslim League and private donations from Saudi princes and mosques were channelled through the Makhtab. A decade later the Makhtab would emerge at the centre of a web of radical organizations that helped carry out the World Trade Centre bombing and the bombings of US Embassies in Africa in 1998.

Until he arrived in Afghanistan, Bin Laden's life had hardly been marked by anything extraordinary. He was born around 1957, the 17th of 57 children sired by his Yemeni father and a Saudi mother, one of Mohammed Bin Laden's many wives. Bin Laden studied for a Masters degree in business administration at King Abdul Aziz University in Jeddah but soon switched to Islamic studies. Thin and tall, he is six feet five inches, with long limbs and a flowing beard, he towered above his contemporaries who remember him as a quiet and pious individual but hardly marked out for greater things.[5]

His father backed the Afghan struggle and helped fund it, so when Bin Laden decided to join up, his family responded enthusiastically. He first travelled to Peshawar in 1980 and met the Mujaheddin leaders, returning frequently with Saudi donations for the cause until 1982 when he decided to settle in Peshawar. He brought in his company engineers and heavy construction equipment to help build roads and depots for the Mujaheddin. In 1986 he helped build the Khost tunnel complex, which the CIA was funding as a major arms storage depot, training facility and medical centre for the Mujaheddin, deep under the mountains close to the Pakistan border. For the first time in Khost he set up his own training camp for Arab Afghans, who now increasingly saw this lanky, wealthy and charismatic Saudi as their leader.

'To counter these atheist Russians, the Saudis chose me as their representative in Afghanistan,' Bin Laden said later. 'I settled in Pakistan in the Afghan border region. There I received volunteers who came from the Saudi Kingdom and from all over the Arab and Muslim countries. I set up my first camp where these volunteers were trained by Pakistani and American officers. The weapons were supplied by the Americans, the money by the Saudis. I discovered that it was not enough to fight in Afghanistan, but that we had to fight on all fronts, communist or Western oppression,' he added.[6]

Bin Laden later claimed to have taken part in ambushes against Soviet troops, but he mainly used his wealth and Saudi donations to build Mujaheddin projects and spread Wahabbism amongst the Afghans. After the death of Azam in 1989, he took over Azam's organization and set up Al Qaeda or Military Base as a service centre for Arab-Afghans and their familes and to forge a broad-based alliance amongst them. With the help of Bin Laden, several thousand Arab militants had established bases in the provinces of Kunar, Nuristan and Badakhshan, but their extreme Wahabbi practices made them intensely disliked by the majority of Afghans. Moreover by allying themselves with the most extreme pro-Wahabbi Pashtun Mujaheddin, the Arab-Afghans alienated the non-Pashtuns and the Shia Muslims.

Ahmed Shah Masud later criticized the Arab-Afghans. 'My jihad faction did not have good relations with the Arab-Afghans during the years of jihad. In contrast they had very good relations with the factions of Abdul Rasul Sayyaf and Gulbuddin Hikmetyar. When my faction entered Kabul in 1992, the Arab-Afghans fought in the ranks of Hikmetyar's forces against us. We will ask them (Arabs) to leave our country. Bin Laden does more harm than good,' Masud said in 1997 after he had been ousted from Kabul by the Taliban.[7]

By 1990 Bin Laden was disillusioned by the internal bickering of the Mujaheddin and he returned to Saudi Arabia to work in the family business. He founded a welfare organization for Arab-Afghan veterans, some 4,000 of whom had settled in Mecca and Medina alone, and gave money to the families of those killed. After Iraq's invasion of Kuwait he lobbied the Royal Family to organize a popular defence of the Kingdom and raise a force from the Afghan war veterans to fight Iraq. Instead King Fahd invited in the Americans. This came as an enormous shock to Bin Laden. As the 540,000 US troops began to arrive, Bin Laden openly criticized the Royal Family, lobbying the Saudi *ulema* to issue fatwas, religious rulings, against non-Muslims being based in the country.

Bin Laden's criticism escalated after some 20,000 US troops continued to be based in Saudi Arabia after Kuwait's liberation. In 1992 he had a fiery meeting with Interior Minister Prince Naif whom he called a traitor to Islam. Naif complained to King Fahd and Bin Laden was declared persona non grata. Nevertheless he still had allies in the Royal Family, who also disliked Naif while he maintained his links with both Saudi Intelligence and the ISI.

In 1992 Bin Laden left for Sudan to take part in the Islamic revolution underway there under the charismatic Sudanese leader Hassan Turabi. Bin Laden's continued criticism of the Saudi Royal Family eventually annoyed them so much that they took the unprecedented step of revoking his citizenship in 1994. It was in Sudan, with his wealth and contacts that Bin Laden gathered around him more veterans of the Afghan war, who were all disgusted by the American victory over Iraq and the attitude of the Arab ruling elites who allowed the US military to remain in the Gulf. As US and Saudi pressure mounted against Sudan for harbouring Bin Laden, the Sudanese authorities asked him to leave.

In May 1996 Bin Laden travelled back to Afghanistan, arriving in Jalalabad in a chartered jet with an entourage of dozens of Arab militants, bodyguards and family members including three wives and 13 children. Here he lived under the protection of the Jalalabad Shura until the conquest of Kabul and Jalalabad by the Taliban in September 1996. In August 1996 he had issued his first declaration of jihad against the Americans whom he said were occupying Saudi Arabia. 'The walls of oppression and humiliation cannot be demolished except in a rain of bullets,' the declaration read. Striking up a friendship with Mullah Omar, in 1997 he moved to Kandahar and came under the protection of the Taliban.

By now the CIA had set up a special cell to monitor his activities and his links with other Islamic militants. A US State Department report in

August 1996 noted that Bin Laden was 'one of the most significant financial sponsors of Islamic extremist activities in the world'. The report said that Bin Laden was financing terrorist camps in Somalia, Egypt, Sudan, Yemen, Egypt and Afghanistan. In April 1996, President Clinton signed the Anti-Terrorism Act which allowed the US to block assets of terrorist organizations. It was first used to block Bin Laden's access to his fortune of an estimated US$250–300 million.[8] A few months later Egyptian intelligence declared that Bin Laden was training 1,000 militants, a second generation of Arab-Afghans, to bring about an Islamic revolution in Arab countries.[9]

In early 1997 the CIA constituted a squad which arrived in Peshawar to try and carry out a snatch operation to get Bin Laden out of Afghanistan. The Americans enlisted Afghans and Pakistanis to help them but aborted the operation. The US activity in Peshawar helped persuade Bin Laden to move to the safer confines of Kandahar. On 23 February 1998, at a meeting in the original Khost camp, all the groups associated with Al Qaeda issued a manifesto under the aegis of 'The International Islamic Front for jihad against Jews and Crusaders'. The manifesto stated 'for more than seven years the US has been occupying the lands of Islam in the holiest of places, the Arabian peninsular, plundering its riches, dictating to its rulers, humiliating its people, terrorizing its neighbours, and turning its bases in the peninsular into a spearhead through which to fight the neighbouring Muslim peoples'.

The meeting issued a fatwa. 'The ruling to kill the Americans and their allies – civilians and military – is an individual duty for every Muslim who can do it in any country in which it is possible to.' Bin Laden had now formulated a policy that was not just aimed at the Saudi Royal Family or the Americans but called for the liberation of the entire Muslim Middle East. As the American air war against Iraq escalated in 1998, Bin Laden called on all Muslims to 'confront, fight and kill' Americans and Britons.[10]

However, it was the bombings in August 1998 of the US Embassies in Kenya and Tanzania that killed 220 people which made Bin Laden a household name in the Muslim world and the West. Just 13 days later, after accusing Bin Laden of perpetrating the attack, the USA retaliated by firing 70 cruise missiles against Bin Laden's camps around Khost and Jalalabad. Several camps which had been handed over by the Taliban to the Arab-Afghans and Pakistani radical groups were hit. The Al Badr camp controlled by Bin Laden and the Khalid bin Walid and Muawia camps run by the Pakistani Harakat ul Ansar were the main targets. Harakat used their camps to train militants for fighting Indian troops in Kashmir. Seven outsiders were killed in the strike – three Yemenis, two Egyptians, one Saudi and one Turk. Also killed were seven Pakistanis and 20 Afghans.

In November 1998 the USA offered a US$5-million reward for Bin Laden's capture. The Americans were further galvanized when Bin Laden claimed that it was his Islamic duty to acquire chemical and nuclear weapons to use against the USA. 'It would be a sin for Muslims not to try to possess the weapons that would prevent infidels from inflicting harm on Muslims. Hostility towards America is a religious duty and we hope to be rewarded for it by God,' he said.[11]

Within a few weeks of the Africa bombings, the Clinton administration had demonized Bin Laden to the point of blaming him for every atrocity committed against the USA in the Muslim world in recent times. In the subsequent indictment against him by a New York court, Bin Laden was blamed for the 18 American soldiers killed in Mogadishu, Somalia in 1993; the deaths of five servicemen in a bomb attack in Riyadh in 1995 and the deaths of another 19 US soldiers in Dhahran in 1996. He was also suspected of having a hand in bombings in Aden in 1992, the World Trade Centre bombing in 1993, a 1994 plot to kill President Clinton in the Phillipines and a plan to blow up a dozen US civilian aircraft in 1995.[12] There was a great deal of scepticism, even amongst US experts that he was involved in many of these latter operations.[13]

But the Clinton administration was desperately looking for a diversion as it wallowed through the mire of the Monica Lewinsky affair and also needed an all-purpose, simple explanation for unexplained terrorist acts. Bin Laden became the centre of what was promulgated by Washington as a global conspiracy against the USA. What Washington was not prepared to admit was that the Afghan jihad, with the support of the CIA, had spawned dozens of fundamentalist movements across the Muslim world which were led by militants who had grievances, not so much against the Americans, but their own corrupt, incompetent regimes. As early as 1992–93 Egyptian and Algerian leaders at the highest level had advised Washington to re-engage diplomatically in Afghanistan in order to bring about peace so as to end the presence of the Arab-Afghans. Washington ignored the warnings and continued to ignore Afghanistan even as the civil war there escalated.[14]

The Algerians were justified in their fears, for the first major eruption from the ranks of the Arab-Afghans came in Algeria. In 1991 the Islamic Salvation Front (FIS) won the first round of parliamentary elections taking some 60 per cent of the seats countrywide. The Algerian army cancelled the results, declared Presidential rule in January 1992 and within two months a vicious civil war began which had claimed some 70,000 lives by 1999. FIS itself was outmanoeuvered by the more extreme Islamic Jihad, which in 1995 changed its name to the Armed Islamic Group (GIA). GIA was led by Algerian Afghans – Algerian veterans from the Afghan war – who were neo-Wahabbis and set an agenda that was to plunge Algeria into a bloodbath, destabilize North Africa and lead to the growth of Islamic extremism in France. Algeria was only a foretaste of what was to come later. Bombings carried out in Egypt by Islamic groups were also traced back to Egyptian veterans trained in Afghanistan.

Bin Laden knew many of the perpetrators of these violent acts across the Muslim world, because they had lived and fought together in Afghanistan. His organization, focused around supporting veterans of the Afghan war and their families, maintained contacts with them. He may well have funded some of their operations, but he was unlikely to know what they were all up to or what their domestic agendas were. Bin Laden has always been insecure within the architecture of Islam. He is neither an Islamic scholar nor a teacher and thus cannot legally issue fatwas – although he does so. In the West his 'Death to America' appeals have been read as fatwas, even though they do not carry moral weight in the Muslim world.

Arab-Afghans who knew him during the jihad say he was neither intellectual nor articulate about what needed to be done in the Muslim world. In that sense he was neither the Lenin of the Islamic revolution, nor was he the internationalist ideologue of the Islamic revolution such as Che Guevera was to revolution in the third world.

Bin Laden's former associates describe him as deeply impressionable, always in the need for mentors – men who knew more about both Islam and the modern world than he did. To the long list of mentors during his youth were later added Dr Aiman al-Zawahiri, the head of the banned Islamic Jihad in Egypt and the two sons of Shaikh Omar Abdel Rehman, the blind Egyptian preacher now in a US jail for the World Trade Centre bombing and who had led the banned El Gamaa Islamiyya in Egypt. Through the Afghan jihad, he also knew senior figures in the National Islamic Front in the Sudan, Hezbollah in Lebanon and Hamas, the radical Islamic Palestinian movement in Gaza and the West Bank. In Kandahar he had Chechens, Bangladeshis, Filipinos, Algerians, Kenyans, Pakistanis and African-American Muslims with him – many of whom were widely read and better informed than Bin Laden, but could not travel outside Afghanistan because they were on US wanted lists. What they needed was financial support and a sanctuary which Bin Laden gave them.

After the Africa bombings the US launched a truely global operation. More than 80 Islamic militants were arrested in a dozen different countries. Militants were picked up in a crescent running from Tanzania, Kenya, Sudan, Yemen, to Pakistan, Bangladesh, Malaysia and the Phillipines.[15] In December 1998, Indian authorities detained Bangladeshi militants for plotting to bomb the US Consulate in Calcutta. Seven Afghan nationals using false Italian passports were arrested in Malaysia and accused of trying to start a bombing campaign.[16] According to the FBI, militants in Yemen who kidnapped 16 Western tourists in December 1998 were funded by Bin Laden.[17] In February 1999, Bangladeshi authorities said Bin Laden had sent US$1 million to the Harkat-ul-Jihad (HJ) in Dhaka, some of whose members had trained and fought in Afghanistan. HJ leaders said they wanted to turn Bangladesh into a Taliban-style Islamic state.[18]

Thousands of miles away in Nouakchott, the capital of Mauritania in West Africa, several militants were arrested who had also trained under Bin Laden in Afghanistan and were suspected of plotting bomb explosions.[19] Meanwhile during the trial of 107 Al-Jihad members at a military court in Cairo, Egyptian intelligence officers testified that Bin Laden had bankrolled Al-Jihad.[20] In February 1999 the CIA claimed that through monitoring Bin Laden's communication network by satellite, they had prevented his supporters from carrying out seven bomb attacks against US overseas facilities in Saudi Arabia, Albania, Azerbaijan, Tajikistan, Uganda, Uruguay and the Ivory Coast – emphasizing the reach of the Afghan veterans. The Clinton administration sanctioned US$6.7 billion to fight terrorism in 1999, while the FBI's counter-terrorism budget grew from US$118 million to US$286 million and the agency allocated 2,650 agents to the task, twice the number in 1998.

But it was Pakistan and Saudi Arabia, the original sponsors of the Arab-Afghans, who suffered the most as their activities rebounded. In March 1997, three Arab and two Tajik militants were shot dead after a 36-hour gun battle between them and the police in an Afghan refugee camp near Peshawar. Belonging to the Wahabbi radical Tafkir group, they were planning to bomb an Islamic heads of state meeting in Islamabad.

With the encouragement of Pakistan, the Taliban and Bin Laden, Arab-Afghans had enlisted in the Pakistani party Harkat-ul-Ansar to fight in Kashmir against Indian troops. By inducting Arabs who introduced Wahabbi-style rules in the Kashmir valley, genuine Kashmiri militants felt insulted. The US government had declared Ansar a terrorist organization in 1996 and it had subsequently changed its name to Harkat-ul-Mujaheddin. All the Pakistani victims of the US missile strikes on Khost belonged to Ansar. In 1999, Ansar said it would impose a strict Wahabbi-style dress code in the Kashmir valley and banned jeans and jackets. On 15 February 1999, they shot and wounded three Kashmiri cable television operators for relaying Western satellite broadcasts. Ansar had previously respected the liberal traditions of Kashmiri Muslims but the activites of the Arab-Afghans hurt the legitimacy of the Kashmiri movement and gave India a propaganda coup.[21]

Pakistan faced a problem when Washington urged Prime Minister Nawaz Sharif to help arrest Bin Laden. The ISI's close contacts with Bin Laden and the fact that he was helping fund and train Kashmiri militants who were using the Khost camps, created a dilemma for Sharif when he visited Washington in December 1998. Sharif side-stepped the issue but other Pakistani officials were more brazen, reminding their American counterparts how they had both helped midwife Bin Laden in the 1980s and the Taliban in the 1990s. Bin Laden himself pointed to continued support from some elements in the Pakistani intelligence services in an interview. 'As for Pakistan there are some governmental departments, which, by the Grace of God, respond to the Islamic sentiments of the masses in Pakistan. This is reflected in sympathy and co-operation. However, some other governmental departments fell into the trap of the infidels. We pray to God to return them to the right path,' said Bin Laden.[22]

Support for Bin Laden by elements within the Pakistani establishment was another contradiction in Pakistan's Afghan policy, explored fully in Chapter 14. The US was Pakistan's closest ally with deep links to the military and the ISI. But both the Taliban and Bin Laden provided sanctuary and training facilities for Kashmiri militants who were backed by Pakistan, and Islamabad had little interest in drying up that support. Even though the Americans repeatedly tried to persuade the ISI to co-operate in delivering Bin Laden, the ISI declined, although it did help the US arrest several of Bin Laden's supporters. Without Pakistan's support the USA could not hope to launch a snatch by US commandos or more accurate bombing strikes because it needed Pakistani territory to launch such raids. At the same time the USA dared not expose Pakistan's support for the Taliban, because it still hoped for ISI co-operation in catching Bin Laden.

The Saudi conundrum was even worse. In July 1998 Prince Turki had visited Kandahar and a few weeks later 400 new pick-up trucks arrived in Kandahar for the Taliban, still bearing their Dubai license plates. The Saudis also gave cash for the Taliban's cheque book conquest of the north in the autumn. Until the Africa bombings and despite US pressure to end their support for the Taliban, the Saudis continued funding the Taliban and were silent on the need to extradite Bin Laden.[23] The truth about the Saudi silence was even more complicated. The Saudis preferred to leave Bin Laden alone in Afghanistan because his arrest and trial by the Americans could expose the deep relationship that Bin Laden continued to have with sympathetic members of the Royal Family and elements within Saudi intelligence, which could prove deeply embarrassing. The Saudis wanted Bin Laden either dead or a captive of the Taliban – they did not want him captured by the Americans.

After the August 1998 Africa bombings, US pressure on the Saudis increased. Prince Turki visited Kandahar again, this time to persuade the Taliban to hand over Bin Laden. In their meeting, Mullah Omar refused to do so and then insulted Prince Turki by abusing the Saudi Royal

Family. Bin Laden himself described what took place. 'He [Prince Turki] asked Mullah Omar to surrender us home or to expel us from Afghanistan. It is none of the business of the Saudi regime to come and ask for the handing over of Osama Bin Laden. It was as if Turki came as an envoy of the American government.'[24] Furious about the Taliban insults, the Saudis suspended diplomatic relations with the Taliban and ostensibly ceased all aid to them, although they did not withdraw recognition of the Taliban government.

By now Bin Laden had developed considerable influence with the Taliban, but that had not always been the case. The Taliban's contact with the Arab-Afghans and their Pan-Islamic ideology was non-existent until the Taliban captured Kabul in 1996. Pakistan was closely involved in introducing Bin Laden to the Taliban leaders in Kandahar, because it wanted to retain the Khost training camps for Kashmiri militants, which were now in Taliban hands. Persuasion by Pakistan, the Taliban's better-educated cadres, who also had Pan-Islamic ideas, and the lure of financial benefits from Bin Laden, encouraged the Taliban leaders to meet with Bin Laden and hand him back the Khost camps.

Partly for his own safety and partly to keep control over him, the Taliban shifted Bin Laden to Kandahar in 1997. At first he lived as a paying guest. He built a house for Mullah Omar's family and provided funds to other Taliban leaders. He promised to pave the road from Kandahar airport to the city and build mosques, schools and dams but his civic works never got started as his funds were frozen. While Bin Laden lived in enormous style in a huge mansion in Kandahar with his family, servants and fellow militants, the arrogant behaviour of the Arab-Afghans who arrived with him and their failure to fulfil any of their civic projects, antagonized the local population. The Kandaharis saw the Taliban leaders as beneficiaries of Arab largesse rather than the people.

Bin Laden endeared himself further to the leadership by sending several hundred Arab-Afghans to participate in the 1997 and 1998 Taliban offensives in the north. These Wahabbi fighters helped the Taliban carry out the massacres of the Shia Hazaras in the north. Several hundred Arab-Afghans, based in the Rishkor army garrison outside Kabul, fought on the Kabul front against Masud. Increasingly, Bin Laden's world view appeared to dominate the thinking of senior Taliban leaders. All-night conversations between Bin Laden and the Taliban leaders paid off. Until his arrival the Taliban leadership had not been particularly antagonistic to the USA or the West but demanded recognition for their government.

However, after the Africa bombings the Taliban became increasingly vociferous against the Americans, the UN, the Saudis and Muslim regimes around the world. Their statements increasingly reflected the language of defiance Bin Laden had adopted and which was not an original

Taliban trait. As US pressure on the Taliban to expel Bin Laden intensified, the Taliban said he was a guest and it was against Afghan tradition to expel guests. When it appeared that Washington was planning another military strike against Bin Laden, the Taliban tried to cut a deal with Washington – to allow him to leave the country in exchange for US recognition. Thus until the winter of 1998 the Taliban saw Bin Laden as an asset, a bargaining chip over whom they could negotiate with the Americans.

The US State Department opened a satellite telephone connection to speak to Mullah Omar directly. The Afghanistan desk officers, helped by a Pushto translator, held lengthy conversations with Omar in which both sides explored various options, but to no avail.[25] By early 1999 it began to dawn on the Taliban that no compromise with the US was possible and they began to see Bin Laden as a liability. A US deadline in February 1999 to the Taliban to either hand over Bin Laden or face the consequences forced the Taliban to make him disappear discreetly from Kandahar. The move bought the Taliban some time, but the issue was still nowhere near being resolved.

The Arab-Afghans had come full circle. From being mere appendages to the Afghan jihad and the Cold War in the 1980s they had taken centre stage for the Afghans, neighbouring countries and the West in the 1990s. The USA was now paying the price for ignoring Afghanistan between 1992 and 1996, while the Taliban were providing sanctuary to the most hostile and militant Islamic fundamentalist movement the world faced in the post-Cold War era. Afghanistan was now truly a haven for Islamic internationalism and terrorism and the Americans and the West were at a loss as to how to handle it.

Part 3

The New Great Game

~11~

DICTATORS AND OIL BARONS: THE TALIBAN AND CENTRAL ASIA, RUSSIA, TURKEY AND ISRAEL

In Ashkhabad, the capital of Turkmenistan, a massive new international airport was completed in 1996. The enormous, luxurious terminal building, was built to meet the expected flow of Western airlines to this oil- and gas-rich desert Republic, but it echoes with the sounds of silence. Within months, half of it was closed down, because it was too expensive to maintain and the rest – with only a few weekly flights arriving – was barely used even in 1999.

In 1995 at Sarakhs, on the Turkmenistan–Iranian border, a spanking new railway station with marbled walls and ticket counters was completed. The howling red sand and shifting dunes of the Karakum or Black Sand desert lapped the building and the heat was stifling. The station was the Turkmen end of a new railway line built by the Iranians, which connects Meshad in north-eastern Iran with Ashkhabad – the first direct communications link between Central Asia and Muslim countries to the south after 70 years of being cut off from each other. Yet with only two goods and passenger trains arriving from Iran every week, the station is closed for much of the week.

Communication links with the outside world were a top priority for all the Central Asian Republics (CARs) after they achieved independence in December 1991, but nearly a decade later it appeared that there was more camel traffic on the fabled Silk Route than today. These monuments to extravagance, grandiose ambition and unrealized dreams were the handiwork of Turkmen President Saparmurad Niyazov, who spends little of his country's dwindling finances on the upkeep of his country's 4.2 million people but much on his thriving personality cult. But these desert mirages also represent the still unfulfilled hopes of Turkmenistan becoming, as Niyazov put it to me as early as December 1991, 'the new Kuwait'.[1]

Since independence Turkmenistan, like other oil rich CARs, has waited in vain for its oil and gas riches to reach outside markets. Landlocked and surrounded by potentially jealous and hostile powers – Russia, Iran, Afghanistan and Uzbekistan – the Central Asian states have manoeuvered relentlessly for pipelines to be built that would end their isolation, free them from economic dependence on Russia and earn hard currency to refloat their economies after the devastation wrought by the break-up of the Soviet Union. For 70 years all their communication links – roads, railways and pipelines – were built heading east to Russia. Now they wanted to build links with the Arabian Sea, the Indian Ocean, the Mediterranean and China.

The energy resources of the Caspian Sea and Central Asia, (which we shall now call the Caspian region and includes Kazakhstan, Turkmenistan, Azerbaijan and Uzbekistan), have been described with breathless hyperbole over the past few years. In the early 1990s the USA estimated that Caspian oil reserves were between 100 to 150 billion barrels (bb). That figure was highly inflated and possible reserves are now estimated to be less than half that or even as low as 50 bb. The Caspian region's proven oil reserves are between 16 and 32 bb, which compares to 22 bb for the USA and 17 bb for the North Sea, giving the Caspian 10–15 times less than the total reserves of the Middle East.

Nevertheless, the Caspian represented possibly the last unexplored and unexploited oil-bearing region in the world and its opening-up generated huge excitement amongst international oil companies. Western oil companies have shifted their interest first to Western Siberia in 1991–92, then to Kazakhstan in 1993–94, Azerbaijan in 1995–97 and finally Turkmenistan in 1997–99. Between 1994–98, 24 companies from 13 countries signed contracts in the Caspian region. Kazakhstan has the largest oil reserves with an estimated 85 bb, but only 10–16 bb proven reserves. Azerbaijan has possible oil reserves of 27 bb and only 4–11 bb proven reserves while Turkmenistan has 32 bb possible oil reserves, but only 1.5 bb proven reserves. Uzbekistan's possible oil reserves are estimated at 1 bb.

Proven gas reserves in the Caspian region are estimated at 236–337 trillion cubic feet (tcf), compared to reserves of 300 tcf in the USA. Turkmenistan has the 11th largest gas reserves in the world with 159 tcf of possible gas reserves, Uzbekistan 110 tcf, Kazakhstan 88 tcf, while Azerbaijan and Uzbekistan have 35 tcf each.[2]

Central Asian leaders became obsessed with projected pipelines, potential routes and the geo-politics that surrounded them. In 1996 the Caspian region produced one million barrels per day (b/d) of oil of which only 300,000 b/d was exported – mainly from Kazakhstan. However only half that (140,000 b/d) was exported outside the former Soviet Union. Caspian production still represented only about 4 per cent of total world oil production. The region's natural gas production in 1996 totalled 3.3 tcf, but only 0.8 tcf was exported outside the former Soviet Union – mostly from Turkmenistan. There was an urgent, almost desperate need for pipelines.

The scramble for oil and influence by the big powers in the Caspian has been likened to the Middle East in the 1920s. But Central Asia today is an even larger complex quagmire of competing interests. Big powers such as Russia, China and the USA; the neighbours Iran, Pakistan, Afghanistan and Turkey; the Central Asian states themselves and the most powerful players of all, the oil companies, compete in what I called in a 1997 seminal magazine article, 'The New Great Game'. The name seemed to stick and was taken up by governments, experts and the oil companies.[3]

I had first visited Central Asia in 1989 during President Mikhail Gorbachov's perestroika reform programme. Convinced that the ethnic issue in Afghanistan was going to become explosive after the withdrawal of Soviet troops, I wanted to understand the ethnic origins of the Afghan Uzbeks, Turkmens and Tajiks and see their original homelands. I returned to the region frequently, exploring the vast vistas and the ethnic and political soup in the region that became more complex and volatile as the Soviet Union fell apart. By chance I was in Ashkhabad where the Central Asian leaders gathered on 12 December 1991, to discuss the dismemberment of the Soviet Union and their independence.

They were all reluctant nationalists, full of fear at the prospects of losing the security and support of the Soviet state system and the prospects of facing the outside world on their own. Within a few months, as their economies crumbled, the importance of their oil resources and the need for pipelines became evident. They began to hold talks with Western oil companies, on the back of ongoing negotiations between Kazakhstan and the US company Chevron. My subsequent visits resulted in a book on Central Asia but with Afghanistan disintegrating into civil war, I concluded that its repercussions would rebound on Central Asia and the issue of pipelines would determine the future geo-politics of the region.[4]

The label – the new Great Game – resonated with history. In the late nineteenth century the British in India and tsarist Russia fought an undeclared war of competition and influence to contain each other in Central Asia and Afghanistan. 'Turkestan, Afghanistan, Transcaspia, Persia – to many these words breathe only a sense of utter remoteness, or a memory of strange vicissitudes and of moribund romance. To me, I confess they are pieces on a chessboard upon which is being played out a game for the domination of the world,' wrote Lord Curzon, before he became the Viceroy of India in 1898.[5] These were expanding empires – the British pushing across India into Afghanistan and the Tsar's armies conquering Central Asia.

The centre of gravity for both powers was Afghanistan. The British feared that a Russian thrust on Herat from the Turkmen region could threaten British Baluchistan, while Moscow gold could turn Kabul's rulers against the British. The Russians feared that the British would undermine them in Central Asia by supporting revolts by the Muslim tribes and the rulers of Bukhara and Kokand. As it is today, the real battle was over communication links as both empires indulged in massive railway projects. The Russians built railway lines across Central Asia to their borders with Afghanistan, Persia and China, while the British built railway lines across India to their border with Afghanistan.

Today's Great Game is also between expanding and contracting empires. As a weakened and bankrupt Russia attempts to keep a grip on what it still views as its frontiers in Central Asia and control the flow of Caspian oil through pipelines that traverse Russia, the USA is thrusting itself into the region on the back of proposed oil pipelines which would bypass Russia. Iran, Turkey and Pakistan are building their own communication links with the region and want to be the preferred route of choice for future pipelines heading east, west or south. China wants to secure stability for its restive Xinjiang region populated by the same Muslim ethnic groups that inhabit Central Asia, secure the necessary energy to fuel its rapid economic growth and expand its political influence in a critical border region. The Central Asian states have their own rivalries, preferences and strategic imperatives. Looming above this is the fierce competition between American, European and Asian oil companies.

But as in the nineteenth century, Afghanistan's instability and the advancing Taliban were creating a new dimension to this global rivalry and becoming a significant fulcrum for the new Great Game. The states and the companies had to decide whether to confront or woo the Taliban and whether the Taliban would impede or help pipelines from Central Asia to new markets in South Asia.

Afghanistan had held Central Asia in a tight embrace for centuries. The territory comprising modern day Tajikistan, southern Uzbekistan and northern Afghanistan was one contiguous territory for centuries, ruled intermittently by amirs or kings in Bukhara or Kabul. The Amir of Bukhara depended on Afghan mercenaries for his army. Persecuted tribal chiefs, bandits and mullahs sought sanctuary in each other's territories, crossing a non-existent border. (Thus Tajikistan's decision in 1997 to hand over the Kuliab airbase in southern Tajikistan to Ahmad Shah Masud so he could receive military supplies from Iran and Russia, was but a continuation of these past linkages.) Afghanistan's contiguity with

Central Asia came to an end after the 1917 Russian Revolution, when the Soviet Union sealed its borders with its southern Muslim neighbours. The reopening of these borders in 1991 heralded the start of the new Great Game.

Afghanistan today borders Turkmenistan, Tajikistan, and Uzbekistan but only Turkmenistan has large energy resources. Along the Pamir mountains Tajikistan's five million people share a rugged 640-mile border with Afghanistan, which is divided by the Amu Darya river. A quarter of Afghanistan's population is Tajik. More Tajiks are scattered throughout the other CARs and another 200,000 live in China's Xinjiang province. The only major ethnic group in Central Asia which is not of Turkic origin, the Tajiks are descended from the first Persian tribes who inhabited Central Asia between 1500 and 1000 BC, but were later pushed to the peripheries by a series of Turkic invasions from Mongolia.

In ancient times, Tajikistan was the military and economic centre of the region. It acted as a gateway for the Silk Route and for Turkic invaders who rode west into Iran, Russia and Europe and south into Afghanistan and India. Russia annexed the northern part of present day Tajikistan in 1868 and it became a part of the province of Russia-controlled Turkestan. As the Great Game intensified, the British and Russians demarcated the border between Afghanistan and Central Asia in 1884, when Russia annexed southern Tajikistan.

After Stalin created the five CARs in 1924–25 by arbitrarily drawing lines on a map, he handed over Bukhara and Samarkand, the two major centres of Tajik culture and history to Uzbekistan, creating a rivalry between the two Republics which has simmered ever since. Modern day Tajikistan represents none of the population or economic centres of ancient Tajik glories. Stalin also created the Autonomous Region of Gorno-Badakhshan in the Pamir mountains, which contains 44 per cent of the land area of Tajikistan but only 3 per cent of the population. While the Tajiks are Sunni Muslims, Gorno-Badakhshan contains various Pamiri ethnic groups many of whom are Shia Muslims. They include the Ismaelis, a Shia sect and followers of the Agha Khan, who also inhabit the contiguous Badakhshan region of Afghanistan.

A few months after the 1917 Revolution, Muslim guerrilla groups sprang up across Central Asia to resist the Bolsheviks. These rebels were called Basmachis by the Bolsheviks, a derogative term meaning bandit. The movement stood for Islam, nationalism and anti-communism. Sixty years later the same inspiration motivated the Mujaheddin in Afghanistan. Determined to undermine Soviet power, the British helped the Basmachis in 1919, by paying Kabul's rulers to send camel caravans of arms and ammunition to the Basmachis. Thousands of Tajik Basmachis took refuge in northern Afghanistan as their struggle continued until 1929, when they were finally crushed by the Bolsheviks. In another replay in the 1980s, the USA encouraged the Afghan Mujaheddin to cross into Central Asia and attack Soviet army posts. And in reply Soviet troops in Afghanistan frequently called the Mujaheddin 'Basmachis'.

Tajikistan remained an underdeveloped, poverty-stricken Republic on the Soviet Union's periphery. Its budget depended on subsidies from Moscow. After 1991, tensions between Uzbeks and Tajiks and intra-clan rivalries within the Tajiks erupted. The resulting civil war (1992–97) between the neo-communist government and an array of Islamicist forces devastated the country. Once again thousands of Tajik rebels and refugees found refuge in northern Afghanistan, while Tajik government forces were backed by Russian troops. President Boris Yeltsin declared in 1993 that the Tajik–Afghan border was 'in effect Russia's border' and the 25,000 Russian troops stationed there would be defending Russia.[6] It was a reassertion of Moscow's role in Central Asia.

Ultimately the neo-communist government and the Islamicist opposition in Tajikistan agreed to a UN-brokered peace settlement, but neither side had been able to promote a national identity for the fragmented Tajik clans. These internal cleavages and the fact that it 'lacked an indigenous intelligentsia to elaborate a nationalism linking the people to the land and each other', left the country vulnerable to influences from Afghanistan.[7] Both sides in the civil war eventually co-operated with Masud, who to many Tajiks became a symbol of Tajik nationalism as he battled the Taliban. The Taliban added to Masud's image by accusing him of trying to divide Afghanistan and create a 'Greater Tajikistan' by joining Afghanistan's Badakhshan province with Tajikistan. Masud denies such aims. For Tajikistan the Taliban represented an Islamic fundamentalism at odds with the moderate, Sufi spiritualism of Central Asia while Pashtun expansionism was at direct odds with Tajik aspirations.

In Uzbekistan Islamic militancy, partly fuelled by Afghanistan, is the most serious challenge to President Islam Karimov. The Uzbeks – the most numerous, aggressive and influential race in the region – occupy today's Islamic heartland and the political nerve centre of Central Asia. Uzbekistan has borders with all the CARs and Afghanistan. Its principal cities of Samarkand and Bukhara have played host to countless civilizations over 2,500 years and became the second centre for Islamic learning after Arabia. Medieval Bukhara contained 360 mosques and 113 *madrassas* and even in 1900 there were 10,000 students studying at 100 active *madrassas*. The 250-mile long Ferghana valley, with its long associations with Islamic learning and militancy such as the Basmachis, is the richest agricultural region in Central Asia and the centre of Islamic opposition to Karimov.

The Uzbeks trace their genealogy to Genghis Khan's Mongols, one branch of which, the Shaybani clan, conquered modern-day Uzbekistan and northern Afghanistan in 1500. Mahmud Ibn Wali, a sixteenth-century historian, described the early Uzbeks as 'famed for their bad nature, swiftness, audacity and boldness' and revelling in their outlaw image.[8] Little has changed in the Uzbek desire for power and influence since then. Uzbekistan is the largest CAR with a population of 22 million. And with some six million Uzbeks living in the other CARs – forming substantial minorities in three of them (Tajikistan, Turkmenistan and Kazakhstan) – Karimov has ethnic allies to pursue his agenda of dominating the region. Some two million Uzbeks live in northern Afghanistan, the result of migrations before and during the Basmachi rebellion. Another 25,000 Uzbeks live in China's Xinjiang province.

Well before Soviet troops withdrew from Afghanistan, Moscow and Tashkent were cultivating Afghan Uzbeks to create a secular Uzbek-controlled 'cordon sanitaire' in northern Afghanistan that would resist any Mujaheddin takeover. For nearly a decade that policy was successful. General Rashid Dostum controlled six provinces and with military aid from Moscow and Tashkent, held off the Mujaheddin and later the Taliban. Karimov meanwhile led the attempt to forge an anti-Taliban alliance amongst the CARs and Russia after 1994. However, with the fall of Mazar in 1998, Karimov's policy collapsed and the Taliban were now Uzbekistan's immediate neighbours. Since then Uzbekistan's influence in Afghanistan has waned considerably as Karimov was unwilling to back Masud, a Tajik.

Karimov has also tried unsuccessfully at throwing his weight around in Tajikistan, where 24 per cent of the population is Uzbek. In 1992 Karimov gave military support to the Tajik government in its crackdown on Islamic rebels. By 1996 when peace talks were under way between the antagonists, Karimov attempted to force both sides to give a greater role to the Uzbek minority by supporting local Uzbek uprisings in northern Tajikistan. Karimov remains opposed to the Tajik attempt to make a coalition administration between the government and the rebels, because it would show the Islamicists in a good light – a lesson that would percolate down to Uzbekistan's own frustrated population.

Karimov runs a tightly controlled, authoritarian police state and cites the civil wars in Afghanistan and Tajikistan as justification for repression at home. The most significant opposition to Karimov has come from underground radical Islamic groups, some of them Wahabbis, entrenched in the Ferghana valley. Many of these Uzbek militants studied secretly in Saudi Arabia and Pakistan or trained in Afghan Mujaheddin camps in the 1980s. Subsequently they developed links with the Taliban.

Karimov has passed the most stringent laws of all the CARs against Islamic fundamentalism, from restricting *madrassa* education to the growth of beards and has blamed all unrest on the Wahabbis, a blanket term which Uzbek authorities increasingly use to describe all Islamic activism. But with half of Uzbekistan's population under 18 years of age and widespread unemployment and inflation, unrest amongst Uzbek youth is growing. The social and economic dissatisfaction amongst young people is unrecognized by the regime. Even though Uzbekistan may be the most powerful state in Central Asia, it faces the most intense political and religious polarization. Karimov's failed forays into Afghanistan and Tajikistan have only encouraged Islamic militancy.

Nevertheless, Uzbekistan is a major player in the new Great Game. It produces sufficient oil and gas for domestic consumption and will soon be an exporter. Initially Uzbekistan was ignored by the oil companies who scrambled to sign contracts with Tashkent's neighbours. Karimov was both jealous and envious of their success in attracting foreign investment, even as he refused to loosen state controls on the economy to attract Western investors. As Tashkent becomes an energy exporter it will have a vested interest in trying to influence routes for pipelines that benefit Uzbekistan, but it will also act as a spoiler in its determination not to see its neighbours prosper and thus become more influential in the region.

Afghanistan's 500,000 Turkmen population also arrived as a result of the 1920s civil war in the Soviet Union. The first migration into Afghanistan was by the Esari tribe in the early nineteenth century, who were followed by the Tekke tribe after their revolt against the Bolsheviks failed. Turkmenistan is a desolate land of desert and mountains inhabited by the nomadic Turkmen tribes, who fiercely resisted but eventually succumbed to Persian, Turkic and finally Russian conquerers. Before the nineteenth century, borders were meaningless for the Turkmen who migrated freely across the region. Some 300,000 Turkmen still live in Iran, 170,000 in Iraq, 80,000 in Syria and several thousand in Turkey.

The Tekke, the largest Turkmen tribe, began to resist Russian advances into their territory in 1870 and wiped out a Russian army at the oasis fort of Geok Tepe in 1881. Six thousand Turkmen horsemen were killed a year later by a Russian retaliatory force. In 1916 the Turkmen under the charismatic leadership of Mohammed Qurban Junaid Khan began another long and bloody resistance against first tsarist Russian and then the Bolsheviks which continued until his defeat in 1927, when he took refuge in Afghanistan.

Throughout the Soviet era Turkmenistan was ignored by Moscow. The Republic had the highest unemployment rate, the highest infant mortality rate and lowest industrialization of any Soviet Republic apart from Tajikistan.[9] As Moscow invested in the oil and gas industry in Siberia, Turkmenistan's potential oil reserves were ignored. Nevertheless 47 per cent of Turkmenistan's revenue in 1989 came from the sale of 3.2 tcf of natural gas to other Soviet Republics. The breakup of the Soviet Union turned Turkmenistan's customers into impoverished, independent states who could not pay their bills. 'We have no idea now who will buy our gas and how they will pay for it,' Foreign Minister Avde Kuliyev told me in December 1991.[10]

Turkmenistan's dilemma was that it was sandwiched between Iran which was unacceptable to the USA as a pipeline route; Afghanistan which was trapped in civil war; and Russia which wanted to limit Turkmenistan's gas exports to the West because they competed with Russia's own exports of Siberian gas. By 1992 Ukraine, Armenia and then even Russia refused to pay their bills for Turkmen gas imports. Moscow had a stranglehold as all Turkmen gas was pumped through the vast former Soviet pipeline network that was now owned by Russia. President Niyazov shut down gas supplies to his neighbours after Turkmenistan accumulated over US$1 billion in unpaid bills and Turkmen gas production slipped to 0.73 tcf in 1994, less than a quarter of what it was five years earlier.

Although the USA was determined to isolate Iran, Turkmenistan could not afford to do so, as Iran offered the nearest and most accessible outlet to the south and the sea. Adroitly Niyazov wooed the USA while seeking Tehran's help in developing road and rail links. In December 1997 the Iranians completed construction of a 119-mile-long gas pipeline between the Korpedzhe gas field in Western Turkmenistan to Kord-Kuy in northeastern Iran. The Turkmen gas that flows through it is consumed in northern Iran.[11] This pipeline is still the only new pipeline built between Central Asia and the outside world after nearly a decade of trying.

Niyazov also courted Western oil companies to build gas pipelines that would free him from the Russian pipeline network. In April 1992 Turkmenistan, Turkey and Iran agreed to build a gas pipeline to Turkey and on to Europe which would cost US$2.5 billion. That pipeline never got built and subsequently saw several variations as the US tried to block any route through Iran. Finally, in February 1999, Turkmenistan signed another agreement, this time with a US consortium, to build a Turkmenistan–Turkey gas pipeline which would go under the Caspian Sea to Azerbaijan and avoid Iran.[12]

As Niyazov saw his economy crumble he sought alternative export routes. On the drawing boards in 1994 were plans for a 5,000-mile-long oil and gas pipeline eastwards to China that would cost over US$20 billion, but the project is still only in the feasibility stage.[13] Also in 1994 Bridas, the Argentinian oil company which had concessions in Turkmenistan, proposed building a gas pipeline that would cross Afghanistan and deliver gas to Pakistan and India. The US company Unocal with support from Washington proposed a similar pipeline in 1995. The battle between the two companies to build this pipeline, which is explored in the next two chapters, sucked in the Taliban and the other Afghan warlords. Thus Afghanistan became the fulcrum of the first battle of the new Great Game.

Weak and impoverished and with no military force to defend its long borders with Iran, Afghanistan and its rival Uzbekistan, Turkmenistan opted for a foreign policy of neutrality. This gave the Turkmens the justification to keep their distance from Russia and avoid being sucked into the economic and military pacts that arose out of the break up of the Soviet Union. Neutrality also allowed Ashkhabad to avoid taking sides in the Afghan conflict, which angered Moscow and Tashkent as Turkmenistan refused to join the anti-Taliban alliance. Ashkhabad had provided the communist regime in Afghanistan with diesel fuel until Kabul fell in 1992. It proceeded to do the same for Ismael Khan who controlled Herat until 1995 and later the Taliban. While the Turkmen Consulate in Herat maintained good relations with the Taliban, its Consulate in Mazar did the same with the anti-Taliban alliance. Turkmenistan was the only CAR that wooed the Taliban rather than confronted them.

Like his Central Asian counterparts, Niyazov was a severe autocratic ruler, allowing no political opposition, censoring the media and maintaining state control over the economy. He developed a crude personality cult in the Stalinist mode, with his portraits and statues on display everywhere. An entire government department was set up to disseminate the President's pictures. Niyazov, like his rival Karimov, was an orphan. Both were bought up in communist orphanages and joined their respective Communist Parties at an early age, rising to become Secretary General well before independence. Their education, upbringing and loyalties lay with the defunct communist system but they both learned to play the new Great Game with skill.

No country in the region has benefited more from the break up of the Soviet Union than Turkey. Russia has been Turkey's most potent enemy for centuries. From the late seventeenth century to World War One, Turkey and Russia fought over a dozen wars and this rivalry had prompted Turkey to join NATO and try and become a member of the EU. However, the independence of the CARs suddenly awakened Turkey to its much older historical legacy.

Until 1991 Pan-Turkism – the idea of a Turkic homeland stretching from the Mediterranean to China – was a romantic dream espoused by a few Turkish scholars and barely figured in Turkey's foreign policy agenda. Suddenly, after 1991, Pan-Turkism became an achievable reality and an integral part of Turkey's foreign policy. Turkish dialects were now spoken by an accessible and vast contiguous belt that stretched from Istanbul across the Caucasus and Central Asia to Xinjiang in China. The CARs saw Turkey as a model for their economic development – Muslim but secular – while Turkey desired to expand its influence in the region and become a major player on the world stage.

Turkey began to send massive aid to the CARs and the Caucasus – starting direct flights to their capitals, beaming TV programmes via satellite, offering thousands of scholarships to students, training their diplomats, soldiers and bankers and initiating an annual Pan-Turkic summit. Between 1992 and 1998 Turkish companies invested more than US$1.5 billion in the region, becoming the single largest state investor. Turkey also realised that to be effective in Central Asia it had to placate Russia which it did by buying Russian gas and expanding trade with Russia, which rose from US$1.9 billion in 1990 to US$4.1 billion in 1997.[14] In 1997, the EU's rejection of Turkey's membership angered the Turks, but also pushed them into forging closer ties with the USA, Russia, Israel and Central Asia.

Turkey has become a major player in the new Great Game. Its need for energy and desire to expand its influence prompted successive Turkish governments to push for becoming the principal route for Central Asian energy exports. In the summer of 1997 the USA and Turkey jointly sponsored the idea of a 'transportation corridor' for a main oil pipeline from Baku in Azerbaijan through Georgia and the Caucasus to Turkey's Ceyhan port on the Mediterranean. Kazakhstan and Turkmenistan would be encouraged to feed their oil into this pipeline. This, the USA argued, would give the expensive and lengthy Baku–Ceyhan route the necessary oil volumes to make the project financially viable.[15] The USA wanted Turkmenistan to build a gas pipeline under the Caspian Sea which would then run along the Baku–Ceyhan corridor to Europe.

The USA also urged Kazakhstan to commit to building a similar under-the-sea Caspian oil pipeline, so that Kazakh oil could be pumped along the Baku–Ceyhan corridor. Kazakhstan's vast oil reserves were being exploited by two major Western oil consortiums in Tenghiz and Karachagnak, while China was developing a third oil-bearing region around Uzen.[16] Kazakhstan already had one planned oil pipeline route from Tenghiz to the Russian port of Novorossiysk on the Black Sea, which was being developed by Chevron, but the Baku–Ceyhan route would offer an alternative that avoided Russia.

The Azerbaijan International Operating Company (AIOC), made up of nearly a dozen of the world's oil companies and which dominated Azerbaijan's oil development, was averse to the Baku–Ceyhan route because it was too expensive, too long and would cross Turkey's volatile Kurdish region.[17] By 1998 it was clear that US plans to develop the Afghanistan route would be delayed and so the Baku–Ceyhan corridor became the main plank of Washington's policy towards the Caspian region.

The controversy over Baku–Ceyhan raged on for two years until late

1998 when international oil prices crashed because of the slump in demand due to the Asian economic crisis. Oil prices sunk to a record low of US$13 a barrel compared to US$25 in 1997, making it uneconomical to immediately exploit Central Asian oil, which was both expensive to produce and transport. The break-even price for Central Asian oil was around US$18 dollars a barrel.[18] Even though the Baku–Ceyhan route was no longer viable commercially, Washington continued to pursue its construction as it became the main plank of US policy in Central Asia.

Turkey had backed the Afghan Mujaheddin in the 1980s, but its role remained limited. However, as it developed a Pan-Turkic foreign policy, Ankhara began to actively support the Turkic minorities in Afghanistan such as the Uzbeks. Ankhara provided financial support to General Dostum and twice gave him a home in exile. Turkey became vehemently opposed to the Taliban, which had created new tensions with its close ally Pakistan. Moreover, the Taliban threat had also pushed Turkey into a greater understanding with its regional rival Iran.

Turkey also played a role in turning around Israel's policy in Afghanistan. Turkey and Israel had developed close military and strategic ties after the 1993 Oslo Accords. The Israelis and more significantly some Jewish lobbies in the USA were not initially critical of the Taliban.[19] In line with the US State Department, Israel saw the Taliban as an anti-Iranian force which could be used to undermine Iranian influence in Afghanistan and Central Asia. Moreover, the Unocal pipeline across Afghanistan would impede Iran from developing its own pipelines from Central Asia.

Israel's intelligence agency Mossad developed a dialogue with the Taliban through Taliban liason offices in the USA and with the oil companies. Pakistan's ISI supported this dialogue. Even though Pakistan did not recognize Israel, the ISI had developed links through the CIA with Mossad during the Afghan jihad. With initial support from Turkey, Israel also developed close diplomatic and economic links with Turkmenistan, Uzbekistan and Kazakhstan. Israeli companies invested in agriculture, the oil industry and communications.

But as US policy towards the Taliban shifted so did Israel's, as the Taliban gave refuge to Bin Laden and encouraged the drugs trade. Turkey convinced Israel that the Taliban were a security threat to the region and could export Islamic fundamentalism to Central Asia. As the Unocal project evaporated and Israel realized the aversion its Central Asian allies and Turkey had towards the Taliban, Mossad opened contacts with the anti-Taliban alliance. Israel now had an interest in seeing that the Taliban did not take control of the whole of Afghanistan, even though it remained suspicious of Ahmad Shah Masud's support from Iran. Both the Taliban and the Northern Alliance were to accuse each other of receiving Israeli support.

With oil prices crashing in 1999, Iran remained the wild card in the new Great Game. Iran sits on the second largest gas reserves in the world and has over 93 bb of proven oil reserves with current oil production at 3.6 million/bd. As pipeline projects waned due to low oil prices, Iran stepped in to urge the CARs to export their oil through a direct north–south pipeline to the Gulf via Iran. This could be built at a fraction of the cost of new pipelines across Turkey, because Iran already had an extensive pipeline network and only needed to add pipeline spurs to connect Iran with Azerbaijan. 'The Iranian route for Central Asian oil is the safest, most economic and easiest. The total cost for Iran would be US$300,000. How does that compare with US$3 billion for a pipeline through Turkey?' Ali Majedi, Iran's Deputy Minister of Oil said in Tehran.[20] Moreover, Iran was also in competition with Turkmenistan to build a gas export pipeline to India and Pakistan – a much more attractive route because it would avoid Afghanistan.[21]

In the first phase of its programme, Iran proposed swapping its crude oil with Central Asian crude. Since 1998 crude from Kazakhstan and Turkmenistan has been transported across the Caspian Sea to Iran's Caspian port of Neka, where it is refined and consumed in Iran. In exchange Iran allowed companies to lift oil from Iranian ports on the Gulf. With pipeline projects indefinitely delayed, this appealed to the oil companies who, despite US pressure not to do so, began to negotiate further swaps with Iran. Two US companies, Chevron and Mobil who have oil concessions in Kazakhstan and Turkmenistan applied to the Clinton administration in May 1998 for a license to carry out swaps with Iran – a move that created a major policy headache for Washington and would become a test case for the future of US sanctions against Iran.[22]

Ultimately the security needed to build pipelines from Central Asia to South Asia rested on ending the Afghan civil war. 'The CARs have two problems with Afghanistan. One is fear and the other is opportunity,' the UN mediator for Afghanistan Lakhdar Brahimi told me. 'Fear is the realization by these new and still fragile countries that the Afghan conflict cannot be contained for ever within its borders. Either it is resolved or it will spill over into the CARs. They want to avoid adventures of any kind from Kabul, be it Islamic fundamentalism, terrorism or drugs. The opportunity is that as landlocked countries who want to break their dependence on Russia, they are looking south for oil and gas pipelines and communication routes. They want a government in Kabul which is responsible and is a good neighbour. They want to open their borders not close them,' Brahimi added.[23]

Despite declining oil prices and Russia's desperate economic plight, the battle of wills between the USA and Russia will dominate future pipeline competition. Russia remains adamant in keeping the USA out of its

Central Asian backyard. 'We cannot help seeing the uproar stirred up in some Western countries over the energy resources of the Caspian. Some seek to exclude Russia from the game and undermine its interests. The so-called pipeline war in the region is part of this game,' said President Boris Yeltsin in 1998.[24] By keeping the conflict in Afghanistan on the boil Russia keeps the region unstable and has the excuse to maintain a military presence in the CARs.

The USA now wants stability, for it is concerned about the repercussions of the continuing Afghan war on its own policies in Central Asia. 'Throughout Central Asia, leaders are on edge about instability in Afghanistan and Tajikistan. They fear an expansion of Iranian influence and the rise of violent extremism in their countries,' said Stephen Sestanovich, Special Adviser to the US State Department on the States of the former Soviet Union (FSU) in March 1999.[25] Only an end to the Afghan civil war would give the CARs and oil companies the confidence to go ahead with pipeline projects to South Asia and that does not appear likely any time soon.

~12~

ROMANCING THE TALIBAN 1: THE BATTLE FOR PIPELINES 1994–96

Carlos Bulgheroni was the Taliban's first introduction to the outside world of high finance, oil politics and the new Great Game. An Argentinian and Chairman of Bridas, he visualized connecting his company's gas fields in Turkmenistan to Pakistan and India – thereby creating a swathe of infrastructure connections that could allow peace to break out in Afghanistan and even between India and Pakistan.

Like American and British oil magnates in the early part of the century, who saw the oil business as an extension of global politics and thereby demanded the right to influence foreign policy, Bulgheroni was a man possessed by an idea. Between 1995 and 1996 he left his business in South America and spent nine months in his executive jet flying from warlord to warlord in Afghanistan and to Islamabad, Ashkhabad, Moscow and Washington, to convince leaders that his pipeline was a realistic possibility. Those around him were equally driven, if not by the same dream, than by the workaholic Bulgheroni.

Bulgheroni is descended from a close-knit family of Italian immigrants to Argentina. Charming, erudite, a philosopher captain of industry, he could talk for hours about the collapse of Russia, the future of the oil industry or Islamic fundamentalism. His father Alejandro Angel had set up Bridas in 1948 as a small service company for Argentina's new oil industry. Carlos and his brother Alejandro Bulgheroni, who was Vice Chairman of Bridas, took the company international in 1978 and Bridas became the third largest independent oil and gas company in Latin America. But until Turkmenistan, Bridas had no experience of operating in Asia.

What had brought these Argentinians halfway across the world to ride around Afghanistan? After the collapse of the Soviet Union, Bridas had first ventured into Western Siberia, 'But there were too many problems there with pipelines and taxes so we arrived in Turkmenistan when it opened up,' Bulgheroni told me in the only interview he has given on Bridas's role in Afghanistan.[1] In 1991, Bridas took a huge risk when it became the first Western company to bid for leases in Turkmenistan. At the time, Western oil companies called the decision crazy. Turkmenistan was distant, landlocked and had passed no legislation to protect foreign investors. 'Other oil companies shied away from Turkmenistan because they thought it a gas place and had no idea where to market it,' said Bulgheroni. 'Our experience in discovering gas and transporting it through cross-border pipelines to multiple markets in Latin America convinced me that the same could be done in Turkenistan.' President Niyazov was flattered by the attention Bulgheroni paid him, when no other Western oil executive even appeared at his door, and the two men struck up a warm friendship.

In January 1992, Bridas was awarded the Yashlar block in eastern Turkmenistan close to the Afghan border and north-east of the massive Daulatabad gas field discovered by the Soviets. A year later, in February 1993, Bridas was awarded the Keimir block in the west of the country near the Caspian Sea. As the first and only entrant to Turkmenistan, Bridas received favourable terms – a 50–50 split in profits in Yashlar and a 75–25 split in profits in Bridas's favour in Keimir. 'We wanted to develop new oil and gas deposits because then Russia could not object to new finds as they would if we just developed old Soviet era fields,' said Bulgerhoni.

Bridas invested some US$400 million in exploring its leases – a staggering sum in those early days for a small oil company, when not even the oil majors were involved in Central Asia. Bridas began to export oil from its Keimir field in 1994, with production rising to 16,800 b/d. Then in July 1995, in the hot, arid Karakum desert, Bridas struck gold – a massive new gas field at Yashlar with estimated reserves of 27 tcf, more than double Pakistan's total gas reserves. 'Unlike oil, gas needs an immediate, accessible market, so we set about devising one,' said Jose Louis Sureda, Bridas's gas transportation manager – a tough, stout engineer who was to criss-cross Afghanistan in the months ahead surveying possible routes.[2]

'After discovering Yashlar we wanted part of the gas to go north through old Russian pipelines, but we wanted to find alternative markets and these were either China or South Asia,' said Bulgheroni. 'A pipeline through Afghanistan could become a peace-making business – difficult but possible,' he added. In November 1994, just as the Taliban captured Kandahar, Bulgheroni persuaded Niyazov to set up a working group to study the feasibility of a gas pipeline through Afghanistan to Pakistan.

Four months later he had persuaded Pakistan's Prime Minister Benazir Bhutto to join forces with Niyazov. On 16 March 1995 Pakistan and Turkmenistan signed a memorandum allowing Bridas to prepare a pre-feasibility study of the proposed pipeline. 'This pipeline will be Pakistan's gateway to Central Asia, it will open up huge possibilities,' Bhutto's husband Asif Zardari told me. Zardari said the Taliban's control of the pipeline route made the pipeline viable. Behind the desk in his office, Zardari had a huge map of the route, which he proudly pointed to.[3]

By now, the Pakistani military and the ISI were backing the Taliban to open up a southern transportation route via Kandahar and Herat to Turkmenistan. At the same time, Pakistan was also negotiating with Qatar and Iran to obtain gas supplies through two separate pipelines, but in geo-strategic terms, with Islamabad's abiding interests in Afghanistan and Central Asia, the Bridas proposal offered the greatest opportunities.[4]

Bridas proposed building an 875-mile-long pipeline from its Yashlar field, crossing southern Afghanistan to Sui in Baluchistan province, where Pakistan's gas reserves and pipeline network originates. The pipeline could later be extended to the even bigger market of India via Multan. Bridas proposed an open-access pipeline so that other companies and countries could eventually feed their own gas into it. This was particularly appealing to the Afghan warlords as Afghanistan had gas fields in the north, which once supplied Uzbekistan but had been shut down. Bulgheroni arrived to woo the Afghan warlords. 'I met with all the leaders, Ismael Khan in Herat, Burhanuddin Rabbani and Masud in Kabul, Dostum in Mazar and the Taliban in Kandahar. I was very well received everywhere because the Afghans understood they needed to rebuild the country and they needed foreign investment,' said Bulgheroni.

By February 1996 Bulghreoni reported to Bhutto and Niyazov that 'agreements have been reached and signed with the warlords which assure us a right of way'.[5] That month, Bulgheroni signed a 30-year agreement with the Afghan government, then headed by President Burhanuddin Rabbani, for the construction and operation of a gas pipeline by Bridas and an international consortium which it would create. Bridas opened negotiations with other oil companies including Unocal, the 12th largest oil company in the USA which had considerable experience in Asia and had been involved in Pakistan since 1976. Turkmen officials had met with Unocal for the first time in Houston in April 1995, on an invitation from Bridas, and a Unocal delegation had visited Ashkhabad and Islamabad apparently to discuss joining Bridas to build the pipeline.

But Bridas was now facing major problems in Turkmenistan. Niyazov had been convinced by his advisers that Bridas was exploiting Turkmenistan and in September 1994 the government blocked oil exports from Keimir and demanded a renegotiation of its contract with Bridas. By

January 1995 the issue appeared to be resolved when Bridas agreed to reduce its take by 10 per cent to 65 per cent. When Bridas discovered gas at Yashlar, Niyazov and his aides refused to join Bridas's celebrations and instead demanded to renegotiate both the Yashlar and Keimir contracts once again. Niyazov stopped Bridas from developing the Yashlar field and again stopped its oil exports from Keimir. This time Bridas said it would not budge from the original contracts which Turkmenistan was obliged to respect.

Niyazov was a communist-style dictator who had little understanding or interest in international law and contracts. But there were other reasons for Niyazov to turn the screws on Bridas at that precise moment. With Unocal expressing interest in building its own pipeline, using Turkmenistan's existing gas fields at Daulatabad, the profit of which would all accrue to Turkmenistan, Niyazov saw that Unocal could become the means to engage a major US company and the Clinton administration in Turkmenistan's development. Niyazov needed the Americans and began an intensive dialogue with US diplomats. The Americans needed to support him if they were to prevent him from becoming dependent on Iran. Niyazov visited the UN and summoned both Bridas and Unocal to New York. There, on 21 October 1995, in front of shocked Bridas executives, Niyazov signed an agreement with Unocal and its partner, the Saudi Arabia-owned Delta Oil Company, to build a gas pipeline through Afghanistan. 'We were shocked and when we spoke to Niyazov, he just turned around and said "Why don't you build a second pipeline,"' said a Bridas executive.[6]

Looking on at the signing ceremony was Henry Kissinger, the former US Secretary of State and then a consultant for Unocal. As Kissinger pondered a route through Afghanistan he quipped that the deal looked like 'the triumph of hope over experience'. However, Bridas was not about to give up, and the first battle of the new Great Game had begun. 'We are just an oil company trying to develop a country's resources, but we got involved in somebody else "Great Game" where the big powers are battering each other,' Mario Lopez Olaciregul, Bridas's Managing Director said later.[7]

Unocal proposed a gas pipeline from Daulatabad, with gas reserves of 25 tcf, to Multan in central Pakistan. Unocal set up the CentGas consortium holding a 70-per-cent stake, giving Delta 15 per cent, Russia's state owned gas company Gazprom 10 per cent and the state-owned company Turkmenrosgaz 5 per cent. Unocal signed a second, even more ambitious agreement with wide appeal across the region. Unocal's Central Asian Oil Pipeline Project (CAOPP) envisaged a 1,050-mile oil pipeline from Chardzhou in Turkmenistan to an oil terminal on Pakistan's coast, delivering one million b/d of oil for export. Existing Soviet-era oil pipelines – from Surgut and Omsk in Russia's Siberian fields, to Chymkent in Kazakhstan and Bukhara in Uzbekistan – could feed into CAOPP – delivering oil from all of Central Asia to Karachi.

'The strategy is to take advantage of the extensive, existing pipeline network to extend the entire regional system to the coast – allowing producers of Russia, Kazakhstan, Uzbekistan and Turkmenistan to access the growing markets of Asia. There would be a commerce corridor across Central Asia,' said Robert Todor, Unocal's Executive Vice-President.[8] To avoid a repetition of Chevron's problems with Russia in Kazakhstan, Unocal wooed Moscow from the start. Russia's Siberian oil would have a new southern outlet to the sea, while Gazprom had a stake in the gas pipeline. 'We don't have a Russian problem just an Afghan problem. For everyone it's a win-win situation,' Henry De La Rosa, Unocal's manager in Turkmenistan told me.[9]

The Clinton administration and Unocal's sudden interest in Turkmenistan and Afghanistan was not accidental. It was preceded by a significant change in US policy towards Central Asia. Between 1991 and 1995 Washington had strategically supported Kazakhstan and Kyrgyzstan as the two states which would swiftly bring about economic and political liberalization, thereby making it easier for US companies to invest there. Kazakhstan still held nuclear weapons left over from the Soviet era and with huge oil, gas and mineral reserves Kazakh President Nursultan Nazarbayev was personally courted by Presidents Bush and Clinton. But by 1995 Nazarbayev was increasingly seen as a failure, as massive corruption riddled his administration and he became increasingly dictatorial.

Kazakhstan had surrendered its nuclear weapons to Russia by 1993 and with 40 per cent of its population made up of ethnic Russians, who were openly hostile to the government, Nazarbayev was forced to bend to Russia's security and economic demands. For four years Kazakhstan was unable to persuade Russia to allow Chevron to transport Tenghiz oil through Russian pipelines to Europe. A frustrated Chevron, which in 1991 had promised to invest US$5 billion in Tenghiz had cut back its commitment and had invested only US$700 million by 1995.[10]

During this period (1991–95) the USA ignored Tajikistan which was involved in a civil war, while Uzbekistan and Turkmenistan, ruled by two dictators, were considered beyond the pale by the US State Department. Moreover, with the Russo-centric Deputy Secretary of State Strobe Talbott in the driving seat of US policy towards the FSU, Washington was not keen to antagonize Moscow and challenge its abiding interests in Central Asia. Talbott's agenda was to enlist Russia in NATO and not create problems in US–Russia relations by encroaching on Russia's backyard.

However, as Russia slipped into chaos, Talbott's pro-Russian policy came under bitter attack from within the US foreign policy establishment, the Jewish and Israeli lobbies in Washington and US oil companies, who all wanted the US to embrace a more multi-dimensional foreign policy towards the FSU. One that would allow them to exploit the Caspian's resources, help the Caspian states assert their independence from Russia and enlist them in the Western camp. US oil companies, who had spearheaded the first US forays into the region now wanted a greater say in US policy-making.

In early 1995, major US oil companies formed a private Foreign Oil Companies group in Washington to further their interests in the Caspian. The group included Unocal and they set about hiring former politicans from the Bush and Carter era to lobby their case in Washington.[11] The group met with Sheila Heslin, the energy expert at the National Security Council (NSC) and later in the summer of 1995 with her boss, the NSC Adviser Samuel Berger. Berger had set up an inter-agency government committee on formulating policy towards the Caspian, which included several government departments and the CIA.[12]

The strategic interest of Washington and the US oil companies in the Caspian was growing and Washington began to snub Russia. The immediate beneficiaries were Uzbekistan and Turkmenistan. Washington had scotched one attempt by US lobbyists to promote Niyazov. In March 1993, a former NSC Adviser, Alexander Haig had been hired by Niyazov and brought him to Washington to try and persuade US companies to invest in Turkmenistan and soften the US position on pipelines through Iran. The visit was a failure and Niyazov was unable to meet US leaders. But by 1995 Washington realized that if it kept Niyazov at arm's length, he would have no choice but to fall back on Iran. Turkmenistan's economic plight was worsening due to its inability to sell its gas. For the USA the prospects of a gas pipeline through Afghanistan was not only attractive because it avoided Iran, but it would signal support to Turkmenistan, Pakistan and the Taliban while clearly snubbing Russia and Iran.

The USA could not develop strategic clout in Central Asia without Uzbekistan, the largest and most powerful state and the only one capable of standing up to Russia. Both cautiously wooed each other. Karimov became supportive of NATO plans to build a Central Asian NATO battalion, a move that was vehemently opposed by Russia. 'We don't accept NATO in our backyard. The US must recognize that Central Asia will remain within the "near abroad" – Russia's sphere of influence,' an angry Russian diplomat told me in Ashkhabad in 1997.[13] US companies took an interest in Uzbekistan's mineral deposits, and trade between Uzbekistan and the USA suddenly blossomed, increasing by eight times between 1995 and 1997. Karimov made his first trip to Washington in June 1996. 'By late 1995 the West, and most notably the US, had clearly chosen

Uzbekistan as the only viable counterweight both to renewed Russian hegemonism and to Iranian influence,' wrote Dr Shireen Hunter.[14]

Thus there were the makings of two coalitions emerging in the region. The US lining up alongside Uzbekistan, Turkmenistan and Azerbaijan and encouraging its allies – Israel, Turkey and Pakistan – to invest there, while Russia retained its grip on Kazakhstan, Kyrgyzstan and Tajikistan. The USA was now prepared to confront Russia as the battle for the Caspian's resources escalated. 'While US policy-makers certainly do not want to see a hegemonic Russia, the potential costs of such hegemony become far greater if Russia is able to dictate the terms and limit Western access to the world's last known oil and gas reserves. Even minimum US involvement here provides for maximum Russian suspicion,' said Dr Martha Brill Olcott, a leading US academic on Central Asia.[15]

I did not begin to investigate this unfolding story until the summer of 1996. The sudden capture of Kabul by the Taliban in September 1996 prompted me to try and unravel two unanswered questions which many Western journalists were grappling with, but failed to answer. Were the Americans supporting the Taliban either directly or indirectly through Unocal or their allies Pakistan and Saudi Arabia? And what was prompting this massive regional polarization between the USA, Saudi Arabia, Pakistan and the Taliban on one side and Iran, Russia, the Central Asian states and the anti-Taliban alliance on the other? While some focused on whether there was a revival of the old CIA–ISI connection from the Afghan jihad era, it became apparent to me that the strategy over pipelines had become the driving force behind Washington's interest in the Taliban, which in turn was prompting a counter-reaction from Russia and Iran.

But exploring this was like entering a labyrinth, where nobody spoke the truth or divulged their real motives or interests. It was the job of a detective rather than a journalist because there were few clues. Even gaining access to the real players in the game was difficult, because policy was not being driven by politicians and diplomats, but by the secretive oil companies and intelligence services of the regional states. The oil companies were the most secretive of all – a legacy of the fierce competition they indulged in around the world. To spell out where they would drill next or which pipeline route they favoured, or even whom they had lunch with an hour earlier, was giving the game away to the enemy – rival oil companies.

Bridas executives never spoke to the press and only issued very occasional statements from a discreet public relations company in London. Unocal was more approachable but their executives were primed to give bland answers which gave nothing away. But there was a marked difference between the two companies which was to affect their future relations with the Taliban. Bridas was a small family company whose executives, brought up in the European tradition, were interested in the politics, culture, history and the personal relations of where and with whom they were dealing. Bridas executives were knowledgeable about all the convolutions of the Game and they took the trouble to explore the ethnic, tribal and family linkages of the leaders they were meeting.

Unocal was a huge corporation which hired executives to run its global oil business. Those sent out to the region were, with a few exceptions, interested in the job rather than the political environment they were living in. While Bridas engineers would spend hours sipping tea with Afghan tribesmen in the desert as they explored routes, Unocal would fly in and out and take for granted what they were told by the notoriously fickle Afghan warlords. Afghans had long ago mastered the art of telling an interlocuter what he wanted to hear and then saying exactly the opposite to their next guest. Unocal was also at a disadvantage because its policy towards the Taliban did not deviate from the US line and consequently Unocal lectured the Taliban on what they should be doing. Bridas had no such compunctions and was ready to sign a deal with the Taliban, even though they were not recognized as the legitimate government by any state.

Unocal tended to depend more on the US Embassy in Islamabad, and Pakistani and Turkmen intelligence for information on what was happening or about to happen, rather than gathering their own information. As my stories were published on the Bridas–Unocal rivalry and the twists and turns of the new Great Game, both companies at first thought I was a spy, secretly working for the other company. Unocal persisted in this belief even after Bridas had realized that I was just a very curious journalist who had covered Afghanistan far too long to be satisfied with bland statements. It took me seven months of travelling, over one hundred interviews and total immersion in the literature of the oil business – of which I knew nothing – to eventually write the cover story for the *Far Eastern Economic Review* which appeared in April 1997.

In July 1997 Strobe Talbott gave a speech that was to become the benchmark for US policy in the region. 'It has been fashionable to proclaim, or at least to predict, a replay of the "Great Game" in the Caucasus and Central Asia. The implication, of course, is that the driving dynamic of the region, fuelled and lubricated by oil, will be the competition of the great powers. Our goal is to avoid, and actively to discourage, that atavistic outcome. Let's leave Rudyard Kipling and George McDonald Fraser where they belong – on the shelves of history. The Great Game which starred Kipling's Kim and Fraser's Flashman was very much of the zero-sum variety.'

But Talbott also knew the Game was on and issued a grim warning to its players, even as he declared that Washington's top priority was conflict resolution. 'If internal and cross-border conflicts simmer and flare, the region could become a breeding ground of terrorism, a hotbed of religious and political extremism and a battleground for outright war.'[16]

On the ground, Niyazov's decision to sign with Unocal infuriated Bulgheroni. In February 1996 he moved to the courts, filing a case against Unocal and Delta in Fort Bend County, near Houston Texas. Bridas demanded US$15 billion in damages alleging 'tortuous interference with prospective business relations' and that 'Unocal, Delta and [Unocal Vice-President Marty] Miller and possibly others engaged in a civil conspiracy againt Bridas.' In its court deposition, Bridas said it had 'disclosed to Miller its strategic planning for the pipeline construction and operation. Bridas invited Unocal to consider joining a joint venture arrangement'.[17] In short, Bridas charged Unocal with stealing its idea.

Later, Bulgheroni explained how he felt. 'Unocal came to this region because we invited them. There was no reason why we and Unocal could not get together. We wanted them in and took them with us to Turkmenistan,' he told me. 'In the beginning the US considered this pipeline a ridiculous idea and they were not interested in either Afghanistan or Turkmenistan,' he added. Bridas also began arbitration against Turkmenistan with the International Chamber of Commerce for breach of contract in three separate cases regarding Turkmenistan's blockade of its Yashlar and Keimir fields.

Unocal maintained that its proposal was different because it involved Daulatabad rather than Yashlar gas field. In a letter, later submitted to court, John Imle, President of Unocal, had written to Bulgheroni saying that Turkmenistan had told him that the government had no agreements with Bridas, so Unocal was free to do what it liked.[18] 'We maintained that the CentGas project was separate and unique from Bridas. We were proposing to purchase gas from existing natural gas reserves and to transport the gas through an export gas pipeline. Bridas was proposing to transport gas from their Yashlar field . . . the CentGas project does not prevent Bridas from developing a pipeline to transport and market its own gas,' said Imle.[19]

The Clinton administration now weighed in on behalf of Unocal. In March 1996 the US Ambassador to Pakistan Tom Simmons had a major row with Bhutto when he asked her to switch Pakistan's support from Bridas to Unocal. 'Bhutto supported Bridas and Simmons accused Bhutto of extortion when she defended Bridas. She was furious with Simmons,' said a senior aide to Bhutto present in the meeting. 'Bhutto demanded a written apology from Simmons, which she got,' added a cabinet minister.[20]

During two trips to Pakistan and Afghanistan in April and August 1996, the US Assistant Secretary of State for South Asia Robin Raphel also spoke in favour of the Unocal project. 'We have an American company which is interested in building a pipeline from Turkmenistan through to Pakistan,' said Raphel at a press conference in Islamabad on 21 April 1996. 'This pipeline project will be very good for Turkmenistan, for Pakistan and for Afghanistan as it will not only offer job opportunities but also energy in Afghanistan,' she added. In August, Raphel visited Central Asian capitals and Moscow where she pitched the same message.

Open US support for the Unocal project aroused an already suspicious Russia and Iran, which became even more convinced that the CIA was backing the Taliban. In December 1996, a senior Iranian diplomat told me in hushed tones that the Saudis and the CIA had channelled US$2 million dollars to the Taliban – even though there was no evidence for such suspicions. But accusations multiplied on all fronts after the USA and Unocal committed several blunders.

When the Taliban captured Kabul in September 1996, Chris Taggert, a Unocal executive, told wire agencies that the pipeline project would be easier to implement now that the Taliban had captured Kabul – a statement that Unocal quickly retracted because it implied that Unocal favoured a Taliban conquest. Just a few weeks earlier Unocal had announced it would give humanitarian aid as 'bonuses' to the Afghan warlords, once they agreed to form a joint council to supervise the pipeline project. Again the implication was that Unocal was ready to dish out money to the warlords.

Then, within hours of Kabul's capture by the Taliban, the US State Department announced it would establish diplomatic relations with the Taliban by sending an official to Kabul – an announcement it also quickly retracted. State Department spokesman Glyn Davies said the US found 'nothing objectionable' in the steps taken by the Taliban to impose Islamic law. He described the Taliban as anti-modern rather than anti-Western. US Congressmen weighed in on the side of the Taliban. 'The good part of what has happened is that one of the factions at last seems capable of developing a government in Afghanistan,' said Senator Hank Brown, a supporter of the Unocal project.[21] Embarrassed US diplomats later explained to me that the over-hasty US statement was made without consulting the US Embassy in Islamabad.

But the damage done was enormous. Unocal's gaffes and the confusion in the State Department only further convinced Iran, Russia, the CARs, the anti-Taliban alliance and most Pakistanis and Afghans that the US–Unocal partnership was backing the Taliban and wanted an all-out Taliban victory – even as the US and Unocal claimed they had no favourites in Afghanistan. Some Pakistani cabinet ministers, anxious to show that the USA supported the Taliban and Pakistan's stance, leaked to Pakistani journalists that Washington backed the Taliban.

The entire region was full of rumours and speculation. Even the ever-neutral wire agencies weighed in with their suspicions. 'Certainly the Taliban appear to serve the US policy of isolating Iran by creating a firmly Sunni buffer on Iran's border and potentially providing security for trade routes and pipelines that would break Iran's monopoly on Central Asia's southern trade routes,' wrote Reuters.[22]

Bridas still faced an uphill climb to ensure that they were still in the race. Its gas and oil fields in Turkmenistan were blocked. It had no agreement with Turkmenistan to buy gas for a pipeline and none with Pakistan to sell gas. With US and Pakistani support, the Taliban were now being courted by Unocal. Nevertheless Bridas continued to maintain its offices in Ashkhabad and Kabul, even though Niyazov was trying to force them out. 'Bridas is out, we have given the Afghan pipeline to Unocal. Our government does not work with Bridas anymore,' Murad Nazdjanov, Turkmen Minister for Oil and Gas told me in Ashkhabad.[23]

Bridas had one advantage with the Taliban. Bridas told them it did not need to raise finances for the project through international lending institutions, which would first demand an internationally recognized government in Kabul. Instead Bridas had set up TAP Pipelines, a 50–50 partnership with the Saudi company Ningarcho, which was extremely close to Prince Turki, the Saudi intelligence chief. Bridas said it could raise 50 per cent of the funding from the Saudis to build the Afghan portion of the pipeline and the rest from an international consortium it would put together, which would build the less risky Pakistan and Turkmenistan ends of the pipeline. 'We will do a complete separation between our problems with the Turkmenistan government and the Afghan pipeline contract. We will make two consortiums, one to build the Afghan line and one to build the Pakistan and Turkmenistan ends of the line,' said a Bridas executive.[24] Bridas was thus offering to start work on the pipeline immediately, without preconditions. It only needed some agreement between the Afghan factions, but even that was to remain unobtainable.

On the other hand, Unocal's position was closely linked to US policy on Afghanistan – that it would not construct the pipeline or discuss commercial terms with the Taliban, until there was a recognized government in Kabul so that the World Bank and others could lend money for the project. 'We made it clear to all parties from the beginning that the ability to obtain financing for the project was critical, that the Afghan factions would have to get together and develop a functioning government that was recognized by lending institutions before the project could succeed,' said John Imle.[25] Unocal's real influence with the Taliban was that their project carried the possibility of US recognition which the Taliban were desperately anxious to secure.

Both Bridas and Unocal now courted regional powers with influence over the Taliban, particularly the Saudis. In their discussions with the Taliban, Bridas made much of their strong links to Prince Turki. 'The Saudis had many years of investment in the Afghan jihad and they really thought this pipeline would help the peace process,' said Bulgheroni. Not to be outdone, Unocal had their own Saudi connection. Delta Oil's President Badr Al'Aiban is close to the Saudi Royal Family, particularly to Crown Prince Abdullah in Abdul Aziz while Badr's brother Mosaed Al'Aiban was a member of King Fahd's court. Thus the competition between Unocal and Bridas also reflected competition within the Saudi Royal Family.

The USA and Unocal had also won over Pakistan. After the dismissal of the Bhutto government in 1996, the newly elected Prime Minister Nawaz Sharif, his Oil Minister Chaudry Nisar Ali Khan, the army and the ISI fully backed Unocal. Pakistan wanted more direct US support for the Taliban and urged Unocal to start construction quickly in order to legitimize the Taliban. Basically the USA and Unocal accepted the ISI's analysis and aims – that a Taliban victory in Afghanistan would make Unocal's job much easier and quicken US recognition.

Apart from wanting US recognition for the Taliban, Pakistan also desperately needed new sources of gas supply. Gas accounts for 37 per cent of Pakistan's energy consumption and the largest fields at Sui in Baluchistan were running out. Pakistan's proven gas reserves of 22 tcf, faced current consumption of 0.7 tcf per year and an annual increase in demand of another 0.7 tcf per year. By 2010 Pakistan would face an annual 0.8 tcf per year shortfall in gas. Islamabad's other options – a gas pipeline from Iran or one from Qatar – were stalled for lack of funding. Pakistan was also desperate for assured supplies of cheaper oil. In 1996 it imported US$2 billion worth of oil, equivalent to 20 per cent of its total imports. Domestic oil production had dropped from 70,000 b/d in the early 1990s to just 58,000 b/d in 1997. The proposed Unocal oil pipeline would not only supply Pakistan, but also turn the country into a major hub for Central Asian oil exports to Asian markets.

President Niyazov also wanted Unocal to start construction immediately and urged Pakistan to force the Taliban to accept the Unocal proposal. Niyazov's wooing of the US began to pay dividends. In January 1997, Turkmenistan signed an agreement with the US oil giant Mobil and Monument Oil of Britain to explore for oil over a large tract of western Turkmenistan. It was the first oil contract Turkmenistan had signed with a major US company as Unocal had still made no direct investment in Turkmenistan.

In November 1996 Bridas said it had signed an agreement with the Taliban and General Dostum to build the pipeline, while Burhanuddin

Rabbani had already agreed. That panicked Unocal and Pakistan. On 9 December 1996, Pakistan's Foreign Secretary Najmuddin Sheikh visited Mullah Omar in Kandahar to persuade him to accept the Unocal proposal, but Omar gave no firm commitment. In the classic Afghan manner the Taliban played their cards adroitly, remaining elusive and non-committal thereby forcing both Unocal and Bridas to up their bids. The Taliban were not just interested in receiving rent for the pipeline route which could be US$100 million a year, but also to involve the oil companies in building roads, water supplies, telephone lines and electricity power lines.

Privately several Taliban leaders said that they preferred Bridas, because Bridas made no demands upon them while Unocal was urging them to improve their human rights image and to open talks with the anti-Taliban alliance – the main plank of US policy. Moreover, Unocal was facing the growing feminist movement in the US which demanded that the USA and Unocal suspend negotiations with the Taliban. The UN was also critical. 'The outside interference in Afghanistan is now all related to the battle for oil and gas pipelines. The fear is that these companies and regional powers are just renting the Taliban for their own purposes,' Yasushi Akashi, the UN Under Secretary General for Humanitarian Affairs told me.[26]

Both companies insisted that their pipeline would bring peace, but no Western bank would finance a pipeline in a country at war with itself. 'The players in the game of pipeline politics must remind themselves that peace can bring a pipeline, but a pipeline cannot bring peace,' said Robert Ebel.[27] The Great Game had entered a new dimension.

~13~

ROMANCING THE TALIBAN 2: THE BATTLE FOR PIPELINES AND THE USA AND THE TALIBAN 1997–99

The attractive mini-skirted Argentinian secretaries at Bridas head-quarters in Buenos Aires had been told to cover up – long dresses and long-sleeved blouses to show as little of their limbs as possible. A Taliban delegation was expected in Buenos Aires. When they arrived in February 1997, Bridas treated them royally, taking them sightseeing, flying them across the country to see Bridas's drilling operations and gas pipelines and visiting the icy, snow-capped southern tip of the Continent.

At the same time, another Taliban delegation was experiencing a different kind of culture shock. They were in Washington where they met with State Department officials and Unocal and lobbied for US recognition for their government. On their return the two delegations stopped off in Saudi Arabia, visiting Mecca and meeting with the Saudi Intelligence chief Prince Turki. The Taliban said they had not yet decided which company's offer to accept. They had quickly learned how to play the Great Game from all angles.[1]

Both companies stepped up their efforts to woo the Taliban. Bridas received a boost in January 1997 when the International Chamber of Commerce issued an interim court order telling Turkmenistan to allow Bridas to resume its oil exports from the Keimir field. But President Niyazov ignored the decision, refusing to compromise with Bridas. In March 1997 Bridas opened an office in Kabul and Bulgheroni arrived to meet Taliban leaders.

Bridas actually began to negotiate a contract with the Taliban. It took weeks of painstaking work through the summer for three Bridas executives to negotiate the 150-page document with 12 Taliban mullahs, who had no technical experts amongst them apart from an engineering graduate, who had never practised engineering. The Taliban had no oil and gas experts and few who spoke adequate English, so the contract was translated into Dari. 'We are going through it line by line so that nobody can accuse us of trying to dupe the Taliban. We will get the same contract approved by the opposition groups so it will be an all-Afghan agreement,' a senior Bridas executive told me.[2] Unocal had declined to negotiate a contract until there was a recognized government in Kabul.

Meanwhile Unocal had donated US$900,000 to the Centre of Afghanistan Studies at the University of Omaha, Nebraska which was headed by Thomas Gouttierre, a veteran Afghanistan academic. The Centre set up a training and humanitarian aid programme for the Afghans, opening a school in Kandahar which was run by Gerald Boardman, who in the 1980s had run the Peshawar office of the US Agency for International Development providing cross-border assistance to the Mujaheddin. The school began to train some 400 Afghan teachers, electricians, carpenters and pipe-fitters to help Unocal lay the pipeline. Unocal gave the Taliban other gifts such as a fax and a generator, which caused a scandal when the story broke later in the year.

Whatever Unocal gave to the Taliban only further convinced the anti-Taliban alliance and Iran and Russia that the company was funding the Taliban. Unocal vehemently denied the charges. Later Unocal specified to me what it had spent on the project. 'We have estimated that we spent approximately US$15–20 million on the CentGas project. This included humanitarian aid for earthquake relief, job-skill training and some new equipment like a fax machine and a generator,' Unocal's President John Imle told me in 1999.[3]

Delta's role also increased external suspicions. Initially Unocal had encouraged Delta Oil, with its Saudi origins and Taliban contacts, to woo the Afghan factions. Rather than hiring eminent Saudis to do the job, Delta hired an American, Charles Santos, to liaise with the Afghans. Santos had worked on and off for the UN mediation effort for Afghanistan since 1988, despite criticism from two subsequent UN mediators that he was too close to the US government and had a personal agenda. Santos had become the political adviser to the UN mediator Mehmood Mestiri, who led the disastrous UN mediation effort in 1995, when the Taliban were at the gates of Kabul. Santos was already intensely disliked by all the Afghan leaders, especially the Taliban, when Delta hired him and nobody trusted him. It was a mistake and Unocal later regretted the decision after Santos failed to make any headway with the Afghans despite repeated trips into the country.

As tensions developed between Unocal and Delta because of Delta's inability to woo the Afghans, Unocal set up its own team of experts to advise the company on Afghanistan. It hired Robert Oakley, the former

US Ambassador to Pakistan and later the US Special Envoy to Somalia. Oakley had played a critical role in providing US support to the Mujaheddin in the 1980s, but that did not endear him to the Afghans as the USA subsequently walked away from Afghanistan. Many Afghans and Pakistanis considered him arrogant and overbearing – his nickname in Islamabad during his tenure as Ambassador was 'The Viceroy'. Oakley travelled to Moscow and Islamabad to win support for the project and helped Unocal hire other experts. These included Gouttierre, Boardman, Zalmay Khalilzad an Afghan-American worked for the Rand Corporation and the Central Asian expert Martha Brill Olcott.

For a US corporation to hire ex-US government officials or academics was not unusual. All the US oil companies playing the Great Game were doing the same in order to lobby Washington and they were hiring even bigger names from the Reagan and Bush administrations than Unocal was. But this was not understood in the region and was viewed with enormous suspicion, reinforcing speculation that Unocal was a policy arm of the US government and that the 1980s network of US–CIA Afghan experts was being revived.

Unocal now also faced immense problems with President Niyazov, who was as far removed from reality as ever. Refusing to accept the problems posed by the constant fighting in Afghanistan, he urged Unocal to start work as quickly as possible. When his terrified Foreign Ministry officials tried to explain that construction could not start in the middle of a civil war, he would shout them down. 'We want the pipeline. We link all of our largest projects to peace and stability in Afghanistan,' Niyazov told me angrily.[4] Subsequently Turkmen officials were too afraid to even inform their boss of the bad news from the Afghan front and Niyazov became more isolated from reality.

Despite these problems Unocal pushed ahead. In May 1997 at an annual regional summit in Ashkhabad, Pakistan, Turkmenistan and Unocal signed an agreement, which committed Unocal to raising the finances and reaching financial closure for the project by December 1997, starting construction by early 1998. The USA and Turkmenistan had been informed by the ISI that the Taliban were on the verge of capturing the northern opposition stronghold of Mazar-e-Sharif. However, two weeks later the Taliban were driven out of Mazar with hundreds of casualties and fighting intensified across Afghanistan. Once again, over-dependence on ISI analysis had embarrased the US.

At the first meeting of the CentGas working group in Islamabad after the debacle in Mazar, Unocal Vice-President Marty Miller expressed grave doubts that Unocal could meet its December 1997 deadline. 'It's uncertain when this project will start. It depends on peace in Afghanistan and a government we can work with. That may be the end of this year, next year or three years from now or this may be a dry hole if the fighting continues,' Miller told a press conference on 5 June 1997. Pakistan and Turkmenistan were forced to sign a new contract with Unocal extending the company's deadline by another year to start the project by December 1988. To most observers even that was considered overly optimistic.

By now, there was growing scepticism in Washington that Pakistan and the Taliban could deliver a unified Afghanistan. As a result, the USA began to explore other options to help Turkmenistan deliver its gas. In a dramatic reversal of policy the USA announced in July 1997 that it would not object to a Turkmenistan–Turkey gas pipeline which would cross Iran. Washington maintained that its decision was not a U-turn on its sanctions regime against Iran. Nevertheless, as European and Asian oil companies scrambled to enter the Iranian market, US companies saw a window of opportunity and intensified pressure on the Clinton administration to ease US sanctions on Tehran.[5]

The opportunity to transport Caspian oil and gas through Iran made an unpredictable Afghan pipeline even less viable. Washington's decision came as a blow to Unocal and a sharp reminder to Islamabad that US support was fickle at the best of times and that time was running out for the Taliban to unify the country through conquest. Moreover, Iran and Australia's BHP Petroleum announced they would sponsor a US$2.7 billion, 1,600-mile-long Iran–Pakistan gas pipeline that would deliver 2 billion cubic feet per day of gas from southern Iran to Karachi and later to India. The advantage of this pipeline, which was in direct competition to Unocal, was that it would run through territory not devastated by a civil war.

On 16 October 1997 Prime Minister Nawaz Sharif paid a one-day visit to Ashkhabad to talk to Niyazov about the Unocal project. As a result, Unocal, Pakistan and Turkmenistan signed a tentative pricing agreement for the import of Turkmen gas, in which the Taliban were given 15 cents per 1,000 cubic feet as a transit fee for the pipeline across their territory.[6] By now there was an air of distinct unreality surrounding the decisions by Sharif and Niyazov, who were ignoring the fighting. The Taliban were incensed because they were not consulted about the gas price and they demanded a larger transit fee.

Unocal company announced an enlarged CentGas consortium on 25 October 1997, which included oil companies from Japan, South Korea and Pakistan.[7] However, Unocal's attempt to woo the Russians had failed. Although 10 per cent shares in CentGas were reserved for Gazprom, the Russian gas giant refused to sign as Moscow criticized US sponsorship of the Taliban and the undermining of Russian influence in Central Asia.[8] Gazprom's chief executive Rem Vyakhirev declared that Russia would not allow Turkmenistan or Kazakhstan to export its oil and gas through non-Russian pipelines. 'To give up one's market . . . would be, at the very least, a crime before Russia,' Vyakhirev said.[9]

US officials had already made their anti-Russia policy clear. 'US policy was to promote the rapid development of Caspian energy . . . We did so specifically to promote the independence of these oil-rich countries, to in essence break Russia's monopoly control over the transportation of oil from that region, and frankly, to promote Western energy security through diversification of supply,' said Sheila Heslin, the energy expert at the NSC.[10]

Bridas remained in the running, this time with a powerful partner which even Washington could not object to. In September 1997 Bridas sold 60 per cent of its company's stake in Latin America to the US oil giant Amoco, raising the possibility that Amoco could influence Niyazov to ease off on Bridas's frozen assets in Turkmenistan. Bridas invited a Taliban delegation headed by Mullah Ahmad Jan, the former carpet dealer and now Minister for Industries, to Buenos Aires for a second visit in September. Pakistani authorities refused to let the Taliban fly out from Peshawar until they had also agreed to visit Unocal. Another Taliban delegation headed by the one-eyed Mullah Mohammed Ghaus arrived in Houston to meeet with Unocal in November 1997 where they were put up in a five-star hotel, visited the zoo, supermarkets and the Nasa Space Centre. They had dinner at the home of Marty Miller, admiring his swimming pool and large comfortable house. The Taliban met with officials at the State Department, where once again they asked for US recognition.[11]

After the winter lull in Afghanistan, fresh fighting broke out in the spring of 1998 and for both companies the project appeared as distant as ever. In March, Marty Miller said in Ashkhabad that the project was on indefinite hold because it was not possible to finance while the war continued. As Niyazov fumed with impatience, Unocal asked for another extension, beyond December 1998, to reach financial closure. Unocal was also facing increasing problems at home. At its annual shareholders' meeting in June 1998, some shareholders objected to the project because of the Taliban's treatment of Afghan women. American feminist groups began to muster American public support against the Taliban and Unocal.

Throughout 1998 the feminist pressure on Unocal intensified. In September 1998 a group of Green activists asked California's Attorney General to dissolve Unocal for crimes against humanity and the environment and because of Unocal's relations with the Taliban. Unocal described the charges as 'ludicrous'. Unocal first attempted to counter the feminists and then became distant in trying to answer their charges. It was a losing battle because these were American women and not foreigners, wanting answers to an issue that the Clinton administration now supported.

'We disagree with some US feminist groups on how Unocal should respond to this issue ... we are guests in countries who have sovereign rights and their own political, social and religious beliefs. No company, including ours, can solve these issues alone. Walking away from Afghanistan – either from the pipeline project or our humanitarian projects, would not help solve the problem,' said John Imle.[12]

The US bombing of Bin Laden's camps in August 1998 forced Unocal to pull out its staff from Pakistan and Kandahar and finally, in December 1998, it formally withdrew from the CentGas consortium, which it had struggled so hard to set up. The plunge in world oil prices which had hit the world's oil industry also hit Unocal hard. Unocal withdrew from a pipeline project in Turkey, closed its offices in Pakistan, Turkmenistan, Uzbekistan and Kazakhstan and announced a 40-per-cent drop in its capital spending plan for 1999 due to low oil prices. Unocal's only victory in these difficult days was over Bridas. On 5 October 1998, the Texas District Court dismissed Bridas's US$15 billion suit against Unocal – on the grounds that the dispute was governed by the laws of Turkmenistan and Afghanistan, not Texas law.

With the USA now preoccupied with capturing Bin Laden, it seemed for the moment that one phase of the Great Game was now over. It was clear that no US company could build an Afghan pipeline with issues such as the Taliban's gender policy, Bin Laden and the continuing fighting. That should have been clearer to Unocal much earlier on, but it never was as the Taliban and Pakistan kept promising them a quick victory. Bridas remained in the running but kept a low profile during the following difficult months. Even though the project was all but over, Pakistan persisted in trying to keep it alive. In April 1999, at a meeting in Islamabad, Pakistan, Turkmenistan and the Taliban tried to revive the project and said they would look for a new sponsor for CentGas, but by now nobody wanted to touch Afghanistan and the Taliban and foreign investors were staying clear of Pakistan.

US strategy in Central Asia was 'a cluster of confusions' according to Paul Starobin and 'arrogant, muddled, naive and dangerous' according to Martha Brill Olcott. Author Robert Kaplan described the region as a 'frontier of anarchy'.[13] Yet the USA, now fervently rooting for the Baku-Ceyhan pipeline despite crashing oil prices and a refusal by oil companies to invest, persisted in the belief that pipelines could be built without a strategic vision or conflict resolution in the region.

After providing billions of dollars' worth of arms and ammunition to the Mujaheddin, the USA began to walk away from the Afghan issue after Soviet troops completed their withdrawal in 1989. That walk became a run in 1992 after the fall of Kabul. Washington allowed its allies in the region, Pakistan and Saudi Arabia, free rein to sort out the ensuing Afghan civil war. For ordinary Afghans the US withdrawal from the scene constituted a major betrayal, while Washington's refusal to harness international pressure to help broker a settlement between the warlords was considered a double betrayal. Other Afghans were furious at the USA for allowing Pakistan a free hand in Afghanistan. The US strategic absence allowed all the regional powers, including the newly independent CARs, to prop up competing warlords, thereby intensifying the civil war and guaranteeing its prolongation. The pipeline of US military aid to the Mujaheddin was never replaced by a pipeline of international humanitarian aid that could have been an inducement for the warlords to make peace and rebuild the country.

After the end of the Cold War, Washington's policy to the Afghanistan–Pakistan–Iran–Central Asia region was stymied by the lack of a strategic framework. The USA dealt with issues as they came up, in a haphazard, piecemeal fashion, rather than applying a coherent, strategic vision to the region. There are several distinct phases of US policy towards the Taliban, which were driven by domestic American politics or attempted quick-fix solutions rather than a strategic policy.

Between 1994 and 1996 the USA supported the Taliban politically through its allies Pakistan and Saudi Arabia, essentially because Washington viewed the Taliban as anti-Iranian, anti-Shia and pro-Western. The USA conveniently ignored the Taliban's own Islamic fundamentalist agenda, its supression of women and the consternation they created in Central Asia largely because Washington was not interested in the larger picture. Between 1995 and 1997 US support was even more driven because of its backing for the Unocal project – even though at the time the USA had no strategic plan towards accessing Central Asian energy and thought that pipelines could be built without resolutions to regional civil wars.

The US policy turnaround from late 1997 to today was first driven exclusively by the effective campaign of American feminists against the Taliban. As always with the Clinton agenda, domestic political concerns outweighed foreign policy-making and the wishes of allies. Clinton only woke up to the Afghanistan problem when American women knocked on his door. President and Mrs Clinton had relied heavily on the American female vote in the 1996 elections and on female support during the Monica Lewinsky saga. They could not afford to annoy liberal American women. Moreover, once Hollywood got involved – its liberal stars were key financiers and supporters of the Clinton campaign and Vice-President Albert Gore was anxious to retain their support for his own election bid – there was no way the US could be seen as soft on the Taliban.

In 1998 and 1999 the Taliban's support for Bin Laden, their refusal to endorse the Unocal project or compromise with their opponents and the new moderate government in Iran provided additional reasons for the

USA to get tough with the Taliban. In 1999 'getting Bin Laden' was Washington's primary policy objective, even as it ignored the new Islamic radicalism Afghanistan was fostering, which would in time only throw up dozens more Bin Ladens. Nevertheless, late as it was, for the first time the USA was genuinely on the peace train and gave full support to UN mediation efforts to end the war.

US policy has been too preoccupied with wrong assumptions. When I first spoke to diplomats at the US Embassy in Islamabad after the Taliban emerged in 1994, they were enthusiastic. The Taliban had told the stream of US diplomats who visited Kandahar that they disliked Iran, that they would curb poppy cultivation and heroin production, that they were opposed to all outsiders remaining in Afghanistan including the Arab-Afghans and they had no desire to seize power or rule the country. Some US diplomats saw them as messianic do-gooders – like born-again Christians from the American Bible Belt. US diplomats believed that the Taliban would meet essential US aims in Afghanistan – 'eliminating drugs and thugs', one diplomat said. It was a patently naive hope given the Taliban's social base and because they themselves did not know what they represented nor whether they wanted state power.

There was not a word of US criticism after the Taliban captured Herat in 1995 and threw out thousands of girls from schools. In fact the USA, along with Pakistan's ISI, considered Herat's fall as a help to Unocal and tightening the noose around Iran. Washington's aim of using the Taliban to blockade Iran was equally shortsighted, because it was to pitch Iran against Pakistan, Sunni against Shia and Pashtun against non-Pashtun. 'Whatever the merits of the isolation policy towards Iran in the fight against terrorism, they incapacitate the US in Afghanistan,' wrote Barnett Rubin.[14] Iran, already paranoid about CIA plots to undermine it, went into overdrive to demonstrate CIA support for the Taliban while stepping up its own arming of the anti-Taliban alliance. 'US policy is forcing us to join Russia and the anti-Taliban alliance against Pakistan, Saudi Arabia and the Taliban,' an Iranian diplomat said.[15]

Some US diplomats, concerned with the lack of direction in Washington on Afghanistan, have admitted that there was no coherent US policy, except to go along with what Pakistan and Saudi Arabia wanted. In a confidential 1996 State Department memo written just before the Taliban captured Kabul, parts of which I read, analysts wrote that, if the Taliban expanded, Russia, India and Iran would support the anti-Taliban alliance and the war would continue; that the USA would be torn between supporting its old ally Pakistan and trying to prevent antagonizing India and Russia with whom the USA was trying to improve relations. In such a situation, the State Department surmised, the USA could not hope to have a coherent pólicy towards Afghanistan. In a US election year a coherent Afghan policy was not particularly necessary either.

There was another problem. Few in Washington were interested in Afghanistan. Robin Raphel, the US Assistant Secretary of State for South Asia and the key policy maker for Washington's Afghan policy at the time, privately admitted that there was little interest in her initiatives on Afghanistan higher up the chain of command in Washington. Secretary of State Warren Christopher never mentioned Afghanistan once during his entire tenure. Raphel's attempts to float the idea of an international arms embargo on Afghanistan through the UN Security Council drew little support from the White House. In May 1996 she managed to push through a debate on Afghanistan in the UN Security Council – the first in six years. And in June, Senator Hank Brown, with support from Raphel, held Senate Hearings on Afghanistan and conducted a three-day conference in Washington between leaders of the Afghan factions and US legislators, which Unocal helped fund.[16]

Raphel recognized the dangers emanating from Afghanistan. In May 1996 she told the US Senate, 'Afghanistan has become a conduit for drugs, crime and terrorism that can undermine Pakistan, the neighbouring Central Asian states and have an impact beyond Europe and Russia.' She said extremist training camps in Afghanistan were exporting terrorism.[17] But Raphel's perserverance turned into patchwork diplomacy, because it was not underpinned by a serious US commitment towards the region.

When the Taliban captured Kabul in September 1996, the CIA, again encouraged by ISI analysis, considered that a Taliban conquest of the country was now possible and that the Unocal project could reach fruition. The USA was silent on the Taliban's repression of Kabul's women and the dramatic escalation in fighting and in November Raphael urged all states to engage the Taliban and not isolate them. 'The Taliban control more than two-thirds of the country, they are Afghan, they are indigenous, they have demonstrated staying power. The real source of their success has been the willingness of many Afghans, particularly Pashtuns, to tacitly trade unending fighting and chaos for a measure of peace and security, even with severe social restrictions,' said Raphel. 'It is not in the interests of Afghanistan or any of us here that the Taliban be isolated,' she added.[18]

Several concerned American commentators noted the inconsistency of US policy at the time. 'The US, although vocal against the ongoing human rights violations, has not spelled out a clear policy towards the country and has not taken a strong and forthright public stand against the interference in Afghanistan by its friends and erstwhile allies – Saudi Arabia and Pakistan, whose aid – financial and otherwise – enabled the Taliban to capture Kabul.'[19]

The US and Unocal wanted to believe that the Taliban would win and went along with Pakistan's analysis that they would. The most naive US policy-makers hoped that the Taliban would emulate US–Saudi Arabia relations in the 1920s. 'The Taliban will probably develop like the Saudis did. There will be Aramco, pipelines, an emir, no parliament and lots of Sharia law. We can live with that,' said one US diplomat.[20] Given their suspicions, it was not unexpected that the anti-Taliban alliance, Iran and Russia, should view the Unocal project as an arm of US-CIA foreign policy and as the key to US support for the Taliban. Unocal's links with the US government became a subject of massive speculation. US commentator Richard Mackenzie wrote that Unocal was being regularly briefed by the CIA and the ISI.[21]

Unocal neither admitted nor denied receiving State Department support, as any US company would have in a foreign country, but it denied links with the CIA. 'Since Unocal was the only US company involved in the CentGas consortium, State Department support for that route became, de facto, support for CentGas and Unocal. At the same time, Unocal's policy of political neutrality was well known to the US Government,' Unocal President John Imle told me.[22] Unocal's failure was that it never developed a relationship with the Afghan factions, which were independent of the US and Pakistan governments.

There was a bigger problem. Until July 1997 when Strobe Talbott made his speech in Washington, the USA had no strategic plan for accessing Central Asia's energy. US oil companies were faced with what they could not do, rather than what they could do since they were forbidden to build pipelines through Iran and Russia. When Washington finally articulated its policy of 'a transport corridor' from the Caspian to Turkey (avoiding Russia and Iran), the oil companies were reluctant to oblige given the costs and the turbulence in the region. The essential issue which the USA declined to tackle was peace-making in the region. Until there was an end to the civil wars in Central Asia and the Caspian (Afghanistan, Tajikistan, Georgia, Chechnya, Nagorno-Karabakh, the Kurdish issue) and there was a broad consensus with Iran and Russia, pipelines would neither be safe to build nor commercially feasible, as every step of the way Iran and Russia would block or even sabotage them.

It was in the interests of Iran and Russia to keep the region unstable by arming the anti-Taliban alliance, so that US pipeline plans could never succeed. Even today the USA is muddled on the critical question of whether it wants to save Central Asia's depressed economies by letting them export energy any way they like or to keep Iran and Russia under blockade as far as pipelines are concerned.

The USA and Unocal were essentially faced with a simple question in Afghanistan. Was it preferable to rely on Pakistan and Saudi Arabia to deliver the Taliban and obtain a temporary Afghan concensus in the old-fashioned way by reconquering the country? Or was it preferable for the USA to engage in peacemaking and bring the Afghan ethnic groups and factions together to form a broad-based government, which might ensure lasting stability? Although Washington's broad-brush policy was to support a widely based, multi-ethnic government in Kabul, the USA for a time believed in the Taliban and when it ceased to do so, it was not willing to rein in Pakistan and Saudi Arabia.

Although there was no CIA budget for providing arms and ammunition to the Taliban and Unocal did not channel military support to the Taliban, the USA did support the Taliban through its traditional allies Pakistan and Saudi Arabia, accepting their provision of arms and funding to the Taliban. 'The US acquiesced in supporting the Taliban because of our links to the Pakistan and Saudi governments who backed them. But we no longer do so and we have told them categorically that we need a settlement,' the highest ranking US diplomat dealing with Afghanistan said in 1998.[23] In Washington it was perhaps not so much a covert policy as no policy. A covert policy involves planning, funding and taking decisions, but there was no such process taking place at the highest levels in Washington on Afghanistan.

Washington's change of heart over the Taliban in late 1997 also arose because of the deteriorating political and economic crisis in Pakistan. US officials began to voice fears that the drugs, terrorism and Islamic fundamentalist threat which the Taliban posed could overwhelm its old and now decidedly fragile ally Pakistan. The USA warned Pakistan of the increasing dangers it faced, but became frustrated with the ISI's refusal to pressurize the Taliban to be more flexible on the political and gender fronts.

The first public expression of the US change was made by Secretary of State Madeleine Albright when she visited Islamabad in November 1997. On the steps of Pakistan's Foreign Office she called the Taliban 'despicable' for their gender policies. Inside, she warned Pakistani officials that Pakistan was becoming isolated in Central Asia – which weakened US leverage in the region. But the Sharif regime remained at odds with itself, wanting to become an energy conduit for Central Asia, wanting peace in Afghanistan but insisting this would best be achieved by a Taliban victory. Pakistan could not have a Taliban victory, access to Central Asia, friendship with Iran and an end to Bin Laden-style terrorism, all at the same time. It was a self-defeating, deluded and contradictory policy which Pakistan refused even to acknowledge.

The shift in US policy was also because of major changes in Washington. The dour, hapless Warren Christopher was replaced by Albright as Secretary of State in early 1997. Her own experiences as a child in

Central Europe ensured that human rights would figure prominently on her agenda. A new team of US diplomats began to deal with Afghanistan in both Washington and Islamabad and the new US Assistant Secretary for South Asia, Karl Inderfurth, knew Afghanistan as a former journalist and was much closer to Albright than Raphel was to Christopher.

Albright's private criticism of Pakistan's policies and public criticism of the Taliban was followed up by the visit of the US Ambassador to the UN, Bill Richardson, to Islamabad and Kabul in April 1998. But with Pakistan exerting no real pressure on the Taliban, except advising them to give Richardson full protocol, the trip turned into little more than a public relations exercise. Richardson's agreements with the Taliban were rescinded hours later by Mullah Omar. The only positive spin from the trip was that it convinced Iran that the USA now saw Tehran as a dialogue partner in future Afghan peace talks, thereby reducing US–Iranian tensions over Afghanistan.

As with Raphel's initiatives in 1996, the USA appeared to be dipping its fingers into the Afghan quagmire, but wanted no real responsibility. The USA wished to avoid taking sides or getting involved in the nuts and bolts of peace-making. The Pakistanis realized this weakness and tried to negate US pressure. Foreign Minister Gohar Ayub blasted the Americans just before Richardson arrived. 'The Americans are thinking of putting puppets there [in Kabul]. These are people who hover around in Pakistan from one cocktail party to the other, they do not cut much ice because they have no support in Afghanistan,' Ayub said on a visit to Tokyo.[24]

US tensions with Pakistan increased substantially after Bin Laden's attacks against US Embassies in Africa in August 1998. The fact that the ISI had helped introduce Bin Laden to the Taliban in 1996 and had maintained contacts with him, but now declined to help the Americans catch him, created major difficulties in the relationship. The American tone became much harsher. 'There appears to be a pervasive and dangerous interplay between the politics of Pakistan and the turmoil inside Afghanistan. With the emergence of the Taliban there is growing reason to fear that militant extremism, obscurantism and sectarianism will infect surrounding countries. None of those countries has more to lose than Pakistan if "Talibanization" were to spread further,' said US Deputy Secretary of State Strobe Talbott in Janury 1999.[25]

But the Americans were not prepared to publicly criticize Saudi support to the Taliban publicly, even though they privately urged Saudi Arabia to use its influence on the Taliban to deliver Bin Laden. Even US Congressmen were now raising the self-defeating contradictions in US policy. 'I have called into question whether or not this administration has a covert policy that has empowered the Taliban and enabled this brutal movement to hold on to power,' said Congressman Dana Rohrabacher in

April 1999. 'The US has a very close relationship with Saudi Arabia and Pakistan, but unfortunately, instead of providing leadership, we are letting them lead our policy,' he said.[26]

The problem for Pakistan was that Washington had demonized Bin Laden to such an extent that he had become a hero for many Muslims, particularly in Pakistan. US policy was again a one-track agenda, solely focused on getting Bin Laden, rather than tackling the wider problems of Afghanistan-based terrorism and peace-making. Washington appeared to have a Bin Laden policy but not an Afghanistan policy. From supporting the Taliban the USA had now moved to the other extreme of rejecting them completely.

The US rejection of the Taliban was largely because of the pressure exerted by the feminist movement at home. Afghan women activists such as Zieba Shorish-Shamley had persuaded the Feminist Majority to spearhead a signature campaign to mobilize support for Afghan women and force Clinton to take a tougher stance against the Taliban. Three hundred women's groups, trade unions and human rights groups signed up. The campaign got a major propaganda boost when Mavis Leno, the wife of comedian Jay Leno pledged US$100,000 to it. 'The US bears some responsibility for the conditions of women in Afghanistan. For years our country provided weapons to the Mujaheddin groups to fight the Soviets,' Ms Leno told a Congressional hearing in March 1998.[27]

With Leno's help, the Feminist Majority organized a massive star-studded party after the 1999 Oscars to honour Afghan women. 'The Taliban's war on women has become the latest cause célèbre in Hollywood. Tibet is out. Afghanistan is in,' wrote the *Washington Post*.[28] As a celebrity in a celebrity-dominated culture Leno and her opinions went far. Hillary Clinton, anxious to secure feminist support for her future political career weighed in with statement after statement condemning the Taliban. 'When women are savagely beaten by so-called religious police for not being fully covered or for making noises while they walk, we know that is not just the physical beating that is the objective. It is the destruction of the spirit of these women,' said Mrs Clinton in a speech in 1999.[29] US policy appeared to have come full circle, from unconditionally accepting the Taliban to unconditionally rejecting them.

~14~

MASTER OR VICTIM:
PAKISTAN'S AFGHAN WAR

In the last days of June 1998, there was pandemonium in Pakistan's Finance and Foreign Ministries. Senior bureaucrats scuttled between the two ministries and the Prime Minister's Secretariat with bulging briefcases full of files that needed signatures from various ministers. In a few days on 30 June the 1997/8 financial year expired and the new financial year began. Every ministry was trying to use up its funds for the present year and procure higher allocations for the coming year from the Finance Ministry. A few weeks earlier (28 May) Pakistan had tested six nuclear devices following India's tests and the West had slapped punitive sanctions on both countries, creating a major foreign currency crisis for Pakistan and worsening the deep recession that had gripped the economy since 1996.

Nevertheless, on 28 June the cash-strapped Finance Ministry authorized 300 million rupees (US$6 million) in salaries – for the Taliban administration in Kabul. The allocation would allow the Foreign Ministry to dispense 50 million rupees every month for the next six months to pay the salaries of Afghanistan's rulers. The Foreign Ministry needed to hide this money in its own budget and that of other ministries, so that it would not appear on the 1998/9 budget record and be kept away from the prying eyes of international donors, who were demanding massive cuts in government spending to salvage the crisis-hit economy.

In 1997/8 Pakistan provided the Taliban with an estimated US$30 million in aid.[1] This included 600,000 tons of wheat, diesel, petroleum and kerosene fuel which was partly paid for by Saudi Arabia, arms and ammunition, ariel bombs, maintenance and spare parts for its Soviet-era military equipment such as tanks and heavy artillery, repairs and maintenance of the Taliban's airforce and airport operations, road building, electricity supply in Kandahar and salaries. Pakistan also facilitated the Taliban's own purchases of arms and ammunition from Ukraine and Eastern Europe. The money given for salaries was seldom used for that purpose and went directly into the war effort. Taliban officials in Kabul were not paid for months at a time. Officially Pakistan denied it was supporting the Taliban.

This flow of aid was a legacy from the past. During the 1980s the ISI had handled the billions of US dollars which had poured in from the West and Arab states to help the Mujaheddin. With encouragement and technical support from the CIA, that money had also been used to carry out an enormous expansion of the ISI. The ISI inducted hundreds of army officers to monitor not just Afghanistan, but India and all of Pakistan's foreign intelligence as well as domestic politics, the economy, the media and every aspect of social and cultural life in the country.

The CIA provided the latest technology, including equipment that enabled the ISI to monitor every telephone call in the country. The ISI became the eyes and ears of President Zia's military regime and by 1989 it was the most powerful political and foreign policy force in Pakistan, repeatedly overriding later civilian governments and parliament in policy areas it concluded were critical to the country's national security interests. Primarily those areas were India and Afghanistan.

Through the 1990s the ISI tried to maintain its exclusive grip on Pakistan's Afghan policy. However, the end of the Cold War deprived the ISI of its funds and due to Pakistan's severe economic crisis, its secret budget was drastically cut. More significantly the ISI's dwindling resources were now directed towards another war of attrition – this one for the hearts and minds of the Kashmiri people who had risen up in revolt against India in 1989.

During Prime Minister Benazir Bhutto's second term of office (1993–96), the retired Interior Minister General Naseerullah Babar promoted the Taliban. He wanted to free Afghan policy from the ISI. Both Bhutto and Babar were deeply suspicious of the ISI's power and resources, which it had used to fuel discontent against Bhutto in her first term in office, leading to her removal in 1990. Moreover, the ISI was initially doubtful about the Taliban's potential as it was still wedded to backing Gulbuddin Hikmetyar and had few funds to back a movement of Afghan students. Babar 'civilianized' support to the Taliban. He created an Afghan Trade Development Cell in the Interior Ministry, which ostensibly had the task of co-ordinating efforts to facilitate a trade route to Central Asia – although its principal task was to provide logistical backing for the Taliban, not from secret funds but from the budgets of government ministries.

Babar ordered Pakistan Telecommunications to set up a telephone network for the Taliban, which became part of the Pakistan telephone grid. Kandahar could be dialled from anywhere in Pakistan as a domestic call using the prefix 081 – the same as Quetta's prefix. Engineers from the Public Works Department and the Water and Power Development Authority carried out road repairs and provided an electricity supply to Kandahar city. The paramilitary Frontier Corps, directly under the control of Babar, helped the Taliban set up an internal wireless network for their commanders. Pakistan International Airlines (PIA) and the Civil Aviation Authority sent in technicans to repair Kandahar airport and the fighter jets and helicopters the Taliban had captured. Radio Pakistan provided technical support to Radio Afghanistan, now renamed Radio Shariat.

After the Taliban capture of Herat in 1995, Pakistani efforts intensified. In January 1996 the Director General of the Afghan Trade Development Cell travelled by road from Quetta to Turkmenistan accompanied by officials from Civil Aviation, Pakistan Telecom, PIA, Pakistan Railways, Radio Pakistan and the National Bank of Pakistan. Ministries and government corporations took on further projects to help the Taliban with budgets that were supposedly for developing Pakistan's economy.[2]

Despite these efforts to help and control the Taliban, they were nobody's puppets and they resisted every attempt by Islamabad to pull their strings. Throughout Afghan history no outsider has been able to manipulate the Afghans, something the British and the Soviets learnt to their cost. Pakistan, it appeared, had learnt no lessons from history while it still lived in the past, when CIA and Saudi funding had given Pakistan the power to dominate the course of the jihad. Moreover, the Taliban's social, economic and political links to Pakistan's Pashtun borderlands were immense, forged through two decades of war and life as refugees in Pakistan. The Taliban were born in Pakistani refugee camps, educated in Pakistani *madrassas* and learnt their fighting skills from Mujaheddin parties based in Pakistan. Their families carried Pakistani identity cards.

The Taliban's deep connections to Pakistani state institutions, political parties, Islamic groups, the *madrassa* network, the drugs mafia and business and transport groups came at a time when Pakistan's power structure was unravelling and fragmented. This suited the Taliban who were not beholden to any single Pakistani lobby such as the ISI. Whereas in the 1980s Mujaheddin leaders had exclusive relationships with the ISI and the Jamaat-e-Islami, they had no links with other political and economic lobbies. In contrast the Taliban had access to more influential lobbies and groups in Pakistan than most Pakistanis.

This unprecedented access enabled the Taliban to play off one lobby against another and extend their influence in Pakistan even furthur. At times they would defy the ISI by enlisting the help of government ministers or the transport mafia. At other times they would defy the federal government by gaining support from the provincial governments in Baluchistan and the NWFP. As the Taliban movement expanded it became increasingly unclear as to who was driving whom. Pakistan, rather than being the master of the Taliban, was instead becoming its victim.

Pakistan's security perceptions were initially shaped by Afghanistan's territorial claims on parts of the NWFP and Baluchistan and there were border clashes between the two states in the 1950s and 1960s. Afghanistan insisted that Pakistan's Pashtun tribal belt should be allowed to opt either for independence or join Pakistan or Afghanistan. Diplomatic relations were severed twice, in 1955 and 1962, as Kabul advocated a 'Greater Pashtunistan', which was supported by left-wing Pakistani Pashtuns. The Zia regime saw the Aghan jihad as a means to end these claims for ever, by ensuring that a pliable pro-Pakistan Pashtun Mujaheddin government came to power in Kabul.

Military strategists argued that this would give Pakistan 'strategic depth' against its primary enemy India. Pakistan's elongated geography, the lack of space, depth and a hinterland denied its armed forces the ability to fight a prolonged war with India. In the 1990s an addition to this was that a friendly Afghanistan would give Kashmiri militants a base from where they could be trained, funded and armed.

In 1992–93, under Indian pressure, the USA had come close to declaring Pakistan a state sponsor of terrorism, as Kashmiri militants based in Pakistan carried out guerrilla attacks in Indian Kashmir. Pakistan tried to resolve this problem in 1993 by moving many of the Kashmiri groups' bases to eastern Afghanistan and paying the Jalalabad Shura and later the Taliban to take them under their protection. The government also privatized its support to the Kashmir Mujaheddin, by making Islamic parties responsible for their training and funding. Bin Laden was encouraged to join the Taliban in 1996, as he too was sponsoring bases for Kashmiri militants in Khost.

Increasingly, the Kashmir issue became the prime mover behind Pakistan's Afghan policy and its support to the Taliban. The Taliban exploited this adroitly, refusing to accept other Pakistani demands knowing that Islamabad could deny them nothing, as long as they provided bases for Kashmiri and Pakistani militants. 'We support the jihad in Kashmir,' said Mullah Omar in 1998. 'It is also true that some Afghans are fighting against the Indian occupation forces in Kashmir. But these Afghans have gone on their own,' he added.[3]

To many, the concept of 'strategic depth' was riddled with fallacies and misconceptions as it ignored obvious ground realities that political stability at home, economic development, wider literacy and friendly relations with neighbours ensured greater national security than imaginary mirages of strategic depth in the Afghan mountains. 'The attainment of strategic depth has been a prime objective of Pakistan's Afghanistan policy since General Zia ul Haq. In military thought it is a non-concept, unless one is referring to a hard-to-reach place where a defeated army might safely cocoon,' wrote Pakistani scholar Eqbal Ahmad. 'The outcome is a country caught in an iron web of wrong assumptions, maginotic [sic] concepts, failed policies, fixed postures and sectarian violence. Far from improving it, a Taliban victory is likely to augment Pakistan's political and strategic predicament,' he added.[4]

The military assumed that the Taliban would recognize the Durand Line – the disputed boundary line between the two countries created by the British and which no Afghan regime has recognized. The military also assumed that the Taliban would curb Pashtun nationalism in the NWFP and provide an outlet for Pakistan's Islamic radicals, thus forestalling an Islamic movement at home. In fact just the opposite occurred. The Taliban refused to recognize the Durand Line or drop Afghanistan's claims to parts of the NWFP. The Taliban fostered Pashtun nationalism, albeit of an Islamic character and it began to affect Pakistani Pashtuns.

Worse still, the Taliban gave sanctuary and armed the most violent Sunni extremist groups in Pakistan, who killed Pakistani Shias, wanted Pakistan declared a Sunni state and advocated the overthrow of the ruling elite through an Islamic revolution. 'The apparent victor, Pakistan, could pay dearly for its success. The triumph of the Taliban has virtually eliminated the border between Pakistan and Afghanistan. On both sides, Pashtun tribes are slipping towards fundamentalism and becoming increasingly implicated in drug trafficking. They are gaining autonomy, already small fundamentalist tribal emirates are appearing on Pakistani soil. The de facto absorption of Afghanistan will accentuate centrifugal tendencies within Pakistan,' predicted Olivier Roy in 1997.[5] In fact the backwash from Afghanistan was leading to the 'Talibanization' of Pakistan. The Taliban were not providing strategic depth to Pakistan, but Pakistan was providing strategic depth to the Taliban.

Pakistan became a victim not only of its strategic vision, but of its own intelligence agencies. The ISI's micro-management of the Afghan jihad was only possible because under a military regime and with lavish funding from abroad, the ISI was able to subdue political opposition at home. Zia and the ISI had the power to formulate Afghan policy and implement it, something which no other intelligence agency, not even the CIA, had the power to do. This gave the ISI enormous unity of purpose and scope for operations. The ISI then faced no independent powerful lobbies or political rivals, as in the Taliban era, when they had to compete with an array of Pakistani lobbies which independently supported the Taliban and had their own agendas.

By running both Afghan policy and operations, the ISI had no room for critical reappraisals, accommodating dissent from the status quo, nor the imagination or flexibility to adapt to changing situations and the ever-evolving geo-political environment. The ISI became a victim of its own rigidity and inflexibility, even as its power to actually control the Taliban dwindled. The agency's operatives in Afghanistan were all Pashtun officers, while many were also motivated by strong Islamic fundamentalist leanings. Working closely with Hikmetyar and later the Taliban, this Pashtun cadre developed its own agenda, aimed at furthering Pashtun power and radical Islam in Afghanistan at the expense of the ethnic minorities and moderate Islam.

In the words of one retired ISI officer, 'these officers became more Taliban than the Taliban.' Consequently their analysis of the anti-Taliban alliance and pipeline politics became deeply flawed, riddled with rigidity, clichés and false assumptions which were driven more by their strong Islamic ideological assumptions than by objective facts. But by now the ISI was too powerful for the government of the day to question and too intrusive for any army chief of staff to clean up.

When the Taliban emerged the ISI was initially sceptical about their chances. It was a period when the ISI was in retreat, with the failure of Hikmetyar to capture Kabul and a shortage of funds. The ISI retreat gave the Bhutto government the opportunity to devise their own support for the Taliban.[6] During 1995 the ISI continued to debate the issue of support for the Taliban. The debate centred around the Pashtun-Islamic field officers inside Afghanistan, who advocated greater support for the Taliban and those officers involved in long-term strategic planning, who wished to keep Pakistan's support to a minimum so as not to worsen relations with Central Asia and Iran. By the summer of 1995, the Pashtun network in the army and the ISI determined to back the Taliban, especially as President Burhanuddin Rabbani sought support from Pakistan's rivals – Russia, Iran and India.[7]

But by now the ISI faced all the other Pakistani lobbies which the Taliban were plugged into, from radical mullahs to drug barons. The fierce competition between the ISI, the government and these lobbies only further fragmented Islamabad's decision-making process on Afghanistan. Pakistan's Foreign Ministry was so weakened by this confusion that it became virtually irrelevant to Afghan policy and unable to counter the worsening diplomatic environment as every neighbour – Russia, Iran, the Central Asian states – accused Islamabad of destabilizing the region. Efforts to defuse the criticism such as secret trips to Moscow, Tehran, Tashkent and Ashkhabad by successive ISI chiefs proved a failure.

As international criticism increased, the newly elected Nawaz Sharif government and the ISI became more adamant in backing the Taliban.

In May 1997 when the Taliban tried to capture Mazar, the ISI calculated that by recognizing the Taliban government, it would force hostile neighbours to deal with the Taliban and need Islamabad to improve their own relationships with the Taliban. It was a high stakes gamble that badly misfired when Pakistan prematurely recognized the Taliban, who were then driven out of Mazar.[8]

Pakistan reacted by lashing out at its critics including the UN which was now openly critical of all external support for the Afghan factions. Pakistan accused UN Secretary General Kofi Annan of being partisan. 'The UN has gradually marginalized itself in Afghanistan and lost credibility as an impartial mediator,' said Ahmad Kamal, Pakistan's Ambassador to the UN in January 1998. Later Kamal told a conference of Pakistani envoys in Islamabad that it was not Pakistan which was isolated in Afghanistan, but that the rest of the world was isolated from Pakistan and they would have to come round to accepting Pakistan's position on the Taliban.[9]

As Pakistan advocated the Taliban's policies in the teeth of widespread international criticism, the government lost sight of how much the country was losing. The smuggling trade to and from Afghanistan became the most devastating manifestation of these losses. This trade, which now extends into Central Asia, Iran and the Persian Gulf represents a crippling loss of revenue for all these countries but particularly Pakistan, where local industry has been decimated by the smuggling of foreign consumer goods. What is euphemistically called the Afghan Transit Trade (ATT) has become the biggest smuggling racket in the world and has enmeshed the Taliban with Pakistani smugglers, transporters, drug barons, bureaucrats, politicans and police and army officers. This trade became the main source of official income for the Taliban, even as it undermined the economies of neighbouring states.

The border post between Chaman in Baluchistan province and Spin Baldak in Afghanistan is a prime location for watching the racket at work. On a good day, some 300 trucks pass through. Truck drivers, Pakistani customs officials and Taliban mix in a casual, friendly way guzzling down endless cups of tea, as long lines of trucks wait to cross. Everybody seems to know everybody else as drivers tell stories which would make the World Trade Organisation's hair stand on end. Many of the huge Mercedes and Bedford trucks are stolen and have false number plates. The goods they carry have no invoices. The drivers may cross up to six international frontiers on false driving licenses and without route permits or passports. The consignments range from Japanese camcorders to English underwear and Earl Grey tea, Chinese silk to American computer parts, Afghan heroin to Pakistani wheat and sugar, East European kalashnikovs to Iranian petroleum – and nobody pays customs duties or sales tax.

This Wild West of free trade expanded due to the civil war in Afghanistan, the drugs business and the collapse and corruption of Pakistani, Iranian and Central Asian state institutions along their borders with Afghanistan. It coincided with a hunger for consumer goods throughout the region. Pakistani and Afghan, transport and drugs mafias merged to fuel this need. 'It's completely out of control,' an official of Pakistan's Central Board of Revenue told me as early as 1995. 'The Taliban are funded by transporters to open the roads for smuggling and this mafia is now making and breaking governments in Afghanistan and in Pakistan. Pakistan will face a 30-per-cent shortfall in revenues this year, because of customs duties lost to the ATT,' he said.[10]

Trade has always been critical to the Islamic heartland. The Silk Route which linked China to Europe in the Middle Ages passed through Central Asia and Afghanistan and was run by the same tribesmen and nomads who are the truck-drivers of today. The Silk Route influenced Europe almost as much as the Arab conquests, for these caravans transported not just luxury goods, but ideas, religion, new weapons and scientific discoveries. A camel caravan might consist of five or six thousands camels, 'its total capacity equalling that of a very large merchant sailing ship. A caravan travelled like an army, with a leader, a general staff, strict rules, compulsory staging posts, and routine precautions against marauding nomads,' wrote French historian Fernand Braudel.[11] Little seems to have changed in nearly 2,000 years. Today's smugglers operate with a similar military type infrastructure even though trucks have replaced camels.

In 1950, under international agreements, Pakistan gave land-locked Afghanistan permission to import duty-free goods through the port of Karachi according to an ATT agreement. Truckers would drive their sealed containers from Karachi, cross into Afghanistan, sell some goods in Kabul and then turn around to resell the rest in Pakistani markets. It was a flourishing but limited business giving Pakistanis access to cheap, duty-free foreign consumer goods, particularly Japanese electronics. The ATT expanded in the 1980s, servicing Afghanistan's communist-controlled cities. The fall of Kabul in 1992 coincided with new markets opening up in Central Asia and the need for foodstuffs, fuel and building materials as Afghan refugees returned home – a potential bonanza for the transport mafias.

However, the transporters were frustrated with the civil war and the warlords who taxed their trucks dozens of times along a single route. Although the Peshawar-based transport mafia were trading between Pakistan, northern Afghanistan and Uzbekistan, despite the continuing war around Kabul, the Quetta-based mafia were at a loss with the rapacious, Kandahar warlords who had set up dozens of toll chains along the highway from Pakistan. The Quetta-based transport mafia were keen to open up safe routes to Iran and Turkmenistan, just as the Bhutto government were advocating a similar policy.

Taliban leaders were well connected to the Quetta mafia, who were the first to provide financial support to the Taliban movement. Initially, the Quetta mafia gave the Taliban a monthly retainer but as the Taliban expanded westwards they demanded more funds. In Apil 1995, witnesses I spoke to in Quetta said the Taliban collected 6 million rupees (US$130,000) from transporters in Chaman in a single day and twice that amount the next day in Quetta as they prepared for their first attack on Herat. These 'donations' were quite apart from the single all-inclusive customs duty the Taliban now charged trucks crossing into Afghanistan from Pakistan, which became the Taliban's main source of official income.

With routes now safe and secure, the volume and area of smuggling expanded dramatically. From Quetta, truck convoys travelled to Kanda-har, then southwards to Iran, westwards to Turkmenistan and to other CARs, even Russia. Soon the Quetta transport mafia were urging the Taliban to capture Herat in order to take full control of the road to Turkmenistan.[12] Even though the ISI initially advised the Taliban not to attack Herat, the Quetta mafia had more influence with the Taliban. In 1996, the transporters urged the Taliban to clear the route north by capturing Kabul. After taking the capital, the Taliban levied an average of 6000 rupees (US$150) for a truck travelling from Peshawar to Kabul, compared to 30,000–50,000 rupees, which truckers paid before. The transport mafia gave Taliban leaders a stake in their business by encouraging them to buy trucks or arranging for their relatives to do so. And with the drugs mafia now willing to pay a zakat (tax) to transport heroin, the transit trade became even more crucial to the Taliban exchequer.

Pakistan was the most damaged victim of this trade. The Central Board of Revenue (CBR) estimated that Pakistan lost 3.5 billion rupees (US$80 million) in customs revenue in the financial year 1992/3, 11 billion rupees in 1993/4, 20 billion rupees during 1994/5 and 30 billion rupees (US$600 million) in 1997/8 – a staggering increase every year that reflected the Taliban's expansion.[13] An enormous nexus of corruption emerged in Paki-stan due to the ATT. All the Pakistani agencies involved were taking bribes – Customs, Customs Intelligence, CBR, the Frontier Constabulary and the administrators in the tribal belt. Lucrative customs jobs on the Afghan border were 'bought' by applicants who paid bribes to senior bur-eaucrats to get the posting. These bribes, considered an investment, were then made up by the newly appointed officials who extracted bribes from the ATT.

This nexus extended to politicians and cabinet ministers in Baluchistan and the NWFP. The chief ministers and governors of the two provinces issued route permits for trucks to operate and wheat and sugar permits for the export of these commodities to Afghanistan. Senior army officers complained to me in 1995 and again in 1996, that the competition between the chief ministers and governors of the two provinces in issuing route permits was a major source of corruption paralyzing the entire administrative machinery, interfering and often at odds with the ISI's policy on Afghanistan and creating widespread Taliban 'control' over Pakistani politicans.

As the mafia extended their trade, they also stripped Afghanistan bare. They cut down millions of acres of timber in Afghanistan for the Pakistani market, denuding the countryside as there was no reforestation. They stripped down rusting factories, destroyed tanks and vehicles and even electricity and telephone poles for their steel and sold the scrap to steel mills in Lahore. Car-jacking in Karachi and other cities flourished as the mafia organized local car thieves to steal vehicles and then shifted the vehicles to Afghanistan. The mafia then resold them to clients in Afghanistan and Pakistan. Sixty-five thousand vehicles were stolen from Karachi alone in 1992–98 with the majority ending up in Afghanistan, only to reappear in Pakistan with their number plates changed.[14]

The transport mafia also smuggled in electronic goods from Dubai, Sharjah and other Persian Gulf ports while exporting heroin hidden in Afghan dried fruit and seasoned timber – on Ariana, the national Afghan airline now controlled by the Taliban. Flights from Kandahar, Kabul and Jalalabad took off directly for the Gulf, moving the Taliban into the jet age and giving Silk Route smuggling a modern commercial edge.

The ATT fuelled the already powerful black economy in Pakistan. According to an academic study, the underground economy in Pakistan has snowballed from 15 billion rupees in 1973 to 1,115 billion rupees in 1996, with its share in GDP increasing from 20 per cent to 51 per cent.[15] During the same period, tax evasion – including customs duty evasion – has escalated from 1.5 billion to 152 billion rupees, accelerating at a rate of 88 billion rupees per year. The smuggling trade contributed some 100 billion rupees to the underground economy in 1993, which had escalated to over 300 billion rupees in 1998. That is equivalent to 30 per cent of the country's total imports of US$10 billion or equal to the entire revenue collection target for 1998/9 (300 billion rupees). In addition, the Afghanistan–Pakistan drugs trade was estimated to be worth an annual 50 billion rupees.

In the NWFP, smugglers markets or baras were flooded with imported consumer goods causing massive losses to Pakistani industry. For example, in 1994 Pakistan, which manufactured its own air-conditioners, imported just 30 million rupees' worth of foreign air-conditoners. Afghanistan, a country then totally bereft of electricity, imported through the ATT 1 billion rupees' worth of air-conditioners, which all ended up in Pakistani *baras*, thus crippling local manufacturers. When duty-free Japanese TV sets or dishwashers were available at virtually the same price as Pakistani manufactured ones, consumers would naturally buy Japanese products. The bara at Hayatabad outside Peshawar set up brand-name shops to attract customers such as Britain's Marks and Spencer and Mothercare, and Japan's Sony where the original products were available duty-free. 'The ATT has destroyed economic activity in the province and people have give up the idea of honest earnings and consider smuggling as their due right,' said NWFP Chief Minister Mahtab Ahmed Khan in December 1998.[16]

A similar undermining of the economy and widespread corruption was taking place in Iran. The transport mafia's smuggling of fuel and other goods from Iran to Afghanistan and Pakistan led to revenue losses, crippled local industry and corrupted people at the highest level of government. Iranian officials privately admitted to me that the Bunyads or the state-run industrial foundations as well as the Revolutionary Guards were among the beneficiaries from the smuggling of petroleum products, whose sale in Afghanistan earned 2,000–3,000-per-cent profit compared to Iran. Fuel was devoured in huge quantities by the war machines of the Afghan warlords and soon petrol pump owners in Baluchistan were ordering cheap fuel from Iran through the mafia, bypassing Pakistani companies (and customs duties) altogether.

Pakistan made several half-hearted attempts to rein in the ATT by stopping the import of items such as electronics, but the government always backed down as the Taliban refused to comply with the new orders and the mafia pressurized government ministers. There were no lobbies in Islamabad willing to point out the damage being inflicted upon Pakistan's economy or prepared to force the Taliban to comply. The ISI was unwilling to use the threat of withholding support to the Taliban until they complied. To bewildered foreign and Pakistani investors the government appeared willing to undermine Pakistan's own economy for the sake of the Taliban, as Islamabad was allowing a de facto transfer of revenues from the Pakistan state to the Taliban. It was a form of unofficial aid, which benefited the Taliban and made those Pakistanis involved extremely rich. They created the most powerful lobby to continue Pakistan's support to the Taliban.

The backlash from Afghanistan added fuel to the spreading fire of instability in Pakistan. In the 1980s the fall-out from the Soviet invasion of Afghanistan had created 'the heroin and kalashnikov culture' that undermined Pakistan's politics and economy. 'Ten years of active involvement in the Afghan war has changed the social profile of Pakistan to such an extent that any government faces serious problems in effective governance. Pakistani society is now more fractured, inundated with sophisticated weapons, brutalized due to growing civic violence and overwhelmed by the spread of narcotics,' wrote American historian Paul Kennedy.[17]

In the late 1990s the repercussions were much more pervasive, undermining all the institutions of the state. Pakistan's economy was being crippled by the ATT, its foreign policy faced isolation from the West and immediate neighbours, law and order broke down as Islamic militants enacted their own laws and a new breed of anti-Shia Islamic radicals, who were given sanctuary by the Taliban, killed hundreds of Pakistani Shias between 1996 and 1999. This sectarian bloodshed is now fuelling a much wider rift between Pakistan's Sunni majority and Shia minority and undermining relations between Pakistan and Iran.[18] At the same time over 80,000 Pakistani Islamic militants have trained and fought with the Taliban since 1994. They form a hardcore of Islamic activists, ever ready to carry out a similar Taliban-style Islamic revolution in Pakistan.[19]

Tribal groups imitating the Taliban sprang up across the Pashtun belt in the NWFP and Baluchistan. As early as 1995 Maulana Sufi Mohammed had led his Tanzim Nifaz Shariat-i-Mohammedi in Bajaur Agency in an uprising to demand Sharia law. The revolt was joined by hundreds of Afghan and Pakistani Taliban before it was crushed by the army. The Tanzim leaders then sought refuge in Afghanistan with the Taliban. In December 1998, the Tehrik-i-Tuleba or Movement of Taliban in the Orakzai Agency publicly executed a murderer in front of 2,000 spectators in defiance of the legal process. They promised to implement Taliban-style justice throughout the Pashtun belt and banned TV, music and videos in imitation of the Taliban.[20] Other pro-Taliban Pashtun groups sprang up in Quetta – they burned down cinema houses, shot video shop owners, smashed satellite dishes and drove women off the streets.

Yet after the Taliban captured Mazar in 1998, Pakistan declared victory, demanding that the world recognize the movement which now controlled 80 per cent of Afghanistan. Pakistan's military and civilian leaders insisted that the Taliban's success was Pakistan's success and that its policy was correct and unchangeable. Pakistan considered Iranian influence in Afghanistan to be over and that Russia and the Central Asian states would be obliged to deal with the Taliban through Islamabad while the West would have no choice but to accept the Taliban's interpretation of Islam.

Even though there was mounting public concern about the Talibanization of Pakistan, the country's leaders ignored the growing internal chaos. Outsiders increasingly saw Pakistan as a failing or failed state like Afghanistan, Sudan or Somalia. A failed state is not necessarily a dying state, although it can be that too. A failed state is one in which the repeated failure of policies carried out by a bankrupt political elite is never considered sufficient reason to reconsider them. Pakistan's elite showed no inclination to change its policy in Afghanistan. General Zia had dreamed like a Mogul emperor of 'recreating a Sunni Muslim space between infidel "Hindustan", "heretic" [because Shia] Iran and "Christian" Russia'.[21] He believed that the message of the Afghan Mujaheddin would spread into Central Asia, revive Islam and create a new Pakistan-led Islamic block of nations. What Zia never considered was what his legacy would do to Pakistan.

~15~

SHIA VERSUS SUNNI: IRAN AND SAUDI ARABIA

There was a sense of change and renewal in Tehran in the spring of 1999. For nearly 20 years since the Islamic revolution, Tehran's women had shrouded themselves in the dictated garb of *hijab* – the uniform black tents. Now suddenly the *hijab* was sprouting faux-leopard-skin trimmings and fur. Some women were wearing raincoats or donning the *hijab* like a cape revealing short skirts, tight jeans, black silk stockings and high heels. Rather than an imposed dress code, female modesty now appeared to be up to the individual. The loosening up of the *hijab* was only one sign of the transformation of Iranian society after the election of Sayed Mohammed Khatami to the Presidency in May 1997, when he took 70 per cent of the popular vote in a stunning victory against a more hardline conservative candidate. Khatami had garnered the votes of the youth, who were fed up with 25-per-cent unemployment and high inflation and hopeful that he would usher in economic development and a more open society.

Khatami's victory created an immediate thaw in Iran's relations with the outside world as it opened up to the West, wooed its old enemy the USA with the need for 'a dialogue between civilizations' and sought an improvement in relations with the Arab world. Afghanistan was to become the primary issue in helping thaw relations between Iran, the USA and the Arab world. During his visit to Kabul in April 1998, US Ambassador Bill Richardson had already signalled that the USA saw Iran as a dialogue partner to help resolve the Afghan crisis. Iran was also talking to an old foe, Saudi Arabia.

'The positive climate between Iran and Saudi Arabia is encouraging and both sides are ready to co-operate for the resolution of the conflict in Afghanistan,' Iran's new Foreign Minister Kamal Kharrázi said in May 1998.[1] A suave, English-speaking diplomat who for 11 years had represented Iran at the UN, Kharrazi's soft diplomatic manner and style were representative of a revolution that had mellowed.

Iran's new leaders were deeply antagonistic to the Taliban, but they were pragmatic enough to realize that peace in Afghanistan was necessary for economic development and political liberalization in Iran. Stability in their neighbourhood would also help Iran end its international isolation. Khatami was far from looking for a fight with the Taliban, yet just six months later, after the Taliban killed nine Iranian diplomats in Mazar, Iran had mobilized a quarter of a million soldiers on its border with Afghanistan and was threatening to invade. As tensions with the Taliban escalated, the new relationship between Iran and Saudi Arabia took on even more importance.

Afghanistan has been just one area of conflict in the intense rivalry between the Persians and the Arabs. Both peoples have conquered and ruled one another against a background of dispute between Sunni Arabia and Shia Persia. In 1501 Shah Ismail of the Safavid dynasty turned Iran into the first and only Shia state in the Islamic world. Both the Persians and the Arabs had ruled over Central Asia and Afghanistan, although Persian rule and its culture and language was much more long-standing and left a permanent mark.

In the twentieth century the long war between revolutionary Iran and Iraq (1981–88), which led to some 1.5 million casualties, only deepened this rivalry as all the Arab states had supported Saddam Hussein's Iraq. As that war began, another was just beginning in Afghanistan and here too the age-old rivalries would continue – this time in the context of the Cold War and the US aim to isolate Iran with the help of the Arab states.

Ostensibly both Iran and Saudi Arabia were on the same side in the Afghan conflict. They strongly opposed the Soviet invasion of Afghanistan, supported the Mujaheddin and backed international measures to isolate the Afghan regime and the Soviet Union. But they supported opposing factions of the Mujaheddin and Iran never severed its diplomatic links with the Kabul regime. Saudi support to the Mujaheddin was in line with the US and Pakistani strategy of providing the bulk of funds and weapons to the most radical Sunni Pashtun groups and ignoring the Shia Afghans. The Saudis also separately funded Afghans who promoted Wahabbism.

Dollar for dollar, Saudi aid matched the funds given to the Mujaheddin by the US. The Saudis gave nearly US$4 billion in official aid to the Mujaheddin between 1980 and 1990, which did not include unofficial aid from Islamic charities, foundations, the private funds of Princes and mosque collections.[2] There were also direct funds given to the ISI, as in 1989 when the Saudis handed over US$26 million dollars to bribe Afghan leaders during the negotiations to form the Mujaheddin interim government in exile in Islamabad.[3] The Mujaheddin leaders were obliged to appoint an Afghan Wahabbi as interim Prime Minister.

In March 1990, the Saudis came up with an additional US$100 million for Hikmetyar's Hizb-e-Islami party who were backing an abortive coup attempt from within the Afghan army against President Najibullah by Hikmetyar and General Shahnawaz Tanai in Kabul.[4] After 1992 the Saudis continued to provide funds and fuel to the Mujaheddin government in Kabul. The fuel, chanelled through Pakistan, became a major source of corruption and patronage for successive Pakistani governments and the ISI.

Due to the estranged relations between Iran and the USA, the Afghan Mujaheddin groups based in Iran received no international military assistance. Nor did the two million Afghan refugees who fled to Iran receive the same humanitarian aid which their three million counterparts in Pakistan received. Tehran's own support to the Mujaheddin was limited on account of budgetary constraints because of the Iraq–Iran war. Thus throughout the 1980s, the USA effectively blocked off Iran from the outside world on Afghanistan. It was a legacy which only further embittered the Iranians against the USA and it would ensure much greater Iranian assertiveness in Afghanistan once the Cold War had ended and the Americans had left the Afghan stage.

Iran's initial support to the Mujaheddin only went to the Afghan Shias, in particular the Hazaras. It was the era in which Iran's Revolutionary Guards funded Shia militants worldwide – from Lebanon to Pakistan. By 1982, Iranian money and influence had encouraged a younger generation of Iran-trained radical Hazaras, to overthrow the traditional leaders who had emerged in the Hazarajat in 1979 to oppose the Soviet invasion. Later, eight Afghan Shia groups were given official status in Tehran, but Iran could never arm and fund them sufficiently. As a result, the Iran-backed Hazaras became marginal to the conflict inside Afghanistan and fought more amongst themselves than against the Soviets. Hazara factionalism was exacerbated by Iran's short-sighted, ideological policies in which the Hazaras loyalty to Tehran was viewed as more important than unity amongst themselves.

By 1988, with the Soviet withdrawal now imminent, Iran saw the need to strengthen the Hazaras. They helped unite the eight Iran-based Hazara groups into the single Hizb-e-Wahadat party. Iran now pressed for Wahadat's inclusion in international negotiations to form a new Mujaheddin government, which was to be dominated by the Peshawar-based Mujaheddin parties. Even though the Hazaras were a small minority and could not possibly hope to rule Afghanistan, Iran demanded first a 50-per-cent and then a 25-per-cent share for the Hazaras in any future Mujaheddin government.

As the rivalry between Iran and Saudi Arabia intensified with the Saudis importing more Arabs to spread Wahabbism and anti-Shiism inside Afghanistan, Pakistan kept the balance between them. A close ally of both states, Pakistan stressed the need to maintain a united front against the Kabul regime. The Iran–Saudi rivalry escalated after the 1989 withdrawal of Soviet troops when Iran drew closer to the Kabul regime. Iran considered the Kabul regime as the only force now capable of resisting a Sunni Pashtun takeover of Afghanistan. Iran rearmed Wahadat and by the time Kabul fell to the Mujaheddin in 1992, Wahadat controlled not only the Hazarajat but a significant part of western Kabul.

The Saudis meanwhile suffered a major set back as their two principle neo-Wahabbi protégés, Gulbuddin Hikmetyar and Abdul Rasul Sayyaf, split. Hikmetyar opposed the newly constituted Mujaheddin government in Kabul and joined up with the Hazaras to bombard the city. Sayyaf supported the Mujheddin government. This division was an extension of the much larger Saudi foreign policy debacle after Iraq invaded Kuwait in 1990. For 20 years the Saudis had funded hundreds of neo-Wahabbi parties across the Muslim world to spread Wahabbism and gain influence within the Islamic movements in these countries.

But when Riyadh asked these Islamic groups for a payback and to lend support to Saudi Arabia and the USA led coalition against Iraq, the majority of them backed Saddam Hussein, including Hikmetyar and most Afghan groups. Years of Saudi effort and billions of dollars were wasted because Saudi Arabia had failed to evolve a national interest-based foreign policy. The Saudi predicament is having a westernized ruling elite whose legitimacy is based on conservative fundamentalism, while those not part of the elite are radically anti-Western. The elite has promoted radical Wahabbism, even as this undermined its own power at home and abroad. Ironically only the moderate Afghan groups, whom the Saudis had ignored, helped out the Kingdom in its hour of need.[5]

As the Afghan war intensified between 1992 and 1995, so did the rivalry between Iran and Saudi Arabia. The Saudis and the Pakistanis made frequent attempts to bring all the factions together. However, they also made every effort to keep Iran and the Hazaras out of any potential agreements. In the 1992 Peshawar Accord which Pakistan and Saudi Arabia negotiated between the Mujaheddin on how to share power in Kabul and in the subsequent, but abortive, 1993 Islamabad and Jalalabad Accords to end the civil war, Iran and the Hazaras were sidelined. The exclusion of Iran in the 1990s by Pakistan and Saudi Arabia, similar to treatment by the USA of Iran in the 1980s, was to further embitter Tehran.

The Iranians had also become more pragmatic, backing not just the

Afghan Shias but all the Persian-speaking ethnic groups who were resisting Pashtun domination. Iran had a natural link with the Tajiks – they originate from the same ancient race and speak the same language – but the Iranians had been incensed by Ahmad Shah Masud's brutal attacks on the Hazaras in Kabul in 1993. Nevertheless, Tehran now realized that unless it backed the non-Pashtuns, Pashtun Sunnis would dominate Afghanistan. In 1993, for the first time, Iran began to give substantial military aid to the President Burhanuddin Rabbani in Kabul and the Uzbek warlord General Rashid Dostum and urged all the ethnic groups to join with Rabbani.

Iran's new strategy intensified its conflict of interest with Pakistan. Islamabad was determined to get its Pashtun protégés into Kabul and both the Pakistanis and the Saudis were determined to keep the Hazaras out of any power-sharing arrangement. Pakistan's adroit diplomacy in the 1980s in providing a balance between Saudi and Iranian interests was now abandoned in favour of the Saudis.

The collapse of the Soviet Union and the opening up of Central Asia had given Iran a new impetus to end its international isolation. Iran moved swiftly into Central Asia with a path-breaking trip by Foreign Minister Ali Akbar Velayti in November 1991, who signed an agreement to build a railway line between Turkmenistan and Iran. But here too the USA tried to block Iran with US Secretary of State James Baker declaring in 1992 that Washington would do everything to block Iranian influence in Central Asia.[6] The neo-communist rulers in Central Asia were initially deeply suspicious of Iran, fearing it wanted to spread Islamic fundamentalism.

But Iran resisted this temptation and also forged close ties with Russia, following the 1989 ice-breaking visit to Tehran by Soviet Foreign Minister Eduard Shevardnadze when he met with Ayatollah Khomeini. The Ayatollah's sanction of closer Iranian–Soviet ties just before his death, gave the new Russia a legitimacy in Iranian eyes. Also between 1989 and 1993, Russia provided Iran with US$10 billion worth of weapons to rebuild its military arsenal. Iran improved its standing in the region by forging links with other non-Muslim former Soviet states such as Georgia, Ukraine and Armenia. Tehran declined to support Azerbaijan in its war with Armenia, even though 20 per cent of the Iranian population is Azeri and helped Russia and the UN to end the civil war in Tajikistan.[7] Crucially, Iran and the CARs shared a deep suspicion of Afghan-Pashtun fundamentalism and the support it received from Pakistan and Saudi Arabia. Thus, an alliance between Iran, Russia and the CARs in support of the non-Pashtun ethnic groups existed well before the Taliban emerged.

In contrast, Saudi Arabia made few state-to-state attempts to improve relations with Russia or the CARs. The Saudis took nearly four years before they established embassies in Central Asian capitals. Instead the Saudis sent millions of Korans to Central Asia, funded Central Asian Muslims on the Haj and gave scholarships for their mullahs to study in Saudi Arabia – where they imbibed Wahabbism. These measures only perturbed Central Asia's rulers. Within a few years the rulers of Uzbekistan, Kazakhstan and Kyrgyzstan were to call Wahabbism the biggest political threat to stability in their countries.[8]

Saudi Arabia viewed the Taliban as an important asset to their dwindling influence in Afghanistan. The first Saudi contacts with the Taliban were through princely hunting trips. Maulana Fazlur Rehman head of Pakistan's JUI organized the first bustard hunting trips for Saudi and Gulf princes to Kandahar in the winter of 1994–95. The Arab hunting parties flew into Kandahar on huge transport planes bringing dozens of luxury jeeps, many of which they left behind along with donations for their Taliban hosts, after the hunt. Saudi Intelligence chief Prince Turki then began to visit Kandahar regularly. After Turki visited Islamabad and Kandahar in July 1996, the Saudis provided funds, vehicles and fuel for the successful Taliban attack on Kabul. Two Saudi companies, Delta and Ningarcho, were now involved in the gas pipeline projects across Afghanistan, increasing local business pressure on Riyadh to help ensure a Taliban victory.

But it was the Wahabbi *ulema* in the Kingdom who played the most influential role in urging the Royal Family to back the Taliban. The *ulema* play a leading advisory role to the Saudi monarch in the Council of the Assembly of Senior *Ulema* and four other state organizations. They have consistently supported the export of Wahabbism throughout the Muslim world and the Royal Family remains extremely sensitive to *ulema* opinion.[9] King Fahd had to call a meeting of 350 *ulema* to persuade them to issue a fatwa allowing US troops to be based in the Kingdom during the 1990 war with Iraq.[10] Saudi Intelligence co-operated closely with the *ulema* as did numerous state-run Islamic charities, which had funded the Afghan Mujaheddin in the 1980s and now began to do the same for the Taliban. Moreover, the *ulema* had the vast network of mosques and *madrassas* in the Kingdom under their control and it was here during Friday sermons that they built up public grass-roots support for the Taliban.[11]

According to the Saudi analyst Nawaf Obaid, the key players in the *ulema* who pushed for Saudi support to the Taliban were Sheikh Abdul Aziz Bin Baz, the Grand Mufti and Chairman of the Council of Senior *ulema* and Sheikh Mohammed Bin Juber, the Minister of Justice and a key member of the Council of the *ulema*.[12] In return, the Taliban demonstrated their reverence for the Royal Family and the *ulema* and copied Wahabbi practices such as introducing religious police. In April 1997,

Taliban leader Mullah Rabbani met with King Fahd in Riyadh and praised the Saudis effusively. 'Since Saudi Arabia is the centre of the Muslim world we would like to have Saudi assistance. King Fahd expressed happiness at the good measures taken by the Taliban and over the imposition of Sharia in our country,' Rabbani said.[13] Meeting King Fahd five months later, Taliban leaders said the Saudis had promised more aid. 'King Fahd was too kind. The Saudis have promised us as much as they can give us,' said Mullah Mohammed Stanakzai.[14]

Riyadh's support for the Taliban made them extremely reluctant to exert any pressure on the Taliban to deport Osama Bin Laden, even though the USA was urging them to do so. Only when Prince Turki was personally insulted by Mullah Omar in Kandahar did the Saudis curtail diplomatic links with the Taliban. Significantly, it was a personal insult that guided Saudi decision-making rather than an overall change in foreign policy. Saudi Arabia still appeared to have learnt little from its negative experiences of trying to export Wahabbism.

Saudi Arabia's initial support for the Taliban convinced Iran that the USA was also backing them in an intensification of its 1980s policies to surround Iran with hostile forces and isolate it. The USA, according to Tehran, had a new aim to promote oil and gas pipelines from Central Asia which would bypass Iran. After the Taliban captured Kabul, Iranian newspapers echoed the long-held views of officials. 'The Taliban capture of Kabul was designed by Washington, financed by Riyadh and logistically supported by Islamabad,' wrote the Jomhuri Islami newspaper.[15]

However, for Tehran the real fall-out with Afghanistan was internal. The leadership was divided between hardliners, who still hankered after supporting Shias worldwide and moderates who wanted a more measured support for the anti-Taliban alliance and less confrontation with the Taliban. Iran suffered from the same problems as Pakistan in having multiple departments and lobbies trying to push their personal vested interests in the making of Afghan policy. The Iranian military, the Revolutionary Guards, the intelligence agencies, the Shia clergy and the powerful Bunyads or Foundations which are run by the clergy and control much of the state sector economy and also finance foreign policy adventures with their large, unaccounted funds, were just some of the contending lobbies.

All these lobbies had to be kept on an even keel by the Foreign Ministry and Alaeddin Boroujerdi, the Deputy Foreign Minister for Afghanistan. Boroujerdi, who ran Afghan policy for more than a decade was a smart diplomat. He had outlasted the earlier regime of President Akbar Ali Rafsanjani to take up the same appointment under President Khatami, until he was forced to resign after the Iranian diplomats were killed in Mazar. He could be both a dove and a hawk on Afghanistan – depending on whom he was talking to and he also had to ensure that Iran's conflict of interests with Pakistan and Saudi Arabia did not get out of hand. In contrast, in Saudi Arabia, the Foreign Minister Prince Saud al Faisal, deferred Afghan policy to his younger brother Prince Turki and Saudi Intelligence.[16]

The collapse of the Afghan state increased Iran's own insecurity by creating a massive influx of drugs and weapons. The spectre of Afghanistan's ethnic conflict threatened to spill into Iran along with the economic burden of supporting millions of Afghan refugees, who were deeply disliked by ordinary Iranians. There are an estimated three million heroin addicts in Iran – the same number as in Pakistan although Iran, with 60 million people, has half the population of Pakistan. The smuggling of fuel, foodstuffs and other goods out of Iran to Afghanistan created losses in revenue and periodic economic problems – just when Iran faced a dramatic fall in revenue because of the drop in world oil prices and was trying to rebuild its economy.

Of even greater concern to the Iranians was that, since 1996, the Taliban were also secretly backing Iranian groups who were anti-regime. In Kandahar, the Taliban had given sanctuary to Ahl-e-Sunnah Wal Jamaat, which recruited Iranian Sunni militants from Khorasan and Sistan provinces. Its spokesmen from Iran's Turkmen, Baluchi and Afghan minorities, claimed that their aim was to overthrow the Shia regime in Tehran and impose a Taliban-style Sunni regime. This was a bizarre aspiration given that over 90 per cent of Iran's population was Shia, although it presumably helped to bolster support among the small band of insurgents. The group received weapons and support from the Taliban and the Iranians were convinced that the Pakistanis were also sponsoring them.

Iranian military aid to the anti-Taliban alliance escalated after the fall of Kabul in 1996 and again after the fall of Mazar in 1998. However, Iran had no contiguous border with the alliance and was forced to either fly in or rail supplies to Masud's forces, which involved getting permission from Turkmenistan, Uzbekistan and Kyrgyzstan. In 1998, Iranian Intelligence flew in plane-loads of arms to Ahmad Shah Masud's base in Kuliab in Tajikistan and Masud became a frequent visitor to Tehran. The danger which the Iran supply line faced was highlighted when Kyrgyzstan's security forces stopped a train in October 1998, in which were discovered 16 railcars loaded with 700 tons of arms and ammunition. The train had been travelling from Iran to Tajikistan with the weapons disguised as humanitarian aid.[17]

The Taliban were incensed with Iran's support for the alliance. In June 1997, the Taliban closed down the Iranian Embassy in Kabul, accusing Iran of destroying peace and stability in Afghanistan'.[18] A Taliban statement in September 1997 after their failure to capture Mazar was explicit. 'Iranian planes in gross violation of all internationally accepted norms intrude our country's air space to airlift supplies to airports controlled by the opposition. The grave consequencs of such interference will rest with Iran which is the enemy of Islam. Afghanistan is capable of harbouring opponents of the Iranian government inside Afghan territory and thus of creating problems for Iran,' the statement said.[19]

However, it was the killing of the Iranian diplomats in Mazar in 1998 that nearly forced Iran into war with the Taliban. There was enormous popular support for an Iranian invasion of western Afghanistan, which was further manipulated by hardliners in Tehran wanting to destabilize President Khatami. Even the reticent Foreign Minister Kamal Kharrazi was forced to adopt extremely tough language. 'The Taliban are Pushtuns and cannot sideline all the other ethnic groups from the political scene without sparking continuing resistance. In such circumstances there will be no peace in the country. I warn the Taliban and those who support them that we will not tolerate instability and conspiracy along our borders. We had an agreement with Pakistan that the Afghan problem would not be resolved through war. Now this has happened and we cannot accept it,' Kharrazi said on 14 August 1998.[20]

Iran felt betrayed by Pakistan on several counts. In 1996, just when President Burhanuddin Rabbani, under Iranian advice, was trying to broaden the base of his government and bring in Pashtuns and other groups, the Taliban captured Kabul. Iran was convinced that Pakistan had sabotaged Rabbani's effort. In June 1997, Prime Minister Nawaz Sharif visited Tehran. Together with President Khatami the two leaders called for a cease-fire in Afghanistan and declared that there could be no military solution. But Iran considered that Pakistan had no intention of sticking to the agreement. 'Pakistan has left no room for our trust and has destabilized its position with the Iranian people. We cannot accept seeing Pakistan cause problems for our national security,' wrote the Jomhuri Islami.[21]

Then, in the summer of 1998, Pakistan persuaded Iran to participate in a joint diplomatic peace mission. Mid-level Iranian and Pakistani diplomats travelled together for the first time to Mazar and Kandahar on 4 July 1998 to talk to the opposing factions. Just a few weeks later, the Taliban attacked Mazar and slaughtered the Iranian diplomats, scuttling the initiative. The Iranians were convinced that Pakistan had duped them by pretending to launch a peace initiative, just as the ISI was preparing the Taliban for the attack on Mazar. Moreover, Iran claimed that Pakistan had promised the safety of its diplomats in Mazar. When they were killed, Iran was furious and blamed the Taliban and Pakistan. Iranian officials said that Mullah Dost Mohammed, who allegedly led the Taliban seizure of the Iranian Consulate, had first gathered the diplomats in the basement of the building and spoken by wireless to Kandahar before shooting them dead.[22]

The Taliban replied, correctly as it appeared, that the Iranians were not diplomats but intelligence agents involved in ferrying weapons to the anti-Taliban alliance. Nevertheless, in the diplomatic skirmishing that followed, trust between Iran and Pakistan evaporated.[23] The Iranians were also furious that the Taliban actions had endangered its growing rapprochement with the USA. US Secretary of State Madeleine Albright had said in June 1998, the critical role that Iran plays in the region, 'makes the question of USA–Iran relations a topic of great interest and importance to this Secretary of State.[24]'

The Iranians had been encouraged that the USA was taking them seriously for the first time. USA–Iran co-operation on Afghanistan, 'certainly can be an exemplary case and shows that the US has a better understanding of the reality in this region and the role that Iran can play for the promotion of peace and security,' Kamal Kharrazi told me. 'We have been trying for a long time to tell them [the USA] that Iran is a key player in the region.'[25] Iran and the USA had also drawn closer because of Washington's changed perceptions about the Taliban. Both countries now shared the same views and were critical of the Taliban's drug and gender policies, their harbouring of terrorists and the threat that the Taliban's brand of Islamic fundamentalism posed to the region. Ironically for the USA, the new threat was no longer Shia fundamentalism, but the Sunni fundamentalism of the Taliban.

The Taliban were now even proving an embarrassment to Saudi Arabia, which helped bring Tehran closer to Riyadh. The Taliban's harbouring of Bin Laden had exposed their extremism and posed a threat to Saudi stability. Significantly, the rapprochement between Iran and Saudi Arabia did not falter, even when Iran was threatening to invade Afghanistan in 1998. In May 1999, President Khatami visited Saudi Arabia, the first Iranian leader to do so in nearly three decades.

The Taliban pose a security threat to the Saudis, especially through their support for Saudi dissidents. In the past the Saudis had deferred to the Taliban's fundamentalism, without giving due thought to what kind of state, political compromises and power-sharing should evolve in Afghanistan, but they could no longer afford to take such a casual attitude. With so much of Saudi foreign policy run on the basis of personal relationships and patronage rather than state institutions, it has become difficult to see how a policy towards Afghanistan, geared more to Saudi national self-interest and stability in the region, rather than Wahabbism, can evolve.

If President Khatami were to push forward his reform agenda at home, the Iranian regime would increasingly desire and need a peace settlement in Afghanistan – to end the drain on its resources from funding the anti-Taliban alliance, stop the drugs, weapons and sectarian spillover from Afghanistan and move towards a further rapprochement with the USA. Ironically, the Taliban's extremism had also helped bring Iran and Saudi Arabia closer together and weakened Pakistan's relationship with both countries. The big loser from Iran's return to the diplomatic mainstream was Pakistan. However, to end its isolation from the West, Iran needed to demonstrate that it was a responsible and stabilizing member of the international community. Its first and biggest test could be in helping to bring peace to Afghanistan.

~16~

CONCLUSION:
THE FUTURE
OF AFGHANISTAN

Afghanistan has become one of 'the world's orphaned conflicts – the ones that the West, selective and promiscuous
in its attention happens to ignore in favour of Yugoslavia', said
former UN Secretary General Boutros Boutros-Ghali in 1995.[1] The world
has turned away from Afghanistan, allowing civil war, ethnic fragmentation and polarization to become state failure. The country has ceased to
exist as a viable state and when a state fails civil society is destroyed.
Generations of children grow up rootless, without identity or reason to
live except to fight. Adults are traumatized and brutalized, knowing only
war and the power of the warlords. 'We are dealing here with a failed
state which looks like an infected wound. You don't even know where to
start cleaning it,' said UN mediator Lakhdar Brahimi.[2]

The entire Afghan population has been displaced, not once but many
times over. The physical destruction of Kabul has turned it into the
Dresden of the late twentieth century. The crossroads of Asia on the
ancient Silk Route is now nothing but miles of rubble. There is no semblance of an infrastructure that can sustain society – even at the lowest
common denominator of poverty. In 1998 the ICRC reported that the
number of Afghan families headed by a widow had reached 98,000, the
number of families headed by a disabled person was 63,000 and 45,000
people were treated for war wounds that year alone. There was not even
an estimate of those killed. The only productive factories in the country
are those where artificial limbs, crutches and wheelchairs are produced by
the aid agencies.[3]

Afghanistan's divisions are multiple – ethnic, sectarian, rural and
urban, educated and uneducated, those with guns and those who have

been disarmed. The economy is a black hole that is sucking in its neighbours with illicit trade and the smuggling of drugs and weapons, undermining them in the process. 'It will take at least ten to 15 years before there will be a functioning central authority capable of doing the minimum of the administration needed for the development of the country. And that is, in my view, a rather optimistic statement,' said Swedish aid-worker Anders Fange.[4]

Complex relationships of power and authority built up over centuries have broken down completely. No single group or leader has the legitimacy to reunite the country. Rather than a national identity or kinship-tribal-based identities, territorial regional identities have become paramount. Afghans no longer call themselves just Afghans or even Pashtuns and Tajiks, but Kandaharis, Panjshiris, Heratis, Kabulis or Jowzjanis. Fragmentation is both vertical and horizontal and cuts across ethnicity to encompass a single valley or town. The Pashtun tribal structure has been destroyed by the loss of common tribal property and grazing grounds, and by war and flight. The non-Pashtun identify their survival with individual warrior leaders and the valley of their birth.

The tribal hierarchy which once mediated conflicts has been killed or is in exile. The old, educated, ruling elite fled after the Soviet invasion and no new ruling elite has emerged in its place which can negotiate a peace settlement. There is no political class to compromise and make deals. There are lots of leaders representing segments of the population, but no outright leader. In such a scenario, with no end to the war in sight, the question of whether Afghanistan will fragment and send waves of ethnic fragmentation and instability spinning through the region, becomes paramount.

Much of the blame for the continuation of the war lies in the hands of outsiders who continue to back their proxies in an ever-increasing spiral of intervention and violence. The FSU began the process with its brutal invasion of Afghanistan, but suffered hugely. 'We brought Afghanistan with us – in our souls, in our hearts, in our memory, in our customs, in everything and at every level,' said Alexander Lebed, who served as a major in the Soviet army in Afghanistan and is now a presidential candidate. 'This feeble political adventure, this attempt to export a still unproved revolution, marked the beginning of the end,' he added.[5]

The Afghan Mujaheddin contributed to the demise of the Soviet Union, the Soviet empire and even communism itself. While the Afghans take all credit for this, the West has gone the other way, barely acknowledging the Afghan contribution to the end of the Cold War. The withdrawal of Soviet troops from Afghanistan heralded the end of the Gorbachov experiment in perestroika and glasnost – the idea that the Soviet system could be changed from within. There is a lesson to be learnt here for today's meddlers – those who intervene in Afghanistan can face disin-tegration themselves – not because of the power of the Afghans, but because of the forces that are unleashed in their own fragile societies.

By walking away from Afghanistan as early as it did, the USA faced within a few years dead diplomats, destroyed embassies, bombs in New York and cheap heroin on its streets, as Afghanistan became a sanctuary for international terrorism and the drugs mafia. Afghans today remain deeply bitter about their abandonment by the USA, for whom they fought the Cold War. In the 1980s the USA was prepared 'to fight till the last Afghan' to get even with the Soviet Union, but when the Soviets left, Washington was not prepared to help bring peace or feed a hungry people. Regional powers took advantage of the political vacuum the US retreat created, saw an opportunity to wield influence and jumped into the fray.

Today the USA, by picking up single issues and creating entire policies around them, whether it be oil pipelines, the treatment of women or terrorism, is only demonstrating that it has learnt little. The abortive Unocal project should have taught many lessons to US policy-makers, but there appear to be no signs of it as US diplomats scurry across Central Asia trying to persuade oil companies and governments to commit to building a main export pipeline from Baku to Ceyhan. But even that is likely to be indefinitely delayed. The start-up for construction scheduled for the year 2000 has been progressively delayed to 2003 and most recently to 2005.[6]

The lessons from the Unocal project are several. No major pipeline from Central Asia can be built unless there is far greater US and interna-tional commitment to conflict resolution in the region – in Afghanistan, Tajikistan, Nagorno-Karabakh, Chechnya, Georgia and with the Kurds. The region is a powder keg of unresolved conflicts. Nor can secure pipe-lines be built without some degree of strategic consensus in the region. Iran and Russia cannot be isolated from the region's development for ever. They will resist and sabotage projects as long as they are not a part of them. Nor can pipelines be built when ethnic conflicts are tearing states apart. Ethnicity is the clarion call of the modern era. Trying to resolve ethnic problems and keep states together needs persistent and consistent diplomacy rather than virtual bribes to keep various warlords quiet.

Oil companies cannot build pipelines which are vulnerable to civil wars, fast-moving political changes and events, instability and an environ-ment beset by Islamic fundamentalism, drugs and guns. The old Great Game was about perceived threats in which force was never directly used. Russia and Great Britain marked out borders and signed treaties, creating Afghanistan as a buffer between them. The new Great Game must be one where the aim is to stabilize and settle the region, not increase tensions and antagonism. The USA is the only world power which has the ability to influence all the neighbouring states to stop interfering in Afghanistan. It has to do so with far more commitment than it has demonstrated so far.

Pakistan, weakened by the demise of its strategic partnership with the USA after the end of the Cold War and in the throes of a deep economic crisis, was nevertheless determined to extend its zone of influence by trying to nominate the next government in Kabul. Faced with a belligerent Indian neighbour seven times its size, Pakistan's obsession with security has naturally shaped its domestic politics and foreign policy concerns since it was created in 1947. But the military-bureaucratic-intelligence elite that has guided Pakistan's destiny since the 1950s has never allowed civil society to function. Only this elite has had the right to determine the nature of the threat to Pakistan's national security and its solutions – not elected governments, parliament, civic organizations or even common sense.

Since 1988, four elected governments have been dismissed, ten governments have come and gone and domestic stability is still as distant a dream as ever.[7] With such deep crises of identity, political legitimacy, economic mismanagement and social polarization, the elite has nevertheless indulged in the worst example of imperial overstretch by any third world country in the latter half of this century. Pakistan is now fighting proxy wars on two fronts, in Kashmir and Afghanistan and even though the repercussions from these wars – Islamic fundamentalism, drugs, weapons and social breakdown – are now aggressively spilling into the country, there is no reappraisal or policy review. Pakistan is now ripe for a Taliban-style Islamic revolution, which would almost certainly jeopardize stability in the Middle East, South and Central Asia.

What Pakistan's policy-makers have failed to realize is that any stable government in Kabul will have to depend on Pakistan for reconstruction, foodstuffs, fuel and access to the outside world. Pakistan's own economy would benefit as it would provide workers, technicians and materials for Afghanistan's reconstruction. The Afghan refugees would return, easing the financial burden of sustaining them and Pakistan could begin to reassert some control over its dilapidated state institutions and borders.

While Pakistan has had a forward policy in Afghanistan, Iran's interference has essentially been defensive, maintaining a limited influence and resisting a total Taliban takeover. But Iran has contributed heavily to the fragmentation of Afghanistan by playing the Shia card, the Persian language card and keeping the very ethnic groups it supports divided amongst themselves. The disparateness of the Hazaras and the Uzbeks, the two ethnic groups Iran has provided the most aid to, is sufficient to show how Iran's policy of divide and rule has devastated the anti-Taliban alliance.

Iran's policies have reflected the intense power struggle within the Iranian elite which has only intensified in the last two years.

Moreover, the complete breakdown of trust and understanding between Iran and Pakistan has set back the peace process and proved ruinous for the Afghans. There is no common ground between the two states on a solution to the Afghan civil war and even more ominously both states are funding proxy wars between Shias and Sunnis in each other's countries as well as in Afghanistan, increasing the likelihood of a major sectarian explosion in the region. With the advent of the Taliban, sectarianism and ethnic/sectarian cleansing has reared its ugly head for the first time in Afghanistan's history.

The Central Asian states are the new players on the block, but they have quickly taken to protecting what they see as threats to their national interests. Pashtun domination of Afghanistan does not suit them and they abhor the kind of Islamic sentiments the Taliban espouse. Until their ethnic cousins in Afghanistan are part of some power-sharing formula in Kabul, the Central Asian states will not cease to aid them to resist the Taliban. This places in jeopardy Pakistan's plans for accessing pipeline and communication routes across Afghanistan from Central Asia. If the Taliban were to conquer the entire country, the Central Asian states would have to accept the Taliban reality, but they would be unlikely to trust their energy exports to go through Taliban controlled Afghanistan and Pakistan.

Saudi Arabia, it appears, has proved incapable of evolving a rational foreign policy which suits its national interests rather than merely appeasing its domestic Wahabbi lobby. It took Mullah Omar to personally insult the House of Saud before the Saudis pulled away from the Taliban. The Saudi export of Wahabbism has now boomeranged back home and is increasingly undermining the authority of the Royal Family. Osama Bin Laden's critique of the corruption and mismanagement of the regime is not falling upon deaf ears amongst the Saudi population. And unless Afghanistan moves towards peace, dozens more Bin Ladens are ready and waiting to take his place from their bases inside Afghanistan.

For Muslims everywhere Saudi support for the Taliban is deeply embarrassing, because the Taliban's interpretation of Islam is so negative and destructive. Increasingly, Western popular perception equates Islam with the Taliban and Bin Laden-style terrorism. Many Western commentators do not particularize the Taliban, but condemn Islam wholesale for being intolerant and anti-modern. The Taliban, like so many Islamic fundamentalist groups today, divest Islam of all its legacies except theology – Islamic philosophy, science, arts, aesthetics and mysticism are ignored. Thus the rich diversity of Islam and the essential message of the Koran –

to build a civil society that is just and equitable in which rulers are responsible for their citizens – is forgotten.

The genius of early Muslim-Arab civilization was its multi-cultural, multi-religious and multi-ethnic diversity. The stunning and numerous state failures that abound in the Muslim world today are because that original path, that intention and inspiration, has been abandoned either in favour of brute dictatorship or a narrow interpretation of theology. Muslim history has been a cycle of conquest, renewal and defeat. 'Perhaps it has been the destiny of Islam to attract and use the primitive peoples who surround or cross its territory, but then to fall prey to their violent power. Ultimately order is restored and wounds are healed. The successful primitive warrior is tamed by the all-powerful urban life of Islam,' wrote Ferdinand Braudel.[8]

Following this Muslim tradition, could the Taliban also change or moderate their policies and absorb Afghanistan's rich ethnic and cultural diversity to become the country's legitimate rulers? In their present form that is unlikely. The Taliban are essentially caught between a tribal society which they try to ignore and the need for a state structure which they refuse to establish. Tribal fragmentation amongst the Pashtuns is already coming back to haunt them as they fail to satisfy even the local demands of power-sharing, while they ignore the non-Pashtuns. This was never the case in the past. 'Despite the seeming dominance of the Pashtuns, the actual process of state-building entailed the participation of the elite of all the ethnic groups and a prominent role played by non-Pastuns in both the bureaucracy and the military,' writes Afghan scholar Ashraf Ghani.[9] The Taliban are bucking the entire trend of Afghan history because they have no understanding of it.

At the same time, the Taliban refuse to define the Afghan state they want to constitute and rule over, largely because they have no idea what they want. The lack of a central authority, state organizations, a methodology for command and control and mechanisms which can reflect some level of popular participatation (Loya Jirga or Islamic Shura or parliament), make it impossible for many Afghans to accept the Taliban or for the outside world to recognize a Taliban government. There can be no effective government unless there is a common, acceptable definition of what kind of state is now required to heal the wounds of war. But the Kandahari group around Mullah Omar brooks no outsiders and no advice. Divisions within the Taliban are multiplying fast and it is not unlikely that more moderate Taliban may mount a coup against Mullah Omar and the Kandahari *ulema*.

No warlord faction has ever felt itself responsible for the civilian population, but the Taliban are incapable of carrying out even the minimum of developmental work because they believe that Islam will take care of everyone. This has raised fundamental questions for the UN and the NGO community – that humanitarian aid is in fact prolonging the civil war because foreign aid keeps the population alive, absolving the warlords of the responsibility of having to provide for the people and allowing them to channel all their resources into the war effort. This dilemma is now common for the UN and aid agencies in other failed states such as Sudan and Somalia and presents the greatest challenge to the international humanitarian community in the future.

It seems that the only effective Afghan NGO is based on organized smuggling and the drugs trade. Thus the limited reconstruction which the Taliban has undertaken so far is entirely related to improving the efficiency of smuggling and drugs trafficking, such as repairing roads, setting up petrol pumps and inviting US businessmen to set up a mobile telephone network which will qualitatively speed up the movement of drugs and illicit trade. The benefits of this reconstruction all accrue to the transport and drugs mafia. No warlord is building schools, hospitals, water supply systems or anything remotely related to civic development.

In their present form, the Taliban cannot hope to rule Afghanistan and be recognized by the international community. Even if they were to conquer the north, it would not bring stability, only continuing guerrilla war by the non-Pashtuns, but this time from bases in Central Asia and Iran which would further destabilize the region. Yet in the Pashtun belt of Afghanistan, the only alternative to the Taliban is further disorder and chaos. 'The majority of Afghans south of Kabul would most probably agree that the Taliban, although not as popular today as when they came, are better for the people, their security and welfare, compared to what was there before them and that there is no real alternative but anarchy.'[10] The Taliban cannot be wished away, but a more likely scenario is that the Taliban will form factions with separate and rival Taliban fiefdoms in Kabul, Kandahar and possibly Herat.

The anti-Taliban alliance is incapable of conquering or ruling over the southern Pashtun region. So far Masud has proved unable to galvanize enough Pashtuns who reject the Taliban and who would give him some national legitimacy. The opposition's only chance for survival depends on winning over sections of the Pashtuns, which will doubtless prolong the war, but also weaken the Taliban and offer the possibility that both sides could then negotiate. The anti-Taliban alliance has also failed to set up minimum state structures or a representative leadership which absorbs even all the non-Pashtuns. Their bickering, internal differences and leadership power struggles have decimated them in the eyes of many Afghans, who may loathe the Taliban but have no faith in the anti-Taliban alliance either.

The fear of fragmentation is ever present and the lines have been well drawn since 1996 – a Pashtun south under the Taliban and a non-Pashtun north divided by the Hindu Kush mountains, leaving Kabul contested by the two sides. With the devastating massacres, sectarian pogroms and ethnic cleansing in so many areas, the chances of fragmentation appear extremely high. Fortunately there is no Slobodan Milosevic or Saddam Hussein amongst the warlords, who would be prepared to preserve power and their fiefdoms at the expense of partition of the country. Despite their interference, fragmentation suits none of Afghanistan's neighbours because it would open a Pandora's box of ethnicity that would rapidly spill across Afghanistan's borders, create massive refugee influxes and further spread the culture of drugs, weapons and Islamic fundamentalism in their already fragile states. Formal fragamentation and even partition of the Afghan state is still possible, but so far none of the players desire it. That is the one positive hope for the future of the peace process.

Peace-making by the UN has so far failed to yield any dividends, but not for lack of trying. The reason is simply that as long as outside powers fuel the warlords with money and weapons, the civil war does not have a likelihood of winding down. A possible solution might lie in a process which would have to begin from outside Afghanistan. All the regional states would first have to agree to an arms embargo on Afghanistan, implement it sincerely and allow it to be monitored by the UN effectively. The regional states would have to accept limited areas of influence in Afghanistan rather than continuing to push for their proxies to rule the entire country. An Iran–Pakistan dialogue would be essential in which Pakistan would accept limiting its influence to the Pashtun belt, while Iran accept the same in western and central Afghanistan with guarantees for the Shia minority.

In short, each neighbouring state would have to recognize not only its own national security needs, but also those of its neighbours. Outside influence cannot now be eliminated in Afghanistan, but it must be contained and limited with mutual agreement to acceptable levels. No neighbouring country can presume to undermine the acknowledged security interests of its neighbours. Negotiating such agreements would be extremely tricky because they would involve not just diplomats, but the military and intelligence officials of each state. The UN and the international community would also have to guarantee that such agreements would not be furthering the future disintegration of Afghanistan or interfering with the process of government formation inside Afghanistan.

Afghanistan's internal settlement can no longer be achieved by what is euphemistically called 'a broad-based government.' There is no possibility that Mullah Omar and Masud are going to be able to agree to sit down in Kabul and rule together. Instead, what is needed is a cease-fire, a weak central government for an initial period, the agreed demilitarization of

Kabul and a high degree of autonomy in the regions controlled by the factions. All the factions would have to agree to build up a strengthened central government in the long term, while maintaining their own autonomy in the short term. In this way, they would retain their independent military units, but would also contribute to a central policing force in Kabul.

The factions would receive outside aid for reconstruction on an independent basis, but work together through the central government to rebuild the country's shattered infrastructure. This would in turn generate greater confidence and understanding between them. All the factions would then have to agree to set in motion some form of legitimizing process through elected or chosen representative bodies in their regions, which ultimately could lead to a central Jirga or Shura in Kabul.

It cannot be underestimated how difficult it would be to negotiate such agreements, given that at present there is no will among the belligerents to negotiate. One lure could be a substantial reconstruction package put together by international donors, the World Bank or large private charities, which would not be disbursed until there was a minimum agreement. This would essentially be a bribe for the warlords and an incentive for the Afghan people to pressurize them to accept an agreement. Any serious peace process would need much greater commitment to peace-making in Afghanistan from the international community than it has shown so far.

Peace in Afghanistan would pay enormous dividends across the entire region. Pakistan would benefit economically from the reconstruction in Afghanistan and it could begin to tackle the leftovers of the Afghan war on its own soil – the proliferation of weapons, drugs, terrorism, sectarianism and the black economy. Pakistan's diplomatic isolation in the region would end and it could reintegrate itself into the Central Asian network of communication links, offering as it does the shortest route to the sea. Iran would return to its position in the world community and its role as a great trading state at the centre of South Asia, Central Asia and the Middle East. Turkey would have links and commercial ties to Turkic peoples in Afghanistan with whom it has a historical connection.

China would feel more secure and be able to carry out a more effective economic development programme in its deprived Muslim province of Xinjiang. Russia could build a more realistic relationship with Central and South Asia based on economic realities rather than false hegemonic ambitions, while laying its Afghan ghosts to rest. Oil and gas pipelines crossing Afghanistan would link the country into the region and speed up foreign assistance for its reconstruction. The USA could evolve a more realistic Central Asian policy, access the region's energy in a securer environment and deal with the threat of terrorism.

But if the war in Afghanistan continues to be ignored we can only expect the worst. Pakistan will face a Taliban-style Islamic revolution which will further destabilize it and the entire region. Iran will remain on the periphery of the world community and its eastern borders will continue to be wracked by instability. The Central Asian states will not be able to deliver their energy and mineral exports by the shortest routes and as their economies crash, they will face an Islamic upsurge and instability. Russia will continue to bristle with hegemonic aims in Central Asia even as its own society and economy crumbles. The stakes are extremely high.

Appendix 1

A sample of Taliban decrees relating to women and other cultural issues, after the capture of Kabul, 1996

(This translation from Dari was handed to Western agencies to implement; the grammar and spellings are reproduced here as they appeared in the original.)

1.

Decree announced by the General Presidency of Amr Bil Maruf and Nai Az Munkar (Religious Police.)
Kabul, November 1996.

Women you should not step outside your residence. If you go outside the house you should not be like women who used to go with fashionable clothes wearing much cosmetics and appearing in front of every men before the coming of Islam.

Islam as a rescuing religion has determined specific dignity for women, Islam has valuable instructions for women. Women should not create such opportunity to attract the attention of useless people who will not look at them with a good eye. Women have the responsibility as a teacher or co-ordinator for her family. Husband, brother, father have the responsibility for providing the family with the necessary life requirements (food, clothes etc). In case women are required to go outside the residence for the purposes of education, social needs or social services they should cover themselves in accordance with Islamic Sharia regulation. If women are going outside with fashionable, ornamental, tight and charming clothes to show themselves, they will be cursed by the Islamic Sharia and should never expect to go to heaven.

All family elders and every Muslim have responsibility in this respect. We request all family elders to keep tight control over their families and avoid these social problems. Otherwise these women will be threatened, investigated and severely punished as well as the family elders by the forces of the Religious Police (*Munkrat*).

The Religious Police (*Munkrat*) have the responsibility and duty to struggle against these social problems and will continue their effort until evil is finished.

2.

Rules of work for the State Hospitals and private clinics based on Islamic Sharia principles. Ministry of Health, on behalf of Amir ul Momineen Mullah Mohammed Omar. Kabul, November 1996.

1. Female patients should go to female physicians. In case a male physician is needed, the female patient should be accompanied by her close relative.

2. During examination, the female patients and male physicians both should be dressed with Islamic *hijab* (veil).

3. Male physicians should not touch or see the other parts of female patients except for the affected part.

4. Waiting room for female patients should be safely covered.

5. The person who regulates turn for female patients should be a female.

6. During the night duty, in what rooms which female patients are hospitalized, the male doctor without the call of the patient is not allowed to enter the room.

7. Sitting and speaking between male and female doctors are not allowed, if there be need for discussion, it should be done with *hijab*.

8. Female doctors should wear simple clothes, they are not allowed to wear stylish clothes or use cosmetics or make-up.

9. Female doctors and nurses are not allowed to enter the rooms where male patients are hospitalised.

10. Hospital staff should pray in mosques on time.

11. The Religious Police are allowed to go for control at any time and nobody can prevent them.

Anybody who violates the order will be punished as per Islamic regulations.

3.

General Presidency of Amr Bil Maruf. Kabul, December 1996.

1. To prevent sedition and female uncovers (Be Hejabi). No drivers are allowed to pick up women who are using Iranian *burqa*. In case of violation the driver will be imprisoned. If such kind of female are observed in the street their house will be found and their husband punished. If the women use stimulating and attractive cloth and there is no accompany of close male relative with them, the drivers should not pick them up.

2. To prevent music. To be broadcasted by the public information resources. In shops, hotels, vehicles and rickshaws cassettes and music are prohibited. This matter should be monitored within five days. If any music cassette found in a shop, the shopkeeper should be imprisoned and the shop locked. If five people guarantee the shop should be opened the criminal released later. If

cassette found in the vehicle, the vehicle and the driver will be imprisoned. If five people guarantee the vehicle will be released and the criminal released later.

3. To prevent beard shaving and its cutting. After one and a half months if anyone observed who has shaved and/or cut his beard, they should be arrested and imprisoned until their beard gets bushy.

4. To prevent keeping pigeons and playing with birds. Within ten days this habit/hobby should stop. After ten days this should be monitored and the pigeons and any other playing birds should be killed.

5. To prevent kite-flying. The kite shops in the city should be abolished.

6. To prevent idolatory. In vehicles, shops, hotels, room and any other place pictures/ portraits should be abolished. The monitors should tear up all pictures in the above places.

7. To prevent gambling. In collaboration with the security police the main centres should be found and the gamblers imprisoned for one month.

8. To eradicate the use of addiction. Addicts should be imprisoned and investigation made to find the supplier and the shop. The shop should be locked and the owner and user should be imprisoned and punished.

9. To prevent the British and American hairstyle. People with long hair should be arrested and taken to the Religious Police department to shave their hair. The criminal has to pay the barber.

10. To prevent interest on loans, charge on changing small denomination notes and charge on money orders. All money exchangers should be informed that the above three types of exchanging the money should be prohibited. In case of violation criminals will be imprisoned for a long time.

11. To prevent washing cloth by young ladies along the water streams in the city. Violator ladies should be picked up with respectful Islamic manner, taken to their houses and their husbands severely punished.

12. To prevent music and dances in wedding parties. In the case of violation the head of the family will be arrested and punished.

13. To prevent the playing of music drum. The prohibition of this should be announced. If anybody does this then the religious elders can decide about it.

14. To prevent sewing ladies cloth and taking female body measures by tailor. If women or fashion magazines are seen in the shop the tailor should be imprisoned.

15. To prevent sorcery. All the related books should be burnt and the magician should be imprisoned until his repentance.

16. To prevent not praying and order gathering pray at the bazaar. Prayer should be done on their due times in all districts. Transportation should be strictly prohibited and all people are obliged to go to the mosque. If young people are seen in the shops they will be immediately imprisoned.

Appendix 2

Structure of the
Taliban

The Taliban leader is Mullah Mohammed Omar, also known as the Amir-ul Momineen, or Commander of the Faithful. A ten-member interim ruling council or Supreme Shura is the most powerful ruling body and is based in Kandahar. Two committees report to this Shura. The first is an interim cabinet or Kabul Shura. The second is a Military Shura.

SUPREME SHURA OF THE TALIBAN'S FOUNDING
MEMBERS, KANDAHAR 1994–1997
Mullah Mohammed Omar. Amir-ul Momineen. Leader of the Faithful. Head of Taliban Movement.

Mullah Mohammed Rabbani Akhund	**Chairman Ruling Council and Deputy Head of Taliban**
Mullah Mohammed Ghaus Akhund.	Acting Minister of Foreign Affairs until June 1997
Mullah Mohammed Hassan Akhund	Military Chief of Staff
Mullah Mohammed Fazil Akhund	Head of the Army Corps
Mullah Abdul Razaq	Head of Customs Department
Mullah Sayed Ghiasuddin Agha	Acting Minister of Information
Mullah Khairullah Khairkhwa	Acting Minister of the Interior
Maulvi Abdul Sattar Sanani	Acting Chief Justice of Afghanistan.
Maulvi Ehsanullah Ehsan	Governor State Bank
Mullah Abdul Jalil	Acting Minister of Foreign Affairs after June 1997

MILITARY COMMAND STRUCTURE OF THE TALIBAN: MILITARY SHURA

Commander in Chief: Mullah Mohammed Omar
Military Chief of Staff: Mullah Mohammed Hassan
Chief of Army Staff: Mullah Rahmatullah Akhund
Head of the Army Corps: Mullah Mohammed Fazil

Army Division chief: Mullah Jumma Khan
Army Division chief: Mullah Mohammed Younas
Army Division chief: Mullah Mohammed Gul
Army Division chief: Mullah Mohammed Aziz Khan
Armoured Force No.4: Mullah Mohammed Zahir

KABUL SHURA OF ACTING MINISTERS 2000

Mullah Wakil Ahmed Mutawakkil	Foreign Minister
Mullah Mohammed Abbas Akhund	Public Health
Mullah Abdur Razzaq	Interior
Mullah Obaidullah Akhund	Construction
Mullah Tahir Anwari	Finance
Mullah Qodratullah	Information and Culture
Mullah Abdul Latif Mansur	Agriculture
Mullah Mohammed Essa	Water and Power
Maulana Ahmadullah Muti	Communications
Mullah Nuruddin Turabi	Justice
Maulvi Hamdullah Numani	Higher Education
Maulvi Ahmad Jan	Mines and Industries
Maulvi Jalaluddin Haqqani	Frontier Affairs
Maulana Abdur Razzaq	Commerce
Qari Din Mohammed	Planning

Origins of Members of the Taliban Movement

D = Durrani Pashtun; G = Ghilzai Pashtun; N = Pashtun but neither Ghilzai nor Durrani; T = Tajik; U = Uzbek; O = Other ethnic group; FM = Founding Member of Taliban; Muj = Former Mujaheddin commander against Soviet troops.

Former Mujaheddin party affiliations.
Hizbe (K) = Hizb-e-Islami (Younis Khalis), Hizbe (H) = Hizb-e-Islami (Gulbuddin Hikmetyar), Jam = Jamaat-e-Islami (Rabbani), Nifa = National Islamic Front of Afghanistan (Gailani), Har = Harakat (Maulvi Mohammed Nabi Mohammedi)

Name	Office	Origin/Age	Tribe/Rank	Remarks
M. Mohammed Omar	Leader	Mewand/Kandahar, FM, 37	G. Hotak Muj. Ex-Hizbe (K)	Educated Kandahar *madrassa*. One-eyed. Head of government
M. Mohammed Rabbani	Chairman of Kabul Shura	Kandahar, FM, 38	N. Kakar Muj. Ex-Hizbe (K)	
Mohammed Hassan	Foreign Minister after 1997	Kandahar	G. Hotak Muj Ex-Hizbe (K)	Educated *madrassa* Quetta. Relative of Omar.
M. Mohammed Ghaus	Foreign Minister, retired 1997	Kandahar, Khushab, FM, 50	D. Nurzai Muj. Ex-Hizbe (K)	Blind in one eye, little sight in other. Close friend of Omar. Captured Mazar 1997.
M. Abdul Razaq	Customs Dept.	Kandahar	D. Popalzai Muj. Ex-Hizbe (K)	
M. Sayed Ghiasuddin	Education	Faryab	U. Muj Ex-Har.	No formal education. Businessman. Wears earring.

Name	Office	Origin/Age	Tribe/Rank	Remarks
M. Khairula Khairkhwa	Interior	Kandahar	D. Popalzai Muj. Ex-Har.	Graduated Haqqania.
Ehsanullah Ehsan	Gov. State Bank	Kandahar, Panjwaj	D.	Former Gov of Khost. Killed Mazar 1997.
Maulvi Abdul Sattar Sanani	Chief Justice Kandahar Supreme Court.	Kandahar, 80	D. Ishaqzai	Educated Kandahar *madrassa*.
Mohammed Abbas	Health. Dealing with UN agencies.	Urozgan, FM, 40	G. Hotak Muj. Ex-Hizbe (K)	Educated *madrassa* Zabul, later Haqqania. Trader in Kandahar. Mayor of Kandahar, later Attorney General. Commander of Baghlan force.
Obaidullah	Defence	Kandahar	G. Hotak Muj Ex-Har.	Educated *madrassa* Quetta. Captured Mazar. Military liaison between Taliban and ISI.
Dadullah Mohammedullah Akhond	Construction Finance	Kandahar	D. Alkozai Muj.	Educated *madrassa*.
Amir Khan Mutaqqi	Information Culture	Logar, FM	Ex-Har. N. Kochi nomad tribe. Muj. Ex-Har.	Quetta. Educated Haqqania, old friend of Omar. Commander Baghlan force after Mazar.

Name	Office	Origin/Age	Tribe/Rank	Remarks
Abdul Latif Mansur	Agriculture	Paktia	G.	Educated in Haqqania.
Mohammed Essa	Water, Power	Kandahar	G. Hotak Muj. Ex-Har.	
Alla Dad Akhund	Communications	Kandahar	G. Hotak Muj. Ex-Hizb (K)	Ran his own *madrassa* in the NWFP.
Nuruddin Turabi	Justice	Urozgan	G. Hotak.	One-eyed.
Hamidullah Nemani	Higher Education	Zabul	D. Daftani.	No formal education.
Ahmed Jan	Mines and Industries	Pakhtia, 40	G. Zadran.	Educated Haqqania. Carpet dealer in Saudi Arabia. Taliban trade commissioner in Peshawar. Negotiator with oil companies.
Jalaluddin Haqqani	Frontier Affairs	Pakhtia, 55	G. Zadran Muj. Ex-Hizbe (K)	Led Islamic movement against Daud 1974. Migrated to Pak. Educated Pakhtia and six years in Haqqania. Leading Mujaheddin commander. Captured Khost 1991. Joined Taliban 1995.
Sadeq Akhond	Commerce	Kandahar	G. Hotak Muj Ex-Har.	Uneducated. Captured Mazar 1997.
Qari Din Mohammed	Planning	Badakhshan	T. Muj. Ex-Jam.	Leading Tajik in council.
Maulvi Qalamuddin	Head of Religious Police	Logar, Bariki Barak, 38	G. Mohmand Muj Ex-Har.	Educated Logar and Haqqani. Secretary to Nabi Mohammedi in Rabbani government. Joined Talibs in Zabul.

Name	Office	Origin/Age	Tribe/Rank	Remarks
Maulvi Jalilullah Maulvizai	Attorney General	Herat, 68	Khawaja.	Educated Deobandi *madrassa*, India. Adviser to Mujaheddin Interim govt 1988. Education minister under Rabbani.
Mohammed Hassan	Gov. Kandahar	Urozgan, FM, 45	D. Achakzai Muj. Ex-Har.	Educated *madrassa* Quetta. Fought Russians in Urozgan. One leg, fingertip missing.
Wakil Ahmed	Secretary to Omar	Kandahar	N. Kakar FM	Chief aide to Omar, spokesman for Talibs.
Sher Mohammed Stanakzai	Dep. Foreign Minister	Logar	G. Stanakzai	Ex-police officer. Trained in India.
Arifullah Arif	Dep. Finance Minister	Pakhtia, Zamrud.	G. Suleiman Har.	Passed 6th grade, then for 14 years in Haqqani. Worked for jihad in Pak.

Appendix 3

A CHRONOLOGY OF THE TALIBAN

1992
April. Afghanistan and Kabul fall to the Mujaheddin as President Najibullah seeks shelter in UN compound in Kabul.

1993
Bitter fighting between President Rabbani and Gulbuddin Hikmetyar leaves 10,000 civilians dead.

1994
January. Factional fighting reduces Kabul to rubble as Dostum and Hikmetyar attack Kabul.

February. UN appoints Mehmoud Mestiri to head Special Mission to Afghanistan. Pakistan Embassy in Kabul sacked.

October. Six Western ambassadors in Islamabad accompany Pakistan Interior Minister Naseerullah Babar to Herat to meet Ismael Khan.

28 October. PM Benazir Bhutto meets Ismael Khan and Dostum in Ashkhabad.

4 November. A 30-truck Pakistani convoy to Central Asia waylaid by warlords near Kandahar, 20 dead in fighting. Taliban emerge.

5 November. Taliban take control of Kandahar and free convoy. Fifty dead in four days of clashes.

25 November. Taliban take control of two southern provinces, Lashkargarh and Helmand.

1995
1 January. 3,000 Pakistani Taliban from Peshawar leave for Afghanistan.

2 February. Taliban move into Wardak province, 25 miles from Kabul.

11 February. Taliban capture Logar province. Nine provinces out of 30 captured by Taliban. President Rabbani sends delegation to meet Taliban.

14 February. Taliban take Charasyab and Hikmetyar flees without a fight.

18 February. Taliban put three conditions on joining possible interim government, neutral force made up of Taliban, only good Muslims will participate and all 30 provinces must be represented.

7 March. Taliban advance on Nimroz, Farah, try to capture Herat. Taliban move into south Kabul as Hazaras vacate their positions.

11 March. Masud attacks Taliban near Kabul. Taliban pushed back to Charasyab.

13 March. Hazara leader Abdul Ali Mazari captured by Taliban and dies in helicopter crash while being taken to Kandahar by Taliban. Taliban take Farah.

4 April. Taliban capture part of Shindand airbase near Herat.

29 March. Government forces push back Taliban 80 miles from Shindand.

12 May. Taliban pushed out of Farah.

31 May. Saudi intelligence chief Prince Turki visits Kabul and Kandahar.

10 July. Deputy chief of Saudi intelligence tours Afghan cities in peace mission, meets with Taliban.

2 September. Taliban retake Farah, heavy fighting close to Shindand.

3 September. Taliban capture Shindand. Kabul reshuffles military command and demotes Ismael Khan as troops airlifted into Herat.

5 September. Taliban capture Herat. Ismael Khan flees to Iran without a fight.

6 September. Pakistan embassy in Kabul sacked and burnt down. Iran warns Taliban not to cross Iranian border.

10 October. Taliban shift 400 tanks to Kabul from Kandahar, prepare for assault on city.

11 October. Taliban begin major attack and recapture Charasyab.

11 November. Kabul rocketed by Taliban. Thirty-six killed, 52 wounded in worst day of rocketing by Taliban.

26 November. Worst ever bombing of Kabul by Taliban. Thirty-nine civilians dead, 140 wounded. Government forces push back Taliban from Kabul.

1996

3 March. Rabbani starts visit to Iran, Turkmenistan and Uzbekistan.

20 March. Taliban Shura meets in Kandahar with 1,000 *ulema* and tribal elders to discuss policy.

4 April. Taliban Shura ends, calls for jihad against Rabbani. Mullah Omar made Amir-ul Momineen.

19 April. Senior US diplomats meet Afghan leaders in Kabul and Kandahar.

23 May. UN envoy Mestiri resigns for health reasons.

26 June. Hikmetyar joins Rabbani and becomes Prime Minister. Taliban rocket Kabul, 52 dead.

11 July. German diplomat Norbert Holl appointed as UN envoy to Afghanistan.

4 September. Afghan women in Kabul protest Taliban excesses.

10 September. Taliban capture two districts in Nangarhar. Haji Qadeer flees to Pakistan, heavy fighting near Jalalabad.

11 September. Taliban capture Jalalabad.

25 September. Taliban capture Sarobi and Assadabad.

26 September. From Sarobi, Taliban move to Kabul in one night. Fighting outside city. Kabul falls to Taliban.

27 September. Taliban hang Najibullah. Masud retreats northwards. Mullah Omar declares amnesty and six-man council to run Kabul headed by Mullah Mohammed Rabbani. Iran, Russia, India and Central Asian states condemn Taliban takeover. Pakistan sends delegation to Kabul.

1 October. Taliban tells Masud in the Panjshir to surrender or die. Masud blows up roads into Panjshir as Taliban advance north. Taliban reach Salang tunnel, stand-off with Dostum troops.

4 October. CIS summit in Almaty warns Taliban to keep away from Central Asia.

8 October. Heavy fighting as Taliban try to take Panjshir. Pakistan starts shuttle diplomacy.

10 October. Dostum, Masud and Khalili meet at Khin Jan and form Supreme Council for the Defence of the Motherland. Masud attacks Bagram with 50 men and counter-attacks on Salang highway.

12 October. Masud takes Jabul Seraj.

13 October. Masud recaptures Charikar. Fighting just ten miles from Kabul, hundreds of casualties.

18 October. Bagram falls to Masud as Taliban flee. Dostum armour arives to help Masud.

24 October. Mullah Omar says, 'We will fight to the death and give our last drop of blood for Kabul.' Masud demands demilitarization of Kabul. Taliban capture Baghdis province in heavy fighting with Dostum forces.

31 October. Ismael Khan troops flown from Iran to Maimana to resist Taliban in west.

1997

1 January. Taliban retake Bagram and Charikar, major set-back for Masud.

23 January. Taliban retake Gulbahar at mouth of Salang.

2 February. Hazaras reinforce defences of Bamiyan as Taliban advance via Ghorband valley. Taliban delegation visits USA.

12 March. Assassination attempt on Mullah Abdul Razaq, Governor of Herat.

19 May. General Malik Pahlawan rebels against Dostum, takes Faryab and says he has joined Taliban.

20 May. Baghdis, Faryab, Sar-e-Pul provinces fall to Malik, heavy fighting. Malik hands over 700 prisoners and Ismael Khan to Taliban.

24 May. Taliban sweep into Mazar, impose Sharia and close girls schools.

26 May. Pakistan recognizes Taliban government. Talks in Mazar between Taliban and Malik break down. Fighting starts.

28 May. Taliban driven out of Mazar after 18-hour battle and 300 Taliban dead. Thousands captured. Masud counter-attacks in south.

2 June. Taliban close Iranian Embassy in Kabul. Thousands of Pakistani students join Taliban. Opposition forms new alliance in Mazar.

12 June. Some 3,000 Taliban disarmed in Baghlan. Masud retakes Jabel Seraj. Rabbani meets Malik in Mazar. Opposition forms United Islamic and National Front for the Salvation of Afghanistan.

19 July. Masud takes Bagram and Charikar. Taliban flee leaving heavy weapons.

21 July. Malik in Iran for talks.

28 July. UN appoints Lakhdar Brahimi to prepare report on Afghanistan. Heavy fighting continues around Kabul.

7 August. ICRC says 6,800 people have been wounded in fighting over last three months. CARE suspends women's programmes in Kabul.

12 August. Opposition meeting in Mazar leads to Rabbani reappointed as President.

15 August. Lakhdar Brahami arrives in Islamabad for extensive trip to region.

19 August. Brahimi vists Kandahar. Taliban warn foreign press to report fairly or be thrown out.

4 September. Mullah Rabbani meets King Fahd in Jeddah and says Saudis will help Taliban in health and education. Taliban accuse Iran, Russia and France of helping Masud.

8 September. Taliban recapture Mazar airport after renewed attack from Taliban force from Kunduz. Uzbeks divided between Malik and Dostum.

9 September. Malik leaves Mazar as home burnt down by Hizb-e-Wahadat, extensive looting in city as UN agencies leave. Taliban pushed back from airport.

12 September. Dostum arrives back in Mazar from Turkey. Taliban kill 70 Hazara villagers in Qazil Abad. After three days of looting order in Mazar, peace restored as Taliban pushed back and Dostum rallies troops.

18 September. Heavy fighting again near Mazar. Taliban say King Fahd will give full financial and political backing to them.

23 September. Taliban bomb Bamiyan heavily. Fighting ten miles from Mazar.

28 September. Emma Bonino arrested in Kabul and held by Taliban for three hours with 19 other EC delegates.

30 September. Three UN workers expelled from Kandahar by Taliban.

1 October. Brahimi completes mission after visiting 13 countries. Heavy fighting continues around Mazar.

8 October. Dostum pushes Taliban back to Kunduz. Kabul rejects transit trade agreement with Pakistan.

21 October. Dostum seizes Shebarghan as Malik flees to Iran.

16 November. Dostum uncovers 2,000 dead bodies of Taliban in 30 mass

graves near Shebarghan, offers to return bodies to Taliban. Prisoner exchanges take place.

18 November. US Secretary Madeleine Albright in Pakistan calls Taliban human rights 'despicable'.

26 November. UN Secretary General Kofi Annan issues tough UN report on outside interference in Afghanistan.

17 December. UN Security Council condemns foreign arms supplies to Afghan factions, calls for cease-fire.

1998

6 January. President Rabbani visits Iran, Pakistan and Tajikistan to gather support for regional conference on Afghanistan under UN. Taliban accused of massacring 600 Uzbek civilians in Faryab province. Siege of Bamiyan by Taliban worsens as food supplies run out.

7 January. Kofi Annan appeals to Taliban to allow safe delivery of food to Bamiyan.

13 January. Taliban plane crashes near Quetta, 80 soldiers killed. Shoot-out near Kandahar between Taliban and villagers resisting recruitment drive.

27 January. Two hundred and fifty prisoners freed on both sides for Eid.

4 February. Earthquake in north-east Afghanistan. Four thousand dead and 15,000 homeless. Relief agencies hampered by snow.

20 February. Second earthquake hits.

8 March. International Women's day celebrated for Afghan women worldwide.

14 March. Heavy fighting in Mazar between Uzbeks and Hazaras.

22 March. Brahimi returns for mediation between Taliban and opposition.

1 April. Taliban name team to negotiate with opposition for *Ulema* Commission.

17 April. US envoy Bill Richardson visits Kabul and Mazar.

26 April. *Ulema* Commission meets in Islamabad under UN auspices.

4 May. *Ulema* Commission talks collapse.

17 May. Taliban jets bomb Taloquan, 31 people killed, 100 injured. Heavy fighting around Kabul and in north.

30 May. Major earthquake hits north-eastern Afghanistan again, 5,000 dead.

18 June. Saudi intelligence chief Prince Turki in Kandahar.

30 June. Taliban demand that NGOs have to move to destroyed polytechnic building. NGOs refuse to move.

3 July. Five-nation Central Asian summit in Almaty calls for end to Afghan war.

9 July. UN plane rocketed at Kabul airport. Omar issues edicts on scrapping TV, all Christians to be deported and former communists to be punished. Former communist Afghan Defence Minister murdered in Quetta.

12 July. Taliban capture Maimana, take 800 Uzbek prisoners and capture 100 tanks.

18 July. EU suspends all humanitarian aid to Kabul because of unacceptable restrictions.

20 July. NGOs pull out of Kabul. EU closes its office.

21 July. Two Afghan workers kidnapped and killed in Jalalabad.

31 July. Taliban leaders visit *madrassa* of Dar-ul-Uloom Haqqania, Akora Khattak in Pakistan where they appeal for manpower. Five thousand Pakistanis leave to fight in Afghanistan.

1 August. Taliban take Shebarghan, Dostum flees with troops to Hairatan on Uzbekistan border.

7 August. Bomb blasts at US embassies in Kenya and Tanzania, Osama Bin Laden held responsible.

8 August. Taliban capture Mazar, kill 11 Iranian diplomats and a journalist. Taliban massacre thousands of Hazaras as thousands more flee Mazar.

10 August. Taloquan falls to Taliban.

11 August. Russia warns Pakistan not to help Taliban. Central Asian states on high state of alert.

12 August. Pul-e-Khumri and Hairatan fall to Taliban.

18 August. Ayatollah Ali Khomeinei accuses US and Pakistan of using Taliban to plot against Iran. Iran–Taliban tensions escalate. Mullah Omar says Taliban will protect Bin Laden.

20 August. US launches 75 cruise missiles against Jalalabad and Khost camps run by Bin Laden. Twenty-one dead, 30 wounded in attack.

21 August. Taliban condemn US attack and vow to protect Bin Laden. UN military officer killed in Kabul. All foreigners evacuate Afghanistan and also Peshawar and Quetta.

26 August. New York Grand Jury hands over a sealed indictment against Bin Laden accusing him of terrorism.

1 September. Iran begins war-games on Afghan border with 70,000 troops.

6 September. Danger of war grows as Iran says it has right under international law to protect its citizens. USA advises restraint. Taliban again appeal to UN for recognition.

10 September. Taliban say they have found the bodies of nine Iranian diplomats in Mazar.

13 September. Bamiyan falls to Taliban after fighting. Omar asks troops to restrain themselves.

20 September. Heavy rocketing of Kabul by Masud, 66 killed and 215 wounded.

22 September. Saudi Arabia expels Taliban envoy and expresses anger at Taliban refusal to hand over Bin Laden following Prince Turki's visit to Kandahar.

27 September. Taliban have 30,000 troops on Iran border to resist Iranian exercises.

2 October. Iran gunships and planes violate Herat airspace. Iranian army exercises begin with 200,000 troops.

14 October. Lakhdar Brahimi holds talks with Mullah Omar in Kandahar in

Omar's first meeting with a foreign diplomat. Taliban agree to free all Iranian prisoners.

21 October. Feminist Majority Foundation in USA representing 129 women's organizations calls for increased economic and social pressure on Taliban. Mavis Leno, wife of Jay Leno, gives US$100,000 dollars for campaign against the Taliban's gender policy.

23 October. Masud undertakes successful offensive in north-east and enters Kunduz province. Taliban arrest 60 of General Tanai's supporters in coup attempt in Jalalabad.

25 October. Taliban ban use of landmines. Masud takes Imam Saheb on Tajikistan border.

7 November. UN says Taliban responsible for killing 4,000 people earlier in Mazar. Omar accuses UN of bias and says 3,500 Taliban killed. Omar again rejects broad-based government.

13 November. Mohammed Akbari, leader of faction of Hizb-e-Wahadat surrenders to Taliban in Bamiyan.

23 November. UNESCO chief Frederico Mayor urges world to stop human rights abuses by Taliban.

1 December. Taliban shoot students outside Jalalabad University, four dead, six injured.

9 December. UN General Assembly passes tough Resolution on Afghanistan.

29 December. UNICEF says education in Afghanistan has collapsed.

1999

10 January. Taliban reject new Peace and National Unity Party formed in Peshawar and say only military solution acceptable. Masud offensive continues in north.

12 January. Family of leading former Mujaheddin commander Abdul Haq gunned down in Peshawar.

19 January. Taliban cut off limbs of six highway robbers in Kabul and hang limbs on trees in the city.

21 January. UN Security Council again calls for cease-fire after briefing by Lakhdar Brahimi.

31 January. First Chinese delegation arrives in Kabul to meet Taliban.

2 February. Iranian officials meet Taliban in Dubai. US Deputy Secretary of State Strobe Talbott meets with Taliban in Islamabad. He hands over letter to Taliban demanding they extradite Osama Bin Laden.

9 February. Taliban reject US letter and say Bin Laden will not be forced out but they will impose restrictions on him.

11 February. Earthquake in Maiden Shahr in Logar kills 50 people and injures 200.

13 February. Bin Laden goes underground. Taliban say they do not know his whereabouts. Masud visits Tehran for talks.

15 February. Ten-year anniversary of Soviet withdrawal from Afghanistan.

21 February. UN mediator Lakhdar Brahimi arrives in Islamabad after meeting King Fahd in Riyadh.

28 February. Anti-Taliban alliance say they will form a leadership council and a 150-man parliament.

3 March. Turkmenistan's Foreign Minister Sheikhmuradov meets with Mullah Omar for the first time in Kandahar.

4 March. Hillary Clinton criticizes Taliban's gender policy.

11 March. Talks between the Taliban and the opposition begin in Ashkhabad under UN mediation.

14 March. Talks end on hopeful note with both sides agreeing to release some prisoners; structure of government to be decided in later talks.

24 March. Lakhdar Brahimi meets with Mullah Omar in Kandahar.

30 March. Next round of Ashkhabad talks stalled as both sides criticize one another.

7 April. Russian Defence Minister Igor Sergeyev meets with Masud in Dushanbe as Russia announces it will build new military base in Tajikistan.

10 April. Mullah Omar rules out further talks with opposition. Heavy fighting in and around Bamiyan.

15 April. President Clinton criticizes Taliban's abuse of human rights. Taliban condemn Clinton.

21 April. Bamiyan falls to Hizb-e-Wahadat as Taliban withdraw, dozens killed and dozens more captured.

28 April. Taliban bomb Bamiyan in bid to retake it. Thirty civilians killed.

29 April. Taliban, Pakistan and Turkmenistan sign agreement to revive gas pipeline through Afghanistan and pledge to find new sponsor for project. Hillary Clinton criticizes gender policy of Taliban in Washington.

5 May. Iran and Uzbekistan issue joint statement in Tashkent to resist any Taliban takeover of Afghanistan.

9 May. Bamiyan retaken by Taliban after they launch attacks from north ad south.

12 May. Taliban delegation sign agreements with Turkmenistan to buy gas and electricity.

14 May. USA issues first warning to Pakistan not to support the Taliban and says it favours the return of ex-King Zahir Shah.

20 May. Heavy fighting erupts. Masud fires 12 rockets into Kabul, Bagram bombed by Taliban and fighting in the north.

22 May. Taliban crush abortive uprising in Herat, execute eight people in public and kill another 100. Taliban accuse Iran of distributing arms.

28 May. Amnesty International accuse Taliban of killing civilians during their capture of Bamiyan. Mullah Omar holds meeting of several thousand Taliban commanders and mullahs in Kandahar for three days to discuss the movement's future.

2 June. Uzbekistan's Foreign Minister Aziz Kamilov meets with Mullah Omar for first time in Kandahar. Taliban insist that they will only attend next 'Six plus Two' conference in Tashkent if recognized as government of Afghanistan.

8 June. US FBI places Bin Laden on top of ten most wanted fugitives. Fears of US attack on Bin Laden increase.

26 June. Ex-King Zahir Shah holds consultative meeting in Rome, but Taliban reject any peace-making role for him. USA closes seven embassies in Africa for three days because of Bin Laden threats.

6 July. US imposes trade and economic sanctions against Taliban and freeze their assets in the USA. Taliban prepare for massive summer offensive against Masud as thousands of Pakistani and hundreds of Arab recruits join Taliban.

15 July. Former Senator Abdul Ahad Karzai, a leading Afghan nationalist, murdered in Quetta after meeting with Zahir Shah.The US State Department and the UN condemn the murder.

16 July. The Foreign Ministers of Russia, Tajikistan and Uzbekistan meet in Tashkent and pledge co-operation in combating Islamic extremism in Central Asia.

19 July. The 'Six plus Two' talks begin in Tashkent. President Islam Karimov calls for cease-fire and UN session on Afghanistan.

20 July. Tashkent talks without firm conclusions.

23 July. Masud in Tashkent and meets President Karimov.

27 July. UN planes stop flying to Kabul as rockets fired by Masud hit airport. Taliban offensive imminent.

28 July. Taliban offensive begins on three fronts as they advance towards Bagram. 130 killed on both sides in first day of fighting.

1 August. Bagram falls to Taliban, but heavy fighting as Masud tries to recapture it.

2 August. Taliban capture Charikar as Masud retreats to Panjshir. 200,000 people flee the Shomali valley creating new refugee crisis.

3 August. Taliban advance in north from Kunduz and take Imam Sahib and Sher Khan Bandar, cutting Masud's supply links to Tajkistan. 3000 casualties in fighting so far.

5 August. Masud counter-attacks and retakes Charikar and pushes Taliban back to former positions near Kabul. 400 Taliban killed and 500 captured.

8 August. Masud recaptures lost ground in the north.

10 August. Washington freezes assets of Taliban airline Ariana in the USA because of its links to Bin Laden.

13 August. Taliban retake Bagram.

15 August. UN appeals to Taliban not to create more refugees and halt fighting as Taliban pursue scorched-earth policy in Shomali valley. Thousands arrested in Kabul.

17 August. Pakistan attempts mediation but rejected by Northern Alliance.

24 August. Massive bomb blast in Kandahar outside Mullah Omar's home, killing 40 people including Omar's two step-brothers and six Arabs.

5 September. Heavy fighting as both sides launch renewed offensives in north and around Kabul.

10 September. UNDCP says Afghanistan's opium production doubles to 4600 tons in 1999. Ninety-seven per cent of cultivation under Taliban control.

20 September. Russia says Afghanistan-based Afghans, Pakistanis and Arabs fighting in Dagestan and Chechnya.

25 September. Taliban advance towards Taloquan, capital of Northern Alliance. Heavy fighting.

27 September. UN criticizes outside support for Afghan factions. Taliban recapture Imam Sahib.

29 September. Northern Alliance shoot down Taliban SU-22 fighter over Taloquan as fighting intensifies.

4 October. Pakistan's ISI chief visits Kandahar and demands extradition of Pakistani terrorists from Afghanistan. Mullah Omar agrees to co-operate.

12 October. Military coup in Pakistan overthrows government of Prime Minister Nawaz Sharif.

15 October. US Security Council imposes limited sanctions on Taliban.

2000

18 January. Francesc Vendrell appointed new UN Secretary General's Special Representative to Afghanistan.

6 February. Afghan civilians hijack internal flight from Kabul and force plane to fly to London where hijacking ends peacefully after 4 days.

March. Organisation of the Islamic Conference hold unsuccessful talks between Taliban and NA.

27 March. Ismail Khan escapes from Taliban jail in Kandahar and arrives in Iran. Taliban launch abortive offensive against Masud.

April. Severe draught grips Afghanistan and Taliban appeal for international help.

1 July. Taliban launch their summer offensive north of Kabul but repulsed with heavy casualties.

10 July. Bomb blasts in Pakistan embassy in Kabul.

28 July. Tabliban launch attack in the north against Masud's forces. Islamic Movement of Uzbekistan based in northern Afghanistan launches attacks in Uzbekistan.

5 September. After four week seige and heavy fighting. Taliban capture Taloqan in Takhar province from Masud, who retreats to Badakhshan province. 150,000 refugees flee and put pressure on Tajikistan. Central Asia and Russian leaders condemn Taliban advances.

Appendix 4

The New
Great Game

TABLE 1. PROPOSED GAS PIPELINES FROM TURKMENISTAN IN 1996

Firm	Route	Details
1. Enron/Wing Merril BOTAS/ Gama Guris	Turkmenistan–Azerbaijan–Turkey	Under Caspian Sea. Cost US$1.6 billion
2. Unocal, Delta Oil, Turkmenrosgaz	Turkmenistan–Pakistan–Afghanistan	937 miles. Cost US$2.5 billion
3. Bridas-TAP	Turkmenistan–Pakistan–Afghanistan	750 miles. Cost US$2.5 billion
4. Royal Dutch Shell, Gaz de France, Snamprogetti, Turkmenistan	Turkmenistan–Iran–Turkey	1875 miles. Cost US$2 billion
5. Mitsubishi, Exxon, China, Turkmenistan	Turkmenistan–Kazakhstan–China–Japan	5,000 miles. Cost US$22 billion
6. China–Iran–Turkmenistan	Kazakhstan–Turkmenistan–Iran–Persian Gulf	1,500 miles. Cost 2.5 billion

7. 120-mile-long gas pipeline connecting Iran–Turkmenistan opened in December 1997.

STATUS OF PIPELINES IN 1999
1. Contract for a Turkmenistan–Turkey pipeline under the Caspian Sea signed in 1999 by consortium made up of Bechtel Group and US General Electric. Cost US$2.5 billion.
2. Suspended.
3. Suspended.
4. Stalled.
5. Stalled.
6. Stalled.

Source: Ahmed Rashid

TABLE 2. TURKMENISTAN GAS PRODUCTION

	Billion cubic metres/year	Trillion cubic feet/year
1989	89.6	3.20
1990	55.7	2.00
1994	20.6	0.73
1995	22.0	0.78
1996	26.0	0.91
1997	17.0	0.60
1998	13.6	0.48

Source: Turkmen government

TABLE 3. CHRONOLOGY OF UNOCAL–BRIDAS COMPETITION FOR AFGHANISTAN PIPELINE

1992	13 January	Bridas awarded gas exploration rights for Yashlar block in eastern Turkmenistan, 50–50 split in production profits.
1993	February	Bridas awarded Keimir oil and gas block in western Turkmenistan. 75–25 split in profits in Bridas favour.
	March	President Niyazov visits USA. Former US National Security Adviser Alexander Haig hired by President Niyazov to head campaign to encourage US investment in Turkmenistan and soften US position on pipelines via Iran.
1994	September	Bridas prevented from exporting oil from Keimir block.
	November	Turkmenistan establishes working group to study gas pipeline routes. Group includes Haig and Bridas. Taliban capture Kandahar.

1995	January	After renegotiating Keimir block, Bridas reduces its share of profits to 65 per cent. Oil exports allowed.
	16 March	President Niyazov and Pakistan's PM Benazir Bhutto sign agreement for Bridas to carry out pre-feasibility study of Afghan gas pipeline.
	April	Turkmenistan and Iran sign agreement to build first 180 miles spur of proposed gas pipeline via Iran to Turkey.
		USA sets up working group including National Security Council, State Department and CIA to study US oil and gas interests in Caspian region. US tells Turkmenistan it will oppose financing for pipelines through Iran and urges it look to the west.
		Turkmen officials visit Houston, Texas, at invitation of Bridas and meet with Unocal for first time.
	June	Unocal delegation in Ashkhabad and Islamabad discuss joining Bridas for Afghan pipeline. Bridas presents feasibility study to Turkmen government.
	August	Bridas makes oil and gas discovery at Yashlar. Bridas meets with Taliban for first time in Kandahar. Bridas executives travel to Kabul, Herat and Mazar.
	21 October	President Niyazov in New York signs Afghan pipeline agreement with Unocal/Delta.
	December	Turkmenistan bans Bridas's oil exports from Keimir block for second time.
1996	February	Bridas signs agreement with Afghan government for construction of pipeline. Bridas files suit in Houston againt Unocal/Delta interference with its business in Turkmenistan.
	March	US Ambassador Tom Simmons urges PM Bhutto to give exclusive rights to Unocal. Bhutto demands a written apology for Simmons's rudeness.
	April	Bridas begins arbitration against Turkmenistan for breach of contract. US Assistant Secretary of State Robin Raphel visits Kabul and Kandahar.
	May	Iran opens new 100-mile railway route linking Turkmenistan and Iran. Turkmenistan, Uzbekistan, Pakistan and Afghanistan sign agreeement giving Turkmenistan the right to nominate the consortium to build the pipeline.
	August	Russia's Gazprom signs agreement with Unocal/Delta and Turkmenistan's Turkmenrosgaz for pipe-

line project. US Assistant Secretary of State Robin Raphel visits Afghanistan and Central Asia. She refers to US interest in the Unocal pipeline.

September — Unocal presents pipeline definition report to President Niyazov. Unocal says it will give humanitarian aid as bonuses to Afghan warlords once they agree to form a council to supervise the project.

27 September — Kabul falls to the Taliban. USA says it will re-establish diplomatic relations with Afghanistan soon.

1 October — Unocal expresses support for Taliban takeover of Kabul, says pipeline project now easier. Later Unocal says it was misquoted.

26 October — President Niyazov and Unocal/Delta sign agreement giving them exclusive rights to form consortium for Afghan pipeline.

Robert Oakley, former US Ambassador to Pakistan, heads first meeting of Unocal's Afghan Advisory Committee.

November — Bridas signs agreement with Taliban and General Rashid Dostum to build pipeline.

9 December — Pakistani Foreign Secretary Najmuddin Sheikh in Kandahar for talks with Taliban on pipeline.

29 December — Iran, Turkey, Turkmenistan sign agreement for Turkey to buy Turkmen gas through Iran.

1997 20 January — Turkmenistan signs agreement with Mobil and Monument Oil for oil and gas exploration.

January — Interim order of International Chamber of Commerce gives Bridas right to export oil from Keimir. Turkmenistan rejects order.

UN Under Secretary General Yasushi Akashi criticizes oil companies and Afghan warlords for pipeline projects.

February — A Taliban delegation in Washington seeks US recognition and meets with Unocal. Second Taliban delegation visits Argentina as guests of Bridas. On return Taliban meet with Saudi Intelligence chief Prince Turki in Jeddah.

March — Unocal to set up office in Kandahar and training centres for Afghans. Bridas sets up office in Kabul as Carlos Bulgheroni visits Kabul, Kandahar.

April 8 — Taliban say they will award pipeline contract to the company which starts work first. Unocal President John Imle says he is baffled by Taliban statement.

	Unocal to set up new headquarters for Asia in Kuala Lumpur.
May 14	ECO summit in Ashkhabad. Pakistan, Turkmenistan and Unocal sign agreement to build oil and gas pipelines to start work during the year.
May 24	Taliban seize Mazar-e-Sharif but are driven out four days later with heavy casualties.
4 June	First meeting of working group of Pakistan, Turkmenistan, Unocal and Delta in Islamabad.
8 June	Marty Miller of Unocal says pipeline could take years to construct unless there is peace.
9 June	Bridas's Carlos Bulgheroni meets Taliban leaders in Kabul and says Bridas 'interested in beginning work in any kind of security situation'. Promises to help Afghans build roads and revive industry. Bridas negotiating contract with Taliban.
22 July	New association formed to promote Turkmen–US business interests. Unocal elected first Chairman.
23 July	Pakistan, Turkmenistan and Unocal sign new contract extending Unocal's deadline by one year to start project by December 1998. Unocal's Marty Miller tours Mazar, Kandahar to win support for extension from Afghan groups.
27 July	In major policy shift, USA says it will not object to a Turkmenistan–Turkey gas pipeline through Iran. USA later says this will help its friends, but is not a signal for any opening towards Iran.
14 August	Shell President Alan Parsley meets Niyazov and promises help on Turkmenistan–Turkey gas pipeline.
28 August	Taliban say Bridas have given better terms for pipeline than Unocal and will sign with Bridas soon. Unocal say they are still in the game.
1 September	Turkmenistan opens tenders for oil companies to take up new concessions along the Caspian. Niyazov, 57, has heart operation in Munich. Concern grows about his health and succession.
5 September	Bridas sell 60 per cent of their company's stakes in Latin America to Amoco. Both will form a new company to run operations jointly.
12 September	A five-man Taliban delegation arrives in Argentina to discuss pipeline with Bridas. Pakistani authorities hold them back for five days in Peshawar refusing to let them go.
15 September	Pakistan concludes a 30-year gas pricing agreement with Unocal. Pakistan will pay US$2.05 per 1,000

cubic feet of gas for delivery at Multan, with 15 cents as royalty to Taliban which they reject.

16 October   Prime Minister Nawaz Sharif travels for one day to Ashkhabad to meet President Niyazov to discuss the pipeline project.

22 October   Taliban delegation visits Ashkhabad and agrees to set up tripartite commission with Pakistan and Turkmenistan to explore Unocal gas pipeline project.

25 October   Central Asia Gas (CentGas) Pipeline Ltd. Formed in Ashkhabad. Unocal 46.5 per cent, Delta Oil 15 per cent, Turkmenistan 7 per cent, Japan's Itochu Oil 6.5 per cent, Indonesia Petroleum (Inpex) 6.5 per cent, Crescent Group 3.5 per cent, Hyundai Engineering and Construction Co 5 per cent. Gazprom will sign later. Unocal's Marty Miller says gas transit price not fixed and CentGas will not sign with Taliban. Taliban say they are undecided which consortium to join.

28 November   Taliban delegation leaves for USA to visit Unocal in Sugarland. Taliban later meet US State Department officials.

December   Unocal gives University of Nebraska US$900,000 for setting up technical training programme in Afghanistan.

29 December   Turkmenistan and Iran inaugurate 120-mile-long gas pipeline with 0.3 tcf capacity per year between the two countries.

1998   6 January   International Court of Arbitration in Paris rules in favour of Bridas on case to release monies owed by Turkmen government for refined products provided to Keimir refinery. Bridas awarded US$47 million and US$3 million in costs.

3 February   Gazprom pulls out of Unocal consortium and its 10-per-cent shares redistributed giving Unocal 54 per cent stake.

3 March   Senior team from Australia's BHP meets with PM Nawaz Sharif to push for Iran-Pakistan gas pipeline.

11 March   In Ashkhabad, Unocal's Marty Miller says pipeline project on indefinite hold because it is unfinanciable while Afghan war continues. Construction work and financial closure cannot be achieved this year. Turkmen insist work must start soon.

30 March   Unocal asks Pakistan for an extension for achieving financial closure by October 1998. It cannot meet the deadline because of Afghan civil war.

June	At Unocal's annual meeting, some shareholders object to company's plans for an Afghan pipeline because of human rights abuses by the Taliban. Unocol says it has spent US$10–15 million on the project since 1995 and plans to donate US$1 million to Afghan charities in 1998.
21 August	Unocal suspends pipeline project and pull out staff from Islamabad and Kandahar after US missile strikes against Osama Bin Laden in Afghanistan.
10 September	A group of Green activists demand that California's Attorney General dissolve Unocal for crimes against humanity and the environment and because of Unocal's relations with the Taliban. Unocal describes the charges as 'ludicrous'.
5 October	Texas District Court in Fort Bend County dismisses a US$15 billion Bridas suit against Unocal for allegedly preventing them developing gas fields in Turkmenistan. Case dismissed on the grounds that the dispute was governed by laws of Turkmenistan and Afghanistan, not Texas law.
23 November	Unocal withdraws from a US$2.9 billion pipeline project to bring natural gas from Turkmenistan to Turkey as the company cuts spending.
4 December	Unocal withdraws from Afghan pipeline consortium, citing low oil prices, concern about Osama Bin Laden in Afghanistan and pressure from US feminist groups. Unocal closes offices in Uzbekistan, Turkmenistan and Kazakhstan.
22 December	Unocal announces a 40-per-cent drop in capital spending plan for 1999 due to low oil prices.
1999 1 January	First Chinese delegation arrives in Kandahar to meet Taliban officials.
24 January	Turkmen Foreign Minister Sheikhmuradov visits Pakistan and says pipeline project still intact.
February	Carlos Bulgheroni visits Turkmenistan, Kazakhstan and Russia for talks with leaders.
3 March	Turkmenistan's Foreign Minister Sheikhmuradov meets with Mullah Omar for the first time in Kandahar and discusses gas pipeline.
11 March	UN sponsored talks in Ashkhabad, Turkmenistan start between Taliban and opposition. Talks later fail.
March	The BP-led North Apsheron Operating Company (NAOC) in Azerbaijan shuts down because of low oil prices. Unocal and Delta, who are partners pull out.

	29 April	Pakistan, Turkmenistan and Taliban sign agreement in Islamabad to revive gas pipeline project.
	April-May	Heavy fighting for control of Bamiyan in Hazarajat.
	12 May	Taliban delegation sign agreements with Turkmenistan to buy gas and electricity.
	May	Uprising in Herat against Taliban, 100 civilians killed, 8 civilians put on trial and executed.
	2 June	Uzbekistan's Foreign Minister Aziz Kamilov meets with Mullah Omar.
	8 June	US FBI places Osama Bin Laden on top of most wanted list and offers US$5 million reward for his capture.
	6 July	US imposes trade and economic boycott on Taliban for refusing to hand over Bin Laden.
	19 July	Six plus Two group of countries meet in Tashkent; meeting also attended by Taliban who remain determined to start offensive.
	28 July	Taliban summer offensive begins, heavy fighting.
	5 August	Masud launches counter-offensive and retakes all lost territory around Kabul. More than 2,000 Taliban casualties.
	25 August	Massive truck bomb explodes outside Mullah Omar's house in Kandahar killing 10, wounding 40 including several of Omar's aides and relatives.
2000	16 January	Chechen breakaway Republic recognised by Taliban and opens embassy in Kabul.
	18 January	Spanish diplomat Francesc Venrell appointed as the UN Secretary General's new Special Representative for Afghanistan.
	6 February	Internal flight of Ariana Afghan Airlines hijacked to London and hijackers demand political asylum.
	27 March	Former Governor of Herat Ismael Khan escapes from Taliban jail in Kandahar and arrives in Iran.
	1 July	Taliban begin summer offensive.
	10 July	Taliban order all foreign relief organisations to sack their Afghan female staff.
	1 August	Islamic Movement of Uzbekistan launches attacks in Central Asia from bases in Afghanistan. Mullah Omar bans poppy cultivation.
2001	8 January	After capturing Yakowlang, Taliban massacre 210 civilians.
	19 January	UN Security Council passes Resolution 1333 imposing sanctions and arms embargo against the Taliban only.

26 February	Mullah Omar orders destruction of two ancient giant statues of Buddha in Bamiyan.
1 March	UN says Taliban have enforced ban on poppy cultivation and virtually zero opium production this year.
10 March	Two Buddha statues destroyed by dynamite.
4 April	Ahmad Shah Masud arrives in Europe for tour of capitals.
16 April	Mullah Mohammed Rabbani, Taliban deputy leader dies of cancer in Pakistan.
22 May	Taliban order all Hindus to wear yellow badges for identity purposes.
1 June	Taliban summer offensive begins.
31 July	UN Security Council passes Resolution 1363 setting up monitoring of sanctions on Taliban.
5 August	Taliban arrest 8 foreigners and 16 Afghans belonging to Christian relief agency on charges of spreading Christianity.
9 September	Ahmad Shah Masud assassinated by Taliban-sponsored suicide bombers in the Takhar Province in the far north of the country.
11 September	Terrorist bombings in New York and Washington prompt US military action against Taliban and Osama Bin Laden.

Appendix 5

Glossary of Afghan terms

Amir-ul Momineen. Commander of the Faithful. An Islamic title.

Baitul Mal. Islamic charitable fund raised from taxes paid by the public.

Bara. A smuggler's market in Pakistan.

Basmachi. Islamic guerrillas who resisted Soviet rule in Central Asia in the 1920s.

Burkha. All-enveloping head-to-toe veil worn by Afghan women under the Taliban.

Dari. The Afghan dialect of Persian.

Fatwa. Legal ruling issued by *ulema*.

Jihad. Effort or struggle to become a good Muslim. Also holy war to defend or spread Islam.

Jirga. Council of tribal elders or whole tribe to discuss political and legal issues.

Halal. The ritual Islamic way to kill an animal, by slitting its throat and letting the blood pour out.

Istakhbarat. The Saudi Intelligence Service.

Kafirs. Non-Muslims or unbelievers.

Khan. Formerly a Pashtun tribal chief, now a common tribal name.

Lashkar. Traditional tribal militia force.

Loya Jirga. Great Council. The traditional meeting of tribal chiefs, *ulema* and other representatives to choose a new Afghan king. Also the primary law-making body in the country.

Madrassa. Islamic schools which teach religious subjects.

Malik. A Pashtun tribal notable. In the past used to be tribal or clan chief.

Mehram. A male blood relative who should accompany a woman during travel, according to strict Islamic law.

Mujaheddin. Holy warriors fighting jihad or holy war.

Mullah. Traditional leader of prayer at local mosque.

Munafaqeen. Muslims who are hypocrites.

Nan. Unleavened baked bread. The staple diet of Afghans.

Pashtunwali. The tribal social code of the Pashtuns often at odds with Sharia law.

Pir. Honorific title given to the head of a Sufi sect.

Qazi. Islamic judge who dispenses justice under Sharia law.

Ramadan. The month of fasting in the Islamic calendar.

Registan. Desert region.

Serai. Staging post for camel caravans on the old Silk Route.

Shalwar kameez. Baggy pants and long shirt worn by Afghan and Pakistani men and women.

Shura. Islamic council.

Sharia. The canon of Islamic law.

Sufism. The mystical trend of Islam.

Tor. High-grade opium.

Ulema. Islamic scholars. Singular is *alim*.

Ummah. The community of all Muslims, the wider Islamic world.

Zakat. Islamic tax given to the poor, equivalent to 2.5 per cent of individual's personal wealth.

Appendix 6

Bibliography

Akiner, Shireen, *Islamic Peoples of the Soviet Union*, Kegan Paul International, London 1983.

Allworth, Edward, *The Modern Uzbeks from the 14ᵗʰ Century to the Present*, Hoover Institute Press 1990.

Arney, George, *Afghanistan*, Mandarin, London 1990.

Arnold, Anthony, *The Fateful Pebble, Afghanistan's Role in the Fall of the Soviet Empire*, Presidio Press, California 1993.

Babur, *Babur-Nama*, translated by Nette Beveridge, Sang-e-Meel Publications, Lahore 1979.

Battuta, Ibn, *Travel in Asia and Africa 1325–1354*, Routledge and Kegan Paul, London 1984.

Bennigsen, Alexandre and Wimbush, Enders, *Muslim National Communism in the Soviet Union, a Revolutionary Struggle for the Post-Colonial World*, University of Chicago Press, Chicago 1979.

Bennigsen, Alexandre and Wimbush, Ender, *Muslims of the Soviet Empire*, C. Hurst and Co, London 1985.

Bennigsen, Alexandre and Wimbush, Enders, *Mystics and Commissars, Sufism in the Soviet Union*, University of California Press, Berkeley 1985.

Byron, Robert, *The Road to Oxiana*, Macmillan, London 1937.

Chase, Robert and Kennedy, Paul and Hill, Emily, *The Pivotal States. A New Framework for US Policy in the Developing World*, W. Norton and Co. 1999.

Cordovez, Diego, and Harrison, Selig, *Out of Afghanistan, The Inside Story of the Soviet Withdrawal*, Oxford University Press 1995.

Dupree, Louis, *Afghanistan*, Princeton University Press 1980.

Dupree, Nancy Hatch, *A Historical Guide to Afghanistan*, Afghan Tourist Organization, Kabul 1970.

Dupree, Nancy Hatch, *A Historical Guide to Kabul*, Afghan Tourist Organization, Kabul 1970.

Elleston, Harold, *The General against the Kremlin. Alexander Lebed: Power and Illusion*, Little Brown and Co., London 1998.

Ghani, Abdul, *A Brief Political History of Afghanistan*, Najaf Publishers, Lahore 1989.

Goodwin, Jan, *Caught in the Crossfire*, E.P. Dutton, New York 1987.

Grousset, Rene, *The Empire of the Steppes, a History of Central Asia*, Rutgers University 1970.

Hopkirk, Peter, *The Great Game*, John Murray, London 1970.

Hopkirk, Peter, *Setting the East Ablaze*, John Murray, London 1984.

Huntington, Samuel P, *The Clash of Civilizations and the Remaking of the New World Order*, Simon and Shuster, New York 1966.

Ignatieff, Michael *The Warrior's Honor, Ethnic War and the Modern Conscience*, Vintage, New York 1999.

Kaplan, Robert, *The Ends of the Earth, a Journey to the Frontiers of Anarchy*, Vintage Books 1997.

Khan, Riaz, *Untying the Afghan Knot, Negotiating Soviet Withdrawal*, Duke University Press 1991.

Khilji, Jalaluddin, *Muslim Celebrities of Central Asia*, University of Peshawar 1989.

Magnus, Ralph and Naby, Eden, *Afghanistan, Mullah, Marx and Mujahid*, Harper Collins, India 1998.

Maley, William (ed.), *Fundamentalism Reborn? Afghanistan and the Taliban* C. Hurst, London 1998.

Marsden, Peter, *The Taliban: War, Religion and the New Order in Afghanistan*, Zed Books, London 1998.

McCoy, Alfred and Block, Alan, *War on Drugs, Studies in the Failure of US Narcotics Policy*, Westview Press 1992.

Metcalf, Barbara, *Islamic Revival in British India 1860–1900*, Royal Book Company, Islamabad 1982.

Mousavi, Sayed Askar, *The Hazaras of Afghanistan, an Historical, Cultural, Economic and Political Study*, Curzon Press, London 1998.

Naumkin, Vitaly, *State, Religion and Society in Central Asia*, Ithaca Press, Reading 1993.

Newby, Eric, *A Short Walk in the Hindu Kush*, Picador 1974.

Noelle, Christine, *State and Tribe in Nineteenth-Century Afghanistan*, Curzon Press, London 1997.

Olcott, Martha Brill, *Central Asia's New States*, US Institute of Peace 1996.

Olsen, Asta, *Islam and Politics in Afghanistan*, Curzon Press, London 1995.

Pettifer, James, *The Turkish Labyrinth – Ataturk and the New Islam*, Penguin Books, London 1997.

Polo, Marco, *The Travels of Marco Polo*, Dell Publishing, New York 1961.

Rawlinson, Henry, *England and Russia in the East*, 1875, Reprinted by Indus Publications, Karachi 1989.

Roy, Olivier, *Afghanistan, from Holy War to Civil War*, Princeton University 1995.

Roy, Olivier, *The Failure of Political Islam*, I.B.Tauris, Cambridge, London 1994.

Roy, Olivier, *Islam and Resistance in Afghanistan*, Cambridge University Press 1986.

Royal Geographical Society, *The Country of the Turkomans*, Royal Geographical Society, London 1977.

Rubin, Barnett, *The Fragmentation of Afghanistan, State Formation and Collapse in the International System*, Yale University Press, New Haven 1995.

Rubin, Barnett, *The Search for Peace in Afghanistan, From Buffer State to Failed State*, Yale University Press, New Haven 1995.

Rubin, Barnett and Synder, Jack, *Post-Soviet Political Order, Conflict and State Building*, Routledge, London 1998.

Seward, Desmond, *The Monks of War, the Military Religious Orders*, Penguin, London 1972.

Shafqat, Saeed, *Civil Military Relations in Pakistan. From Z.A. Bhutto to Benazir Bhutto*, Westview Press 1998.

Sikorski, Radek, *Dust of the Saints*, Chatto and Windus, London 1989.

Tapper, Richard, *The Conflict of Tribe and State in Afghanistan*, Croom Helm, London 1983.

Verrier, Anthony, *Francis Younghusband and the Great Game*, Jonathan Cape, London 1991.

Media sources
Pakistan: *Dawn, Frontier Post*, the *Nation*, the *News, Herald*.
USA: *International Herald Tribune, New York Times, Washington Post, Los Angeles Times*.
Other: Agence France Press (AFP), Associated Press (AP), Reuters, Interfax, *Far Eastern Economic Review*, the *Economist*, the *Guardian*, the *Independent*, *Le Monde*.

Notes

Introduction

1. Huntington, Samuel P, *The Clash of Civilizations and the Remaking of the New World Order*, Simon and Shuster, New York 1966.
2. Verrier, Anthony, *Francis Younghusband and the Great Game*, Jonathan Cape, London 1991.
3. Polo, Marco, *The Travels of Marco Polo*, Dell Publishing, New York 1961.
4. *Babur-Nama*, translated by Nette Beveridge, Sang-e-Meel Publications, Lahore 1979.
5. Noelle, Christine, *State and Tribe in Nineteenth Century Afghanistan*, Curzon Press, London 1997.
6. Rubin, Barnett, 'Afghanistan the forgotten crisis,' *Refugee Survey Quarterly*, Vol 15 No.2, UNHCR 1996.

Chapter 1

1. US aid began with US$30 million in 1980, rising to US$80 million in 1983, to US$250 million in 1985, to US$470 million in 1986, to US$630 million in 1987 until 1989. US aid continued until Kabul fell to the Mujaheddin in 1992. Between 1986–89 total aid to the Mujaheddin exceeded US$1 billion dollars a year. Rubin, Barnett, 'Afghanistan the forgotten crisis,' *Refugee Survey Quarterly* Vol 15 No.2. UNHCR 1996.
2. I conducted several interviews with Mullah Hassan in Kandahar in 1995, 1996 and 1997.
3. Dupree, Nancy Hatch, *A Historical Guide to Afghanistan*, Afghan Tourist Organization, Kabul 1970.

4. I conducted several interviews with Mullah Ghaus in 1996 and 1997.

5. Yousufzai, Rahimullah. 'Taliban head says Rabbani sabotaging UN peace efforts,' the *News*, 2 February 1995.

6. This profile of Mullah Omar has been built up over five years after interviews with dozens of Taliban leaders. I am grateful to Rahimullah Yousufzai's articles as he is the only journalist to have interviewed Omar.

7. Goldenberg, Suzanne, 'Place where the Taliban began and certainty ends', the *Guardian*, 13 October 1998.

8. Burns, John and Levine, Steve, 'How Afghans' stern rulers took hold', *New York Times*, 11 December 1996.

9. *Dawn*, 4 November 1994.

10. The Ambassadors were from the USA, UK, Spain, Italy, China, and South Korea. The delegation included officials from the United Nations.

11. Interviews with senior Pakistan government officials and transporters in Quetta, March 1995.

12. Davis, Anthony, 'How the Taliban became a military force', in Maley, William (ed.), *Fundamentalism Reborn? Afghanistan and the Taliban*, C. Hurst, London 1998. Davis's military account is the most detailed to date on the capture of Spin Baldak and Kandahar by the Taliban.

13. Interviews with Pakistani intelligence officers, Kandahar, April 1995.

14. *Muslim*, 17 November 1994.

15. The *Nation*, 18 February 1995.

16. *Dawn*, 18 March 1995.

Chapter 2

1. Seward, Desmond, *The Monks of War, the Military Religious Orders*, Penguin, London 1972. The great military orders, the Templars, the Hospitallers and the Teutonic Knights, were founded in the twelfth century.

2. Interviews with Taliban soldiers, Kandahar, March 1995.

3. Sikorski, Radek, *Dust of the Saints*, Chatto and Windus, London 1989.

4. Byron, Robert, *The Road to Oxiana*, Macmillan, London 1937.

5. Byron wrote on his first sight of the minarets, 'No photograph, no description, can convey their colour of grape-blue with an azure bloom, or the intricate convolutions that make it so deep and luminous. On the bases, whose eight sides are supported by white marble panels carved with baroque Kufic, yellow, white, olive green and rusty red mingle, with the two blues in a maze of flowers, arabesques and texts as fine as the pattern on a tea-cup.' (Byron: *The Road to Oxiana*)

6. Dupree, Nancy Hatch, *A Historical Guide to Afghanistan*, Afghan Tourist Organization, Kabul 1970.

7. Interview with Ismael Khan, September 1993.

8. Interview with Mullah Wakil Ahmad, Kandahar, May 1995.

9. Dupree: *A Historical Guide to Afghanistan*.

Chapter 3

1. Interview with Mehmoud Mestiri in Islamabad, 2 February 1996. See also Rashid, Ahmed, 'Masud ready to launch offensive says Mestiri', the *Nation*, 4 February 1996.

2. AFP, 'Ullema declare Jihad against Rabbani', the *Nation*, 4 April 1996.

3. Interview with Wakil in Kandahar, March 1996.

4. Interviews with Pakistani diplomats and intelligence officials, Islamabad, February 1996.

5. AFP, 'Taliban ready to negotiate', the *Nation*, 3 April 1996.

6. Interviews with US and Pakistan diplomats, Islamabad, February 1995. See also Rashid, Ahmed. 'Afghanistan: Proxy War is back', the *World Today*, The Royal Institute of International Affairs, March 1996.

7. AFP, Kabul, 'Senator Hank Brown meets Masud in Kabul', the *Nation*, 8 April 1996. For a fuller discussion of the US role in the rise of the Taliban, see Chapter 13.

8. AFP, Bagram, 'Raphael says US interest in Afghanistan increasing', the *Nation*, 20 April 1996.

9. Interview with Robin Raphel, Islamabad, 18 April 1996.

10. APP, Washington, 'US wants peace, stable Afghanistan', the *Nation*, 11 May 1996. Raphel spelled out US policy in a Testimony to the Senate Foreign Relations Committee in Washington.

11. Interview with Rabbani, Kabul, August 1996.

12. AFP, Kabul, 'Holl flays Taliban for rocket attacks', the *Nation*, 31 July 1996.

13. Interviews with several Pakistani and Afghan sources. See also: Rubin, Barnett, 'Afghanistan the forgotten crisis', *Refugee Survey Quarterly* Vol 15 No.2, UNHCR 1996.

14. Davis, Anthony, 'How the Taliban became a military force,' in Maley, William (ed.) *Fundamentalism Reborn? Afghanistan and the Taliban*, C. Hurst, London 1998.

15. This account is based on several interviews with UN officials and Masud himself in 1996 and 1997. There are also reports that Najibullah was hoping to do a deal with the Taliban because of their common ethnic origins and that he left the compound voluntarily.

16. Khan, Behroz, 'Taliban commander admits ordering Najib's killing', the *News*, 16 February 1998. Mullah Razaq admitted ordering Najibullah's execution in an interview. 'We had asked our soldiers to kill Najib then and there. It was necessary because he was responsible for the massacre of thousands of Afghans,' Razaq said. Mullah Omar appointed Razaq commander of the Taliban forces that captured Kabul in 1996. He was captured by Dostum's troops in Mazar in May, 1997 and later freed.

17. Burns, John, 'With sugared tea and caustic rules, an Afghan leader explains himself', the *New York Times*, 24 November 1996.

18. Yousufzai, Rahimullah, 'The leader nobody knows', the *News*, 30 March 1997.

Chapter 4

1. Pakistani diplomatic sources told me that Pakistan had provided Dostum with US$10 million dollars in a bid to persuade him to ally with the Taliban. Iran paid him similar sums to keep him opposed to the Taliban.

2. Levine, Steve, 'Enemies of Enemies', Newsweek, 21 October 1996.

3. Dostum had summoned Malik to Mazar from the Baghdis front but he refused to go saying that Dostum would kill him. 'That was the trigger for the coup against Dostum', a senior Pakistani General told me in Islamabad on 19 May 1997.

4. Pakistan's Foreign Minister Gohar Ayub issued a statement on 25 May 1997 extending recognition and stating that the crisis in Afghanistan was now solved as the Taliban had formed a broad-based government. 'We feel that the new government fulfils all criteria for de jure recognition. It is now in effective control of most of the territory of Afghanistan and is representative of all ethnic groups in that country,' said Ayub. Within hours of the statement the Taliban were forced out of Mazar.

5. The Taliban captured Ismael Khan and some 700 of his fighters after Khan had been invited to a dinner by Malik who then allowed the Taliban to arrest him. Betraying a guest in your home is anathema for Afghans. See Rashid, Ahmed, '550 Pakistani students captured by Afghan opposition', the Nation, 14 July 1997.

6. According to interviews with officials from the UN and the ICRC in Kabul, July 1997, Malik held 1,000 Taliban in Maimana, 1,000 in Sheberghan and 800 in Mazar. Masud held between 600 and 700 prisoners in the Panjshir. General Naderi's Ismaeli forces north of the Salang tunnel held 100 Taliban and Hizb-e-Wahadat held around 100 Taliban. According to the UN, Malik held 200 Pakistanis in Mazar, another 225 in Maimana while Masud held 100 Pakistanis in the Panjshir valley and Khalili held nearly 50.

7. Interview with Haqqani, Kabul, 12 July 1997.

8. Interview with Abbas, Kabul, 15 July 1997.

9. Interview with Uzbek diplomat, Islamabad, 5 July 1997. See also Rashid, Ahmed, 'Highly explosive. Renewed fighting alarms Central Asian neighbours', Far Eastern Economic Review, 12 June 1997.

10. Interview with Haqqani, Kabul 12 July 1997. See also Rashid, Ahmed, 'Afghan factions face serious internal divisions', the Nation, 16 July 1997.

11. Peters, Gretchen, 'Massacres prompt fears of ethnic escalation', AP, 15 February 1998.

12. Yousufzai, Rahimullah, 'Dostum unearths mass graves', the News, 16 November 1997.

13. AFP, 'Taliban massacre site discovered in Afghanistan', 16 December 1997.

14. Peters, Gretchen, 'Massacres prompt fears of ethnic escalation', AP, 15 February 1997.

15. Press conference by Norbert Holl, Islamabad, 18 October 1997.

16. Reported by news agencies. See also Rashid, Ahmed, 'Taliban hold Bonino

in hospital ward', *Daily Telegraph*, 30 September 1997. Those held included Christiane Amanpour of CNN.

17. Taliban leaders alluded to these feelings as early as July in conversations with me in Kabul. In Pakistan, Maulanas Fazlur Rehman and Samiul Haq, leaders of separate factions of the Jamiat-e-*Ulema* Islam which backed the Taliban, said that the UN was a nest of spies and anti-Islam and that they had asked Mullah Omar to kick out the UN agencies.

18. The six neighbours were Pakistan, Iran, Turkmenistan, Uzbekistan, Tajikistan and China.

19. AFP, 'UN Chief slams outside forces for fuelling Afghan conflict', 9 November 1997.

20. Report of the Secretary General, 'The situation in Afghanistan and its implications for international peace and security', 14 November 1997.

Chapter 5

1. Mousavi, Sayed Askar, *The Hazaras of Afghanistan, an Historical, Cultural, Economic and Political Study*, Curzon Press, London 1998. This is the only recent work on the Hazaras, who remain little known outside Afghanistan.

2. Dr Rahi gave me a sheaf of her Dari poems when I was in the Hazarajat in December 1997. I am grateful to UN officials for the translation.

3. Interview with Lakhdar Brahimi, 8 April 1997.

4. Crossete, Barbara, 'UN's impatience grows over Afghan restrictions on Aid workers', the *New York Times*, 14 July 1998.

5. AFP, 'Taliban reject warnings of aid pull-out', 16 July 1998.

6. Interviews with Pakistani officials and foreign diplomats in Islamabad, March 1998. See also Rashid, Ahmed 'Massive arms supplies reach all Afghan factions', the *Nation*, 13 March 1998.

7. Winchester, Michael, 'Ethnic cleansing in Afghanistan', *Asiaweek*, 6 November 1998.

8. Interviews with survivors who eventually escaped to Pakistan, conducted by the UNHCR. Private report by the UNHCR sent to the UN Secretary General.

9. Halal is the ritual Islamic way of killing an animal for meat by slitting its throat so that it bleeds.

10. Human Rights Watch Report, 'Afghanistan, the massacre in Mazar-e-Sharif', November 1998.

11. Human Rights Watch Report, as above.

12. Human Rights Watch Report, as above.

13. Interviews with Pakistani diplomats and intelligence officials, and Iranian and Turkmen diplomats, Ashkhabad and Islamabad, August 1998.

14. Personal communication by an international official who interviewed inmates of Kandahar jail.

15. Reuters, 'Taliban blame Clinton scam for attacks', 21 August 1998.

16. Personal communication from Bamiyan.

17. UN Security Council Report, 8/December 1998.
18. Boustany, Nora, 'Busy are the peacemakers', the *Washington Post*, 10 January 1998.
19. UN Security Council Report, 9 December 1998.

Chapter 6

1. The four schools of Islamic law which evolved in the ninth century were Hanafi, Maliki, Shafi and Hanbali. Hanafi was based on customary practices and the easiest to follow.
2. The syllabi of these *madrassas* are learning the Koran by heart, interpretating the Koran, Islamic jurisprudence, Islamic law, life and sayings of the Prophet Mohammed, spreading the word of God, Islamic philosophy, Arabic language and mathematics.
3. Magnus, Ralph and Naby, Eden, *Afghanistan, Mullah, Marx and Mujahid*, Harper Collins, India 1998. I am grateful to the authors for their perceptive history of Islam in Afghanistan.
4. Battuta, Ibn, *Travel in Asia and Africa 1325–1354*, Routledge and Kegan Paul, London 1984. See also Rashid, Ahmed, 'The Revival of Sufism', *Far Eastern Economic Review*, 17 December 1992.
5. Roy, Olivier, *Afghanistan, from Holy War to Civil War*, Princeton University Press, 1995.
6. Roy, Olivier, *The Failure of Political Islam*, I.B.Tauris, London 1994.
7. Roy: *The Failure of Political Islam*.
8. Huntingdon, Samuel, *The Clash of Civilizations and the Remaking of the World Order*, Simon and Schuster, New York 1996.
9. Metcalf, Barbara, 'Islamic Revival in British India 1860–1900', Royal Book Company, Islamabad 1982.
10. Metcalf, as above.
11. Olsen, Asta, *Islam and Politics in Afghanistan*, Curzon Press, London 1995. This is the best book on the historical relationship between Islam and the Afghan state.
12. Shafqat, Saeed, *Civil Military Relations in Pakistan, from Z.A. Bhutto to Benazir Bhutto*, Westview Press, USA 1998.
13. Intelligence report presented to the cabinet of Prime Minister Nawaz Sharif in 1992.
14. The JUI have consistently only won a small number of seats in the National Assembly and the Baluchistan Provincial Assembly. The JUI won ten seats in the Baluchistan Provincial Assembly in the 1988 elections, six seats in the 1990 elections, three seats in the 1993 elections and seven seats in the 1997 elections with the help of Taliban votes. In the National Assembly the JUI won four seats from Baluchistan in 1988, two seats each in the elections in 1990, 1993 and 1997.
15. These included Mullahs Khairkhwa, Minister of Interior, Abbas, Health, Mutaqqqui, Information, Ahmed Jan, Industries, Haqqani, Frontier Affairs, Qala-

muddin, Religious Police, Mansur, Agriculture and Arif, Deputy Finance Minister. See Appendix for further details.

16. Interview with Maulana Samiul Haq, February 1999.

17. *Herald* magazine, 'Binori madrassa', December 1997.

18. After the Clinton administration classified them as a group supporting international terrorism in 1998, they changed their name to Harkat-ul-Mujaheddin.

Chapter 7

1. Sikorski, Radek, *Dust of the Saints*, Chatto and Windus, London 1989. This is the most comprehensive account of the field commanders' meeting.

2. Magnus, Ralph and Naby, Eden, *Afghanistan: Mullah, Marx and Mujahid*, Harper Collins, India 1998. I am grateful to the authors for providing this helpful division of the Mujaheddin leadership.

3. There are 31 provinces (*wilayat*) in Afghanistan, each governed by a governor (*wali*). Each province is divided into districts (*uluswali*) and sub-districts (*alaqdari*). Kabul is divided into *karts* and subdivided into smaller districts call *nahia*.

4. At every opportunity during my visits to Kabul I would ask ministers their views on how they saw the future government of the Taliban. No two ministers had the same opinion and clearly there was very little thought being put into the subject.

5. *Al-Majallah*, 23 October, 1996. Interview given to Arabic magazine.

6. Interview with author. Kandahar, March 1997.

7. The *Nation*, 'Four killed in revolt against Taliban', 10 January 1998.

8. Interviews with international aid workers in Kandahar, who had met the village elders. Islamabad, February 1998.

9. Interview with former inmate of Kandahar jail.

10. AFP, 'Taliban arrest dozens of alleged coup plotter', 23 October 1998.

Chapter 8

1. Rubin, Barnett, *The Fragmentation of Afghanistan: State Formation and Collapse in the International System*, Yale University Press, 1995.

2. Braudel, Ferdinand, *A History of Civilizations*, Penguin Books, London 1993.

3. Interview with Maulvizada, Kabul, June 1997.

4. UNDP Country Development Indicators, 1995.

5. UNOCHA statement, October 1996.

6. UNICEF statement, 11 December 1998.

7. Rubin, Barnett: *The Fragentation of Afghanistan: State Formation and Collapse in the International System*.

8. 'In The Firing Line: War and Children's Rights', Amnesty International 1999.

9. Anders, Fange, 'Difficulties and Opportunities; Challenges of Aid in Afghanistan'. Paper for Stockholm Conference on Afghanistan, 24 February 1999.

10. Wali, Sima, 'Statement on Afghanistan' to the US Congressional Human

Rights Caucus, 30 October 1997. Wali is head of the Refugee Women in Development.

11. Interview with Maulvizada, Kabul, June 1997.

12. UNICEF issued an official communique on 10 November 1995 and Save the Children on 8 March 1996.

13. Interview, Kabul, June 1996.

14. Dupree, Nancy Hatch, 'Afghan women under the Taliban', in *Fundamentalism Reborn? Afghanistan and the Taliban*, (Maley, William ed.) C. Hurst, London 1998. This is the best essay on the history of the gender issue under the Taliban.

15. Power, Carla, 'City of Secrets', *Newsweek*, 13 July 1998. Power's beautiful, tragic piece written with enormous flair, had a major influence on American feminists.

16. UNOCHA statement, 31 October 1996.

17. AFP, 'One survives Taliban death sentence for sodomy', 28 February 1998.

18. Burns, John, 'With sugared tea and caustic rules, an Afghan leader explains himself', the *New York Times*, 24 November 1996.

19. AP, 'Taliban restrict music', 18 December 1996.

20. Reuters, 'Iranian leader accuses Taliban of defaming Islam', 4 October 1996.

Chapter 9

1. I am grateful for interviews with officials from the UN International Drug Control Programme (UNDCP) in Islamabad for their help in describing the opium-growing process.

2. Interviews, Kandahar May 1997. See also Rashid, Ahmed, 'Drug the infidels', *Far Eastern Economic Review*, May 1997.

3. As above.

4. Lifschultz, Lawrence, 'Pakistan, the Empire of Heroin,' in McCoy, Alfred and Block, Alan, *War on Drugs, Studies in the Failure of US Narcotics Policy*, Westview Press 1992.

5. Rubin, Barnett, *The Fragmentation of Afghanistan, State Formation and Collapse in the International System*, Yale University Press 1995.

6. Lifschulz, Lawrence, 'Pakistan: the Empire of Heroin,' in McCoy, Alfred and Block, Alan, *op.cit.*

7. Rashid, Ahmed, 'Dangerous Liaisons', *Far Eastern Economic Review*, 16 April 1998.

8. Interviews with UNDCP and DEA officials, March 1998.

9. Interviews with Iranian officials, Tehran, March 1998. Rashid, Ahmed: 'Dangerous Liaisons'.

10. Observatorie Geopolitique de Drogues, Paris, 'Report on Turkmenistan', March 1999.

11. Interview with President Akayev in Davos, Switzerland, 29 January 1999.

12. Interview with Ambassador, Islamabad, May 1998.

13. UNDCP Report, 25 October 1998.

14. Interview with Pino Arlacchi in Davos, January 1999.

15. Interview with Arif, Kabul, May 1997.

16. Interview with Jan, Kabul, May 1997.

17. UN Demining office for Afghanistan. For several years the UN and other NGOs said there were more than ten million mines in Afghanistan. In 1997 they said that is an exaggerated figure, which at current clearance rates of mines would take 5,000 years to clear. The World Bank is now funding a more detailed survey but it is estimated that several thousand square miles of land are still mine infested. Only 19 per cent of that area, mostly in major cities, was cleared between 1992 and 1999.

18. Interview with Cestari, Islamabad, June 1997.

Chapter 10

1. Interviews with Pakistani cabinet ministers who served under Zia.

2. Roy, Olivier, *Afghanistan, from Holy War to Civil War*, Princeton University Press 1995.

3. Roy, as above.

4. Huntington, Samuel, *The Clash of Civilizations and the Remaking of World Order*, Simon and Schuster, New York 1996.

5. Personal interviews with Bin Laden's friends in Saudi Arabia and London in 1992, 1993 and 1999.

6. AFP, 'Laden planned a global Islamic revolution in 1995,' 27 August 1998.

7. *Al-Ahram*, 'Interview with Masud', by Yahya Ghanim, 19 August 1997.

8. Giacomo, Carol, 'US lists Saudi businessman as extremist sponsor', *Washington Post*, 14 August 1996.

9. AFP, 'Bin Laden training young Islamists, alleges Egypt', 18 February 1997.

10. Hiro, Dilip, 'Islamic militants, once encouraged by the US, now threaten it', the *Nation*, New York, 15 February 1999.

11. *Time* magazine, 'Interview with Bin Laden', 11 January 1999.

12. *Time* magazine, 'Inside the hunt for Osama', 21 December 1998.

13. *Newsweek* magazine, 'Making a symbol of terror', 1 March 1999. The article, using US sources, disputes that Bin Laden was involved in all these terrorist acts.

14. Interviews with Algerian and Egyptian diplomats and politicans in Islamabad in 1992–93.

15. *Global Intelligence Update*, 'Bangladesh Movement highlights new Pan-Islamic identity', 27 January 1999.

16. *Global Intelligence Update*, 'Possible Bin Laden group attempts transit through Malaysia', 13 January 1999.

17. Reid, Tim, 'Yemeni kidnappings were revenge for Iraq bombing', *Daily Telegraph*, 3 January, 1999. The FBI claimed that the Yemenis had lap-top computers and communication equipment and were directly in touch with Bin Laden.

18. AFP, 'Bin Laden may be targeting Bangladesh', 19 February 1999.

19. AFP, 'Suspected Bin Laden supporters held in Mauritania', 5 March 1999.

20. AFP, 'Osama bankrolled Egypt's Jihad', 15 February 1999.

21. AFP, 'Kashmir militant group issues Islamic dress order', 21 February 1999. Pakistani diplomats grew increasingly concerned about the activities of the Wahabbis in Kashmir. Interviews with diplomats, Islamabad March 1999.

22. *Time* magazine, 'Interview with Bin Laden', 11 January 1999.

23. Interviews with senior Pakistani officials, Islamabad, December to March 1998–99. See also Mcgirk, Tim 'Guest of Honour', *Time* magazine, 31 August 1998.

24. *Time* magazine, 'Interview with Bin Laden', 11 January, 1999.

25. Interviews with senior US diplomats, Islamabad January 1999.

Chapter 11

1. Interview with President Niyazov by the author, Ashkhabad, December 1991.

2. US Energy Department, 'The Caspian Sea Region', October 1997.

3. Rashid, Ahmed, 'The new Great Game – the Battle for Central Asia's Oil,' *Far Eastern Economic Review*, 10 April 1997.

4. Rashid, Ahmed, *The Resurgence of Central Asia, Islam or Nationalism?* Zed Books, London 1994.

5. Verrier, Anthony, *Francis Younghusband and the Great Game*, Jonathan Cape, London 1991.

6. Rubin, Barnett, 'Russian hegemony and state breakdown in the periphery: Causes and consequences of the civil war in Tajikistan', in Rubin, Barnett and Synder, Jack, *Post Soviet Political Order, Conflict and State Building*, Routledge, London 1998.

7. Barnett, as above.

8. Allworth, Edward, *The Modern Uzbeks from the 14th Century to the Present*, Hoover Institute Press, 1990.

9. In 1989 unemployment in Turkmenistan stood at 18.8 per cent, infant mortality was 54 per one thousand rising to 111 per one thousand in some desert regions or ten times higher than in Western Europe, child labour was widespread and 62 per cent of the population suffered from jaundice or hepatitis due to the inadequate health system. A quarter of the hospitals had no running water or electricity. See Rashid, Ahmed: *The Resurgence of Central Asia, Islam or Nationalism?*

10. Interview with Kuliyev, Ashkhabad, December 1991.

11. During the first three years (1998–2000), 58 per cent of the gas supplied will go towards paying Iran for the US$190 million construction costs of the pipeline. Exports from Korpedzhe, which reached 2 bcm/year in late 1998, were projected to rise to 8 bcm/year in 2000.

12. The consortium was led by PSG International, a joint venture by two US companies Bechtel Enterprises and General Electric Capital Structured Finance Group.

13. The Japanese company Mitsubishi and the US company Exxon are preparing a feasibility study.

14. Pettifer, James, *The Turkish Labyrinth – Ataturk and the New Islam*, Penguin Books 1997.

15. Petroleum Finance Company, ''The Baku–Ceyhan Pipeline,' Washington, May 1998.

16. The Tenghiz–Chevroil joint venture is the single largest US-led investment in the former Soviet Union. It groups Chevron, Mobil and Arco through LukArco giving US companies a 72 per cent share. The Tenghiz–Chevroil Production Sharing Contract was signed in September 1993.

17. AIOC is led by BP–Amoco and includes US companies Amerada Hess, Exxon, Pennzoil and Unocal with a total US share of 40 per cent. The other companies are Statoil, Itochu, Delta-Hess, Ramco, Socar and TPAO.

18. It costs about US$5 dollars to produce a barrel of Caspian oil compared to US$1.5 a barrel for Saudi Arabia. Transport costs would add another US$5 per barrel.

19. American Jewish groups such as B'nai B'rith and the American Jewish Congress took a strong public stance against Iran.

20. Interview in Tehran, 26 April 1998.

21. The Australian company BHP and Royal Dutch Shell were separately keen to build such a pipeline and BHP presented a feasibility study to Iran and Pakistan in 1998. The gas would be pumped from Iran's South Pars field in the Gulf.

22. The two major Western consortia which presently produce oil in Central Asia are both dominated by US companies. The Tenghiz field in western Kazakhstan (Chevron/Mobil 70 per cent) and the Azerbaijan International Operating Company (Amoco/Unocal/Pennzoil/Exxon 40 per cent) in the Caspian Sea, could potentially produce 1.4 milion barrels per day by 2010. Other ventures such as Karachagnak field in Kazakhstan with a 20 per cent Texaco share and Mobil's stake in Turkmenistan will also need export outlets.

23. Interview with Lakhdar Brahimi, Lahore 8 April 1998.

24. Kinzer, Stephen, 'Caspian Competitors in race for power on sea of oil', *New York Times*, 24 January 1999.

25. Csongos, Frank, ''Official outlines US policy,' RFE/RL Newservice, 18 March 1999.

Chapter 12

1. I interviewed Carlos Bulgheroni in Islamabad in June 1997 over several days and again on 30 January 1999 in Davos, Switzerland. Both times we spoke extensively on and off the record. I believe these are the only times he has spoken to a journalist at length on the Afghanistan pipeline. All the following quotes from Bulgheroni are drawn from these two interviews.

2. Interview with Sureda, Islamabad, 27 February 1997.

3. Interview with Zardari, Islamabad, 1 May 1995.

4. The Qatar proposal was an undersea pipeline across the Gulf to Baluchistan. The Australian company BHP proposed to build an overland gas pipeline from southern Iran to Baluchistan.

5. Interviews with Pakistani diplomats, Islamabad, June 1996.

6. Interview with Bridas executives, Islamabad, 27 February 1997.

7. Kissinger's comments were quoted to me by Bridas executives in Islamabad February 1997. The interview with Olaciregul was at the same time.

8. Interview with Tudor, Islamabad, 27 February 1997.

9. Interview with De La Rosa, Ashkhabad, 22 January 1997.

10. Moscow became more amenable in April 1996, but only after Chevron gave Russia a 24 per cent stake in the consortium to build a US$1.5 billion pipeline to transport Tenghiz oil to Novorossiysk on the Black Sea. Mobil later bought a 25 per cent stake in Chevron's Tenghiz lease.

11. Those hired by the oil companies working in the Caspian included Zbigniew Brzezinski, a former NSC Adviser, former Assistant Defence Secretary Richard Armitage, former Chief of Staff John Sununu, former Senate majority leader Howard Baker, former Secretaries of State Lawrence Eagleburger and Henry Kissinger.

12. The working group included officials from the Departments of State, Energy, Commerce, CIA and the NSC.

13. Interview with diplomat, Ashkhabad, January 1997.

14. Hunter, Shireen, *Central Asia since Independence*, Praeger 1996.

15. Interview with Olcott, Ashkhabad, 27 May 1997.

16. Talbott, Strobe, 'Deepening US engagement with the States of Central Asia and the Caucasus: A Roadmap for the Future,' speech delivered in Washington, 21 July 1997.

17. Case No. 94144 deposited in the District Court of Fort Bend County, Texas. Bridas Corporation, plaintiff v Unocal Corporation, Marty Miller, and Delta Oil Company Ltd, defendants.

18. Letter sent by John Imle to Carlos Bulgheroni on 11 October 1995 and submitted in court by Bridas. The letter stated 'that Unocal should look solely to the Government regarding potential pipeline projects from Turkmenistan to Pakistan and that the Government has not entered into any agreements, which would preclude or interfere in any way with any pipeline projects being discussed between Unocal and Turkmenistan'.

19. Interview with John Imle, Davos, Switzerland 31 January 1999. I had sent 30 questions to Imle and he gave me written answers to some of them and answered others verbally.

20. I interviewed the aide and the cabinet minister on separate occasions in January and February 1997. I also interviewed Benazir Bhutto about the incident, which she confirmed but would not be quoted.

21. Dobbs, Michael, 'Kabul's fall to end the anarchy,' *Washington Post*, 29 September 1996. Senator Brown, in his capacity as Chairman of the Senate Foreign Relations Subcommittee on the Near East and South Asia, had invited all the Afghan warlords to Washington for a three-day round table discussion June 25–

27 1996. Pakistani diplomats in Washington told me that the air tickets of some of the participating Afghans had been paid by Unocal. Brown was one of the few US legislators who took an interest in Afghanistan at the time, partly because he backed the Unocal project.

22. Reuters, 'US sending envoy to Taliban,' Washington, 1 October 1996.

23. Interview with Nazdjanov, Ashkhabad, 22 January 1997.

24. Interview with Bridas executive, Islamabad, June 1997. Bridas held talks with Mobil, Amoco and Coastal oil companies in the USA in order to win backing from a major US oil company to offset Unocal's links with the US government. Bridas was also talking to British, French and Malaysian oil companies to join its consortium. It was also talking to a Russian oil company about joining, in order to offset Russian opposition to its pipeline project.

25. Interview with Imle, Davos, Switzerland, 29 January 1999.

26. Interview with Akashi, Ashkhabad, 22 January 1997.

27. Ebel, Robert, 'Energy Choices in the Near Abroad. The Haves and Havenots face the future,' Centre for Strategic and International Studies, Washington, April 1997.

Chapter 13

1. Both companies had built up lobbies within the Taliban. 'We have still not decided which company we will accept, but we prefer Bridas. They give us confidence because they are neutral,' Mullah Mohammed Sadeq, who had visited Buenos Aires, told me on 27 February 1997.

2. Interview with Bridas executive, Islamabad June 1997.

3. Interview with John Imle, in Davos, Switzerland, 31 January 1999.

4. Interview with President Niyazov, Ashkhabad, 22 January 1997. Turkmenistan hosted a meeting of the UN-sponsored 'International Forum of Assistance to Afghanistan' in a bid to play a larger role in Afghanistan.

5. Three European companies were involved in the Turkey–Turkmenistan pipeline, Italy's Snamprogetti, Gas de France and Royal Dutch Shell.

6. The breakdown of the deal gave Turkmenistan US$1 for supplying the gas, Unocal 65–85 cents for transport costs and the Taliban 15 cents as royalty. This would have given the Taliban an estimated US$105 million dollars a year, but the Taliban rejected it.

7. The new CentGas consortium announced on 25 October 1997, included Unocal 46.5 per cent, Delta Oil 15 per cent, Turkmenistan 7 per cent, Itochu (Japan) 6.5 per cent, Indonesia Petroleum (Japan) 6.5 per cent, Crescent Group (Pakistan) 3.5 per cent and Hyundai Engineering and Construction Co. (South Korea) 5 per cent. Ten per cent shares were reserved for Gazprom.

8. After Gazprom's pullout, the CentGas shares were rearranged. Unocal 54.11 per cent, Delta Oil 15 per cent, Turkmenistan 7 per cent, Indonesia Petroleum (Japan) 7.22 per cent, CIECO TransAsia Gas Ltd (Japan) 7.22 per cent, Hyundai Ltd (South Korea) 5.56 per cent, Crescent Group (Pakistan) 3.89 per cent.

9. Reuters, 9 August 1997. Quoted in *Dawn* newspaper.

10. Heslin, Sheila. Testimony at Senate hearings into illegal fund-raising activities, 17 September 1997.

11. Lees, Caroline, 'Oil barons court Taliban in Texas', *Sunday Telegraph*, 14 December 1997.

12. Interview with Imle, 29 January 1999, Davos, Switzerland.

13. Starobin, Paul, 'The New Great Game', the *National Journal*, 12 March 1999. The Kaplan quote is from his book. Kaplan, Robert, *The Ends of The Earth, A Journey to the Frontiers of Anarchy*, Vintage Books, 1997.

14. Rubin, Barnett, 'US Policy in Afghanistan', *Muslim Politics Report*, Council of Foreign Relations, New York January 1997.

15. Interview with Iranian diplomat, Islamabad, January 1997.

16. Although publicly Pakistan supported the arms embargo, the ISI warned the CIA privately that such a measure would complicate its arming of the Taliban and delay a Taliban victory and the Unocal project. The US still supports an arms embargo, but subsequently it has not been pushed by the Clinton administration. Pakistan diplomats told me that Unocal had paid for some air tickets for Afghan speakers for the Hank Brown hearings.

17. Raphel, Robin, Testimony to the Senate Foreign Relations Subcommittee on the Near East and South Asia, 11 May 1996.

18. Raphel, Robin, text of speech at the closed door UN meeting on Afghanistan, obtained by the author, 18 November 1996.

19. Rubin, Barnett, 'US Policy in Afghanistan', Muslim Politics Report, Council of Foreign Relations, New York, January 1997.

20. Interview with US diplomat, Islamabad, 20 January 1997. Aramco was the consortium of US oil companies which controlled Saudi oil development until it was nationalized by the Saudi government.

21. 'While the CIA did not embark on a new Afghan operation of its own, Unocal officials were briefed extensively by US intelligence analysts. Unocal and Delta hired as consultants every available member of the inner circle of those Americans involved in Afghan operations during the jihad years.' Mackenzie, Richard, 'The United States and the Taliban,' in Maley, William (ed.), *Fundamentalism Reborn? Afghanistan and the Taliban*, C. Hurst, London 1998.

22. Interview with John Imle, 29 January 1999, Davos, Switzerland.

23. Interview with US official, Islamabad, 27 January 1998.

24. AFP, 'US wants puppet government in Afghanistan,' 11 March 1998. Ayub's reference was to an abortive American attempt to talk to neutral Pashtun figures, who might play a role in diluting the Taliban's hardliners.

25. Talbott, Strobe Speech at Stanford University, California, 23 January 1999, US Information Service.

26. Rohrabacher, Dana, 'US Policy towards Afghanistan', Senate Foreign Relations Subcommittee on South Asia, Washington, 14 April 1999.

27. Testimony of Mavis Leno to US Senate Foreign Relations Committee on gender apartheid in Afghanistan, 2 March 1998.

28. Waxman, Sharon, 'A cause unveiled – Hollywood women have made the plight of Afghan women their own', *Washington Post*, 30 March, 1999.

29. AP, 'Mrs Clinton takes on Afghan government', 28 April 1999.

Chapter 14

1. Interviews with cabinet ministers and bureaucrats in June 1998. Much of this subsequent information was gathered by me from civil and military officials beween 1995 and 1999. See Rashid, Ahmed, 'Pakistan and the Taliban,' in Maley, William (ed.), *Fundamentalism Reborn? Afghanistan and the Taliban,* C. Hurst, London 1998.

2. Babar, Mariana, 'The Battle for economic gains in Afghanistan', the *News*, 15 January 1996.

3. Yousufzai, Rahimullah, 'We have no intention of exporting jihad', the *News*, 19 August 1998.

4. Ahmad, Eqbal, 'What after strategic depth?' *Dawn*, 23 August 1998.

5. Roy, Olivier, *Middle East Report*, Winter 1997.

6. This above assessment, which I have written about widely in the past, is a result of dozens of interviews over the years with senior military and intelligence officials, diplomats and bureaucrats involved in Afghan policy.

7. Both the army chief General Abdul Waheed and the head of Military Intelligence Lieutenant General Ali Kuli Khan were Pashtuns, as were all operational ISI field officers involved with the Taliban.

8. Rashid, Ahmed, 'Isolated in Asia, Pakistan's Afghan policy fails to reflect regional realities', *Far Eastern Economic Review*, 5 March 1998.

9. Rashid, Ahmed, 'Pakistan undermines UN in peace process', the *Nation*, 23 January 1998.

10. Interview with Pakistan official, Quetta, April 1995. See also Rashid, Ahmed, 'Nothing to declare', *Far Eastern Economic Review*, 11 May 1995.

11. Braudel, Fernand, A *History of Civilizations*, Penguin Books, London 1993.

12. Ismael Khan, the warlord who controlled Herat, was charging exorbitant customs fees, having raised his customs duty from 5000 to 10,000 rupees per truck.

13. Interviews with CBR officials in 1996, 1997, 1998. In 1993 US$1 was worth 40 rupees. In 1999, US$1 was worth 50 rupees.

14. The racket involved the police, customs officials and bureaucrats who all got a cut from the mafia. After my nephew's car was stolen in Lahore in 1997, he was told by his local police station that his car was now in Afghanistan and he could get it back if he paid the police a 'recovery fine', in cash. Otherwise it would be resold.

15. Pakistan Institute of Development Economics, 'Study on informal economy', December 1998.

16. *Business Recorder*, 'Afghan transit trade destroyed local industry, says NWFP Chief Minister', 15 December 1998.

17. Chase, Robert and Kennedy, Paul and Hill, Emily, *The Pivotal States. A New Framework for US Policy in the Developing World*, W. Norton and Co., 1999.

18. The Lashkar-e-Jhangvi and Sipah-e-Sahaba, offshoots of the JUI who demanded the expulsion of all Shias from Pakistan, sent thousands of volunteers to fight with the Taliban and in return the Taliban gave sanctuary to their leaders in Kabul.

19. Rashid, Ahmed, 'Afghan conflict eroding stability in Pakistan', the Nation, 21 January 1998.

20. Yousufzai, Rahimullah, 'Pakistani Taliban at work', the News, 18 December 1998. See also AFP, 'Murder convict executed Taliban style in Pakistan', 14 December 1998.

21. Roy, Olivier, 'Domestic and Regional Implications of the Taliban regime in Afghanistan', conference paper delivered at St Antony's College, Oxford University, 24 April 1999.

Chapter 15

1. Interview with Kharrazi, Tehran, April 30 1998. See also Rashid, Ahmed, 'Iran trying to improve ties with old enemies', the Nation, 5 May 1998.

2. Between 1984 and 1986 the Saudis gave US$525 million to the Afghan resistance; in 1989 they agreed to supply 61 per cent of a total of US$715 million or US$436, with the remainder coming from the USA. In 1993 they provided US$193 million to the Afghan government. The total amount they contributed during the course of the war was at least as much as and probably more than the US$3–3. 3 billion spent by the US,' Huntingdon, Samuel, The Clash of Civilizations and the Remaking of World Order, Simon and Schuster, New York 1996.

3. Interviews with Pakistani intelligence officers 1989. Also quoted in Rubin, Barnett, The Fragmentation of Afghanistan: State Formation and Collapse in the International System, Yale University Press, 1995.

4. Interviews with cabinet ministers in 1990. Also see Rubin, Barnett: The Fragmentation of Afghanistan.

5. The Saudis appealed to the Mujaheddin to send a military contingent to Saudi Arabia to help their fight with Iraq, in order to show Islamic solidarity and counter propaganda in the Islamic world that the Saudis were solely dependent on Western troops. All the Afghan parties declined, except for the moderate National Islamic Front of Afghanistan led by Pir Gailani which the Saudis had always sidelined.

6. Hunter, Shireen T, 'The Islamic Factor in Iran's Relations with Central Asia', February 1999. Unpublished paper. I am grateful to Hunter for many of these ideas.

7. Rashid, Ahmed, The Resurgence of Central Asia, Islam or Nationalism?' Zed Books, London 1994. In this book I deal extensively with the early period of independent Central Asia's relations with Iran, Turkey, Pakistan and Saudi Arabia.

8. As none of the Central Asian leaders allowed a democratic opposition to flourish, all the opposition to their regimes took the shape of underground Islamic fundamentalism which these leaders conveniently dubbed Wahabbism even though the Islamic opposition was not made up solely of Saudi-trained Wahabbis.

For a discussion of Wahabbism in Central Asia between 1991–94 see, Rashid, Ahmed: *The Resurgence of Central Asia, Islam or Nationalism?*

9. The other bodies are the Higher Council of Qadis, the Institute for Scientific Study, the Supervision of Religious Affairs and the Committee for the Prevention of Vice and Propagation of Virtue. The latter was copied by the Taliban.

10. The result was a fatwa issued by the most powerful *ulema* leader, Sheikh Abdul Aziz Bin Baz which read, 'Even though the Americans are, in the conservative religious view, equivalent to non-believers as they are not Muslims, they deserve support because they are here to defend Islam.' I am indebted to a private paper on Saudi Arabia. Obaid, Nawaf, 'Improving US Intelligence Analysis on the Saudi Arabian Decision Making Process', Harvard University 1998.

11. Several Saudi sources told me that after the Taliban captured Kabul, Saudi mosques regularly took up collections from the congregation after Friday prayers, for the Taliban – just as they did for the Muslims in Bosnia.

12. Obaid, Nawaf, 'Improving US Intelligence Analysis on the Saudi Arabian Decision Making Process,' Harvard University, 1998.

13. AFP, 'Taliban claim Saudi support', 21 April 1997.

14. AFP, 'Taliban battling for northern city', 17 September 1997.

15. Quoted in Rashid, Ahmed, 'Afghanistan – Road to Disaster', *Herald* magazine, November 1996.

16. I interviewed Prince Saud in Jeddah in 1986 and Prince Turki in Islamabad in 1989. Both men are extremely intelligent and articulate, but poorly informed on the details of what was happening in Afghanistan. As with the CIA, Saudi intelligence depended to a large extent on the ISI for its information and analysis.

17. AFP, 'Convoy carrying weapons stopped', 12 October 1998.

18. AFP, 'Taliban shut down Iran embassy in Kabul', 2 June 1997.

19. AFP, 'Taliban warn of retaliation against Iran', 22 September 1997.

20. AFP, 'Iran says Taliban threat to the region', 14 August 1998.

21. AFP, 'Iran presses Nawaz over Afghan policy', 15 June 1997.

22. Iran based this assessment on the evidence of one Iranian diplomat who had escaped the massacre by feigning death. Although wounded, he arrived back in Tehran and talked to reporters. Ironically Mullah Dost Mohammed was jailed when he returned to Kandahar. His wife complained to Mullah Omar that he had brought back with him two Hazara concubines whom she refused to accept in her home.

23. Interviews with senior Iranian diplomats in September 1998 in Islamabad and January 1999 in Davos, Switzerland.

24. Albright, Madeleine, Speech to the Asia Society, New York, 17 June 1998.

25. Interview with Kharrazi, Tehran, 30 April 1998.

Chapter 16

1. Ignatieff, Michael, *The Warrior's Honor, Ethnic War and the Modern Conscience*, Vintage, New York 1999.

2. Interview with Brahimi, Islamabad, 14 May 1998.

3. AFP, 'Afghan casualty figures show no signs of easing', the *News*, 13 October 1998.

4. Fange, Anders, 'Challenges of Aid in Afghanistan', Paper for Stockholm Conference on Afghanistan, 24 February 1999.

5. Elleston, Harold, 'The General against the Kremlin. Alexander Lebed: Power and Illusion', Little Brown and Co, London 1998.

6. AFP, 'Oil pipeline not ready for main production', 20 May 1999.

7. The elected governments dismissed are those of Mohammed Khan Junejo May 1988, Benazir Bhutto August 1990, Nawaz Sharif April 1993, Benazir Bhutto November 1996.

8. Braudel, Ferdinand, *A History of Civilizations*, Penguin Books, London 1993.

9. Private communication, 6 March 1999.

10. Fange, Anders, 'Difficulties and Opportunities; Challenges of Aid to Afghanistan', Paper for Stockholm Conference on Afghanistan, 24 February 1999.

Index